The Don Juan Legend Before Mozart

The Don Juan Legend Before Mozart

With a Collection of Eighteenth-Century Opera Librettos

Charles C. Russell

Ann Arbor

THE UNIVERSITY OF MICHIGAN PRESS

Published in the United States of America by
The University of Michigan Press
Manufactured in the United States of America

1996 1995 1994 1993 4 3 2 1

Library of Congress Cataloging-in-Publication Data

Russell, Charles C.

The Don Juan legend before Mozart / Charles C. Russell. With a collection of eighteenth-century opera librettos.

p. cm.

Librettos in Italian with commentary in English.

Includes bibliographical references (p.) and index.

Partial Contents: La pravità castigata / Eustachio Bambini—Il convitato di pietra o sia Il dissoluto / Vincenzo Righini and Nunziato Porta—Il convitato di pietra / Giuseppe Calegari—Il Don Giovanni / Gioacchino Albertini—Il convitato di pietra / Giacomo Tritto and Giambattista Lorenzi—Il nuovo convitato di pietra / Francesco Gardi and Giuseppe Maria Foppa—Il capriccio drammatico / Giovanni Valentini and Giovanni Bertati—Don Giovanni o sia Il convitato di pietra / Giuseppe Gazzaniga and Giovanni Bertati.

ISBN 0-472-10413-6

1. Operas—18th century—Librettos. 2. Opera—18th century. 3. Drama—18th century—History and criticism. 4. Don Juan (Legendary character)—Drama. 5. Don Juan (Legendary character)—Legends—History and criticism. 6. Libretto—18th century. 7. Mozart, Wolfgang Amadeus, 1756–1791. Don Giovanni. I. Title.

ML48.R87 1993 <Case>
782.1′026′8—dc20 93-22344
CIP
MN

A CIP catalogue record for this book is available from the British Library.

Some of the material in this book appeared in different form in *Music & Letters* 65, no. 1 (January 1984): 17–27; and in *Mozart-Jahrbuch 1980–83* (Kassel: Bärenreiter, 1983), 385–92. This material is used by permission of Oxford University Press and by permission of the Internationale Stiftung Mozarteum Salzburg, respectively.

Decorative motifs from original librettos.

For Anthony and Mario

Ma credete voi forse
che si badi alle regole?
Si bada a quel che piace, e spesse volte
si fanno più denari
con delle strampalate
di quello che con cose
studiate, regolate e giudiziose.

Do you think
we pay attention to rules?
We pay attention to what people like,
and we often make more money
with nonsense,
than with careful,
well-put-together, sensible things.

—Policastro, an impresario, *Il capriccio drammatico*

Preface

There is something about the story of a man who lives life on his own terms, totally indifferent to others, that fascinates the imagination: a man who is young, handsome, healthy, energetic, and virile, who never lacks for money, good food, good entertainment, or beautiful women, a man whose boundless independence becomes, in a way, our own vicarious freedom, while his final damnation pleases us equally because, since we know we cannot live as he does, he must not be allowed to either. Hence the enormous popularity of the Don Juan story, first put into theatrical form by Tirso de Molina in the early years of the seventeenth century. New versions followed rapidly, some of them well written, some of them rather poorly done. For some we know the author's name: Cicognini, Perrucci, Dorimond, Villiers, Molière, Shadwell, Thomas Corneille, Córdoba y Maldonado, Goldoni. Other versions are nameless, such as those played time and again by the commedia dell'arte, by the troupes foraines, or by pantomime companies and puppet theaters. No version was completely original, not even the first. Every version sprang from the past, whether by deliberately imitating it or by deliberately ignoring it; each version added something new, either something as unimportant as a humorous routine or a simple plot twist or as important as a new set of scenes or a new character. Finally, a legend was born: a Don Juan who was all versions and no version. And so he remains.

Because Don Juan is a legend, one goes to the theater not to see *who* he is, one goes *because* he is who he is. What he is, I think, is all of us. Only thus considered does his unlikely tale or does his extraordinary character make any sense. To try to fathom him as an individual, as one tries to fathom the mind and the motives of a Hamlet, is to try to understand who or what man himself is, is to try to grasp air. Don Juan passes beyond mere understanding.

If one reads only the letter of the text of Mozart's *Don Giovanni,* one is forced to admit that, in many respects, the story is ridiculous. The walking and talking statue is absurdly improbable, the twenty-four-hour activities of Don Giovanni himself are beyond belief, and his claim to have seduced, in his travels through Italy, Germany, France, Turkey, and Spain, a total of 2,065 women is so preposterous as to be irritating in its presumption of our gullibility.

But the fact is that neither this man nor this number reflects a literal truth. They are expressions of a broader idea. The number 2,065 is really a symbol of infinity; the five countries mentioned in Leporello's list are tokens of all the nations of the world. For Don Juan is every man and woman, he is every human being; as such he has visited not only these few places but all countries on earth, and his conquests are indeed without number, infinite.

Don Juan lives in us all. He is our daydream of adventure, he is our nighttime dream of escape; he is the sexual act of conquest or of submission that we have all longed for; he is the act of daring we have never attempted and the fulfillment of successes we have never achieved; he is the irresponsibility, indifference, egotism, all the unlawful things that we put aside because unattainable in a world with real spouses, real neighbors, real police, and real ministers. He is our ego asserting itself in its most elemental and selfish fashion.

Since he is all of us, there are many Don Juans; there is no one, single figure. The Don Juan of legend corresponds to no Don Juan of history or of literature. He is always the latest dream of his re-creator. Each dreamer creates Don Juan to his own measure, according to his own ideas and needs: Molière's is pensive and disturbed, Thomas Shadwell's violent and crazed, José Zorilla's anguished and tormented by sin, Edmond Rostand's a boastful failure, Max Frisch's cool and resigned. The true Don Juan exists only in our minds, formed there in an image that only we ourselves can fully understand and that we can communicate only imperfectly to others, like dreams; an image built, however, upon the myriad examples of the story created over the last one, two, three, or three-and-a-half centuries. Each of us creates his or her own Don Juan that draws on all preceding versions and yet is none of them.

For, in the last analysis, Don Juan is not a man but a dream, the dream of what we could have been or what we might have done, if only. . . . And every man and woman's dream is different. Perhaps, then, Don Juan is even more than what his legend tells us he is: the irresistible seducer of women and the courageous defier of the divine. He is, perhaps, a sad image of the yearning that is in each of us; he is a faint expression of the dissatisfactions that we feel with life, an image of lost hopes, lost chances, lost dreams, an image of lost youths and lost eternities. But he is magnificent even in his losses: self-absorbed, disloyal, cruel, wicked; strutting and flaunting his youth, his strength, his sensuality, his beauty, his courage; a horrible, an attractive man; a wicked man there on the stage, but, because he and I are one, truly magnificent. Thus has he been admired and reviled for centuries.

As an image of the triumph of the self, as a statement of the rude primacy of the ego, his very name is synonymous with absolute freedom, and it is freedom that he offers to Donna Anna, Don Ottavio, Donna Elvira, and to all who enter his kingdom. How narrow-minded and mistaken are those who consider Mozart's *Don Giovanni* a record of failures! They understand Don Juan even less than Catalinón or Passarino or Sganarelle or Leporello. Mozart would have been astounded, Da Ponte appalled. At no time in history did the legendary figure ever fail. His very name has always meant success, and audiences have always recognized unquestionably that he was a success. There was no other reason to watch his adventures. Don Juan exists precisely because he never fails, not even in death.

No one understood this better than Mozart; no one better understood the beauty of his strengths and the beauty of his evils and the beauty of his death. Not even Lorenzo Da Ponte, who prepared for Mozart a solid, well-written libretto, a robust but pliable text that permitted Mozart's music to seek out and illuminate the multifaceted personality, the dark psyche of this ambiguous and fascinating figure who was, for Mozart too as he is for all of us, I am sure, Mozart himself.

Yet if Mozart expressed the meaning of the legend more profoundly than anyone had before, he, too, in the creation of his opera, based his work upon the multitude of versions that preceded; it is those versions that make up the subject of this book. It is not about Mozart's *Don Giovanni* of 1787. Rather, it is concerned with the story of Don Juan as it was played before Mozart and with the way the story developed and changed for a century-and-a-half as it worked its way from Tirso de Molina in Spain to Mozart and Da Ponte in Vienna. Chapter 1 explores nonmusical expressions of the tale that were created in Spain, Italy, France, and elsewhere between the early years of the seventeenth century and 1787. It touches not only upon well-known Don Juan versions such as those by Tirso de Molina and Molière, it also examines the important contribution of many lesser known writers, such as Giacinto Andrea Cicognini, Dorimond, and Villiers. In chapter 2, musical versions of the legend are explored, Don Juan in ballet and opera, from a single, first appearance on the lyric stage in Rome in 1669 to multiple appearances in 1787. That Don Juan had a rich libretto tradition has been largely ignored or forgotten. Both chapters 1 and 2 trace the historical progress of the story, changes in character, plot, style, and meaning, and put into relief many developing aspects of the legend that found major expression in Da Ponte's text. For, like Mozart's music, Da Ponte's text is also a product of the past, an understanding of which serves to illuminate the true originalities of their opera. The libretto tradition culminating in Da Ponte's work is the subject of chapter 3. Here are gathered together, in carefully edited form, the librettos for every eighteenth-century Don Juan opera that preceded Mozart's. Here can be found all the Don Juan libretto texts that operagoers were reading in Prague and Venice and Vienna. There were no others. Most of them rapidly disappeared from circulation. In fact, only one original libretto of *La pravità castigata* is known to exist. It is now in the University Library of Brno, Czechoslovakia. With the exception of the libretto by Giovanni Bertati, all appear here for the first time in a modern edition. It is hoped that this collection of texts will serve as a useful tool for scholars of the Don Juan legend, of Mozart, and of Da Ponte. The long-ago popularity of these first musical versions of the legend and the shifting popularity of the story itself as a subject for musical expression are attested to in chapter 4. This final section of my study is a carefully documented record of every known musical performance of the story from the first in Rome in 1669 up through Mozart to the end of the eighteenth century. Unless otherwise noted, translations are my own.

Although Mozart's *Don Giovanni* is the point of arrival and not the point of departure, Mozart's presence and that of his librettist are felt throughout; all early versions seem to echo forward toward theirs. For Mozart and Da Ponte did not create a new and original Don Juan, as Molière had. Their version was a distillation of all past Don Juans, an expression of their essences. Theirs was the culmination of a 150-year-old tradition, the summation of all Don Juans who had come before and a figure so powerful in its essentiality and intensity that those of the following centuries exist only because their Don Juan existed; those that followed are illumined by the light of his strength and passion. For, as the eighteenth century came to a close, Don Juan was growing tired and trivial. Like all mortal things, and legends are mortal too, he was on the path toward death. It was Mozart who brought him back to new life; it was the genius of Mozart that gave him renewed life and meaning and made him eternal, with the universal language of his music, by means of which Don Juan continues to shape himself to the needs and desires of us all forever.

Acknowledgments

This book has taken a long time to complete. It would have taken even longer without the help of my wife, Camilla, and many others: the American Council of Learned Societies, Stefania Amodeo, Cordell Black, Wanda Bogdany-Popielowa, Marianne Bosshard, Judith Cmero and the Interlibrary Loan of the University of Maryland, the Casa Goldoni, the Conservatorio Luigi Cherubini of Florence, Francesco Cortellazzo, Vladislav Dokoupil, the Fondazione Cini, Marina Foschi-Albert, the Graduate School of the University of Maryland for a Semester Research Award, Janina Hoskins, Jan Kozubek, Boguslaw Madey, Antonio Maffei, Linda Martz, Stefan Neuschl, Teresa Nowogorska, Delys Ostlund, Armand E. Singer, the staff of the Music Library at the Library of Congress and at the University of Maryland, Ralph Tarica, Madeleine Therrien, Dorothea Zitta. I am very grateful to all of them.

Contents

1. Don Juan and Nonmusical Theater Before Mozart 1

2. Don Juan and Musical Theater Before Mozart 55

3. Don Juan Librettos 129

A Note on the Texts 131

La pravità castigata
Eustachio Bambini 133

Il convitato di pietra o sia Il dissoluto
Vincenzo Righini and Nunziato Porta 183

Il convitato di pietra
Giuseppe Calegari 227

Il Don Giovanni
Gioacchino Albertini 277

Il convitato di pietra
Giacomo Tritto and Giambattista Lorenzi 289

Il nuovo convitato di pietra
Francesco Gardi and Giuseppe Maria Foppa 327

Il capriccio drammatico
Giovanni Valentini and Giovanni Bertati 381

Don Giovanni o sia Il convitato di pietra
Giuseppe Gazzaniga and Giovanni Bertati 407

4. Don Juan in Music: Performance Data, 1669 to 1800 445

Bibliography 493

Index 505

I

Don Juan and Nonmusical Theater Before Mozart

It was a Spanish monk who first gave cohesive literary form to a story that, in bits and pieces, had long been part of Spanish folklore. Gabriel Téllez, who was born in Madrid in 1580 and died in Almazán in 1648, lived most of his life as a monk of Our Lady of Mercy, of the Mercedarian Order, which he joined in 1601. Around 1610 he began to write for the stage, and, under the name Tirso de Molina, he soon became a popular and successful playwright whose works were bought and produced by the best acting companies of his day. He wrote a variety of stage works including historical dramas, lives of the saints, comedies of morals, religious plays, plays of intrigue, and pastoral comedies. His output was prolific. Toward the end of his life he claimed to have written more than four hundred works. However, it is now thought more likely that he composed around two hundred. Fifty-four plays exist today, with another twenty-three whose attribution is less certain.

Tirso's most famous work is *El burlador de Sevilla y Convidado de piedra.* It is in this three-act verse play that he introduced to the world the figure and the story of Don Juan and the many other characters, scenes, and situations that became standard elements of the later legend. No copy of his original play exists. What does exist are two later versions that, although not perfectly similar, are obviously from the same stock. The first bears the title noted above. It was printed in 1630, and it is to this version that reference is usually made when speaking of Tirso's Don Juan. The second version, *¿Tan largo me lo fiáis?,* seems to have been printed some decades after *El burlador,* yet the original text of this printed version is generally believed to have preceded *El burlador.* In fact, most critics agree that the texts of both plays descend from a single, lost original that Tirso prepared probably sometime after 1616.[1]

I do not know why Don Juan came to life in Spain. Perhaps a story like his was necessary as a criticism of what was a particularly abusive nobility in seventeenth-century Spanish society; perhaps his tale was useful in pointing up a particularly oppressive and corrupt Spanish code of honor; perhaps his irresponsible and ultimately fatal adventures were the clucking voice of a powerful clergy. But I think not. Tirso's Don Juan is too youthful, too energetic, too full of life, in a word, too fascinating to have been meant to serve merely as a reminder, and nothing more, that the cost of sin is death. In spite of his damnation, I suspect that most men and women who watched his adventures on stage did so first with curiosity, then with sympathy, and finally with a kind of aching admiration and envy. After all, not for nothing did *El burlador* immediately become, as the noted Tirsoan critic Gerald E. Wade put it with blunt and attractive succinctness, "the most important drama ever written";[2] not for nothing did the character of Don Juan soon turn legendary, a figure with a life of its own, the central figure of a legend that has lasted down to the present day and that became so firmly embedded in the Western conscience and language that no modern fussing with it in the last 150 years—Don Juan repentant, Don Juan philosophical, Don Juan married, Don Juan old and tired—has managed to dislodge the fundamental image and idea of Don Juan as a youthful and handsome seducer of women.

Perhaps Giacomo Casanova had the answer why Don Juan first appeared in Spain. Casanova's answer is simple and certainly clear and sufficient for our needs. Speaking of Spain, and of Madrid in particular, he writes that

> both men and women are subject to passions and desires as keen as the air they breathe. . . . The women are very pretty, burning with desires, and all ready to lend a hand in schemes intended to deceive all those who surround them to spy on their doings. The lover who most boldly faces and defies dangers is the one they prefer to all those who are timid, respectful, guarded. Their coquetry makes them want to keep them, but at bottom they despise them. In the public walks, in churches, at the theaters, they speak with their eyes to those to whom they wish to speak, possessing that

1. Both texts may be found in Tirso de Molina, *Obras dramaticas completas,* ed. Blanca de los Rios, vol. 2 (Madrid: Aguilar, 1962). For a further discussion of the play and its dates, see Gwynne Edwards, ed., *The Trickster of Seville and the Stone Guest,* by Tirso de Molina (Warminster: Aris and Phillips, 1986); Margaret Wilson, *Tirso de Molina* (Boston: Twayne, 1977).

2. Gerald E. Wade and Robert J. Mayberry, "*Tan Largo Me Lo Fiais* and *El Burlador De Sevilla Y El Convidado De Piedra,*" *Bulletin of the Comediantes* 14, no. 1 (1962): 1.

> seductive language to perfection; if the man, who must understand it, can seize the occasion and take advantage of it, he is sure to be successful; he need not expect the slightest resistance; if he neglects the opportunity or does not profit by it, it is not offered him again.[3]

In Spain the women offered.

Passion, intrigue, trickery, and opportunity. That is indeed the atmosphere and the subject matter of the first Don Juan play, which begins with an act of passion consummated and an act of trickery nearly so. It is worth recounting the story in some detail, since all later versions are variations of it. The good monk Gabriel Téllez was the father of them all.

Act I takes place in Naples. It is night. Don Juan has just boldly seduced a lady of the court, Doña Isabela, by pretending to be the lady's fiancé, Duque Octavio. As the play opens, Doña Isabela has suddenly realized her error and screams for help. Don Juan is arrested by the King of Naples but manages to escape from the palace with the connivance of his uncle, the Spanish ambassador. He and his servant, Catalinón, then set sail for Spain, but, off the coast of Tarragona, their ship is capsized. Though nearly drowned, the two are washed ashore and given aid by a lovely but haughty fishergirl, Tisbea, whose beauty immediately arouses Don Juan. In spite of her lofty moral principles, she almost immediately succumbs to his physical beauty and his ardent words. Having enjoyed Tisbea, Don Juan sets fire to her hut as a diversion and then gallops off to Seville with horses acquired by Catalinón. Distraught, Tisbea tries to throw herself into the sea. Meanwhile, Duque Octavio has also left Naples for Seville in order to avoid imprisonment; he has been falsely accused of being the seducer of Doña Isabela. Also recently arrived in Seville is Don Gonzalo de Ulloa, Grand Commander of the Order of Calatrava and a highly respected member of the Spanish court. To reward his faithful service, the King of Castile offers to arrange a marriage between Don Gonzalo's daughter, Doña Ana, and Don Juan, whose father, Don Diego Tenorio, is a close and trusted advisor to the king. Don Gonzalo is delighted.

But bad news travels rapidly. By the beginning of the second act, the King of Castile has learned that the defiler of Doña Isabela's honor was not Duque Octavio but Don Juan Tenorio. His father is heartsick; the king is enraged, withdraws his promise to wed Don Juan to Doña Ana, and orders Don Juan banished from Seville. Doña Ana is offered to the newly arrived and innocent

3. Giacomo Casanova, *History of My Life,* trans. Willard R. Trask (New York: Harcourt Brace Jovanovich, 1970), 10:310–11.

Duque Octavio, who is so delighted with the change of events that he entirely forgets his Neapolitan Isabela. Don Juan, meanwhile, has come across an old friend, the Marqués de la Mota, and together they salaciously discuss a number of women Don Juan used to know in Seville. The Marqués then confesses that a secret love exists between himself and Doña Ana, whom he describes so effectively that Don Juan's libido is immediately aroused. The two make plans for further erotic adventures that evening, but Don Juan's secret intention is to trick and seduce Doña Ana as soon as possible. Adopting an innocent pretext, he borrows the Marqués de la Mota's crimson cloak and, pretending to be the Marqués, he gains access to Doña Ana's rooms. Yet Doña Ana is not deceived. She screams from offstage (she never appears on stage); her father, the Comendador, rushes in with sword drawn and challenges Don Juan, but he is easily and contemptuously slain by the younger man who slips out quickly and returns the crimson cloak to the Marqués. The unsuspecting Marqués is soon arrested and sentenced to death by the king, who promises to erect (at his own expense) a noble statue of the Comendador with a proper inscription promising vengeance. In the last scene of the act, Don Juan is on his way to his place of exile. He and Catalinón come across the country wedding of Batricio and Aminta. Aminta is too lovely to be ignored. To the rage of Batricio, Don Juan takes his place beside Aminta at the wedding table as the act comes to a noisy conclusion.

Don Juan uses the time that elapses between the second and third acts to woo Aminta from Batricio. As the third and final act begins, he musters all his seductive skills. He grandly swears an oath of eternal faithfulness: should he be untrue, let God send someone to strike him dead—provided, he adds in an aside, that the someone be a dead man. Aminta gives in. Afterward, in spite of the king's banishment, Don Juan decides to return to Seville for more adventures. He is accompanied as usual by a reluctant Catalinón who, now and as throughout the play, continues to remonstrate with his master for the wicked life he leads. As usual, Don Juan does not listen: there is plenty of time for repentance, plenty of time to pay debts. Near Seville they find themselves in a church where they see a stone effigy of the Comendador with an inscription threatening vengeance.

> Aquí aguarda del Señor,
> el más leal caballero,
> la venganza de un traidor.
>
> (III.xi)

[Here a most loyal knight
awaits the vengeance of God
on a traitor.]

In a moment of fun, Don Juan tweaks the statue's beard and invites it to dinner, after which, he suggests, the two gentlemen can fight a proper duel.

At Don Juan's inn, dinner has been prepared. As he and Catalinón are about to eat, they hear a loud knocking and the statue enters. Don Juan gallantly and fearlessly invites it to dine. Catalinón, though, is so frightened that he evacuates in his pants. In turn, the statue invites Don Juan to dinner at his church. The young man agrees and seals his promise with a bold handshake. However, after the statue departs, he confesses to his first real moment of fear. Meanwhile, at the palace, the king has now decided that Don Juan, to make amends, must marry Doña Isabela and that not Duque Octavio but the Marqués de la Mota, whom the king now knows to be innocent, should marry Doña Ana. Aminta and her father also appear at the court. They are looking for Don Juan and for justice. A foolish Aminta declares to one and all that she is a lady, since her "husband," Don Juan, is a member of the nobility. Back at the inn, Don Juan has been getting ready for his wedding; he then sets off for the ceremony but first stops, as agreed, at the tomb of the Comendador. The banquet that has been prepared for him is horrible—a black bedecked table with snakes and scorpions. The statue asks Don Juan for his hand, which he proffers fearlessly. But as soon as he is gripped by the statue he realizes that his end is near. Desperate, he swears that he never touched Doña Ana. "Your intention alone condemns you," replies the statue. "Let me make confession," begs Don Juan. "Too late," intones the statue, "your time has run out." Statue and Don Juan sink down into hell. At the king's palace, Catalinón, a terrified witness to these events, recounts them to the astonished and horrified listeners, who all agree that, with Don Juan's death, order finally reigns anew.

Thus Tirso brings about the very theatrical and properly didactic stage death of his young seducer, who, though, has really just come to life, literary life that is. He is not yet fully grown. Still an adolescent, he is an appealing figure of bounding energy and strength, indifferent to the future, uninterested in repentance—plenty of time for that, he keeps repeating—disinterested in God, a lukewarm believer whose final plea to be allowed to confess is rather pitiful. The heavenly resonances of the Stone Guest are not yet fully heard by him. In Tirso's long title, *El convidado de piedra* is an afterthought. His Don Juan is first of all *El burlador de Sevilla*—a trickster, a playboy ready for (and seeking) adventures. Seducing women is fine, but it is the trick itself that thrills. In fact, says

Catalinón, his master is not only the trickster of Seville, he is "el burlador de España." "You have given me a fine name," replies Don Juan proudly (II.xii).

In Molière's hands, in Thomas Shadwell's, in Da Ponte's and Mozart's, Don Juan will become a man, and the trick alone will no longer be sufficient. By then, Tirso's name and his play will have been generally forgotten, but his story and his Don Juan will have entered the realm of legend.

At first sight it would seem that Da Ponte knew Tirso's text quite well. Similarities abound, of plot, of character, of scene and action: in Catalinón we foresee Leporello, in the country folk and their wedding celebration are foreshadowed Zerlina and Masetto, and so on and so forth. But there is no evidence that Da Ponte had ever read Tirso's play. What he must have read was a once famous Florentine playwright by the name of Giacinto Andrea Cicognini. Cicognini was quite familiar with contemporary Spanish drama and had read Tirso closely.

El burlador de Sevilla reached Italy and Cicognini by way of Naples, long under Spanish dominance and influence. Plays from Spain were often presented by Spanish actors in Naples, and it is there that Tirso's drama probably arrived in performances at the Teatro di San Bartolomeo in 1625 and 1626.[4] Not long following, versions in Italian began to circulate. Cicognini's was the first.[5] His three-act prose play was clearly based on Tirso's, part of whose very title he appropriated for his own: *Il convitato di pietra*.

Cicognini, who was born in Florence in 1606 and died in Venice in 1651, was a much admired and very successful dramatist. He experimented with a variety of popular theatrical styles, including texts for music for some important seventeenth-century composers. He wrote *Giasone* for Francesco Cavalli and *Orontea* for Marcantonio Cesti. In a letter dated 24 March 1632, Cicognini's father, Jacopo, who was likewise a successful dramatist, indicated that sometime earlier his young and promising son had presented a *Convitato di pietra* in Florence that "pleased beyond expectation" and that he was now trying to arrange for a performance of the comedy in Pisa.[6] Unfortunately, the text for these early performances has not survived; only later editions are available.[7] Jacopo's letter

4. Joseph G. Fucilla, "*El Convidado de Piedra* in Naples in 1625," *Bulletin of the Comediantes* 10, no. 1 (1958): 5.

5. Although Benedetto Croce (*Aneddoti di varia letteratura* 2d ed. [Bari: Laterza, 1953], 2:126) believed that the play in question was not by Cicognini—he spoke of a "pseudo-Cicognini"—Cicognini's legitimacy has been almost conclusively proved by Anna Maria Crinò ("Documenti inediti sulla vita e l'opera di Jacopo e di Giacinto Andrea Cicognini," *Studi secenteschi* 2 [1961]: 255–86).

6. Letter by Jacopo Cicognini, quoted in Crinò, "Documenti," 282.

7. The text can be found in Georges Gendarme De Bévotte, *Le Festin de Pierre avant Molière* (Paris: Cornély, 1907); Giovanni Macchia, *Vita avventure e morte di Don Giovanni* (Bari: Laterza, 1966).

made it clear that he himself did not much admire his son's play. Jacopo was, in fact, the first of a long procession of critics who did not care for the tale at all.

In truth, Cicognini's version was not nearly as good as Tirso's, but "good" had nothing to do with success. Good or bad, Cicognini's play served as a model for countless versions that followed. Although it lacked the elegance, the insights, the breadth, and the complexities of Tirso's *Burlador,* it nonetheless caught the popular Italian imagination, probably because it was not elegant or complex, but energetic, direct, and amusing. In addition, it contained some very entertaining comic figures. And then there was the increased importance Cicognini gave to the wonderful ambulatory statue. All versions of the Don Juan legend have their spiritual roots in Tirso's play, but most, at least most Italian ones, have their physical roots in Cicognini's. They are children of his version or the children of his numerous offspring and their descendants. That is true for Lorenzo Da Ponte's libretto as well. While it cannot be proved that Da Ponte ever directly read a copy of Cicognini's *Convitato,* many of the things that he put in his *Don Giovanni* were first invented by the Florentine playwright. Editions of his play must have been numerous. The Casa Goldoni in Venice has four poor-quality eighteenth-century reprints of it among its holdings, one of which is dated 1787, the same year as Da Ponte's libretto.

The general story of Cicognini's Don Juan, now called Don Giovanni, is much the same as before. Because his version is a kind of launching pad for many later versions, a brief plot summary may again be useful. Once more we are in Naples. Don Giovanni has violated Donna Isabella. As before, he is caught by the King of Naples but secretly allowed to escape by his uncle. Duca Ottavio is accused of the crime, but he is also permitted to flee. On his way to Spain, Don Giovanni, accompanied by his servant, Passarino, is shipwrecked. He is rescued by a young peasant girl, Rosalba. Though until then content with the simple country innocence of her life, she instantly falls in love with his good looks. Passarino immediately recognizes that she will end up on the list of his master's conquests, and, in fact, she soon does. When Don Giovanni leaves her, she throws herself into the sea out of desperation.

In the second act, Don Giovanni and Duca Ottavio meet in Castile. Duca Ottavio confides to Don Giovanni that he is now in love with Donna Anna. His confession arouses Don Giovanni, who decides that he must have her, asks to borrow Duca Ottavio's hat and cloak (ostensibly for another conquest), and enters Donna Anna's house. He is discovered by her father, the Commendatore Oliola. After a brief and ruthless struggle, the Commendatore is killed. Donna Anna pleads with the King of Castile for justice. Don Giovanni, fearing that the king's men may be closing in, exchanges cloaks with Passarino and slips away in the dark. He later comes across a group of festive peasants. In a dumb show that concludes the act, Don Giovanni starts to dance with the peasants and then runs off with Brunetta, the young bride promised to Pantalone.

In the third act, Passarino warns Don Giovanni to be less foolhardy, but he refuses to listen. In an open temple he comes upon the recently erected statue of the Commendatore and observes the usual vengeance-promising epitaph. Piqued by the statue's threats, he strikes it with his glove, although believing full well that his gesture is foolish. To prove to Passarino that he is unafraid of the dead man, he invites it to dinner. Unexpectedly, the statue nods. At dinner, Don Giovanni is thoroughly enjoying himself as Passarino humorously reviews the women he has known. Things turn serious when the statue arrives and invites Don Giovanni to another dinner. The second one is a ghoulish affair, but Don Giovanni is not afraid. He ignores the statue's triple request to repent and, after his third refusal, is swallowed up into hell. The play's last scene takes place in hell itself. Now suffering inexpressible torments, Don Giovanni curses his former wickedness and warns the living to avoid his fate.

From even this brief summary, it is obvious that both the plot and the characters of the comedy derive from Tirso's *El burlador.* Although Cicognini's play does not vary from Tirso's to any significant degree, he did make some changes. Some things he compressed: the role of the peasant folk has been considerably reduced, while the figure of the Marqués de la Mota has been eliminated altogether as has Don Juan's father. A few things he added, and some of his additions were later adopted by Lorenzo Da Ponte. There was no list in *El burlador;* it shows up here for the first time. The role of Donna Anna has been increased; she now appears on stage, if only briefly. Don Giovanni escapes the palace guard by changing capes with Passarino, just as he will make an exchange for the same reason a century or so later with Leporello. In the churchyard, the statue nods its assent to Don Giovanni's thoughtless invitation. In Tirso it had shown no sign of life. At the second dinner, the statue three times orders Don Giovanni to repent; in Tirso it made no such request.

The statue, in fact, now plays a more prominent role. It dominates nearly the entire third act, whereas in Tirso's third act many different stories were woven together. There has been a slight shift in emphasis, as the very title of the new play suggests. As Cicognini rewrote it, his adaptation was not so much about a *burlador* of Seville as about an avenging stone guest of Seville, a *convitato di pietra,* the second part of Tirso's title, not the first. Cicognini must have felt that the statue was one of the genuine novelties of the Spanish drama and a real drawing card, hence his own, new title. The central character of his drama is no longer exclusively the *burlador.* Don Juan is not now the single, dominating, fascinating figure of the play as he was before. No longer during the course of the action do we wonder whether this young man will repent or not. In the new play, we have no reason to expect that he will. We wonder not *if* he will be struck down but, rather, *when* it will happen. We await the stone guest's arrival from the beginning of the play, from its very title. We know that a "just avenger" (III.x) is bound to appear sooner or later. Tirso's statue was a stiff, stern, scolding headmaster. Cicognini needed something more for a Don Giovanni who was no longer an adolescent prankster, indifferent to religious matters, but a truly lascivious, truly wicked individual. Cicognini intended his statue to be properly heavenly, a solemn and dignified instrument of divine justice whose thrice repeated call for repentance fairly begged for music.

STATUA: Don Giovanni, dammi la mano.
D. GIO: Eccola; ma, oh Dio, che stringo un ghiaccio,
un freddo marmo? Lasciami, traditore!

(Don Giovanni pone mano a uno stile, e gli tira nel petto.)

STATUA: Pentiti, Don Giovanni.
D. GIO: Lasciami dico, ohimè.
STATUA: Pentiti, Don Giovanni.
D. GIO: Ohimè io moro, aiuto!
STATUA: Pentiti, Don Giovanni.

(III.viii)

[STATUE: Don Giovanni, give me your hand.
D. GIO: Here it is; oh, my God, am I gripping ice,
cold marble? Let me go, traitor!

(Don Giovanni takes hold of a dagger and strikes at his breast.)

STATUE: Repent, Don Giovanni.
D. GIO: Let me go, I say; oh God!
STATUE: Repent, Don Giovanni.
D. GIO: Oh God, I'm dying; help!
STATUE: Repent, Don Giovanni.]

In spite of the compelling presence of the statue, Cicognini's play is far inferior to Tirso's. He stripped down the plot, ruthlessly abbreviated dialogues, and virtually eliminated any subtlety of characterization. Yet the result was probably exactly what he wanted it to be: a play that was simple, easy to follow, entertaining, and shallow. He placed a great deal of emphasis on the comic. The country folk tell riddles with salacious double meanings and servants turn somersaults; two servants, Don Giovanni's Passarino and Duca Ottavio's Fichetto, have roles equal in importance to the roles of their masters. They engage in frequent *lazzi,* typical of the commedia dell'arte, often abetted in their nonsense by Don Giovanni and Duca Ottavio themselves. At the dinner for the statue, Passarino eats twelve eggs, drinks twelve glasses of wine, and smartly farts to the accompaniment of horns after draining each glass.

Yet foolish or not, inferior or not, moments added to the story by Cicognini endured all the way to Mozart. In fact, it is hard not to hear faint echoes of his music in the statue's lines (quoted previously) or in these solemn words also uttered by the statue: "Non ha bisogno di cibi terreni, chi è fuori di vita mortale" [One who is beyond mortal life has no need of terrestrial foods]; or a moment later: "Don Giovanni: m'invitasti teco a cena, io venni; t'invito meco a cena, verrai?" [Don Giovanni, you invited me to dinner with you; I have come. I invite you to dinner with me; will you come?][8] (III.v). Cicognini established

8. In Da Ponte the equivalent verses are as follows.

IL COM:	Dammi la mano in pegno!
D. GIO:	Eccola! Ohimè!
IL COM:	Cos'hai?
D. GIO:	Che gelo è questo mai!
IL COM:	Pentiti, cangia vita: è l'ultimo momento!
D. GIO:	No, no, ch'io non mi pento: vanne lontan da me!
IL COM:	Pentiti, scellerato!
D. GIO:	No, vecchio infatuato!
IL COM:	Pentiti.
D. GIO:	No.
IL COM:	Sì.
D. GIO:	No.
IL COM:	Ah, tempo più non v'è!

(II.xvii)

IL COM:	Non si pasce di cibo mortale chi si pasce di cibo celeste.

(II.xvii)

IL COM:	Tu m'invitasti a cena: il tuo dover or sai. Rispondimi: verrai tu a cenar meco?

(II.xvii)

Text from Lorenzo Da Ponte, *Tre libretti per Mozart,* ed. Paolo Lecaldano (Milan: Biblioteca Universale Rizzoli, 1956).

an Italian basis for the legend; nearly all future Italian librettists, most of whom were certainly not familiar with Tirso, looked back to him for essential elements of the story, and they are in his debt.

In addition to Cicognini's version, *scenari* from the commedia dell'arte may also have begun to circulate quite soon after Tirso's *El burlador* reached Italy, although none has survived.[9] Those that have survived are probably of a slightly later date. At any rate, it is clear that by 1641 the story and its title, *Il convitato di pietra,* were so well known that they could be alluded to in an off-hand way for humorous effect, as Bartolomeo Bocchini did in his mock-epic poem, when he described an elderly figure in *Le pazzie de' savi overo Il Lambertaccio.*

Qui tacque il veglio e col suo cul sentato
rimase senza moto e senza lena
che pareva di pietra il convitato
ma non vi fu chi l'invitasse a cena.

(Canto I, 17)

[At this, the old man fell silent, and seated on his rear end,
he remained motionless and without breathing,
so that he seemed like the stone guest,
but there was no one who invited him to dinner.]

A later annotator, glossing these lines, complained that they referred to a "very vulgar tragedy" frequently played by the comedians of the commedia dell'arte.[10] From these verses and their gloss two things are evident: by the fourth decade of the century, the play was extremely popular, as it would continue to be for the next 150 years, and it was already being treated with contempt by those who pretended to be arbiters of good taste, as was also to be its destiny.

Not everyone chose to follow Cicognini's simple comic manner. Among the very earliest Italian versions of the legend was one by a famous *capocomico,* head of the Compagnia dei Fedeli, Giambattista Andreini. Born around 1579, he achieved true international success both as an impresario—his stage settings were particularly renowned—and as a prolific writer of religious dramas, comedies, tragedies, and every genre in between. Yet his *Convitato di pietra* has remained almost totally unknown. It exists today only in manuscript form in

9. Croce, *Aneddoti,* 127–28. Croce also mentions that Tiberio Fiorilli, a famous Scaramouche, was said to have begun his career in a *Convitato di pietra* well before 1640.

10. Unknown annotator, quoted in Fucilla, "*El Convidado,*" 6.

the Biblioteca Nazionale in Florence. It was written, apparently, some time before 1651.[11]

Andreini was familiar with Tirso's version of the story and with Cicognini's, from whom he borrowed several scenes. What he did not borrow was Cicognini's earthy representation of the legend. Instead, into what had heretofore been a relatively realistic narrative, Andreini inserted scenes with mythological figures—Vulcan speaking with the Titans, Neptune promising justice to Tisbea. He favored settings of the most elaborate and grotesque fullness, and he couched his story in language that was involuted, artificial, and pompous.[12] The legend

---

11. Antonio García Berrio ("El Primer *Convidado de piedra* no Español," *Revista de Filología Española* 50 [1967]: 25–56), who, as far as I know, is the only critic to have studied this manuscript and to have published part of the text, reports that the library catalog entry quotes a dedicatory letter dated Florence, 17 December 1651. The letter refers to "Il nuovo Risarcito convitato di Pietra in versi composto. Al ser. signor Principe Leopoldo dedicato: autore Gio. Batt. Andreini fiorentino, per li Theatri detto Lelio Fedele" (see p. 26). The date indicated by this letter is puzzling. Andreini died in 1654; he had retired from the stage some years before. He did most of his work in the 1620s and 1630s. I suspect, therefore, that his *Convitato* was written some years earlier than 1651, although after Cicognini's version, and that the date of 1651 refers only to this "Risarcito" copy of his play. No mention of it appears in Lione Allacci's *Drammaturgia,* first published in Rome in 1666, though Allacci's volume includes other works by Andreini.

12. This, for example, is the setting for the statue's dinner.

> Qui veder si dourà una gran mensa con due seggiole nere e uno scagno nero, che dourano seruir quelli per Comend. e per D. Gio. e per Grillo [Don Giovanni's servant]. Coprirà la tauola un gran tapetto nero con touaglia, touagliuoli, piatti tutti neri; per uiuande altro non ci sarà che corui, maluecchie, rondoni, storni, merli, alcioni, guffi, civette, barbagianni; teste di morti per candeliere li quali col porui dentro lumini accesi seruir dourano per luce, douendosi il theatro tutto obtenebrarsi, non douendosi quello rischiarare se non per così fatti lumi. Sopra la stessa mensa come per uiuande grasse seruir dourano questi uccelami. . . . A destra a sinistra pur ci saranno due gran credenze di nero addobate, quella a destra d'ossi di morti tra quelli intermezzati di fiaschi neri, bichieri neri, e pani neri con teste pur di morti con quei lucernini per entroui, onde per gli occhi e per le bocche serua ad illuminare l'oppacità del teatro. La credenza a sinistra guernita sarà da bacini pur neri tra quali altre teste de morti esser dourannoui con la stessa illuminatione. . . . (42–43)

This is a bit of the final conversation between Don Giovanni and the Commendatore.

D. GIO: Cauaglier, tu perdona
S'a te nel apparire il piè fu tardo.
COM: A tempo tu venisti in punto appunto,
Ch'io per tumoli erraua,
E i morti resuegliaua,
Per mirar tutto fiamme quel sentiero
Che a Dite de' condur gran Caualliero.
Hora t'auuicina.
D. GIO: Ecco m'inoltro.
GRILLO: O sasso maladetto,

did not come alive in his hands. It seems, incidentally, that among those who witnessed Don Giovanni's downfall was his mother, Lisidora. I believe that this play may be the only one in which Don Juan's mother appears. But neither this fact nor any other in it seems to have sparked the invention of later writers.

A third *Convitato* circulated more or less at the same time and was apparently much more successful than Andreini's. It was by Onofrio Giliberto di Solofra and was published by Francesco Savio in Naples in 1652. His version is often considered to have been a principal source for commedia dell'arte *scenari* performed by Italian troupes in France and a basis for two full French adaptations of the legend prior to Molière's. The text has been lost, but Italian playwright Carlo Goldoni, who had read both this play and Cicognini's and who believed that both were taken from a Spanish original, indicated that there was "very little difference . . . between these two translations."[13] Most modern commentary on Giliberto's presently nonexistent text is purely speculative.

Three *scenari* performed in Italy by the *improvvisi* do exist and give us an idea of what the legend was like around 1650.[14] The first, entitled (as expected)

Che per non stare in piede
O in arcione o in su seggiola risieda.
D. Gio: O pomposo apparecchio, che m'incita
A depor mense regie,
Per trar da' cimiteri ogn'hor mia uita.
Com: Del pasteggiare i' godo
Che ti diletti, e sodisfaccia il modo.
Grillo: Di uomitar già sento
Che le uiscere mie hanno talento.
Nero pan, neri piatti,
Neri corui piumosi,
E che forse n'ha Vglioa per tanti gatti?
Com: Auuicinati, e siedi
Grillo tu pur.
Grillo: Io sempre mangio in piedi
Per poter correr uia.
D. Gio: Un incentiuo i' sento
L'epa di cotai cibi sattollare,
Nè so più ritardare,
Onde seggomi pronto a te uicino;
Drago apparecchia il sanguinoso uino.
Com: O così Don Giovanni, inuitto siedi;
Tu che fai insedente?

(47–48)

13. Carlo Goldoni, "L'autore a chi legge," in *Don Giovanni Tenorio o sia Il dissoluto,* vol. 9 of *Tutte le opere di Carlo Goldoni,* ed. Giuseppe Ortolani, 2d ed. (Milan: Mondadori, 1960), 215.

14. All three may be found in Marcello Spaziani, *Don Giovanni dagli scenari dell'arte alla "foire"* (Rome: Edizione di storia e letterature, 1978): 99–134.

Il convitato di pietra, is part of the Ciro Monarca collection in the Biblioteca Casanatense in Rome. Only a few pages long, it presents a very abbreviated version of Cicognini's play and offers nothing new in terms of cast or plot. What does strike a reader, however, are the many statements in the text itself that this or that character plays his "usual" scene or "does his routines" (*lazzi*); yet no explanation is given about what the scene is or what the routines are. By the middle of the century, the stone guest had visited everywhere, and every actor knew by heart what he and his companion players were supposed to do and say on stage.

The second *scenario,* also a *Convitato,* is from Naples and is part of a collection known as the *Cibaldone comico di varij suggetti di commedie ed opere bellissime.* It was gathered together by a comic actor, Antonino Passanti. Passanti prepared his collection in 1700, but his *scenari* are considered to be copies of mid-seventeenth-century originals. His text has a Neapolitan flavor in language and character. Several of the country folk, Spanish in Tirso and Cicognini, have now been turned into comic Neapolitan figures. They are journeying to Castile to seek redress from the king for various unspecified wrongs. Don Giovanni comes across them as he too travels toward Castile. Passanti's version, somewhat more extensive than the *scenario* of Rome, also owes much of its story to Cicognini; nonetheless, some elements of it, not found in the Italian version, hark back directly to Tirso.

Once again, plot and character follow the standard lesson, yet an occasional new and interesting detail has been added. The statue at its first appearance is now on horseback. Da Ponte's Don Giovanni will find himself in a cemetery surrounded by "diverse equestrian monuments, among them that of the Commendatore" (II.xii). For the first time the statue speaks; in reply to Don Giovanni's dinner invitation, it utters a clear and unequivocal "Sì." Heretofore it had only nodded in assent. At the end of the play it flies upward toward heaven as Don Giovanni falls below. Duca Ottavio has become more and more the ineffectual aristocrat that he will be in Mozart. He can hardly imagine Don Giovanni guilty of the crimes of which he is accused because he knows him to be "un ben nato cavaliere" [a well-born gentleman] (III.iii). Don Giovanni's dinner for the statue takes place in a "villa con casino" (III.iv), perhaps the same "casino" (I.iv) that Da Ponte's Don Giovanni will use for seductions. When the statue arrives, Don Giovanni brazenly raises a toast to the most beautiful woman he has enjoyed in Castile. He means, of course, the statue's own daughter, Donna Anna. While this last idea is not taken up by Da Ponte, it became popular with other opera librettists as a good occasion for song and for toasting and flattering the lovely ladies of their city.

But what one notes in particular in these two *scenari* is the consistently low level of humor: Don Giovanni passes himself off as a dancing master at a country wedding celebration, Pulcinella stumbles against the dead body of the Commendatore and takes a pratfall, the peasant girl, Rosetta, talks about the "occhialone," the telescope, that Don Giovanni placed in her hand during the night they spent together. The *scenari* are crude, low-class entertainment. The performances must have been fun, but hardly moving and very forgettable, much like a good James Bond movie.

The third *scenario,* also part of the Ciro Monarca collection, bears a new and different title: *L'ateista fulminato.* It is not about Don Giovanni, although many of the things that happen to the protagonist, Count Aurelio, also happen to Don Giovanni, in particular his encounters with various statuary. However, unlike his peers, Aurelio is hardly a good-natured, carefree adventurer among the erotic. This Aurelio-Giovanni is violent, cruel, and cold-blooded. The heads of several of his victims are impaled on spikes. Even less is he a reflective adventurer, as some later Don Juans will be. Aurelio does not think; he reacts. He is an animal, crazed, unpredictable in thought and action. The *scenario* is of no real interest except for the appearance of a "romito," a hermit, whose character and actions foreshadow those of Molière's gentle and innocent *pauvre.* At the play's conclusion, a bolt of lightning opens a fissure at Aurelio's feet, and he falls into it headlong. Not many years hence, thunder and lightning will explode directly over the wicked head of Molière's Dom Juan.

Thomas Shadwell, the vigorous English Restoration playwright, may have been familiar with this *scenario.* To parry any suggestion that his own Don Juan play, *The Libertine,* might be criticized as an encouragement to vice, he claimed to have been told by "a worthy Gentleman" that he, the worthy, had seen in Italy a play of similar nature "acted there by the name of *Atheisto Fulminato,* in Churches, on *Sundays,* as a part of Devotion."[15] I suspect either that the memory of the "worthy Gentleman" is very unreliable or that Shadwell is pulling our leg. No record of such performances of *L'ateista fulminato* in Churches in Italy on *Sundays* has come down to us. And certainly this *scenario,* if it is the one the worthy saw, would not have inspired anyone to great Devotion.

Shortly after the middle of the century, perhaps in 1658 or perhaps a few years earlier, the players of the commedia dell'arte took their stone guest to France, where the newest thing about their old play was its title. *Il convitato di pietra* became *Le Festin de Pierre,* it being generally agreed, by default as it were, that, in France anyway, the Commendatore's Christian name was Peter. The

15. Thomas Shadwell, "Preface," in *The Libertine,* vol. 3 of *The Complete Works of Thomas Shadwell,* ed. Montague Summers (London: Fortune Press, 1927), 21.

comedy met with great success. In 1665, a contemporary chronicler declared that the tale was "famous throughout the land";[16] a few years later another observed that the "beau" *Festin de Pierre* "would make a stone laugh," thanks to the extraordinary ability of its actors.[17] The Parfaict brothers, who so carefully documented the history of Italian theater in France, were of the same opinion concerning its success. In their *Histoire de l'ancien théâtre italien* (published in 1767), they noted that "the Italian comedians presented that play in the first years of their permanence in France, and it had such prodigious success that various French theaters competed in putting on copies of it."[18] Then, in 1673, once everyone was familiar with Don Juan's story, the Italian players introduced a new twist. In a follow-up version, they portrayed not the adventures of Don Juan but those of a wicked bastard son.[19]

The story was probably introduced to Paris by a company of Italian actors performing at the Petit Bourbon. Their *capocomico* was Domenico Locatelli, who, when his company put on the *Convitato,* would have played the principal role; that is, he would have taken the part not of Don Giovanni but of his servant, whom Locatelli called Trivellino.[20] Unfortunately we do not know what the Locatelli *scenario,* performed in Italian, was like. All trace of it has disappeared.

Yet we do have a record of some later performances by the same company. These featured a brilliant comic actor who gradually replaced Locatelli as head player and who took over as *capocomico* following Locatelli's death in 1671. This young man was Domenico Biancolelli. He was born in Bologna in 1636 and died in Paris in 1688. In 1661, at the age of twenty-five, Biancolelli, or Dominique as he became known in France, was called to Paris by Cardinal Mazarin, who was well aware of his genius. Dominique soon acquired such fame and prestige that he counted among his intimate friends Louis XIV himself. Dominique was always closely associated with the character of Arlecchino, a role to which he brought new grace and elegance of gesture and movement. He changed Arlecchino's rag-tag costume into the clean, diamond-shaped patches and white

16. Loret, 14 February 1665, quoted in Georges Couton, in Molière, *Oeuvres complètes* (Mayenne: Gallimard, 1971), 2:8.

17. Robinet, 27 November 1669, quoted in Spaziani, *Don Giovanni dagli scenari,* 38.

18. François Parfaict and Claude Parfaict, *Histoire de l'ancien théâtre italien, depuis son origine en France, jusqu'à sa suppression en l'année* 1697 (1765; reprint, New York: AMS, 1978), 265.

19. Robinet, 4 February 1673, quoted in Parfaict and Parfaict, *Histoire,* 411.

20. Virginia Scott (*The Commedia dell'Arte in Paris 1644–1697* [Charlottesville: University Press of Virginia, 1990], 45–46, 77) argues that the servant's role was taken by another member of the troupe, Tiberio Fiorilli. Fiorilli was always associated with the figure of Scaramouche. She also calls into question whether Locatelli should truly be considered the company's *capocomico.*

pleated collar that it has remained. It was as Don Giovanni's servant, now using the name of Arlecchino, that Biancolelli performed in *Il convitato di pietra*.

We know what Biancolelli's Arlecchino was like, because, some years later (between 1662 and 1680), the actor wrote out a prose description in Italian of the nearly eighty *scenari* in which he had appeared in this role. Although the Italian text has since been lost, a French translation of it was made between 1734 and 1750 by Thomas-Simon Gueullette, a Parisian lawyer, man of letters, and passionate theater buff. It is Gueullette's French translation of Biancolelli's Italian *Convitato* that exists today.[21] Although Biancolelli joined Locatelli's company in 1661, it is unclear precisely when he began to perform his version of the story. Did it precede Molière's *Dom Juan,* first given in 1665, and hence serve as an influence on it, or did it, as Marcello Spaziani suggests in *Don Giovanni dagli scenari dell'arte alla "foire,"* postdate Molière's version, of which it would then be, as the critic believes, a parody?[22]

Given Biancolelli's comic brilliance, it is no surprise that the principal figure of his *Convitato/Festin* is Arlecchino/Arlequin, not Don Giovanni/Dom Jouan: a comical Arlequin who drags himself out of the sea wearing ten or twelve air-filled bladders to keep him afloat; a hungry Arlequin who uses a fishhook to snatch away a capon from Dom Jouan's table; a cowardly Arlequin who, holding a chicken in one hand and a lighted candlestick in the other, fearfully approaches the door behind which the Commendatore is knocking.

Biancolelli's story does not differ significantly from the other Italian versions, nor are there notable variations within the plot. There may be one exception. The customary first scene, the seduction of Donna Isabella in Naples, seems to have been eliminated, for the comedy opens, according to Biancolelli, with the arrival of the King of Naples who talks to him about Dom Jouan's libertine behavior. Over the course of time, the Neapolitan scenes will be dropped altogether; they do not appear in Da Ponte's text at all.[23]

One moment does seem new. Whether this moment helped to color Molière's great final scene between Done Elvire and Dom Juan or whether it is a parody of it, I cannot say. The moment is not in and of itself of great importance.

21. See Macchia, *Vita avventura,* or Spaziani, *Don Giovanni dagli scenari,* for the full text.

22. See "Lo scenario degli 'italiens': Biancolelli fra la tradizione italiana e Molière: una 'parodia' di *Dom Juan*?," in Spaziani, *Don Giovanni dagli scenari,* 27–56.

23. It may be, of course, that the Neapolitan seduction scene was of no interest to Biancolelli; he may not have been a part of it and therefore, since his text was to serve as a memory aid, he may have simply skipped over it. In fact, in an addendum to the original text known as "La Suite du festin de Pierre," Biancolelli added a long monologue as part of what he defined as "ma première scène." It is spoken "quand mon maistre a donné la sérénade et s'est retiré" (see Spaziani, *Don Giovanni dagli scenari,* 136). This scene could well have taken place outside Donna Isabella's house.

Yet it wonderfully illustrates how, in some mysterious way, elements of the legend worked their way through the decades, joining and separating, suggesting and influencing, sometimes operating in plain sight, sometimes hidden from view, in such a way that a comic scene played by an Italian comedian in Paris in the 1660s eventually touched an Italian librettist and an Austrian musician in Vienna in 1787. In the third act, writes Biancolelli,

> I want to reprove Dom Jouan for his vices. . . . He pretends to be open to my remonstrances. I throw myself before him, he gets on his knees too and pretends to implore Jupiter. I give thanks to Heaven for his conversion. He gets up, gives me a kick in the rear and makes fun of me. Then I get up again and say: "Let's go to a bordello." He orders me to serve dinner.[24]

We are witness to an unedifying scene of human baseness, a mocking of man's spiritual dignity: Arlequin's shallowly pious remonstrances, Dom Jouan's affected contrition, Arlequin and Dom Jouan on their knees, Dom Jouan's vulgar kick in the rear followed by Arlequin's blunt confession that it is time for sex. The scene is coarse, yet it has a rhythm and a sharpness of intent, an abruptness and, I am inclined to say, an insightfulness into the human character that clearly reflect the moment in Da Ponte's libretto when Donna Elvira last encounters Don Giovanni. She kneels and begs him to reform; he mockingly drops to his knees, swears he is listening seriously, and, "with affected tenderness," he asks: "What do you want, my love?" Then, having risen, harshly, no longer playacting: "Let me eat, and if you like, you eat with me" (II.xvi). A false act of contrition, an act of mockery, and then the coarse voice of the senses; for that "eat with me" is nothing more or less than a request for sex, for Donna Elvira to remain and dine and spend the night, the equivalent of Arlequin's long ago "Let's go to a bordello."

Around the same time as the *commedie improvvisate* of Locatelli and Biancolelli were being performed, four *commedie sostenute* were produced in France. As works of art, three were negligible, important only in that they too, like so many others, helped to give form and shape to a legend that was really bigger, at this point, than the sum of its parts. Yet the first two did have a certain historical importance, for they served as a prompt for the third, a profound and moving study of human searching and of human despair, Molière's *Dom Juan* of 1665. Next to his, the other three were hack work: Dorimond's *Le Festin de Pierre ou*

24. Spaziani, *Don Giovanni dagli scenari,* 144, 145.

Le fils criminel (1658), Villiers's *Le Festin de Pierre ou Le fils criminel* (1659), and Rosimond's *Le Nouveau festin de Pierre ou L'athée foudroyé* (1670).

Dorimond—his real name was Nicolas Drouin—was born in Paris around 1628 and died sometime before 1673. He was an obscure actor and playwright, a member of the Troupe de Mademoiselle. He is credited with seven or more plays, among them this *Festin de Pierre.*[25] The actors of the commedia dell'arte played their Don Juans in Italian. Dorimond's was the first to be played in French. It was probably produced at the end of 1658 in Lyons and published there early the next year. It was republished four more times in the next twenty-five years.

Dorimond's play was quite different from its predecessors, most notably for the fact that, unlike the plays of the commedia, his was almost never light-hearted. He called it a *tragi-comédie* and adapted it to classical French theatrical forms: five acts of rhymed alexandrine couplets. In Dorimond's hands, alexandrine couplets were not congenial to Don Juan's personality. Could this be the reason that his Dom Jouan lacked charm? Molière wrote his play in prose. Although Dorimond's protagonist is not without boldness, not without a certain reflective intellectual curiosity, he is not very likeable: harsh with his father, disdainful with other men, indifferent to the souls of women, in speech more prone to the grandiose than to the personal. He is even a touch the hypocrite, a fact that seems to have pleased and impressed Molière. All this could be forgiven if there were moments of gaiety; but Dom Jouan never smiles; he is deadly serious, ice cold. Perhaps it is the fault of the alexandrines or of the fact that, as he says of himself, "I have never known violent love" (I.iii). He does not know what true passion is.

Dom Jouan's story, as Dorimond tells it, is more of the same; but though once again the traditional plot is adopted, there are occasional variations and modifications. Dom Jouan's father, here called Dom Alvaros, returns to play the fairly prominent role of disappointed parent. Dom Jouan, unmoved by his father's complaints, rebuffs him with a slap and a curse, hence the play's subtitle, *Le fils criminel.* He dies of heartbreak. The figure of Donna Isabella has been completely removed, as have all the scenes once set in Naples. Dorimond's play takes place entirely in Spain. The first act is a series of actionless, plot-setting, character-explaining conversations. The true action of the drama begins in the second act, as Dom Jouan attempts to violate Amarille, the daughter of Dom Pierre. Amarille has become a strong, onstage presence, a forceful and robust

25. For the complete text, see Enea Balmas, *Il mito di Don Giovanni nel seicento francese,* vol. 1, *Testi* (Milan: Cisalpino-Goliardica, 1977).

personality, no longer the brief, offstage voice she had been as Doña Ana in Tirso's *Burlador* or the brief, onstage figure she was in Cicognini. It is almost as if the legend, with an instinctive life of its own, were now beginning to realize that the heart of the drama lay in a deadly contest of personalities and wills between Donna Anna, pillar of public virtue, though privately not without hidden faults and hypocrisies, and Don Juan, scourge of public virtue, though privately not without a certain melting fascination. All extraneous matters are being cast away.

In fact, as the legend goes shaping itself into the form in which it will present itself to Mozart, it is not difficult to hear, as can be heard in this play, echoes of things to come, echoes from the future, a faint Dapontian voice searching about for usable words and phrases and forms. The present words and forms are seeds that finally mature in Da Ponte's mind and blossom beneath the heat of Mozart's music. Dorimond opens his second act exactly as Da Ponte will open his first: Dom Jouan's complaining servant, Briguelle, is waiting outside Amarille's house, as Leporello will wait outside the house of Donna Anna. Leporello grumbles that he has to put up with wind and rain, with eating and sleeping badly. He does not want to serve this so-called "fine gentleman" of his any longer. It is not fair, he has had enough.

> Voi star dentro con la bella,
> ed io far la sentinella!
>
> (I.i)

> [You inside with the lovely lady,
> and me acting as sentinel!]

Leporello is echoing, albeit with far sharper wit and concision, Briguelle's similar complaint. At one point he even echoes a rhyme that Briguelle had used.

> Il est allé duper une Amante nouvelle,
> Cependant que je fais icy la sentinelle.[26]
>
> (II.i)

26. Briguelle's full speech is as follows.

> C'est tout de bon, destin, tu me fais enrager.
> Tout mon mal seroit peu si j'avois à manger!
> Mais icy m'exposer au vent d'une cuisine,
> C'est bien entierement conclure ma ruine.

[He has gone to trick a new lady,
while I'm here acting as sentinel.]

Likewise beginning to mature is Da Ponte's first act recitative and *scena* in which Donna Anna finally explains to Don Ottavio what happened between her and Don Giovanni. To Dom Philippe's request, "Mais, Madame, comment s'est fait cette action?," Amarille now replies, not as she had to the king in Cicognini's version, briefly and rather colorlessly, but fully, intimately, and breathlessly, with words that here and there seem to glow like sparks.

A la faveur de l'ombre il s'est glissé chez nous,
Dedans l'obscurité j'ay creu que c'estoit vous:
Pensant donc vous trouver, j'ay trouvé le perfide.
D'une lasche action il paroissoit avide.

Dedans cette maison j'oys remüer les plats,
Et cependant je n'ay que l'air pour mon repas.
Si dans nostre Almanach je puis voir la Planette
Qui m'expose aux rigueurs d'une telle disette,
Elle aura mille coups, je la déchireray
Et j'en feray du feu dont je me chaufferay.
Ah! Planette maudite et peu considerante,
Si de mon appetit tu ne remplis l'attente,
Au moins guarantis-moy des mains d'un maistre fou,
Qui m'a plus de cent fois pensé rompre le cou.
Il est allé duper une Amante nouvelle,
Cependant que je fais icy la sentinelle;
Si son rival venoit, je craindrois bien pour luy,
Et pour mon dos aussi. Toutesfois pour autruy
Ne soyons pas si sot; évitons la querrelle,
Et si nous en voyons, enfilons la venelle. . . .

Leporello's speech is as follows.

Notte e giorno faticar
per chi nulla sa gradir;
piova e vento sopportar,
mangiar male e mal dormir . . .
voglio far il gentiluomo,
e non voglio più servir.

Oh, che caro galantuomo!
Voi star dentro con la bella,
ed io far la sentinella! . . .
Ma mi par che venga gente . . .
Non mi voglio far sentir.

Il m'a voulu forcer; mais, et de ses discours,
Et de ses trahisons, j'ay sçeu rompre le cours.[27]

(II.iii)

[Under cover of night he slipped into our apartment;
in the darkness I thought that he was you.
Expecting therefore to find you, I found this perfidious man.
He seemed intent on a wicked act.
He tried to bend me to his will, but I was able to break
the course of both his speech and his treasonable actions.]

"Ah! Dieu!" breathes out Dom Philippe after her "J'ay sçeu rompre le cours," as will Don Ottavio—"Ohimè! respiro"—after Donna Anna's "Da lui mi sciolsi."

The mania for list making is growing. Lists are getting longer and more specific. Women are not the only thing that Dom Jouan catalogs. To Briguelle contemptuously: "Your relatives are scattered all over the world, in Germany, in Flanders, in France, in England, even in Turkey and Japan" (III.ii). But the important list is the one of conquests. It is now lengthier, more detailed and critical. Names are carefully cataloged: Angelique, Benoiste, Clorianne, Dorinde, etc., etc., as well as some of the girls' characteristics: "Glodine the cripple and Catin the pugnosed."[28]

---

27. Donna Anna's recitative begins as follows.

Era già alquanto
avanzata la notte,
Quando nelle mie stanze, ove soletta
Mi trovai per sventura, entrar io vidi
In un mantello avvolto
Un uom che al primo istante
Avea preso per voi:
Ma riconobbi poi
Che un inganno era il mio . . .

(I.xiii)

28. The full text is as follows.

Je vous les vais nommer: dans son pays natal
L'aure, dont le bel oeil au vostre estoit esgal,
Dorinde, Clorianne, Amarante, Isabelle,
Selimene, Selye et Lucresse et Marcelle,
Angelique, Lucelle, Aminthe, Amarillis,
Et celle dont on fit des chançons, c'ét Fillis,
Glodine la boiteuse, et Catin la camuse

The second Don Juan play in French was very similar to Dorimond's. It too was a five-act *tragi-comédie* in rhymed alexandrine couplets; it too bore the title *Le Festin de Pierre ou Le fils criminel.*[29] These plays were similar because the second playwright, a popular French actor whose stage name was Villiers, kept a copy of Dorimond's close at hand while writing his own. He claimed that both versions were translations of an Italian original (often thought to have been the lost version by Onofrio Giliberto), but boasted that his version "infinitely surpasses" that of his rivals Dorimond and Locatelli.[30]

Villiers—his real name was Claude Deschamps—was born around 1600 and died in 1681. His whole life was dedicated to the theater, and he achieved a very respectable reputation as both writer and actor of comedies and tragedies. In 1642 he began working in one of the best-known theaters of Paris, l'Hôtel de Bourgogne, and it is there that his Don Juan play was first performed in 1659. Villiers took the part of Dom Juan's servant, Philipin, a servant role he performed in other comedies as well and that very much contributed to the success of his career. His comedy was published the following year, in 1660, in both Paris and Amsterdam and again in Paris in 1665.

Villiers had no illusion about the lasting artistic value of his work. He considered the story of Don Juan nothing more than a good drawing card. As a practical man of the theater he was quite aware of "the French in the country and the Italians in Paris, who have stirred up so much excitement with it." He was referring to Dorimond's success with the legend in Lyons and to the successes in Paris of the comedians from Italy. He wanted the same for his company, and it did not much matter to him if the play was, as indeed he thought it was, irregular, awkward, and morally offensive. In fact, for our purposes, Villiers's version is most interesting precisely for what he has to say about the state of the legend in the two prefaces, one to Pierre Corneille and one to his readers, from which I have been citing.[31] Villiers confirms the legend's popularity, while at

---

Qui se laissa duper comme une pauvre buse,
Jannete, Marion, Perrette, Janneton,
Jacqueline, Margot, Perronnelle, et Suzon,
Germaine, Violante, Anne, Fanchon, Gillette,
Benoiste, Marinnette, Argine et Guillemette,
Et celles que le temps m'oste du souvenir,
Sont dedans cette Liste.

(IV.vi)

29. The complete text of the play with its two prefaces, "A Monsieur de Corneille" and "Au Lecteur," can be found in Gendarme de Bévotte, *Le Festin.* The play, without prefaces, can also be found in Balmas, *Il mito di Don Giovanni* 1.

30. Gendarme de Bévotte, *Le Festin,* 154.

31. Gendarme de Bévotte, *Le Festin,* 153–59.

the same time he once again confirms the contempt in which it was held by those who claimed to arbitrate what was and what was not in good taste. He apologizes for having written such a play and apologizes that his troupe was "reduced to putting on show a man and a horse, for the lack of something better."[32] By "a man and a horse" he meant the stone statue on its stone horse, two ridiculous aspects of the legend that, however, in his opinion helped to guarantee the tale's popularity. It was precisely these sorts of foolish things that attracted large crowds; even though most were "des ignorans,"[33] he could not do without them because crowds meant profits. With a certain detached fastidiousness he explained how the play came about.

> My companions . . . , after having seen all of Paris rush en masse to see what the Italian comedians did with [the Don Juan story], were persuaded that if the subject were put into French for the comprehension of those who do not understand Italian, of which there is a large number in Paris, and particularly if it were in simple verses such as these, it would draw in a large number of people who do not put great stock in the question of proper form, so often sought after but so little found up to now; and that provided the figure of Dom Pierre and his horse were well conceived and well proportioned, the play would be within the rules that they require. Large numbers of people bring in money; it is this money in part which helps keep our theater going.[34]

Villiers's play—its plot and its characters—is not markedly different from Dorimond's. His Dom Juan is perhaps even colder, vainer, and more self-centered. He is either disinterested in others or downright contemptuous of them. He suffers no authority: "I am my own king, my master, and my fate and my gods" (I.v). He kills Amarille's father, Dom Pierre, and also kills her betrothed, Dom Philippe, even though the latter is unarmed. He holds no one in affection. He cannot tolerate his father, whom he brutally punches with his fists and on whom he wishes death. His seductions are brief, libidinous acts of physical release: his anger at Amarille's rejection is that of wounded pride, not of hurt affection. Yet he is enormously attractive, a fact generally implied but rarely stated in other versions. Here is Amarille's description of him to Dom Philippe *after* he has killed her father.

---

32. Gendarme de Bévotte, *Le Festin,* 155.
33. Gendarme de Bévotte, *Le Festin,* 153.
34. Gendarme de Bévotte, *Le Festin,* 158–59.

D. PHILIPPE:	His cut?
AMARILLE:	Rich and handsome.
D. PHILIPPE:	His air?
AMARILLE:	Bold.
D. PHILIPPE:	And his hair?
AMARILLE:	Rather blond.
D. PHILIPPE:	And his bearing?
AMARILLE:	Glorious.
	But as for the rest, he is wicked, brutal.

(II.iii)

In spite of all that has befallen her, there is a flutter of fascination in her speech.

Because this play is so much like Dorimond's, it too, here and there, echoes forward toward Da Ponte's, although in no way was it a source for the Italian librettist. One observes, for example, that an action involving peasants in pursuit of Dom Juan, who has carried off one of their young brides, is beginning to evolve into what will become, in Da Ponte, the unhappy pursuit of Don Giovanni by Masetto and his gullible peasant allies. In Cicognini this incident was limited to a brief stage direction: "*Passarino sees {the festive peasants}, he calls Don Giovanni, who also starts dancing like Passarino; then Don Giovanni abducts Brunetta and exits. The Dottore and Pantalone start yelling and bring the second act to a close*" (II.xvi). This roughly sketched event has now become, in Villiers, a fully developed scene with dialogue in which Dom Juan spots his prey, trips her father and her fiancé with his foot, and races off in escape. "Help, get the kidnapper, go get that bastard," shouts her outraged father (V.iv). Shortly afterward, Philipin warns Dom Juan to be on guard because he is being sought by "a hundred thousand peasants" (V.vi).

Though Da Ponte did not use Villiers's text as a source, Molière used it extensively, just as he used Dorimond's. Later opera librettists also expropriated several of the new ideas that he introduced into the legend. Not in all operas is Donna Anna so fond of her father as she is in Mozart's. Already in Villiers's text there is a certain friction between father and daughter caused by Amarille's love for Dom Philippe. Her father is jealous of the younger man. That friction will occasionally be developed to such a degree that, as we will see, the Amarille-Anna character will become quite rebellious in some versions. We will also see Don Juan temporarily lose his self control and begin to fear that he is emotionally unstable, even a monster. Such self-doubts appear for an instant in this text; a wave of angst briefly washes over his soul (IV.vii) but then quickly dissolves into a placid sea of sinfulness. This twist on the Don Juan psyche, although later tried several more times, never met with much success. Don Juan's seventeenth- and eighteenth-century public wanted him thoroughly and pleasantly bad, not uncomfortably angst ridden. That was for a later century. More in keeping with public expectation was the nasty song about his conquests that Dom Juan orders Philipin to sing to the statue, Dom Pierre (V.ii). He then asks Dom Pierre if he wants to hear another, this one about his daughter Amarille. In Giuseppe Foppa's libretto, *Il nuovo convitato di pietra,* Don Giovanni will raise his glass before the statue in a mocking toast to his daughter Anna (I.xvii).

In Paris, Molière was well aware of the good fortunes of the Italian troupe and of Dorimond and Villiers. When he unexpectedly found himself in need of a quick success, he too turned for help to the story of Don Juan, as so many others had, and specifically to the texts of his rivals. He plundered them as needed, but in so doing he brought the legend to life, as they had not. He poured fresh spirits into an old and commonplace bottle. In May 1664, in the presence of Louis XIV, Molière had read aloud the first three acts of his newest play, *Tartuffe.* The work proved controversial, and he was forced to withdraw it. Suddenly the players of his company, la Troupe de Monsieur, found themselves without the drawing power of a new comedy. Fearing financial ruin, they appealed to Molière for something to take its place. To fill the gap and to provide what he knew would be a sure source of ticket sales, Molière wrote a new *comédie, Dom Juan ou Le festin de Pierre.* He composed his five-act, prose version of the legend rapidly, perhaps in the matter of a few weeks. As the play went into rehearsal there must have been a certain pleasant sense of anticipation in Paris, or so it would seem from the following commentary, published the evening before the play's opening performance.

> The frightening *Festin de Pierre,* so famous throughout the land and which has succeeded so well at the Théâtre Italien, will make its appearance on our stage next week; it will satisfy and delight those who do not put off going to see this admirable subject that is able, they say, with its wonderful speeches to move hearts of bronze or stone.[35]

The play opened to a full house on 15 February 1665 in the Théâtre de la Salle du Palais-Royal. Molière himself took the part of Sganarelle. Although the first performance was a success, the playwright was swiftly and harshly criticized for having written scenes regarded as irreverent. He immediately introduced modifications into the text for the second performance. Thirteen more perfor-

35. Loret, 14 February 1665, quoted in Couton, in Molière, *Oeuvres complètes* 2:8.

mances followed; they may have included still further modifications. Administrative records indicate that attendance at all performances was quite good and that ticket sales were satisfactory. Then the theater closed for Easter. When it reopened, *Dom Juan* was no longer in the company's repertory. "It is clear," writes Georges Couton in his authoritative edition of Molière's work, "that he had received a piece of advice, as pressing as an order, to abandon *Dom Juan*."[36] A month later, Molière and his play were fiercely attacked in a lengthy pamphlet by an unnamed "avocat en Parlement" who accused him of immorality, atheism, and irreverence. The comedy was never again presented in his lifetime.

Molière's *Dom Juan* is a profound and fascinating play. It is filled with oddities: long discourses on tobacco, medicine, honor, and hypocrisy, which may or may not have anything to do with the story at hand; a Commandeur already six-months dead and whose death by Dom Juan's sword we are not even permitted to witness or to enjoy; a Don Juan, in fact, who does not kill anyone on stage and whose principal vice is not seduction but talking, either not enough or far too much; finally (though many other things could be added), a large cast of Frenchmen playing Spaniards, all of whom reside, for no discernable reason whatsoever, in Sicily. As Oscar Mandel comments in his usual lively and acute fashion, "The play is an anarchy of unrelated scenes, false anticipations, loose ends, and unexplained matters. What are we to say? The versions of Villiers, Dorimon and the pseudo-Cicognini hang together yet they are anemic; Molière's would be laughed out of a graduate class in playwriting, but it is a masterpiece."[37]

Indeed, Molière's is the finest play ever written on the Don Juan theme; it is the most truthful of all and the most disturbing. Molière has pushed the figure of Don Juan to the limit, for he has sensed, as no one else before or since, that what truly drives Don Juan is not his sexuality but a passionate, tormenting desire to comprehend himself and the chaotic universe he inhabits. Once again Oscar Mandel has said it well: "*Dom Juan* is so much a play about irreligion that it almost forgets to be a play about sex. Anna is missing; there are no abductions; . . . no irruptions into a lady's bedroom; no interrupted weddings."[38] He is quite right. The play is not "about sex." If there is sexual activity here, it is only because, in Dom Juan's quest for inner peace, for a comprehension of things—which is a possession of things—he is led to try to obtain his goal through sexual activity, by means of the peace of sexual satisfactions.

36. Couton, in Molière, *Oeuvres complètes* 2:3.

37. Oscar Mandel, ed., *The Theatre of Don Juan: A Collection of Plays and Views, 1630–1963* (Lincoln: University of Nebraska Press, 1963), 110.

38. Mandel, *Theatre of Don Juan,* 115.

Mandel errs in one thing only. This play is not really "about irreligion," but, like Mozart's opera, it too is "about" religion. Molière's Dom Juan is obsessed with a desire to possess absolute metaphysical truths, to know God. That desire is in every action he undertakes, every phrase he speaks, every moment of his life. And because he cannot find what he is seeking, he is in pain. Even Mozart did not sense the depths of Don Juan's pain as Molière has. Dom Juan suffers because he wants to believe and is not able to do so. For the world, he plays the libertine, the cynic, the hypocrite, the swaggerer, rejecting with contempt any notion that does not conform to his comforting and facile principle of faith that two plus two makes four, everywhere and always. Yet inwardly he is in anguish, for he is not entirely certain that he is right. He has, therefore, an urgency to lose himself in his sexuality; he is jealous of young lovers' happiness; he is irritated and contemptuous of the hermit's stubborn piety; he is testy with Sganarelle's pious, silly but probing conundrums. To the tough accusations of Sganarelle, of his father, of Dom Carlos and Done Elvire, his defensive response is either an abrupt change of subject or an agonized silence. He cannot discuss what he has not understood himself, and the material and spiritual worlds, their injustices, their aloofness, make no sense to him; he cannot fathom their intentions. At the same time, it is evident that he too senses, but refuses to accept without absolute proof, that even in the life of a rational man not all two plus twos make four. Certainly Done Elvire knows it is so; how otherwise can one explain her remarkable change by the play's conclusion? No longer vindictive, she pardons Dom Juan for the wrongs he has done her. Sganarelle knows it is so. "Are you not convinced even by a stone statue which moves and talks?" he asks his master, whose reply is a bitter revelation that his comprehension of the metaphysical is lit only by a dim, half-light: "Il y a bien quelque chose là-dedans que je ne comprends pas" [There is indeed something there that I do not understand]. His pride then struggles to reassert itself—though perhaps it is wrong to speak of pride; it is his self-esteem as a man, his dignity as a rational, free-thinking human being. He continues: "Mais quoi que ce puisse être, cela n'est pas capable ni de convaincre mon esprit, ni d'ébranler mon âme" [But whatever it may be, it is not capable of convincing my mind or of shaking my soul] (V.ii). As his end approaches, he is still seeking unequivocal proof that two plus two equals four, not only on earth but in divine matters as well. But he is, I think, tired of the search, tired of the struggle: "Si le Ciel me donne un avis, il faut qu'il parle un peu plus clairement, s'il veut que je l'entende" [If Heaven is giving me a warning, it must speak a little more clearly, if it wants me to understand it] (V.iv). In death he is heroic, a noble, tragic figure, for even as a disbeliever he has believed more honestly and fully than many who have claimed always to believe.

Da Ponte was not capable of understanding the agonies of heart of Molière's Dom Juan. In fact, nothing of any great importance from Molière's Don Juan character resurfaced in Da Ponte's libretto. What did touch the librettist was the warm, full-blooded figure of Done Elvire who, as Donna Elvira, is essentially the same woman that Molière's Dom Juan briefly married and abandoned, the same vibrant and embracing woman whose intense anger is only matched by the intensity of her forgiveness and whose final ardor of charity can only have been equaled by a similar ardor of sexual intensity for the man she once believed her husband to be. For her, Sganarelle and Leporello wept.

Not long after Molière's unexpected death in February 1673, his widow, Armande Béjart, asked Thomas Corneille, brother of the more famous Pierre Corneille, to prepare a safe, inoffensive version of her late husband's work. One supposes that she was well aware that she had a popular drawing card in her hands and that she also knew that it was not in marketable condition. By turning to Thomas Corneille, she was turning to first-rate help. Although now eclipsed by his older brother, in 1673 Thomas was a highly regarded playwright who throughout a long career (he was born in 1625 and died in 1709) had many successful works to his credit. One of his first, a tragedy entitled *Timocrate,* had held the stage in Paris in 1656 for an extraordinary six-month run. He rapidly completed a properly emasculated verse adaptation of Molière's virile prose comedy within the year, but, for reasons unknown, the revision was not offered publicly until 12 February 1677. It was performed at the theater in Rue Guénégaud where what was left of Molière's company was then playing. With that performance, Thomas Corneille's adaptation became Molière's play. It was Corneille's version that held the stage exclusively for 164 years. Molière's was forgotten until 1841, when the original text was finally rediscovered and once more returned to performance.[39]

It is to Corneille's credit that he himself never pretended that his version was anything but a copy of Molière's. In a preface to the edition published in Paris in 1692, while noting that he had softened "certain expressions that had offended the scrupulous" and that he had added some new scenes to the third and fifth acts, he modestly claimed to have followed "rather precisely" Molière's

39. See Balmas, *Il mito di Don Giovanni,* vol. 2, *Nascita ed evoluzione del mito, dagli scenari a Rosimond,* 116–31, or Couton, in Molière, *Oeuvres complètes* 2, for a detailed history of the problems and controversies that have surrounded Molière's text, its variants, its performance history, and its publication.

"excellent original."[40] From his point of view he was right. The story was much the same, and much of the text was indeed quite similar.

But in its essence the play was no longer Molière's. Some changes were negligible. Corneille modified its title. He called it simply *Le Festin de Pierre.* He switched Don Juan's last name, for no apparent reason, from Tenorio to Giron (III.v). Other changes were more serious. He adapted Molière's vigorous prose to alexandrine couplets; he eliminated the fearful figure of the specter and the scythe-bearing figure of time. But worst of all, he altered the spirit of the work. In order not to offend the scrupulous, he mitigated or removed all the moments in which Dom Juan had bluntly expressed his terrifying religious doubts, and he exorcised the figure of the hermit, whose piety had so exacerbated Molière's Dom Juan. In other words, Corneille removed anything that would have made the play a public scandal once again. He did what he had been hired to do and for which he and Molière's wife shared 200 écus d'or paid over by the acting company for the revised text. But in Corneille's hands, Molière's new and brilliant Dom Juan became once again an old Don Juan, little more than a rutting libertine who this time chases after a provocative fourteen-year-old by the name of Leonore. She is bound for a nunnery against her will and is delighted to run off with Don Juan instead.

Four years after Molière's *Dom Juan* had been withdrawn, Claude de la Rose, or Rosimond as he was generally called, drawing on the experiences of Dorimond, Villiers, and Molière, offered Paris what he claimed was a new version of the legend. Like his predecessors, he recognized the story's popularity in France and wanted to profit from it. In the introduction to his play, he complained that, as of 1669, his acting company was the only one in the city that had not played it at all.[41]

Rosimond, born in Paris in 1640, was, like his predecessors, also a well-known actor and playwright. He was at first associated with the Théâtre du Marais, but, following Molière's death in 1673, he left that troupe and joined the one at the Palais Royal, where he took over some of the great playwright's roles until his own death in 1686. He was an excessive drinker, and it is said that when he died his wine merchant wept copious tears, not for the man, but because he was losing 800 livres per year.[42] Denied a normal burial by his parish

40. Thomas Corneille, "Avis," in *Le Festin de Pierre,* vol. 2 of *Théâtre de Pierre et de Thomas Corneille avec notes et commentaires* (Paris: Didot, 1852), 464.

41. This preface, "Au lecteur," along with the play itself, can be found in Victor Fournel, *Théâtre du Marais,* vol. 3 of *Les Contemporains de Molière* (Paris: Firmin-Didot, 1875), 323. The only modern edition of the play, without preface however, is in Balmas, *Il mito di Don Giovanni* 1.

42. Fournel, *Théâtre du Marais,* 316.

priest, he was interred at night, without lights, in a graveyard reserved for children who had died without baptism.[43]

Like Dorimond and Villiers, Rosimond offered his public the usual five-act verse play in alexandrine couplets. He published the text in Paris in 1670. The title he chose is curious: *Le Nouveau festin de Pierre ou L'athée foudroyé.* It is evident that he had in mind one of the older but less popular Italian *scenari, L'ateista fulminato,* the same one that a few years hence Thomas Shadwell also claimed to have been familiar with. But what is especially curious about Rosimond's title is the adjective *nouveau.* To theatergoers in Paris, familiar with three recent versions of the legend, the word implied that something interesting and different would be found in this new play and that it was therefore worth going to see again; to us today the word *nouveau* is proof that the basic characters and events of the story had by that time become fixed in an agreed-upon form, as indeed they had been and were so to remain. Rosimond was the first to use this adjective, which then reappeared from time to time. We will see it in Venice in 1787 when Francesco Gardi and Giuseppe Maria Foppa use it to advertise their new musical product, a ridiculous opera they entitled *Il nuovo convitato di pietra* so as to distinguish it from a similar product with a nearly similar title by Giuseppe Gazzaniga and Giovanni Bertati, *Don Giovanni o sia Il convitato di pietra,* which was opening the same evening in the very same city.

In truth, Rosimond's version was not excitingly new; in fact, a great deal of it was old. He borrowed generously from Dorimond, Villiers, and Molière, although in his preface he generously conceded that Molière's version contained "des beautez toutes particulières."[44] He made no pretense that his own work was of any great value, and, in a criticism echoed by others throughout the following century, he stated that the legend was impossible to fix within "les règles," within the rules of classical form. What Rosimond added of his own to the story were two debauched friends of Dom Juan's. Their presence created greater movement and confusion on stage. Together, the three form a very ignoble gang of vicious young libertines. Their most disturbing adventure has to do with the abduction of a young woman from a nunnery, which they first burn to the ground. During Don Juan's fourth-act dinner—also new in that it is far more sumptuous than any other heretofore (in fact Rosimond is quite proud of "ces superbes ornemens" used by his company)—the statue drags the two rakes down to hell as a warning to Dom Juan. But he is not impressed. Thomas

43. Balmas, *Il mito di Don Giovanni* 2:192.

44. "Au lecteur," in Fournel, *Théâtre du Marais,* 323. The other quotations in this paragraph can also be found there.

Shadwell was. He adapted a good bit of Rosimond's work, including Dom Juan's two friends, for his own version of the legend in 1676.

Rosimond's Dom Juan is not a pleasant man. Dorimond and Villiers had each created, in Enea Balmas's phrase, a "sumptuous baroque figure."[45] Molière then brought that figure back down to earth as a thinking and tormented human creature. Rosimond's Dom Juan now refuses torment, for he refuses to recognize the heavens altogether. Indeed, according to his servant, Carrille, "Il n'a ny foy ny loy" [He has neither faith nor law] (I.i). Dom Juan agrees with Carrille.

> J'obéis à mes sens, il est vray; mais quel crime?
> La nature m'en fait une nécessité,
> Et nostre corps n'agit que par sa volonté.
>
> (I.ii)

> [I obey my senses, it is true; but what crime is that?
> Nature makes it a necessity for me,
> and our body only acts according to its will.]

He then adds: "Everything is lawful for me when an object [of desire] can give me pleasure." His only law is his instinct, what Da Ponte's Don Giovanni will refer to as his "buon natural" (II.i). Rosimond's Dom Juan has no spiritual life; the playwright has entirely eliminated the encounter with the hermit, so significant a moment of spiritual probing in the three earlier French plays. Dom Juan is not troubled with concepts of sin or guilt; as a result he is unafraid of death. He mocks the statue to the very end, for he regrets nothing and would do again and again what he has always done: "Spirit, you are wasting your time with foolish speeches! You think you can touch my heart; I laugh at your words."[46]

---

45. Balmas, *Il mito di Don Giovanni* 2:165.

46. His full speech is as follows.

> Ombre, tu pers ton temps à des discours frivoles!
> Tu crois toucher mon coeur, je ris de tes paroles,
> Et pour te détourner d'y prétendre plus rien,
> Apprens mon sentiment, mais écoute-moy bien,
> Car la redite icy ne m'est pas nécessaire:
> Je n'ay rien fait encor que je ne veuille faire;
> Je fus ton assassin, et si l'occasion
> Faisoit naistre à ce prix ma satisfaction,
> Je remplirois d'horreur et de deuil ta famille,
> Et ferois périr tout pour jouir de ta fille.
> Les forfaits les plus noirs ont des charmes pour moy;

In Rosimond, previews of things to come are slight. Da Ponte infused his text and his protagonist with greater charm. Nonetheless, even Rosimond assisted Da Ponte. Carrille is caught by two angry peasants; he is recognized as Dom Juan's servant-accomplice and nearly hanged, just as in Da Ponte Leporello will be caught and accused of various crimes by Masetto, Zerlina, and others. Both servants manage to get away.

Rosimond's play was the last seventeenth-century Don Juan play in France. The legend then moved to England, where it was introduced to a London public by Thomas Shadwell in a work he called *The Libertine.* Shadwell, who was born around 1642 and died in 1692, was an active figure in Restoration theater, author of more than seventeen plays. He is not much esteemed today, for he still suffers from the wrath of a better known contemporary, John Dryden, who had nothing for him but contemptuous words: a drunken "mass of foul corrupted matter," he called him among other things.[47] Indeed, he was a rather obese, coarse, and indecent individual, but likewise a thorough professional with many theatrical successes.

Shadwell was quite attuned to the theatrical activities of Paris and based several of his plays on works by Molière. For *The Libertine,* a five-act tragedy in prose and verse, he used as his point of departure the versions of Dorimond and Villiers and especially the swaggering Don Juan of Rosimond. He did not use Molière's because the text was not available to him. Shadwell wrote quickly, finishing his play in just under three weeks; it was produced in June 1675 and published the following year. It was a very great success both immediately and in the following years and had numerous revivals up to 1740.

Like so many other writers who chose to work with the Don Juan theme, Shadwell must have been attracted to it by its very popularity. "The story from which I took the hint of this play, is famous all over Spain, Italy and France," he noted in the play's preface. Like Villiers, he too apologized for the "irregularities" of his work and claimed that "the extravagance of the subject forced me to it." He hoped that no reader would be offended by the scurrilous material, since, as he observed hypocritically, vice is properly punished at the play's conclusion.[48]

It is not the immorality of the play that offends. Rather, it is hard not to

---

Et, loin que tes advis me donnent de l'effroy,
Je prétens dès demain, dans l'ardeur qui m'anime,
Entasser mort sur mort, et crime sur le crime.

(V.vii)

47. John Dryden, quoted in George Atherton Aitkin, *The Dictionary of National Biography* (Oxford: Oxford University Press, 1960), 17:1279.

48. Shadwell, "Preface," 21.

be often offended, and eventually somewhat bored, by Don John's loud, ceaseless, and obnoxious promotion of self and self-pleasures. His egotism trumpets throughout the play. He boasts, for example, of a rape: "Mine, my lads, was such a rape, it ought to be registred; a noble and heroick rape" (I). The noise becomes tiresome. Other egos mean nothing to him: his servant Jacomo's, his companions', that of the entire female gender that he regards with contempt. Yet it is equally hard not to be stunned into attentiveness by the intensity, variety, and sheer physical energy of his actions: glutton, drunkard, rapist, arsonist, murderer, and patricide. He never stops to draw breath. "My bus'ness is my pleasure, that end I will always compass, without scrupling the means; there is no right or wrong, but what conduces to, or hinders pleasure" (I). He has no conscience, he has no soul; he is a brute of nature whose primary interest in life is copulation. He is impelled, it seems, by a perpetual erection, the force of which drives him from action to action. The tension and perverse fascination of the play is to witness Don John, screwed up to madness by his libido, perpetually on the verge of erotic explosion, furiously seeking a release that, when it comes, never satisfies. Yet without this drive he would be nothing. The grandeur and fearlessness of his end is remarkable. There is no worse Don Juan. To the statue who has just hurled his two companions down to hell as a warning:

> These things I see with wonder, but no fear.
> Were all the elements to be confounded,
> And shuffl'd all into their former chaos;
> Were seas of sulphur flaming round about me,
> And all mankind roaring within those fires,
> I could not fear or feel the least remorse.
> To the last instant I would dare thy power.
> Here I stand firm, and all thy threats contemn;
> Thy murderer stands here; now do thy worst.
>
> (V)

Shadwell, too, has done his worst. Perhaps it is for that reason that his *Libertine* left no legacy. No one borrowed from it or built upon it to create new Don Juans. There was nowhere else to go. Mozart and Da Ponte had probably not read the play. Nonetheless, in some way or other, Don John's compulsive, animal sexual drive found its way into their opera. Leporello makes the following comments about Don Giovanni.

> Delle vecchie fa conquista
> pel piacer di porle in lista:

ma passion predominante
è la giovin principiante.
Non si picca se sia ricca,
se sia brutta, se sia bella:
purchè porti la gonnella . . .

(I.v)

[He seduces old ladies
for the pleasure of putting them on his list.
But his main passion
is the young beginner.
He doesn't care if she is rich,
if she is ugly, if she is beautiful;
as long as she wears a skirt . . .]

And so had said Don John's servant, Jacomo: "If he were to live here one moneth longer, he wou'd marry half the town, ugly and handsome, old and young: nothing that's female comes amiss to him" (I). Later, during an orgy of sexuality with his two companions in the second act, Don John, as if to give credence to Jacomo's words, rapes an ugly old woman simply because she happens to be present, for the pleasure of putting her on his list, so to speak. Unaccompanied by music, especially Mozart's music, the scene is horrible.

The original production of *The Libertine* actually included a large amount of incidental music, songs, and choruses written by William Turner. When the play was revived in 1692, new music was composed by Henry Purcell: two songs, ensembles, and choruses, all for the fourth and fifth acts. This music quickly became some of Purcell's most celebrated, especially the soprano air "Nymphs and Shepherds, Come Away." According to Curtis Price, who has studied all of Purcell's theater music, the composer's "obvious lack of compassion for Don John produced music which attempts nothing like pathos or ennoblement, the Don's behavior being beyond the pale of good taste."[49]

After Shadwell, the remaining decades of the seventeenth century saw only a smattering of new versions, none of any significance. The last Italian *commedia sostenuta* of the century was by Andrea Perrucci who, though born in Palermo in 1651, lived much of his productive artistic life in Naples where he was employed by the Teatro San Bartolomeo, the same theater that may have been the first in Italy to present Tirso de Molina's *El burlador de Sevilla*. Perrucci was

49. Curtis A. Price, *Henry Purcell and the London Stage* (Cambridge: Cambridge University Press, 1984), 116.

the author of many dramas both sacred and profane, of intermezzos and of librettos, as well as of poetry composed in Latin, Italian, Sicilian, and Neapolitan. His most famous work, *Il vero lume tra le ombre ossia La nascita del verbo umanato,* was performed in Naples for well over 200 years on Christmas night. He died in Naples in 1704.

Perrucci's first known work, written when he was still a young man, was a three act *opera tragica* in prose, *Il convitato di pietra,* performed in Naples in 1678. (How often has Don Juan attracted a writer or a composer in the very earliest stages of his career?) In 1690, adopting the anagram Enrico Prendarca (only the *u* of Perrucci is missing), he republished his tragedy "ridotta in miglior forma e abbellita," in an improved new form.

His very talky version of the legend drew on Tirso and Cicognini as a source for character and plot, with additions of original, often comic detail. Here, for example, is the way Don Giovanni replies to his servant's remonstrances.

> Why are you talking to me about heaven? Heaven needs to correct its own imperfections, since it has a sun that eclipses, a moon that wanes, stars that bode evil influences. In any case, how can I offend heaven if it is so far away from us? Heaven should mind its own business. Doesn't it have anything else to think of besides me?[50]
>
> (II.iii)

Nonetheless, as Gendarme de Bévotte observes, this *Convitato* "is more a drama than a comedy" and is filled with annoying erudition and literary affectations.[51] It lacks the verve of a Cicognini, and really offers nothing new. In fact, the work left no mark on the general history and development of the legend and was soon almost entirely lost sight of. No modern edition exists.[52]

The seventeenth century had opened with a Don Juan play by a Spanish writer and so did it close. While in the intervening decades the legend multiplied rapidly elsewhere, in Spain there was nothing in-between. After Tirso's *El burlador,* the only other Spanish play was an odd and now totally forgotten three-act drama in verse entitled *La venganza en el sepulcro* by Alonso de Córdova y Maldonado. No one knows who Córdova y Maldonado was or when he was born or died, and no other literary works have been attributed to him. On the title sheet of his manuscript he lists himself as "criado de Su Majestad." What

50. Quoted in Georges Gendarme de Bévotte, *La Légende de Don Juan, son évolution dans la littérature des origines au romantisme* (1906; reprint, Geneva: Slatkine, 1970), 302.

51. Gendarme de Bévotte, *La Légende de Don Juan,* 305.

52. Gendarme de Bévotte, whose synopsis and analysis in *La Légende de Don Juan* (296–306) I have relied on, used an edition published in Naples in 1706.

he did as *criado* has not been ascertained. Arcadio Baquero, who published the full text of the drama in *Don Juan y su evolución dramática,* uncovered only one or two certifiable facts about him: in 1662 he was an inspector and an accountant for the king in the city of Segovia and, in the same year, he published a small book describing the translation of a holy statue of the Virgin from one church to another within the city.[53] It is uncertain precisely when he wrote this play. It is thought that he did so sometime within the last thirty years of the century.

La venganza en el sepulcro is a curious work that, as its uncommon title indicates, does not follow the path laid out by Italian *Convitati* or French *Festins.* It stands alone, influenced only by Tirso de Molina and perhaps influencing in turn a later popular Spanish play, José Zorrilla's *Don Juan Tenorio* of 1844. Córdova y Maldonado went his own way, and that is the only reason that his weak and awkward drama has a modicum of interest for us today.

The playwright considerably shortened the Tirsoan cast of characters to an essential five: Don Juan, his servant Colchón, Doña Ana, her fiancé el Marqués de la Mota, and her father Don Gonzalo de Ulloa. He also reduced the sweep and variety of the actions of Tirso's work to one elemental point: the relationship between Don Juan and Doña Ana.

Córdova y Maldonado's Don Juan, now thirty years old, is ready to settle down. He had left home at the age of fifteen and for fifteen years had fought and brawled his way across Europe. He was less interested in seductions. Now he has come back to Seville. His father is dead, but he is looking forward to seeing his mother again. As he approaches Seville, he comes by chance upon Doña Ana, who is enjoying the fresh air and the freedom of the Sevillian countryside outside the city's walls. He immediately falls deeply and seriously in love. The play is about his attempt to marry her in spite of her father and in spite of her fiancé. The old trickster of Seville is nowhere to be seen, nor is the mocker or the doubter or the seducer. A young woman who lets Don Juan know that she is available and willing, no strings attached, is entirely ignored. Doña Ana must first become his wife. Then, if Isabela still wants to become his mistress, fine, but first things first.

As for Doña Ana, it is hard to imagine that she is not in love with Don Juan, in spite of her vigorous denials. Certainly she is fascinated and touched by his hot words, disturbed by his physical presence, and agitated by his attentions. Though she swears to avenge her father's death and swears to love eternally her fiancé, the priggish and verbose Marqués de la Mota, one feels that she swears too much. She weeps when she hears of Don Juan's death.

53. Arcadio Baquero, *Don Juan y su evolución dramática* (Madrid: Editora nacional, 1966), 1:320.

Later writers will develop the implications of a Don Juan–Doña Ana relationship more skillfully and more profoundly than Córdova y Maldonado. Although Da Ponte was apparently not interested in that relationship, one cannot help wondering, as many critics have, precisely what his Donna Anna felt and thought about her attacker, how truthful her explanations were to Don Ottavio concerning that extraordinary night's events, why she insists over and over on postponing their marriage. Córdova y Maldonado was the first to recognize her possible fascination with evil.

As is true of many seventeenth-century versions, there is no reason to think that Da Ponte would have been familiar with this one. Yet once again, in this obscure and forgotten play we find a future echo of Da Ponte's work in a brief scene of hypocrisy and deception between Don Juan and Doña Ana. After killing her father, Don Juan offers condolences to Doña Ana, who is not yet aware that he is her father's murderer, and he adds: "See, then, that you command me; decide what you want, and as soon as you charge me, you will see how you will be avenged" (II.i). In a similar fashion, a blustering Don Giovanni, likewise relieved that he is not yet suspected of having killed the Commendatore, will gallantly fawn before Donna Anna: "Command me. My family, my relatives, this hand, this sword, my possessions, my blood itself I will expend to serve you" (I.xi). The similarity is a brief one, the detail very small, yet like so many others it too contributes to the growing portrait of the Da Ponte–Mozart protagonist.

La venganza en el sepulcro was a poor play that, in a way, was more than a hundred years ahead of its time. No one was yet ready for radical departures from the traditional tale. In the new century, Don Juan remained in essence what he had been in the seventeenth. What he did, though, was to experiment with new kinds of theater: vaudeville, ballet, pantomime, and opera: opera that was sometimes serious, sometimes comic, and sometimes downright farcical.

Don Juan's first appearance in the eighteenth century was very modest. He showed up in France at the fairgrounds outside Paris. In the previous century, French theatrical versions had, for the most part, tried to outdo each other in making him more and more wicked. Then Thomas Shadwell topped them all with a Don John who was the very nadir of nastiness. Nothing was left for him to do but to return to being what he had been before. Therefore, when he appeared at the Foire Saint-Germain in Paris in 1713, he turned comic once again. The legend always held particular appeal to the popular imagination, to a nonliterary public. What appealed were Don Juan's antics and those of his servant, his hectic adventures, his supernatural encounters with the statue, and his startling and dramatic demise. Those who enjoyed the play were not looking for anything introspective or probing. The fairs of Saint-Germain and of Saint-Laurent provided a public looking for easy amusements. Here, small acting companies regularly performed their entertaining plays; also on display were jugglers, acrobats, singers, comics, mimes, and puppeteers, who made up a kind of street theater for the people, as opposed to the licensed and certified theaters of the city of Paris.

The earliest record that attests to Don Juan's arrival at the fair dates from 1713; he may even have come sometime before. He came to the *foire* in a *Festin de Pierre* written by someone known only as Le Tellier and about whom absolutely nothing else is known except that, between 1713 and 1715, he created this and four other comedies for Saint-Germain.[54] *Le Festin* was roundly applauded at its first appearance; its success was repeated the following season, again in 1720, and once more in 1721. In fact, it is thought that Le Tellier's version, modified according to the needs of the moment, continued to be performed for many years in and around Paris, but without attribution given to its original creator. No text of the comedy was published until Marcello Spaziani included three manuscript versions of it in his informative book on the Don Juan legend and the Parisian fairs, *Don Giovanni dagli scenari dell'arte alla "foire."*[55]

The excitement generated by Le Tellier's comedy must surely have been in the performance. It was certainly not in the brief, rough-hewn texts similar to the *canovacci* of the commedia dell'arte: telegraphic prose descriptions of plot and action with numerous references to *lazzi*. The novelty of the performance lay in the fact that the simple plot and the straightforward action were fleshed out with a large number of songs: original and sometimes witty words set to familiar melodies and popular songs that were well known to the watching public, songs of all types and styles, from sad to happy, from serious to amusing. The idea of using new words and old tunes was not Le Tellier's. Other comic companies did so too, and at some performances the audience was asked to sing along with the actors by following the new words written out on large posters. As the creator of the spectacle, Le Tellier probably selected the comic story he wanted to work with, organized the text, and wrote the lyrics, the *couplets;* he would not have composed or arranged the music, nor do we know who did. The result was a kind of vaudeville entertainment, the Don Juan story with song. However, in no way should these performances be considered operatic.

Nothing in the texts is new. Everything in them can be traced back to

54. Spaziani, *Don Giovanni dagli scenari,* 80.

55. See Spaziani, *Don Giovanni dagli scenari,* 163–95, for the texts; 73–95, for problems of dating.

earlier French, Italian, or Spanish versions. What is new is the focus. All Duke Ottavios, all Donna Annas, all Donna Isabellas and Elviras have been eliminated. On the one hand we are left with the statue of the dead Commandeur, Arlequin, and Don Juan, and on the other hand with Don Juan, Arlequin, and a number of country folk, fisherpeople, and shepherds. In other words, Le Tellier reduced the breadth of the traditional tale to only two centers of interest: Don Juan's romp in the country and his spectacular and dramatic encounter with and defeat by the stone statue; everything else is discarded.

The password is humor, just as it had been with the commedia dell'arte, and the humor belongs to Arlequin: Arlequin invites the statue to his master's home to dine on a fried carp; when the statue asks for Don Juan's hand, Arlequin cries out, "Tell him you've got the mange"; Arlequin spills a jug of water on Don Juan's hands, rushes offstage, and then returns with "a napkin attached to his rear end. Don Juan dries his hands and gives him a kick in the pants."[56]

Yet in spite of the nonsense, one hears more strongly than ever, even in a script of this nature, clear future echoes of Mozart and Da Ponte. It may well be that these echoes are heard for the very reason that the text was allowed to run free; there was no pretense that it needed to be anything but entertainment. In the *forain* versions, as in those of the commedia dell'arte, the tale was allowed to assume a natural and spontaneous shape; it was permitted to be illogical or absurd, indifferent to form, style, or subtleties. The legend never wanted to be honed or shackled, as it was in the chiseled and constricting versions of a Dorimond or a Villiers or, a few years later, of a Goldoni. It needed to burst on stage with its own irrepressible vitality regardless of rules, as it does here and as it will do in some operatic versions before Mozart's. Da Ponte thoroughly understood what the legend ought to be and tapped directly into its energy, the fullest source of which was in versions of this sort.

Thus, the giddy and frank admonition of Da Ponte's Zerlina to her girl friends not to let time pass them by, her enthusiasm and Masetto's to find themselves quickly in each other's arms is all here in Le Tellier's *pescheuse.*

Dans notre brillante jeunesse
Livrons nos coeurs à la tendresse,
Laissons murmurer la vieillesse
Qui languit sous le poix de ses ans.

56. Spaziani, *Don Giovanni dagli scenari,* 184 (II.iii), 194 (V), 187 (III.ii).

Dans notre brillante jeunesse
Profitons de notre printemps.[57]

[In our bright youth,
let us give our hearts to love;
let old age complain,
that languishes under the weight of its years.
In our bright youth,
let us take advantage of our springtime.]

In this crude French *scenario,* Da Ponte's country wedding scene was assuming its final shape, asserting and affirming its vitality. Though the scene was not invented by Le Tellier—we have noted it in several earlier versions—he added more and more important detail so that it was finally beginning to have the sense of self that it will have in Da Ponte. It was no longer a throwaway moment. Don Juan and Arlequin interrupt the country festivities. Arlequin must distract the bridegroom, a jealous, suspicious, and angry Pierrot, while Don Juan makes love to the bride, a willing, eager, and easily beguiled Colombine. The rhythms of the two scenes are similar, the rapid movements and the confusion; the sexual energies and tensions are quite like what they will be between Masetto, Zerlina, and Don Giovanni. Then, in a dramatic moment, Don Juan makes a daring escape with Colombine, holding all at bay with a loaded pistol. He leaves behind a deserted and devastated Pierrot-Masetto. Cicognini's short pantomime scene has now truly come to life.

While this old-fashioned comic Don Juan was performing at the Paris fairs, a second attempt was made to turn him into something new. Once again it was a Spanish playwright who tried, Antonio de Zamora. Like Córdova y Maldonado before him, Zamora failed; like Córdova too, Zamora is a shadowy figure of the past. Born in Madrid, probably in 1664, he was an "Oficial de la Secretaría de Nueva España" and "gentilhombre de Cámara."[58] If today he is remembered at

57. Spaziani, *Don Giovanni dagli scenari,* 178. The equivalent verses in Da Ponte are as follows.

Giovinette che fate all'amore,
non lasciate che passi l'età:
se nel seno vi bulica il core,
il rimedio vedetelo qua.
Ah, ah, ah; ah, ah, ah!
Che piacer, che piacer che sarà!

(I.vii)

58. *Gran Enciclopedia Rialp* (Madrid: Ediciones Rialp, 1975), 23:851.

all, it is because he is regarded as the last epigone of the great Spanish playwright Calderón de la Barca. He wrote at least seventeen plays—religious, historical, moral, legendary, *de figurón*—that were performed in Madrid from 1690 on. The work of his that is of most interest to us is *No hay deuda que no se pague y Convidado de piedra*. It is not known for certain when he wrote it, and it was only published in 1744, well after the playwright's death, which probably occurred in 1728. According to Arcadio Baquero, most critics place its composition around 1714.[59] Even if not available in print, *No hay deuda* was very popular in performance and was frequently played in Spain during the first two weeks of November until it was displaced in public popularity after 1844 by José Zorrilla's *Don Juan Tenorio*. In fact, it is generally agreed that Zorrilla's play owes certain debts to Zamora. But Zamora, in turn, has some large debts with Tirso de Molina and perhaps some smaller ones with Córdova y Maldonado, as well as with Dorimond, Villiers, and Molière.

No hay deuda is a very long and straggly play. It is overburdened with plot (or rather with events, with things that happen) but very light in characterization and thought. It principally concerns Don Juan's involvement with two women: Doña Ana whom he comes to love and Doña Beatriz who loves him no matter how badly he behaves. With a certain literary self-consciousness, Zamora's Don Juan proudly defines himself as "el burlador de Sevilla" (I.i), yet one sees in him little of the carefree, energetic *burlador* of the past. Tirso's golden youth has become a blustering and petulant bully whose acts of defiance, whether toward women, his peers, his father, or his king, seem like unattractive childish tantrums. The originalities of the play are scant: a Comendador murdered while defending the honor not of his daughter but of a male guest insulted by Don Juan, Don Juan's father who joins alongside his son in a sword fight, a Don Juan who, gripped by the statue's cold hand, actually begs for pity and salvation.

> Ya lo veo, y, pues, mi muerte
> su justicia satisface,
> ¡Dios mío, haced, pues la vida
> perdí, que el alma se salve!
> . . . .
> ¡Piedad, Señor! Si hasta ahora
> huyendo de tus piedades,

59. Baquero, *Don Juan y su evolución dramática* 2:1. This volume contains the full text of Zamora's play.

mi malicia me ha perdido,
tu clemencia me restaure.

(III.xii)

[Now I understand; my death
satisfies [God's] justice.
My God, since I have lost my life,
let my soul be saved!
. . . .
Have pity, my Lord;
if up to now, fleeing your mercy,
my evil deeds have condemned me,
may your clemency restore me.]

One scarcely cares whether he is saved or not. Of more interest, as in *La venganza,* is an ambiguous relationship between Don Juan and Doña Ana. Like Córdova y Maldonado, Zamora also suspects that Doña Ana has a power and a fascination over Don Juan that heretofore had not been much examined. He likewise suspects that Doña Ana herself may be not unattracted to the young Tenorio, but he is not skillful enough to probe his intuition effectively, and so the matter must be left to the post-Mozart romantics.

Playwrights with better abilities than Zamora's now shunned the story. Only one notable, nonmusical version of the legend was created during the entire eighteenth century. It was by the fine Venetian playwright Carlo Goldoni, who was born in Venice in 1705 and died in Paris in 1793. The play was one of Goldoni's earliest works and not one of his best. He had been writing for the theater for only a few years when he turned to the Don Juan tale. His reason for doing so was a recent and unhappy love affair with a dangerously fascinating young actress by the name of Passalacqua. The play was his revenge; he used Passalacqua's actions and behavior as a model for the by now traditional country figure of Tisbea-Charlotte-Zerlina. He called her Elisa—her real name was Elisabetta—and he made of her a fickle, lying, ambitious, and faithless young woman, just as she had been with him. He also made her very attractive.[60]

Goldoni gave a new and different title to his five-act verse version of the tale: *Don Giovanni Tenorio o sia Il dissoluto.* He considered his play a comedy, and

60. Carlo Goldoni gives many additional and fascinating details of their relationship and its effects on the play in book 1, chap. 39 of his *Mémoires,* vol. 1 of *Tutte le opere di Carlo Goldoni,* ed. Giuseppe Ortolani, 5th ed. (Milan: Mondadori, 1973).

so it is, though it is a somewhat serious comedy, hardly the offspring of the commedia dell'arte—the customary comic servant is nowhere to be found. The play's initial reception was shaky, for Goldoni's Venetian public certainly expected a more traditional Don Juan tale. But aided in particular by the figure of Elisa and by the fact that many spectators knew of her relationship with Goldoni, the comedy lasted throughout the carnival season of 1736 and may have been given sporadic productions in some later seasons. Goldoni was never anxious to have it published and eventually included it in the second collection of his works, the Edizione Paperini published in Florence in 1754, only because a badly mutilated, pirate edition had recently appeared in Bologna.[61]

Goldoni was quite familiar with the legend's Spanish, French, and Italian history. He had read Giacinto Andrea Cicognini's *Convitato* and the now lost version by Onofrio Giliberto. He had seen the versions given by the players of the commedia dell'arte. He had studied Tirso de Molina's play (he thought it was by Calderón de la Barca) as well as Molière's and Corneille's. According to Gendarme de Bévotte, he had even read Perrucci's little-known version and borrowed an idea or two from it.[62]

Goldoni did not care for the legend at all and throughout much of his later life spoke badly of it. In 1754 he characterized Don Juan comedy in general as "sconcia" [lewd], "scorretta ed irregolare" [improper and irregular];[63] in 1772 he said he thought the story was "piena zeppa di improprietà e stolidezze" [chock full of improprieties and stupidities] and "un ammasso . . . d'inezie, d'improprietà, d'indecenze" [a mass . . . of trifles, improprieties, and indecencies].[64] Nor by 1787, then living in Paris, had he changed his mind: "I always regarded [the story] with horror in Italy, and I could never understand how this farce was able to endure for such a long time, attract crowds of people and be the delight of a civilized nation."[65] He had no kind words for the crowds that flocked to see the story on stage and thereby maintained its continuing popularity.

> If we want to take a look at the sorts of people who would run to see it, and still do so in large numbers, we will see that most spectators were servant

61. Goldoni, *Mémoires,* 178.

62. Gendarme de Bévotte, *La Légende de Don Juan,* 304.

63. Goldoni, "L'autore a chi legge," in *Tutte le opere* 9:216.

64. Carlo Goldoni, *Prefazioni di Carlo Goldoni ai diciassette tomi delle commedie edite a Venezia da G. B. Pasquali, Tomo xiv, Tomo xv,* vol. 1, *Tutte le opere,* 730, 735.

65. Goldoni, *Mémoires,* 176.

> girls, domestic help, children and very ignorant low-class folk who enjoy foolishness and are satisfied with spectacle.[66]

Goldoni's objections to the legend were twofold: structural and moral. For the introduction to the published version of his play he prepared a sarcastic summary of the traditional plot.

> By night a man enters the apartments of the king of Naples; he is met in the dark by a noble young damsel, who receives him into her arms in place of another, and who only realizes the deception when he starts to slip away from her. At the querulous voice of such an honest lady, the king of Naples appears with candlestick in hand; Don Giovanni puts out the light with his sword, and his majesty is left in the dark. After being discovered, the dissolute gentleman leaves for Castile; a storm tosses him into the sea, and good fortune throws him on shore with his powdered wig and without even having gotten his shoes wet. Leaving aside the servant, Don Giovanni's companion in the shipwreck and in good fortune, with whom he graciously exchanges insults, abuses, and kicks, what is truly incredible is the speed with which our hero is transported from one kingdom to the other in order for him to start up again in Castile. Finally, so as not to waste time analyzing a comedy, every scene of which has its share of absurdities and improprieties, let one scene suffice for all the rest—the marble statue erected in a moment or two, that talks, that walks, that goes to dinner, that invites to dinner, that threatens, that avenges, and that works miracles. Then, as the play's crowning glory, all the spectators proceed safe and sound to the house of the devil along with the protagonist. Thus, mixing fear with laughter, the devout are saddened, while the disbelievers make fun of the whole thing.[67]

Goldoni hoped to get rid of structural flaws and to give to his version what, in the same preface, he called "proprietà maggiore" [greater propriety]. He also hoped to improve the moral tone of the legend. He recognized—rightly so, I believe—that many spectators thoroughly enjoyed the wickedness of Don Juan's life and his spectacular and entertaining death and that they were scarcely stirred or frightened by his damnation. They did not leave the theater with proper moral uplift. Goldoni, a man of smiling virtues, wanted to make his Don

66. Goldoni, "L'autore a chi legge," in *Tutte le opere* 9:216.
67. Goldoni, "L'autore a chi legge," in *Tutte le opere* 9:215–16.

Giovanni's wickedness a little less attractive and his demise a little more serious, a little less fun. As the title of his new play warned, it was about a *dissoluto,* not about a walking and talking *convitato* of stone. If you wanted thoughtless entertainment, you had best go elsewhere.

What resulted, though an interesting play, was not a very good one. Goldoni struggled to make the best of a bad situation, of a bad story, but in the last analysis the story got the best of him. Because he thought the tale ridiculous, he eliminated from it whatever he deemed outlandish: the vulgar comic servant, the improbable shipwreck, the talking statue of stone, dinners with black-bedecked tables. All miraculous events are gone, all spectacles: in the fifth act he settled for a modest, quick, and efficient bolt of lightning from a clear blue sky. Yet, in spite of his efforts to modify the story, Goldoni's play remained the traditional adventure tale of Don Juan, except that its life force, its energy, was gone. The characters, too, were pale and bloodless, little people of no consequence. It is clear that Goldoni was not touched by the hidden meanings of the legend; its broader themes and ideas did not speak to him, so that he illuminated it with little of his own sun-flooded Venetian personality or humor or insights.

Almost as if annoyed with the tale, he considerably mixed and modified traditional roles. Donna Anna is turned into a headstrong and ambitious young woman who would prefer to marry the king. She feels nothing but "repugnanza" (I.iv) for Duca Ottavio, who likewise has nothing but "avversione" (III.ii) for her. The duke, in fact, is interested in Donna Isabella, seduced by Don Giovanni some time before in Naples, and eventually it is she whom he marries.

Unlike the steely Don Juan of Dorimond or Villiers, Goldoni's Don Giovanni seems, at first sight, a return to the ebullient liar and lover created by Tirso, but as the play progresses his expansive personality gradually degenerates, and so does the play. It is as if Goldoni did not know what he wanted his protagonist to be. In act 4, finding himself alone with Donna Anna, he turns aggressive and threatening. Angry at her refusal of affection, he tears at her clothing and attempts to stab her. She is rescued only by the intervention of her father, the Commendatore di Lojoa, whom Don Giovanni promptly slays. By act 5 he has become a whiner. He is disturbed and upset that all Spain seeks his death for the murder of Donna Anna's father. The fault, he complains, is not his, but that of a "cruel destiny," of a "fierce star," of all "prideful women," and particularly of the behavior of Donna Anna herself (V.i). When a vengeful Donna Anna comes upon him hiding in church, he rather ignominiously tries to play upon her womanly sentiments, first by dramatically offering his breast to her dagger, and then by offering her his hand in marriage. She refuses both, although not without some inner turmoil: "I'm a woman after all," she laments in an aside (V.v). When he realizes that safety and freedom are beyond his grasp, he petulantly curses his destiny, his fate, his mother, his wet nurse, and all lying deities in general. If you really exist, he shouts, strike me with a bolt of lightning. They immediately oblige.

Although Lorenzo Da Ponte had surely read Goldoni's version, there appear to be no direct and obvious borrowings from it. Nonetheless, future echoes can be heard from time to time, especially linguistic echoes. Donna Anna, gazing down upon the blood spilled from her father's body, says to Duca Ottavio: "Il suolo asperso mirate ancor del sangue suo" (IV.vi), just as later in Da Ponte she will say to Don Ottavio: "Rimira di sangue coperto il terreno" (I.xiii). However, this moment and others like it had become part of a story tradition with a generally agreed-upon set of actions and dialogues. One writer was not copying from the other; both were drawing from a common pool.

Another echo is less immediately evident: the moment in which Don Giovanni attempts to assault Donna Anna. In Goldoni, the scene is violent and ugly.

D. GIO: I advise you
to offer me as a gift what a more resolute heart
could take by force.
D. AN: Have you reached
this degree of rashness?
D. GIO: Yes, you resist in vain. I want from you
the gift of your hand, or this knife
will bring you death. *(He seizes a dagger.)*
D. AN: Base betrayer! . . .
Servants, Father, does no one hear me?
D. GIO: You call for father and servants in vain;
in vain will you call upon the gods themselves,
if you do not surrender to my commands;
and this dagger plunged . . . *(Don Giovanni rises.)*
D. AN: Great gods in heaven . . . *(rising to leave)*
D. GIO: *(holding her back by her clothing)* Be careful, stop . . .
D. AN: Villain!
D. GIO: I'll strike you . . .
D. AN: You are vile!
What outrages are these?

(IV.ii)

This played-out violence, brutal in its onstage appearance, becomes reported violence in Da Ponte, as Donna Anna narrates to Don Ottavio what took place in her apartments. As reported violence—moreover as sung reported violence—the actions are tempered, seemingly less tangible, less violent, less demeaning to the grandeur of the Mozartian hero, but in truth the situation and the two Don Giovannis are quite one and the same.[68]

---

68. From Goldoni:

D. GIO: Io vi consiglio
Porgermi in don ciò che rapir potea
Un cuor più risoluto.
D. AN: E a questo segno
Temerario s'avanza il vostro ardire?
D. GIO: Sì, resistete invano: io vo' da voi
La vostra mano in dono; o questo ferro
Vi darà morte. (*impugna lo stile*)
D. AN: Ah traditore, indegno! . . .
Servi, padre, chi ascolta . . . ?
D. GIO: E padre e servi
Chiamate invano, invano i numi istessi
Chiamerete, se al fine a' cenni miei
Non v'arrendete; e questo ferro immerso . . .
(*Don Giovanni s'alza*)
D. AN: Santi numi del cielo . . . (*alzandosi in atto di partire*)
D. GIO: (*Trattenendola per le vesti*) Olà, fermate . . .
D. AN: Ah scellerato!
D. GIO: Io vi ferisco . . .
D. AN: Indegno!
Che violenze son queste? . . .

(IV.ii)

Da Ponte's Donna Anna explains as follows.

Tacito a me s'appressa,
e mi vuole abbracciar; sciogliermi cerco,
ei più mi stringe; io grido:
non viene alcun. Con una mano cerca
d'impedire la voce,
e coll'altra m'afferra
stretta così, che già mi credo vinta.
. . . . Alfin il duol, l'orrore
dell'infame attentato
accrebbe sì la lena mia, che, a forza
di svincolarmi, torcermi e piegarmi,
da lui mi sciolsi.

(I.xiii)

Midway between Goldoni and Da Ponte stands the libretto by Giovanni Bertati, *Don Giovanni o sia Il convitato di pietra,* from which Da Ponte borrowed extensively.

In scenes like these, Don Giovanni is not an appealing or attractive image. In fact, throughout the eighteenth century there was a general decline in the quality of the figure. Only through music would the fascination of his character be restored. Meanwhile, though his general popularity continued unabated, for many decades he led a sort of half-life in nonclassical theater in versions of third- and fourth-rate quality at best. He was almost totally ignored by serious playwrights. As Mandel has aptly noted, "Except for Goldoni and Zamora, Don Juan in the pre-Mozartean eighteenth century was left mostly to the rough care of vagabond comedians, vaudeville performers, shadow-players and puppeteers."[69] The nonmusical legend was in the domain of a kind of literary underclass, impresarios, writers, actors, and a public who conceived of it as a vehicle for unthinking entertainment and nothing more. Nor were musical presentations usually any less mindless.

Nonetheless, between Goldoni and Da Ponte there were myriad versions. Some were original, others were copies or adaptations of older versions, still others were copies of copies, with the inevitable slippage away from the original text. All kinds of versions were available throughout the century, most thrown together without much care. They came and went like television specials and made no more significant an impact. Some versions exist today only in the mind of a critic who supposes that such and such an actor may have played in "a" Don Juan play; some are remembered by a title, but are bodiless and textless; some grew a skeletal outline, while others developed a fully fleshed text. Some of these children of art are legitimate, but many are orphans, fathered by unknown actors and writers. Some that survive need still to be examined in detail, others lead a lonely existence in editions too inaccessible for study; others yet, perhaps heretofore considered peripheral, lie as half-forgotten manuscripts in remote libraries, and there are others, surely, still waiting to be discovered and claimed. No one will ever be able to catalog the total number of Don Juan's offspring.

Respectability was hard to come by. The eighteenth-century French theater historian, Cailhava de l'Estandoux, made it clear in *De L'Art de la comédie* that he could not abide the legend. He was especially contemptuous of its Spanish and Italian versions.

> It is quite natural that a passionate, superstitious country that is fond of the supernatural would have enjoyed watching its innocent daughters corrupted by a wicked man, nighttime rendezvous, fights, a mixture of religion and impiety, the sight of a walking statue, and the miraculous punishment of

69. Mandel, *Theatre of Don Juan,* 255.

> a man hateful for his crimes. It is likewise hardly surprising that the same things have charmed the Italians, who are also passionate, also superstitious, also as fond of the supernatural as the Spanish, but more comical. They even added one more absurdity to the work by mixing morals with buffoonery.[70]

But Cailhava regretted that a fellow countryman, a Frenchman, had allowed himself to be pressured into working with such a story: "Molière, urged on by his comrades to put this dramatic monster on stage, agreed with difficulty. His compliance was punished by the small success of his play."[71] For Cailhava, the figure of Don Juan was shockingly ill mannered: it was unheard of for a gentleman to permit a servant to sit at table with him! Were not those who wrote these sorts of scenes aware of "l'invraisemblance" that there was in such behavior?[72] Cailhava was correct; the figure was indeed vulgar. In the eighteenth century, the thinking, reflective, elegant Don Juan had changed his name and had left the theater for the pages of the novel. He became Lovelace in Samuel Richardson's *Clarissa Harlowe* or Valmont in Choderlos de Laclos's *Les Liaisons dangereuses*.

Because Don Juan occupied a position of lesser importance in eighteenth-century theater, performance information and texts are harder to come by today. Nevertheless, it is clear that the story continued to maintain a sufficient degree of popularity in most countries of Western Europe, including Portugal, Italy, France, England, Germany, Austria, and Holland. Only in Spain, with the marked exception of Zamora's version, does there not seem to have been a strong popular tradition.

The legend was frequently performed in German-speaking countries in the eighteenth century, especially in Vienna and in lower Austria, as Elizabeth Price has carefully documented, although no version has survived today on its own merits.[73] Not only was Molière's comedy given in French and commedia versions in Italian, every local acting company had its own version in German as part of a standard repertory of plays or *Hauptactionen.* Performances of *Hauptactionen* were "improvised to a great extent," explains Price,

> but had certain fixed interpolations such as solo songs and other musical numbers, dances, and dramatic monologues. They made great use of the

70. Cailhava de l'Estandoux, *De L'Art de la comédie,* nouvelle édition ([1786]; reprint, Geneva: Slatkine, 1970), 2:191. *De L'Art* was first published in 1772.

71. Cailhava de l'Estandoux, *De L'Art* 2:175.

72. Cailhava de l'Estandoux, *De L'Art* 2:197.

73. Elizabeth Price, "Don Juan: A Chronicle of his Literary Adventures in Germanic Territory" (Ph.D. diss., Washington University, 1974), 95.

> contrasts between the comic and the serious, the tumultuous and the contemplative, the rustic and the urban, the violent and the tender.[74]

One of the best was by fashionable theater director Karl Marinelli, whose *Dom Juan, oder Der steinerne Gast* was presented in Vienna in 1783. It is the only one of the German popular texts whose authorship has been established.[75] One wonders whether Da Ponte attended a performance of it while living in Vienna.

One wonders, too, if Da Ponte ever stopped to watch a puppet version of the legend. In Germany, the puppet popularity of the story of Don Juan was second only to that of Faust. Its renown was enhanced by the vulgar servant figure of Hans Wurst, who rollicked through these performances (and in the *Hauptactionen* as well) much like Arlecchino in the commedia. The legend was equally popular with Italian puppeteers. Puppet theater had been enthusiastically applauded in Italy from the sixteenth century on, so that it is hard to imagine that Da Ponte would not have at least witnessed Italian puppet performances of the story, particularly in Venice.

Texts in Italian are not readily available. Roberto and Renata Leydi, as part of an informative history of Italian puppetry entitled *Marionette e burattini,* have published an interesting script for puppets that bears the curious title *Don Giovanni il disoluto {sic}, ovvero Il castigo impensato, con Famiola disgraziato in amore.* Famiola is Don Giovanni's goofy Piedmont peasant servant. The Leydis took their text from a very recent manuscript, in turn probably based on an early nineteenth- or even eighteenth-century version. Their text differs in no significant way in language, plot, or style from the texts of Cicognini and the commedia dell'arte. Most puppet versions evidently followed the traditional tale.

Still, variations did exist. The Leydis discuss an interesting scene from a puppet *scenario* entitled *Don Giovanni.* The scene readily calls to mind a similar and significant comic-serious moment in Mozart's opera in which a passionate Elvira seeks to make love to a skittish Leporello disguised as Don Giovanni (II.vii–ix). Mozart's scene has no source in the theatrical versions we have discussed so far. In the puppet play, Don Giovanni has grown tired of women.

> Nonetheless, [he] realizes that his fame as a tireless lover demands of him certain duties that must be respected, even if they have become wearisome. The Castilian gentleman therefore charges his servant . . . to take his place with Donna Eleonora. Though still aflame with passion, she is not able to

74. Price, "Don Juan," 66–67.
75. Price, "Don Juan," 92.

> comprehend, in the darkness of the alcove, how from one day to the next her lover has been transformed from an elegant gentleman into a smelly and ill-mannered lout who takes total advantage of the situation. The lady is heartsick over this inexplicable metamorphosis and as a consolation finds nothing better to do than to offer herself to the false servant of the false Don Giovanni, that is, to the real Don Giovanni.[76]

Although this puppet *scenario* is post–Da Ponte, its origins are not; it derives, explain the Leydis, from a French comedy of 1707 by Alain-René Lesage, *Crispin rival de son maître,* which in turn descends by direct filiation from a *canovaccio* of the commedia dell'arte.[77] Did Da Ponte get an inkling for his scene from the script of some anonymous puppeteer who had, in turn, borrowed from Lesage's *Crispin*? The one scene clearly suggests the other, yet it is equally true that the similarities are imprecise, the correspondences blurred. Unfortunately, no one has yet discussed the influence of puppet plays on Da Ponte's text.

As for Italy's regular theater, no one after Goldoni experimented with the legend, which remained encrusted in forms that were now more than a hundred years old. Throughout the century there were scattered performances in various cities of the peninsula. The story was always well received and loudly applauded, but no performance was noteworthy or original. A *Convitato di pietra* printed by Giammaria Bassaglia in Venice in 1787 was nothing more than a word-for-word copy of Cicognini's text, as was another *Convitato* published in Florence in 1788 and sold at Sereno Sereni's bookstore. Neither booklet mentioned Cicognini's name.[78] A version published in Bologna in 1789 under the name of the prolific Neapolitan playwright Francesco Cerlone was entitled *Il nuovo convitato di pietra,* but, in spite of the title's promise of something new, the play was nothing but warmed over Juan, based as it was on the usual Cicognini and the little-known Andrea Perrucci earlier discussed.[79] Italy's eighteenth-century contribution to the legend lay not in the prose theater, but in opera and opera librettos.

---

76. Roberto Leydi and Renata M. Leydi, *Marionette e burattini* (Milan: Collana del "Gallo Grande," 1958), 266.

77. Leydi and Leydi, *Marionette,* 266.

78. Besides these two holdings, the Casa Goldoni also has a *Convitato di pietra, opera reggia et esemplare* printed in Bologna by Gioseffo Longhi and a *Gran convitato di pietra ad uso d'almanacco* printed in Milan by Pietro Agnelli. The first is a direct copy of Cicognini's, the second an abbreviated and slightly modified version. Both are without date of publication but are certainly eighteenth-century.

79. This text may in fact be Perrucci's, who, as noted, based his own work on Cicognini's. A comparison of the outline of the plays by Perrucci and Cerlone shows them to be nearly identical. Cerlone, author of fifty-six comedies and ten librettos for, among others, Giacomo Tritto and Giuseppe Gazzaniga, was born in Naples in 1722. It is not known when he died. That he is not the

The tired legend showed a bit more vigor throughout the century in France, although there too it attracted no new and outstanding author. It was performed on two levels. Thomas Corneille's version was frequently played at the Théâtre Français,[80] while on a distinctly less sophisticated level, in addition to the vaudeville *pièces foraines* already noted, the Théâtre Italien offered a number of revivals of its *Festin,* especially between 1743 and 1778.[81] Contemporary theatrical chroniclers recorded other occasional performances in and around Paris, the texts of which are no longer extant. While some of these made use of elaborate scenery, music, ballet, and even fireworks, at heart they remained the same old comic versions that harked back to Biancolelli and even to Cicognini. Neither Jean-Auguste Julien Desboulmiers in his *Histoire anecdotique et raisonnée du Théâtre Italien* published in 1769 nor Cailhava de l'Estandoux in his 1772 essay on comedy suggests that there was anything new or different about the legend. If anything, it must have been getting sillier. At the end of the version transcribed by Cailhava de l'Estandoux, after Don Juan drops down to hell, "Arlequin lui souhaite bon voyage" [Arlequin wishes him bon voyage].[82]

Continental versions of the tale held no great appeal to the English theatergoing public. While Shadwell's *Libertine* received many revivals up to 1740, his was the only one played. Throughout most of the century, performances of other versions, perhaps imported from France or Italy, could be counted on little more than the fingers of one hand. In the last two decades of the century the legend underwent a slight revival in the form of pantomime ballet. Two companies competed for London's attention. During the spring season of 1782, an Italian, Charles Antony Delpini, offered a pantomime entertainment, *Don Juan; or, The Libertine Destroy'd,* at the Drury Lane Theater. The music was by "Chevalier Clough," that is, by Christoph Willibald Gluck. The performance was repeated at the Haymarket Theater during the spring season of 1785. During the same season, a Frenchman, Charles Lepicq, presented a ballet, *Il convitato di pietra,* at

author of this *Nuovo convitato* is additionally suggested by the fact that the text is not included among the fourteen volumes of his collected works. Cerlone did the bulk of his work between 1764 and 1778, the year in which the collected edition of his works was published. See entries in the *Enciclopedia dello spettacolo* and especially the *Dizionario biografico degli italiani.* As for Perrucci's comedy, it was last published, according to Gendarme de Bévotte (*La Légende de Don Juan,* 297), in 1706 in Naples. For his study of Perrucci's contribution to the legend, Gendarme de Bévotte used a copy of the Naples edition, which he located in the university library in Bologna. Could a Bolognese publisher also have found that volume and republished a slightly modified text under Cerlone's more popular name?

80. Spaziani (*Don Giovanni dagli scenari,* 58) indicates 158 performances between 1701 and 1750.

81. Spaziani (*Don Giovanni dagli scenari,* 65), based on Clarence Brenner (*The Théâtre Italien: Its Repertory, 1716–1793* [Berkeley: University of California Press, 1961]), lists fifty-seven performances during this period.

82. Cailhava de l'Estandoux, *De L'Art* 2:190.

the King's Theater. He also chose music by Gluck. Delpini retaliated two years later (in 1787) at the Royalty Theater with a totally revised version that included songs, duets, and choruses by a Mr. William Reeve, music by Mr. Gluck, and scenery and machinery designed and executed by a Mr. Dixon, who, after the legend's traditional shipwreck scene, arranged to have Don Juan's servant, Scaramouch, played by Mr. Delpini, carried to the Spanish mainland on the back of a dolphin. Mr. Delpini's version proved to be the more popular of the two and was repeated several more times in the following years of the century. Mozart's *Don Giovanni* never made it to London, even though Mr. Ponte did himself. He was employed as official poet of the King's Theater, for which he prepared a Don Juan libretto. The opera was produced in March 1794, but it was not Mozart's. It was mainly Giovanni Gazzaniga's popular but trifling version, with a smattering of arias by other composers thrown in for good measure. It closed after only two performances.

2

Don Juan and Musical Theater Before Mozart

Throughout much of the eighteenth century, the legend of Don Juan was strictly a product for the popular theater, a subject for low-class comedy. What revitalized the story, gradually allowing the figure of Don Juan to reacquire lost energy and vitality, was his entrance into the musical world. Music raised him from the simply comic; music reinvested him with dignity and fascination. Without the music of Gluck or Mozart, it is likely that, as the century came to a close, the legend would have vanished into nonsense.

Don Juan made several false starts before he found the musical form that fit him best. He made a first operatic appearance in Rome during the carnival season of 1669 in an elaborately staged and lavishly produced *dramma musicale* entitled *L'empio punito.* Carnival was the season in which Roman high society spared no expense in order to entertain itself in the most opulent fashion, with elaborate banquets, public jousts, masked balls, cavalcades, hunts, public allegorical floats, and private theatrical performances. Opera had become an especially significant outlet for the extravagant tastes of the city's nobility due to the fact that it was the special passion of the reigning pope, Clemente IX (Giulio Rospigliosi), who was himself a successful opera librettist. When he ascended to the pontificate in 1667, he immediately saw to it that the climax of his first carnival season was the lavish production of several operas, among them one entitled *La comica del cielo* for which he himself had written the text. The enthusiasm of Clemente IX for this art form created a notable and lasting revival of opera in Rome in the latter half of the century.

L'empio punito was intended to be the high point of the 1669 carnival season.

An enormous amount of money, more than 6,000 scudi, was budgeted for the production. Preparations were begun the preceding November. The best singers from the papal chorus were engaged. For the obligatory dinner-with-the-statue scene, six real statues were moved into the theater.[1] Even a dwarf was hired, for humorous effect, to take the role of a servant.[2] Expectations of a magnificent performance were great.

Three young men, all active figures in Rome's theatrical world, prepared the opera. Filippo Acciaiuoli (1637–1700) sketched out the subject, the framework of the story. Acciaiuoli was a man of many talents and interests who had traveled widely throughout Europe, the Middle East, and Africa. He is thought to have even reached the coast of America. Upon returning to his studies in Rome, he specialized in mathematics, but his predominant enthusiasm was for the theater. He was particularly esteemed by his contemporaries as a designer of marvelous stage machinery and as a librettist. As such, he was among those instrumental in helping to bring about renewed enthusiasm for opera under Clemente IX. During the carnival season of 1668, he produced *Il Girello,* for which he also supplied the text. The opera was a burlesque of the conventions of the *dramma per musica* and turned out to be a very popular and successful entertainment. Acciaiuoli later designed elaborate spectacles for the marionette theater. It was probably he who coordinated all aspects of the production of *L'empio punito.* His outline was turned into verse by Giovanni Filippo Apolloni (ca. 1635–1688), a librettist of some renown, who was employed in Rome in the service of Cardinal Flavio Chigi. Apolloni had already written the libretto for Antonio Cesti's *La Dori* (1657), which became one of the most widely performed Italian operas of the seventeenth century. Last of the trio responsible for *L'empio punito* was Alessandro Melani (1639–1703), *maestro di cappella* at the church of Santa Maria Maggiore in Rome. He prepared the music. His brother, Jacopo, had composed the music for Acciaiuoli's *Girello.*

L'empio punito was first seen on 17 February 1669 in the Palazzo Colonna. Several subsequent performances followed. Present at the first performance were Queen Christina of Sweden, around whom so much of Roman society revolved, twenty-six cardinals of the church, ambassadors, princes, and many others of the

1. Margaret Murata, "Il carnevale a Roma sotto Clemente IX Rospigliosi," *Rivista italiana di musicologia* 12, no. 1 (1977): 94.

2. Alessandro Ademollo (*I teatri di Roma nel secolo decimosettimo* [1888; reprint, Bologna: Forni, 1969], 112) quotes a contemporary who mentions the dwarf. It is evident that the dwarf played Niceste, Cloridoro's servant, for Delfa, another servant, says to him (III.xv): "Dir ti conviene il tutto, / come buffon di corte: / s'io son vecchia, e tu brutto, / commune è la sciagura; / me minchionò l'età, te la natura." A few verses farther on, she refers to him as a "garbato figurino / da portar la livrea / dal bendato fanciul di Citarea."

nobility. A later performance was attended by an equally distinguished public including Caterina Colonna, who was the Venetian ambassadress, the ambassador from Spain, Cardinals Chigi and Rospigliosi, and nearly all the other members of the Rospigliosi family.

The new opera was as opulent as its public. It was presented, according to an eyewitness, "with sumptuous display, the richest vestments, the most delightful and lovely scenery with perspectives, music and magnificent dances."[3] The libretto listed seventeen singing roles plus a chorus of sailors, stable boys, and devils. In addition, there were sixty-seven nonsinging roles for dancers and actors. Much care was given to the scenery and to the stage spectacle. "They worked the side flats and the flies very well," wrote a delighted member of the audience, "they were changed ten times, the one and the other in the same moment."[4] The libretto actually indicated twelve scene changes and promised, among other effects, a flying statue and a sinking ship.

Most people enjoyed the performance, but not everyone. Queen Christina found it too long, and when asked by the Pope's brother, Cardinal Rospigliosi, how she liked it, she is reported to have whispered, "It's the *Convitato di pietra.*"[5] By that she meant that in spite of the opera's new and unusual title, its lovely singing and dancing, its sophisticated stage effects, and its exotic setting, what she was really watching was the same trite story played over and over again by the comedians of the commedia dell'arte in Italy and in France, a story that, by 1669, most educated people were tired of. Her boredom was echoed throughout the next hundred years by many others who considered the tale ridiculous, an unfit subject for serious creative invention.

Another member of the audience was even more critical than the queen. Even before he had seen it, Salvator Rosa, painter, writer, actor, and acquaintance of all the participants involved, was already annoyed that such a story, "in spite of all the new things around,"[6] had been chosen as the subject for a new opera. He did not change his mind after the performance.

> Friday I went to hear that wretched [*castratissimo*] *Convitato di pietra* which, both for the heat of the room and for the tediousness of its first-class stupidity [*solennissima coglioneria*], so affected my head and so deeply infuriated me, that I was forced to stay at home two days to digest my anger. Good God, how little it takes to make a fool out of a man [*con quanto poco*

3. Quoted in Murata, "Il carnevale," 95.
4. Quoted in Ademollo, *I teatri di Roma,* 112.
5. Quoted in Ademollo, *I teatri di Roma,* 113.
6. Aldo de Rinaldis, *Lettere inedite di Salvator Rosa a G. B. Ricciardi* (Rome: Palombi, 1939), 215.

> *l'huomo si fa coglionare*], and yet these people, in order to make a laughing-stock of themselves, have spent five to six thousand scudi. I swear I've never seen such absurdities.[7]

Indeed, as far as concerns the libretto, the opera was truly a "solennissima coglioneria." In this first musical version, the familiar story and the familiar characters were hidden behind aristocratic masks. Acciaiuoli and Apolloni fastidiously avoided any obvious contact with the vulgar Italian versions of the commedia. A fictitious Greece takes the place of a contemporary Italy and Spain, while the familiar characters cavort behind the masks of a fictitious and overblown Grecian nobility. Don Juan or, as he is called here, Acrimante is neither the youthful and energetic trickster of Seville that he was in Tirso de Molina's play nor the cold-hearted seducer of Dorimond's or the enigmatic thinker that he became in Molière's. Rather, he is a shallow, mean-spirited, and often pompous Roman aristocrat amusing himself in a lavish baroque masquerade. In fact, the entire opera, with its spectacular scenery, stage effects, dances, and *intermezzi,* is nothing more than an amusing carnival entertainment in which everyone participates, public and players alike. At the end of the first act, spectators can no longer be distinguished from the actors: tired from his day of hunting, the King of Macedonia relaxes in a lovely garden next to a fountain. The progress of the opera pauses as his servants, six Moors, serve him a drink and then come forward to serve the distinguished members of the audience as well.

The text of *L'empio punito* has not been included in this collection, but a summary of the narrative will give a sufficient idea of its qualities.[8] As in most baroque operas, the plot is complex. The action takes place in and around the city of Pella in Macedonia. In the first act, Atamira, daughter of the King of Corinth, is wandering along a deserted, wooded shore. She is seeking her husband by whom she has been abandoned but with whom she still is desperately in love. From afar she hears cries for help coming from a sinking ship and then sees two figures swimming toward shore. She pulls them in. The first turns out to be her husband, Acrimante, who is less than delighted to see her. The second is Bibi, his servant. Acrimante brutally refuses to have anything to do with his wife and runs off with several peasant girls whose names Bibi immediately adds to his list. Atamira retires under a nearby tree and falls asleep. She is sighted by Atrace, King of Macedonia, who is out hunting with his cousin, Cloridoro. The king immediately falls in love with her and sends her to Pella to stay with

7. De Rinaldis, *Lettere,* 217.

8. A full text may be found in Giovanni Macchia, *Vita avventure e morte di Don Giovanni* (Bari: Laterza, 1966).

his sister, Ipomene. Acrimante has also gone to Pella, and there he catches sight of Ipomene. He too falls deeply in love, unaware, however, that her affections are entirely for Cloridoro. Through Ipomene's nurse, Delfa, Bibi arranges to have Ipomene brought to Acrimante's apartment. He leads her to believe that Cloridoro will be waiting there for her. Grateful to his enterprising servant, Acrimante willingly lends him a cloak, for Bibi has plans to woo Delfa while Acrimante is busy with Ipomene.

In the second act, Bibi, wearing Acrimante's cloak, is flirting with Delfa through the barred window of her lady's apartment. He is sighted by Atrace who mistakes Bibi for Acrimante and supposes the unseen Delfa to be his beloved Atamira. Enraged, he orders Acrimante to appear before him. In the meanwhile, Ipomene hides in Acrimante's apartment to await, as she thinks, the arrival of her faithful Cloridoro. When an unsuspecting Acrimante appears before the king, he is immediately arrested. Thoroughly confused by the king's accusation, Acrimante begs Cloridoro for aid and asks him to inform the lady waiting in his apartment that he is in trouble. At the same time he shamelessly asks Atamira for help, help which she cannot deny him, so strong is her love for him still. When Atrace orders Acrimante's execution, she publicly begs to be allowed to poison him herself. Her secret plan is to administer a sleeping potion and whisk the body away to safety, all of which she does. Cloridoro also wants to die; he has found his Ipomene in Acrimante's rooms. But Bibi sets things right with a few little lies: Acrimante, he claims, had really been trying to arrange an assignation between the two young people. Delighted, the two lovers make up and agree, in Bibi's hearing, to meet again that evening. In the meanwhile, Acrimante's dormant body is lying in Atamira's room. The devil conjures up a vision of all the pleasures of hell for the sleeping Acrimante. Even Persephone seems to be in love with him.

Acrimante awakens in the third act. Having seen the delights of hell, he is now totally in the thrall of the flesh. He still cares nothing for Atamira; his thoughts are only for Ipomene. Bibi informs him of the planned nighttime meeting between the two lovers and suggests that if he pretends to be Cloridoro he may, under cover of darkness, have a chance to make love to her. He tries, but Ipomene screams. When Tidemo, her tutor, rushes to her defense, Acrimante slays him. Later, Acrimante comes across a statue of the dead man in one of the royal gardens. "Why don't you come to dinner?" mocks Acrimante. The statue agrees. To the king of the underworld, Acrimante offers his soul in exchange for a meal worthy of his guest. Six statues bring forth a fully loaded table. But the stone guest is not interested in food. "You have given your soul to Pluto," says the statue. "It is now time for him to receive it." With that,

Acrimante drops beneath the earth down to the banks of the River Styx. Charon receives the sinner into his boat. As Acrimante disappears from sight, he is last heard confessing his guilt and admitting that justice has been done.

What most strikes a reader of this text is that Queen Christina was absolutely right when she whispered to Cardinal Rospigliosi that what they were watching was really the same old *Convitato di pietra.* The traditional legend was clearly visible behind the Grecian facade. Behind the exotic names were most of the standard figures that had been traveling around Italy and France for thirty or forty years. Acrimante, as already noted, behaves like Don Giovanni, aspects of Ipomene reflect the figure of Donna Anna, in Cloridoro can be seen Duca Ottavio or the Marqués de la Mota, Tidemo obviously recalls the Commendatore, while Atamira suggests a Donna Isabella–Done Elvire figure. Many events were first imagined by Tirso de Molina: Acrimante's shipwreck and rescue, his dalliance with the peasant girls, the attempted seduction of Ipomene, the murder of Tidemo, and the final dinner scene with the statue; yet all these scenes were lifted not from Tirso but probably from a later popular Italian version of the legend such as Cicognini's or Giliberto's or from a *scenario* of the commedia dell'arte. Indeed, it is quite clear that, for their very sophisticated opera, Acciaiuoli and Apolloni did not hesitate to raid and pillage Don Juan texts that belonged to the popular theater, for *L'empio punito* contains elements not present in Tirso at all but found exclusively in the popular Italian tradition, such as Bibi's list of his master's conquests or Acrimante's lament in hell.[9] When, on a rare occasion, in the midst of so much Grecian grandeur, a phrase or an idea turns up from Cicognini or from a commedia version, we embrace it like a long lost friend.

But if the story is the same, the style and the energy with which it is related are not. The characters in this complicated opera express themselves in a gush

9. Specifically: Bibi's list (I.iv) can be found in Cicognini (I.xi) and in the Naples *Convitato scenario;* Acrimante's oath on the "uom di pietra" (II.xiv) is in Cicognini (I.xi) and the Naples and Rome *Convitato;* Bibi's reference to the statues as "bambocci" (III.xvi) reflects Cicognini's "bambozzo" (III.v); the vision of Acrimante in hell, his admission of guilt, and his desire for a definitive death (III.xvii–xviii) can be found in the final scenes of Cicognini and in the Rome and Naples *scenari* as well as in *L'ateista fulminato.* No one heretofore has noticed that there are also some curious echoes of Molière's Done Elvire in the figure of Atamira. Like Done Elvire, Atamira was married to Acrimante–Don Juan and abandoned by him. Still thoroughly in love, she is now searching for him everywhere. When she unexpectedly comes face to face with him, he makes fun of her and rejects her brutally, as Dom Juan did Done Elvire. But she too persists. The figure of Done Elvire is one of Molière's most original contributions to the legend. The fact that similarities exist between her and Atamira is puzzling. Although Molière's play was staged in 1665, four years before *L'empio punito,* it was withdrawn after fifteen performances. It was not published until well after the production of the opera.

of lengthy, mellifluous, emotion-fraught verse that suffocates the tale's vitality. For example, this is a melancholy Atamira bewailing the loss of her beloved Acrimante.

Vaghe frondi, amiche piante,
che le mie querele udite,
compatite,
e del mar l'onda spumante
col suo mesto mormorio
serva d'intercalare al pianto mio.
Care selve, onor del monte,
s'il mio ben qui racchiudete,
rispondete.
Se di voi l'altera fronte
d'Euro a forza al suol s'inchina,
dite: l'anima mia fors'è vicina?
Dove sei, mio tesoro,
mio consorte adorato?

(I.iii)

[Lovely foliage, friendly trees,
you who hear my complaints,
have pity on me,
and may the frothy wave of the sea
with its sad sighing
serve as a refrain to my weeping.
Forests dear, honor of the mountain,
if you here enclose my beloved,
answer me.
If Eurus bends
your proud brow earthward,
tell me: Is my very life close by?
Where are you, my treasure,
my adored consort?]

This is a frustrated Atrace, baffled by Atamira's refusal to marry him.

M'uccide un vago volto,
e qual farfalla allo splendor del lume,

da cari lacci avvinto,
m'aggiro intorno all'adorato nume,
per rimaner dalle sue fiamme estinto.

(II.viii)

[A lovely visage slays me,
and like a moth before the splendor of a light,
bound by fond bonds
I circle around my adored goddess,
to be extinguished by her flames.]

Finally, this is an anxious Ipomene awaiting the arrival of her lover.

Aurette tenebrose,
ch'addolorate e chete
sopra guancie di rose
con stille di rugiada il sol piangete,
godete pur, godete,
ch'i luminosi rai
tosto veder potrete;
ma il mio bel sol non si rivede mai.

(III.iii)

[Shadowy breezes,
silent and grief-stricken,
who weep for the sun with drops of dew
on rose cheeks,
be glad, be yet glad,
for soon you will be able to see
its luminous rays;
but my handsome sun never reappears.]

Three different characters, three different subject matters, three different emotions, but all their expressions seem cast from the same die. In this opera libretto, the graceful, stately rhythms rarely change, the music rarely modulates. Nor is it wise to search too intently for solid significance amid the liquid harmonies of these very literate verses.

It is true that among the servants there are moments of vulgarity that temper the sweet monotony of the principal players. Acrimante and Bibi come upon a shepherdess. "What is your name?" asks Bibi. "I won't tell you," she replies, "except to say that I [*io*] am a woman." Bibi's retort is sharp, as he compares her to Io, the daughter of Inachus, first king of Argos, beloved by Zeus and changed by Hera into a heifer: "Perhaps you are that Io [I] who in the lovely forests knew how to bind the heart of a great deity. Behold a new Zeus who for love will now turn you into a cow [*vacca*]"[10] (I.v). Yet the fresh vulgarity of the servants is often vitiated by the intellectualistic quality of their verse. Their thoughts may be crude, but their mode of expression reflects a remarkable education in the classics. What is lacking is the raw, natural earthiness generally associated with the lower-class servant figure and so often present in the legend.

In spite of the fact that the participants in this drama speak at length, they are rarely able to explain themselves with clarity, perceptivity, or profundity. Their emotions are curiously generic and their characters likewise. For that reason, they generate little interest. The librettists of *L'empio punito* have not realized that Don Juan is usually not a man of words but a man of action. He becomes grand not through what he says but through what he does. He and his legend cannot be confined by a literary Greece, by the delights of papal Rome, or by the conventions of baroque opera, nor can he be hedged in by airy verse,

10. The Italian text is as follows.

PASTORELLA: Gran curiosità.
Non te lo voglio dir; donna son io.
BIBI: Forse quell'Io che nell'amene selve
seppe allacciare il cuore
d'un'alta deità?
Ecco un Giove novel, che per amore
diventar una vacca or ti farà.

There is also a fairly rough exchange between Bibi and Ipomene's old nurse, Delfa.

BIBI: Se per drudo mi vuoi,
bella coppia faremo,
nè mai temer potremo
dalli sbirri d'amore affronto alcuno,
che, venendo il citetur,
scritto abbiamo nel volto il: non gravetur.
DELFA: Non più strali, non più dardi,
già per te moro e languisco.
Divenisti con i sguardi
al mio core un basilisco.
BIBI: S'io son serpe, io son almeno
un di quei fatt'alla moda:
se co'l capo io t'avveleno,
la triacha ho nella coda.

(I.viii)

pleasant rhymes, heartfelt declamatory expressions, or artful classical allusions. Can we really believe in a Don Juan in love who speaks such saccharine verses as these?

> Tormentose faville,
> che nel mio seno ardete,
> non più crescete il foco,
> ch'a sì gran fiamma un picciol core è poco.
>
> (I.xiii)
>
> [Tormenting coals
> burning in my breast,
> do not increase the flame,
> for a tiny heart cannot contain such a great fire.]

Or worse, such tripping rhymes as these?

> Se fatali
> sono i strali,
> se 'l mio male è inremediabile,
> senz'aita
> la mia vita
> un sol dì non è durabile.
>
> (II.iv)
>
> [If [Eros's] dart
> has pierced my heart,
> if the wound is now unhealable,
> without assistance
> my existence
> not a single day is endurable.]

When Don Juan is hedged in by this sort of poetry, his expansive personality shrivels, his wickedness turns into meanness, and even his virility becomes suspect. In *L'empio punito,* he is more victim than victimizer; the list of his misdeeds is exceedingly short, and the catalog of women he has seduced is almost nonexistent. On the Roman stage, the legendary Don Juan cut a very poor figure. He lost the grandeur that should make his final fall so disturbing and fearful. He and his legend were forced to wear an ill-fitting disguise, forced to be what they are not. What the legend should be is a tale of supreme egoism, of betrayal, of divine admonition and divine vengeance, a warning here and now. Costumed as *L'empio punito* in order to serve the pleasures of the Roman court, it lost its force both as an adventure story and as a moral tale. For these reasons, in the ongoing tradition of the Don Juan legend, *L'empio punito* was a dead end.

Only occasionally are we reminded of Da Ponte's treatment. Just as Elvira interrupts Don Giovanni's wooing of Zerlina, so Atamira interrupts Acrimante as he tries to seduce a shepherdess (I.v). Some verses may seem to reflect a faint Dapontian light. Bibi reports the statue's answer to Acrimante's dinner invitation: "Ma con la testa sua fece così" [But with his head he did like this] (III.xvi). The statue refuses to dine with these words: "Chi a vivande celesti un dì s'avvezza / ogni cibo terreno odia e disprezza" [Whoever becomes accustomed to heavenly fare / hates and scorns all earthly food] (III.xvi). Especially curious are the opera's very opening verses, which clearly suggest the opening lines of complaint sung by Leporello. In *L'empio punito,* it is a stable-boy and his companions who do the complaining.

Gran tormento che mi par
lavorar
la notte e 'l dì.
. . . .
O che pena, che catena
è la vita d'un Paì.[11]

(I.i)

[What torture
to have to work
night and day.
. . . .
Oh how painful, what a ball and chain
is the life of a Paì!]

11. The texts in Da Ponte are: "Con la marmorea testa / ei fa così, così" (II.xii); "Non si pasce di cibo mortale / chi si pasce di cibo celeste" (II.xvii); "Notte e giorno faticar / per chi nulla sa gradir; / piova e vento sopportar, / mangiar male e mal dormir . . ." (I.i). See Lorenzo Da Ponte, *Tre libretti per Mozart,* ed. Paolo Lecaldano (Milan: Rizzoli, 1956).

But these similarities do not mean a thing. Da Ponte knew nothing of this opera. What we observe here is simply the legend as it begins to assume a librettistic shape.

It took Don Juan more than sixty years to find his way back into opera; when he did, he showed up in a new sort of libretto that, in essence, was not much different from Da Ponte's. With this new libretto, a Don Juan model was set. From then on it simply had to be fine-tuned. In *L'empio punito,* the legend had been presented as a masquerade. In the new opera, *La pravità castigata,* the masks were removed. For the first time in music, here was the legend as we have come to know it, both as it had developed out of Tirso and as it was to become in Da Ponte's text for Mozart. All playacting was eliminated; costumes were put aside. For the first time in music, the characters were characters of their own time and their own society. The King of Naples plays cards in the evening with his courtiers; Duca Ottavio tells time with a London-made watch he carries about in his pocket; Don Giovanni's servant, Malorco, eats macaroni. The characters have come straight from a popular fiction, from the commedia. A reader fresh from the stultifying fakery of *L'empio punito* is immediately struck by the fact that these characters are not afraid to recognize and accept their origins. They are not pretending to be what they are not; they are not ashamed of their plebeian, comedic origins, as they were in *L'empio punito.* As a result, there is a new reality in the action of this libretto, a new sense of contemporality; there is, in its message, even a sense of urgency. Seduction and murder have become a serious business, damnation is frightening. Just as the macaroni eaten by Malorco are real, so his list now contains eighty-seven names of real, living women seduced by Don Giovanni. Thus, in this libretto, Don Juan's story and his character begin to assume the shape and style that they will have in Mozart. For these reasons, *La pravità castigata* and not *L'empio punito* should be considered the first true Don Juan opera. When Da Ponte set about preparing his text in 1787, he was not inventing something new, but drawing on a libretto tradition that had begun more than fifty years earlier.

La pravità castigata was first presented in 1734 in Brno, Czechoslovakia, under the active impresarioship of Angelo Mingotti, who, together with his brother Pietro, was successfully introducing Italian opera of the highest quality into the theaters of Northern Europe in the middle decades of the eighteenth century. Theirs was, writes Giorgio Pestelli in *The Age of Mozart and Beethoven,* "the most dynamic Italian musical troupe of the eighteenth century."[12] In a

12. Giorgio Pestelli, *The Age of Mozart and Beethoven* (Cambridge: Cambridge University Press, 1984), 71.

brief dedicatory letter dated 20 February 1734 and printed at the beginning of the opera libretto, Mingotti indicates that this opera was among the first to be presented in the newly built theater of Brno. The score has not survived, and only one copy of the libretto, in the University Library of Brno, is known to exist.[13] The booklet was rather handsomely prepared, with attractive decorative motifs printed throughout. Each left-hand page provides the Italian text in verse, while the right-hand page furnishes a German translation in prose.

The music was by an obscure Italian composer, Eustachio Bambini. Information about him is scant. He was born in Pesaro in 1697, and he served as *maestro di cappella* between 1723 and 1731, first in Pesaro and then in Cortona. He later seems to have been a fairly successful theater impresario in Italy and in France from 1745 until his death in Pesaro in 1770. In 1750, he was in Strasbourg, where *La pravità castigata* was sung for a second and last time. The attention given to him by music historians is due, however, not to this opera, but to the fact that, in 1752, he took a small company of singers to Paris where, on 2 August, on the stage of the Opéra-Comique, he presented Giovanni Pergolesi's *La serva padrona.* It was this performance that triggered the *querelle des bouffons* during which all Paris argued over the relative merits of French and Italian opera. Bambini and his singers, caught in the middle, were the *bouffons.* No published biographical sketch mentions his Czech experience or the fact that he was also a composer.[14]

It is not known who served as Bambini's librettist. In an introductory page of the printed libretto headed "Lettore Discreto," the unknown author makes some interesting comments about his work. He chose the legend of Don Juan for performance, he informs his readers, precisely because it was so familiar, returning year after year on stages all over Europe and looking, he adds curiously, like "a young bride among a packed crowd of elderly matrons." In other words, he considered the popularity of the story a sure promise of the opera's success. Da Ponte, with his fine sense of what was theatrically expedient, certainly selected the legend for exactly the same reason. Bambini's librettist indicated that he was dispensing with the usual plot summary, since the story could

13. I am deeply indebted to the kindness of Dr. Vladislav Dokoupil of the University of Brno for furnishing me with a microfilm of the libretto.

14. In addition to the opera under discussion, three others, all performed in 1733, have also been attributed to him: an *Artaserse,* a *Partenope,* and an *Armida abbandonata.* For the first two, see Vladislav Dokoupil and Vladimír Telec, *Hudební staré tisky ve fondech universitní knihovny v brně* (Brno: Universitní knihovna, 1975), 143, 174. The third is listed by Jiří Sehnal in "Počátky opery na moravě," *O divadle na moravě,* Acta universitatis palackianae, Facultas philosophica, Supplementum 21 (Prague: Státní pedagogické nakladatelství, 1974), 57.

be easily understood at first listening. He took for granted that everyone already knew what happened. Yet he believed that his version also offered something new; never before, he boasted, had the legend been fitted out so grandly, and he promised that the performance would be morally exemplary, scenically miraculous, visually splendid, and musically charming.

The impresario, Angelo Mingotti, probably did try to make the opera visually splendid. His audience would have expected nothing less; through the years, the public had learned to associate the legend with such things as shipwrecks, flying statues, and ghastly visions of hell. Scenic effects were an essential part of the Don Juan promise. Thirteen scene changes are listed at the beginning of the libretto and two others are added in the body of the text. The first scene is set along a seashore. In the distance, the city of Naples can be seen. A boat is approaching and docks. A later scene takes place in a gothic temple with an equestrian statue of the dead Commendatore and a sepulchre decorated with various marble statues and military trophies. It is clear that the company was especially proud of a "double flight of the Commendatore" and of an "abyss which swallows Don Giovanni and the table." These items are typographically isolated on the page headed *mutazioni di scena* so as to be more immediately noticeable.

Mingotti's small company consisted of eight singers: five women and three men. Since *La pravità castigata* had nine roles, one of the men played two parts. The part of Don Giovanni was sung by a woman, Rosa Cardini, as was that of the King of Naples. His role was taken by Laura Bambini, Eustachio's sister. Naturally, everyone sang in Italian, even Malorco, Don Giovanni's servant, who in comic, nonmusical versions often preferred the dialect of Venice or Naples. In later operatic versions, he sometimes switched back to his hometown speech. The Italianization of Malorco may have been due to the fact that the production was designed for foreign consumption. Among the spectators, a certain knowledge of Italian might have been presumed, but certainly not of a dialect.

While in this version the legend was well on its way to becoming what it will be with Da Ponte and Mozart, *La pravità castigata* is not yet an opera buffa as is theirs. On the title page it is called a "drama per musica." Mingotti speaks of it as an "eroicomica rappresentazione." Unlike the opera buffa, principal male roles have been written for female voices; there is no chorus, there are no duets or ensembles, and there are no finales. Most of the opera consists of recitative dialogue followed by a da capo exit aria, the subject of which is only marginally related to the happenings on stage. These characteristics will later disappear as the operatic Don Juan more and more affirms itself a part of the opera buffa style and tradition.

Nonetheless, this affirmation is starting to take place, even if not completely, in *La pravità castigata.* We see it in the verse. The librettist promises to tell the story in rather plain speech; he recognizes that it cannot be successfully told in an elegant, aristocratic format. For the most part he has been true to his word, not so much in the arias, which at times are a bit heady, opera seria style,[15] as in the dialogue, which is generally straightforward and unadorned, far removed from baroque ingenuities and complexities. All characters, not just servant figures, tend to speak briefly and simply, as they will in Da Ponte's libretto and as they do in opera buffa in general. They make use of relatively short, plainspoken expressions that go to the heart of the matter. As such, their speech reflects the style of the popular theater sources from which this librettist amply borrowed.

In fact, almost nothing in the libretto is original. Plot development, scenes, characters, dialogue, ideas—all have been pieced together from earlier Italian versions of the legend. While there are similarities to Tirso's *El burlador de Sevilla,* this is only because all versions descend from him. The libretto owes no debt to the Spanish playwright; nothing in it comes exclusively from his play. Nor does it owe debts to versions from France, by which it has been completely untouched. Bambini's opera has its roots exclusively in the popular Italian comic theater of its time.

Much of the three acts of *La pravità castigata* directly descends from Cicognini's three-act play in prose. Bambini's librettist knew it well: language and style are similar, plot development and characterization are remarkably alike, and some scenes have been filched almost directly.[16] The librettist may also have

---

15. For example, Manfredi, King of Naples, sings the following lines.

> Pargoletto con mano innocente
> lieto scherza con l'aspide algente,
> ma s'il morde, languendo sen va.
>
> (I.vii)

Meanwhile, Duca Ottavio compares himself to a thirsty deer.

> Come la cerva al fonte
> per isfogar sua sete
> corre dal prato al monte,
> nè mai presta sen riede
> finchè estinta l'ha;
> tal degl'eroi il core . . . etc., etc.
>
> (II.vii)

16. Among the major borrowings from Cicognini are the following: Bambini I.i, v from Cicognini I.xi, xiii; Bambini II.ii from Cicognini I.i, ii; Bambini III.v from Cicognini III.v; Bambini III.ix from Cicognini III.viii; the final inferno scene.

been familiar with Andrea Perrucci's late seventeenth-century, three-act version. In that play, Don Giovanni approaches his servant, Coviello, under the cover of darkness. Just for fun, Coviello imitates the voice of a police officer in pursuit of Don Giovanni and carries out a humorous dialogue between himself and the imaginary officer.[17] Something like this scene is in the opera (II.i). It is night. Don Giovanni's servant, Malorco, is suddenly startled by the footsteps of an approaching court official. In pidgin German, French, and Spanish, he imitates the voices of imaginary comrades-in-arms and scares off the cowardly intruder, who fears he is surrounded by a veritable enemy army.

Of course, Bambini's librettist may have witnessed this bit of comic byplay not in Perrucci but in some performance by the commedia dell'arte. He was certainly familiar with their interpretations. His statue flies through the air just as theirs did in the mid-seventeenth-century scenario from Naples. When his Malorco makes a mess at Don Giovanni's dinner party by mixing a salad too energetically and seasoning it with lamp oil, he is repeating what was a traditional salad *lazzo* used by the commedia for at least seventy-five years. Domenico Biancolelli left a record of the way he played the scene: "I mix the salad with my stick, I cut up a chicken, I upset a lamp, I wipe my mouth with a tablecloth, etc."[18] The libretto was deeply embedded in an Italian comic tradition that freely fed off itself. Versions abounded, all similar in essence, and theatrical performances were numerous. Between Cicognini's first version and *La pravità,* it is impossible to say how many editions were available or which one happened to fall into the hands of Bambini's anonymous librettist. What is clear is that he, too, was a part of the tradition.

The libretto offers a few curiosities. There are some small additions to the traditional plot: the onstage departure by boat of Donna Isabella (Anna) to rejoin her father in Naples and an intrigue involving a misplaced jeweled belt belonging to Donna Beatrice. There are small twists on the old plot: the borrowing by Don Giovanni of Duca Ottavio's watch instead of his cloak. Particularly odd, the entire story is set in and around Naples, not split, as customary, between Naples and Spain. Yet the libretto also acquired a certain economy of action, usually not a strong point in earlier versions. It opens with the shipwreck that so embarrasses Goldoni; it proceeds quickly to the seduction of the fishergirl Rosalba, which in turn is followed in the second act by attempts in rapid succession upon the virtue of Donnas Isabella and Beatrice, ladies of the Neapoli-

17. See Georges Gendarme de Bévotte, *La Légende de Don Juan, son évolution dans la littérature des origines au romantisme* (1906; reprint, Geneva: Slatkine, 1970), 299.

18. See Marcello Spaziani, *Don Giovanni dagli scenari dell'arte alla "foire"* (Rome: Edizioni di storia e letteratura, 1978), 147.

tan court who also happen to be good friends and confidants. The act concludes with the murder of Donna Isabella's father, the Commendatore di Sant'Iago. Totally unexpected is the dying man's pardon of his slayer. However, by the third act, the Commendatore has had a change of heart, thereby allowing the librettist to devote this final act almost entirely to his statue and to vengeance.

More interesting than these few originalities is the fact that, in *La pravità castigata,* characters and scenes of the standard story for the first time take on a form and expression, suitable to the needs of opera, that will remain essentially unaltered by later eighteenth-century librettists working with the same material. The solutions adopted by this librettist are the same as those adopted by the librettists who prepared texts for Don Juan operas by Vincenzo Righini and Giuseppe Calegari, by Giacomo Tritto and Giuseppe Gazzaniga, and, finally, by Mozart. Da Ponte, far from creating a new Don Juan libretto, followed a well-established tradition first formulated here.

It is impossible not to hear echoes of the violent music that Mozart imagined for a similar scene in this staccato exchange between Don Giovanni and Donna Beatrice. He is fleeing her apartment after attempting to violate her.

D. Gio: Lasciami, o donna.
D. Bea: Temerario! In vano
tenti fuggir; palesa
l'iniquo nome.
D. Gio: Lascierai la mano
alle mie vesti appesa,
se a trattenermi tu persisti, o ardita.
D. Bea: Vi lascierò la vita,
pria che lasciarti.
D. Gio: Cedi omai.
D. Bea: Discuopri
chi tu sei.
D. Gio: Nol vuo' dire.
Venni incognito, e tale
voglio di qui partire.
D. Bea: Olà, di corte;
gente, soccorso!
D. Gio: Taci.
D. Bea: Olà, di corte . . .
D. Gio: Taci, dissi, o muori.

(II.ii)

[D. GIO: Lady, let me go.
D. BEA: Coward! In vain
you seek to escape;
reveal your wicked name.
D. GIO: If you persist in holding on to me,
you will find your hand
hanging from my clothing.
D. BEA: I will give up my life
rather than let you go.
D. GIO: Yield.
D. BEA: Disclose
your name.
D. GIO: I will not tell you.
I came incognito,
and so I wish to depart.
D. BEA: Guards,
people, bring help!
D. GIO: Keep silent.
D. BEA: Guards.
D. GIO: Keep silent, I said, or you die!]

Her cry to Duca Ottavio for revenge is as sharp and as angry as Donna Anna's will be. As for the duke, he is introduced as the wordy, ceremonious, and ineffectual aristocrat we are familiar with from Da Ponte's libretto, while the Commendatore enacts his usual paternal role as defender of his daughter's honor and then as minister of divine justice. Malorco plays a prominent part and, like Leporello, is wily, practical, sharp-tongued, amusing, often vulgar, and always hungry. He complains bitterly about the life he is forced to lead, eating little, sleeping hardly at all, and never seeing his salary. Men like Don Giovanni are a "razza porca" [a filthy breed] (II.i). Yet, again like Leporello, he has a certain affection for Don Giovanni himself, and with commonsense morality he too unsuccessfully tries to dissuade him from the ways of the flesh.

The Don Giovanni that Malorco complains about is likewise essentially the figure he will be in Mozart. He is a young, active, and able flatterer and seducer. Listening to him as he offers his hand to the fishergirl, Rosalba, we are also listening to the melody of Mozart's "Là ci darem la mano." He is a man of action, not a thinker; he is violent—to the statue of the dead Commendatore: "Ti sprezzo, ti detesto" (III.i)—indifferent to others, concerned only for his own pleasure and honor, without a trace of conscience, unafraid. In a way, he is already a man possessed. He interrupts Malorco, who is beginning to run down the list of women he has seduced: "Don't talk to me about past joys; once my desire has been satisfied, they no longer please me" (III.iv). He is well on his way to the 2,065 conquests later cataloged by Leporello.

Similarities between the two texts are most striking in the third act, in the scenes involving encounters with the statue of the Commendatore. In these scenes, Don Giovanni begins to embody the same grandiose qualities that will be his in Da Ponte's version. He reads the accusing inscription on the monument pedestal, just as he will do in Da Ponte: "Here lies the body of the Commendatore, whom a wicked traitor deprived of life." His reaction is one of violent disdain: "You call me a traitor? Villain! My blows were not traitorous; why, if you came back to life, I would run you through the heart again face to face" (III.i). Personal honor is all. Just so, Da Ponte's Don Giovanni will say to the Commendatore with arrogant pride: "I will never be accused of cowardice" (II.xvii). Bambini's protagonist insults the dead man: "O vecchio ribaldo," he calls him (III.i). "O vecchio buffonissimo!" are the words in Da Ponte (II.xii). Malorco extends a dinner invitation to the statue, who nods his assent. Don Giovanni refuses to believe it.

D. Gio: Your belief made you see what wasn't there.
Mal: You try it,
you invite him. I'm frightened!
D. Gio: I will. Commendatore,
I invite you to dinner with me.
Will you come?
Statue: I will come.

(III.i)

The moment is much the same in Da Ponte, whose Don Giovanni is also unbelieving.

Lep: Ah! ah! ah! What a sight this is!
Oh God, he nodded his head!
D. Gio: Nonsense, you're ridiculous.
Lep: Look again.
D. Gio: What should I look at?
Lep: With his marble head
he's going like this.

D. GIO: (*to the statue*) Speak! If you are able,
will you come to dinner?
IL COM: Yes.

(II.xii)

Forced to accept the reality of this supernatural event, each man suffers a moment of perplexity, a faint shudder of human fear. "The situation indeed is strange," mutters Da Ponte's hero, and later, when the statue appears at dinner, he adds, "I would never have believed it" (II.xvii). At the beginning of dinner, Bambini's Don Giovanni confesses to Malorco, "I don't know why, but I'm perturbed" (III.iv). Yet both Don Giovannis quickly revert to the fearlessness that is an essential part of their fascination. Each has an image of himself that cannot be denied. The statue must be faced. In Bambini: "I am a gentleman, and I will keep my word. . . . With pride I do not give in to fear" (III.v). In Da Ponte: "My heart is steadfast, I have no fear" (II.xvii). Like Leporello, Malorco cares less for questions of reputation than for practical realities, for saving his own skin. His master, he believes, is either completely reckless or totally mad. And so he asks him a fundamental question: "Why do you seek evil?" (III.viii). For Bambini's Don Giovanni, the question is as meaningless as is Leporello's similar complaint to his master that the life he leads is criminal (I.iv). Neither Don Giovanni seeks evil in and of itself; neither has any idea of the meaning of the word. They pose themselves no moral or ethical questions.

Therefore, come what may, to the extended hand of the Commendatore each boldly extends his own, as a command to repent is given and refused three times.[19] Don Giovanni is not afraid of the statue, of divine vengeance, because what he is, what he has done, is not for him a question of morality. He does not repent because, as far as he is concerned, he has done nothing that requires it. When the statue grips his hand and he finally knows fear, he is not fearful of damnation or of hell. For him they do not exist. He is afraid because he no longer has his two hands free to defend himself. The terror of these Don Giovannis is a brief and awful moment of illumination in which they realize that a man may be caught in a destiny more powerful than his own strength and self-sufficiency. For an instant, Bambini's text has caught that terror just as Da Ponte's will a half-century later.

Except for the one revival in Strasbourg, Bambini's opera was quickly forgotten. It had no influence on the ongoing development of the legend, which continued to be performed in the popular, nonmusical theater for comic effect

19. Bambini III.ix; for Da Ponte's text, see chap. 1, note 8.

and cheap spectacle. It was not until 1761 that Don Juan reappeared on the musical stage, this time not in operatic form but as a ballet. The effect was extraordinary. Christoph Willibald Gluck's pantomime ballet, *Don Juan*, revitalized the story and brought it back before aristocratic audiences in a well-conceived, serious, and compelling work of art.

It happened in Vienna. The historical importance of the performance was manifold. First, the manner of dancing devised for the ballet was new and startling and introduced significant reforms into the art of the dance. Next, for the first time, music of worth was created for what was, in the minds of many educated spectators, a very silly legend; music of grandeur was now linked to the legend, thus unconsciously preparing for Mozart's interpretation. Finally, the legend itself was considerably ennobled by the ballet's choreographer, Gasparo Angiolini, who removed traditional farcical elements and endowed the figure of Don Juan with renewed vigor and tragic stature. Gluck and Angiolini showed that the legend was worthy of serious creative thought. While many later versions did not follow their example (many were in fact not worthy at all), these two men proved that it could be. Angiolini's choreography and Gluck's music changed the way one thought about the story, as the incidental songs by Henry Purcell for Shadwell's *The Libertine* or the tunes of the *foire* never did. Although critics have begun to recognize the significant role of the Gluck-Angiolini *Don Juan* in the history of ballet reform,[20] most have ignored the influence of the ballet on Da Ponte and Mozart.

Vienna was one of the most active and progressive musical centers in Europe in 1761. The director of the imperial theaters was Count Giacomo Durazzo. A man of great culture and intelligence, he was a forward-looking *intendant* tired of the conventions of Metastasian opera seria and of traditional court ballet. He actively encouraged change and spared no effort or expense to bring it about in his theaters. Among his innovative circle of friends were Gluck, whom he invited to Vienna in 1754; Ranieri Calzabigi, adventurer and poet who wrote the librettos for Gluck's reform opera *Orfeo ed Euridice* (1762), *Alceste* (1767), and *Paride ed Elena* (1770); and Angiolini, a young Italian ballet master who, like Durazzo, was concerned with finding a way to revitalize the traditional forms of ballet. In fact, the originality and the lasting success of *Don Juan* was due not only to Gluck and his music but in equal measure to this young and vigorous

20. See, for example, Paul F. Marks, "The Reform of Subject and Style in Ballet-Pantomime at Vienna between 1740–1767," in *Woman in the 18th Century and Other Essays,* ed. Paul Fritz and Richard Morton (Toronto: Hakkert, 1976), 141–85.

ballet master who wrote the story and prepared the choreography in close collaboration with the composer. What is more, the credit for *Don Juan* as a reform ballet should be Angiolini's entirely.

Gasparo Angiolini was a man of remarkable and unflagging talents. Dancer, choreographer, and ballet master, he was the first choreographer to compose his own ballet music. He also wrote a number of treatises in which he elegantly defended the theories and practices of his new style of choreography, a style he called pantomime ballet. He was born into a family of dancers in Florence in 1731, and his early training probably took place in Italy. He then studied in Stuttgart with Franz Hilverding from whom he got the idea for pantomime ballet. In 1754, he married a celebrated dancer, Teresa Fogliazzi, who counted among her close friends two of Italy's most important literary figures, Pietro Metastasio and Giuseppe Parini. She was also one of the very few women mentioned by Giacomo Casanova in his memoirs as having totally rejected his advances. In 1758, Angiolini was appointed to the important position of ballet master at the Viennese court, and it was there that he met the forty-four-year-old Gluck, already in the midst of a brilliant career.

During his first few years at court, Angiolini created nothing out of the ordinary; then, in 1761, he choreographed *Don Juan,* his first pantomime ballet. It was immediately recognized as anything but traditional and is now increasingly considered to have been the first truly modern ballet. The following year, in 1762, he prepared the dances for Gluck's *Orfeo ed Euridice,* itself a milestone in the development of opera, with its new stress on a logical and natural interrelationship between word, music, and dance, as opposed to the artificiality of opera seria. After further successes in Vienna, Angiolini was invited to St. Petersburg, where he was highly acclaimed, especially for a heroic three-act ballet, *Le Départ d'Enée ou Didon abandonnée.* The scenario, choreography, and music were all his. Metastasio, on whose 1724 melodrama Angiolini based his ballet, wrote him the following words, which are quite flattering in light of the fact that the playwright's work had already been set to music by many of the leading composers of the day. "For forty years now my poor *Dido* has been deafening all the theaters of Europe with her laments, and not one of your colleagues has been able to make such admirable use of her as you have done."[21] For the next thirty years, Angiolini traveled between Russia, Vienna, and the principal cities of Italy. He finally settled in Milan, where he directed choreography at La Scala and where he was highly regarded by the leading Milanese figures

21. Pietro Metastasio, quoted in Lorenzo Tozzi, *Il balletto pantomimo del settecento: Gaspare Angiolini* (L'Aquila: Japadre, 1972), 89. The letter is dated 9 December 1766.

of the Enlightenment. He died in Milan in 1803. More than ninety ballets are attributed to him, and he may have written the music for more than fifty.

With *Don Juan,* Angiolini sought to create a new style of dance. He was impatient with the contemporary state of things. He felt that ballet, particularly French ballet, consisted of nothing but abstract forms, posturing, and acrobatics. It was his opinion that the ballet of his day was nothing but "wretched buffoonery."[22] He criticized ballet dances as a succession of unlinked scenes, empty spectacle, and simple entertainment, grafted onto music that preexisted. Performances lacked profundity of subject matter and were incapable of arousing genuine human emotions.

As a corrective, Angiolini advocated the return to a dance form of the ancient Greeks and Romans. In the program published for the first performance of *Don Juan,* he explained what this form was.

> The loftiest form of ancient dance was the pantomime. This was the art of imitating the manners, passions, and actions of gods, heroes, and men by means of movements and postures of the body, by gestures and motions made in time to music and capable of expressing what one intended to represent. These movements and gestures were supposed to form, so to speak, a continuous discourse. It was a kind of declamation, made for the eyes, the comprehension of which was made easier for the spectator by the music, which varied its harmonies accordingly as the pantomime actor intended to express love or hatred, fury or despair.[23]

Angiolini called his new work a pantomime ballet because, without the help of words, the dancers were to tell a story, a full story. They were not simply to present isolated scenes. And the story was to be true to life, "vraisemblable," he said several times. The movements of the dancers, he later wrote, were to be in keeping with the story told and with the characters portrayed in it so as properly and harmoniously to reflect their manners, personalities, and pas-

22. Gasparo Angiolini, *Dissertation sur les ballets pantomimes des anciens, pour servir de programme au ballet pantomime tragique de Semiramis* (1765; reprint, n.p.: Dalle Nogare e Armetti, 1956), 20. The reprint has an introduction by Walter Toscanini.

23. For the entire program, see the facsimile in Richard Engländer, ed., *Don Juan/Semiramis, Ballets Pantomimes von Gasparo Angiolini,* ser. 2, vol. 1 of *Sämtliche Werke* by Christoph Willibald Gluck (Kassel: Bärenreiter, 1966), xxiii–xxvii. For additional information concerning Angiolini and his ballet, see Charles C. Russell, "The Libertine Reformed: *Don Juan* by Gluck and Angiolini," *Music and Letters* 65, no. 1 (January 1984): 17–27.

sions.[24] Angiolini insisted that the choreographer should work hand in hand with the composer, something not customary hitherto. Music and dance had to be perfectly integrated, in perfect unison, for it was up to the music to express the ideas of the ballet. He found a compatible soul in Gluck and in his score for *Don Juan*. Gluck, he wrote in the ballet program,

> has perfectly captured the awesomeness [*le terrible*] of the action. He has striven to express the passions that are at play and the terror that reigns in the denouement. Music is essential for pantomimes; it is the music which speaks, we only make gestures. . . . It would be almost impossible for us to make ourselves understood without the music, and the more it is appropriate to what we want to express, the more we make ourselves intelligible.

The ballet had its premiere on 17 October 1761 at the Burgtheater in Vienna following a performance of Jean François Regnard's 1696 five-act comic opera *Le Joueur*. The scenery was by another member of Gluck's circle of friends, Giovanni Maria Quaglio. Angiolini danced the role of Don Juan. Others in the cast included, among the women, Joffroi-Bodin, Paganini, Clerc, and Buggiano, and among the men, Dupré, Turchi, and Onorato Viganò, who later choreographed his own version of the ballet in Italy to music by Luigi Marescalchi. Count Karl Zinzendorf, who attended the opening night performance (as he did the first Viennese performance of Mozart's *Don Giovanni* more than twenty-five years later), noted in his diary that the music was very well received by the public, the ballet itself less so.[25] Nonetheless, the work was repeated in Vienna ten more times in the following six-week period. A later diary entry by Count Zinzendorf indicated that, at a performance on 3 November, everyone in Vienna who mattered was present.

Further performances followed, first in Vienna and then in many cities throughout the continent, though Angiolini's choreography was sometimes modified or replaced. The success of the ballet turned other composers to the legend, composers who either adapted Gluck's score or wrote new ballet music of their own. It is possible to identify more than thirty-five different Don Juan ballet productions between the first in 1761 and Mozart's opera in 1787. While none of them achieved the prominence of the original Gluck-Angiolini version, and while all probably lacked the tragic intensity of the original, by keeping the

24. Gasparo Angiolini, *Lettere di Gasparo Angiolini a Monsieur Noverre sopra i Balli Pantomimi* (Milan: Bianchi, 1773), 17–18.

25. Karl Zinzendorf, quoted in Engländer, *Don Juan/Semiramis*, x.

legend before a musical public they too were preparing the way for Mozart's version.

It is understandable why Angiolini's choreography puzzled the first-night audience. Contemporary versions of the legend tended to emphasize the comic aspects of the story. Angiolini's, on the other hand, emphasized the tragic. Although he referred to the story as a "tragicomédie" in the ballet program, nothing in his version was amusing or lighthearted. His Don Juan did not follow the common eighteenth-century Italian or German tradition of the carefree libertine accompanied by a slapstick servant; his was a seducer, murderer, and mocker of divine justice, the horror of whose punishment was intended to serve as a warning, much in the manner of Greek tragedy. Gluck's music, Angiolini believed, perfectly reflected the tragic tone of the piece. It caught "the awesomeness of the action" and "the terror that reigns in the denouement." Could Gluck possibly have seen and remembered the dramatic conclusion of Bambini's opera? He had been living and working in Prague when Bambini's opera was given in Brno in 1734. It seems likely that a young and ambitious composer might have wanted to see for himself the dynamic presentations of the Mingotti brothers.

For his first pantomime ballet, one would have expected Angiolini to pick a more fitting subject from classical antiquity, from among the tragedies he so much admired, rather than the awkward legend of Don Juan. Like others before him who had worked with the story, he too recognized that it was filled with faults, that it was unacceptable in terms of the much-admired unities of time and place. Yet, unlike others, there was something about it which held him spellbound: "Its imaginative qualities are sublime," he wrote in the ballet program, "its denouement awe-inspiring, and to our way of thinking it is true to life." One supposes that he, too, like the librettist for *La pravità castigata,* felt that the choice was an expedient one. Since his new ballet was an experiment in which he intended to narrate a detailed story by means of wordless pantomime dance and music, it was perhaps wiser to select a subject that, as he also notes in the program, "has earned the approbation of all nations, . . . has been successful in all theaters, . . . [and] has been well received everywhere in performance." In other words, he could be sure his public was already familiar with the characters and the plot.

But Angiolini and Gluck did more than simply retell a popular tale. Angiolini turned a shallow adventurer into a figure of tragic dimensions, while Gluck ennobled him with the grandeur of his music as no other musician had done before. They eliminated the claptrap associated with the legend in its popular forms and constructed an original work of art particularly suited to the medium of ballet. Angiolini's story was skillfully put together; it is beautifully organized and balanced, taut and dramatic, rightly focused on the figure of Don Juan as a man recognizing no authority, temporal or spiritual, except his own desires. Act 1 details the seduction of a young woman and the murder of her father. The opening of act 2 is in effective contrast: a magnificent ball and dinner at the home of Don Juan at which it becomes evident that the protagonist is a thorough libertine. Festive dancing then abruptly gives way to terror as the avenging statue of the dead man enters and invites Don Juan to dinner. Act 3 is retribution: a horrified Don Juan, assaulted by specters and furies, is dragged below to hell. Unlike other versions, Angiolini makes no concession to entertainment or amusement. Particularly noteworthy is the fact that Don Juan's servant is only briefly mentioned toward the end of the second act and that he is in no way the prominent comic figure he so often was. Angiolini compressed and unified the action by eliminating many scenes common to almost all earlier versions. Later variations of the ballet, choreographed by others, elaborated on his plot and spoiled the harmony of his design.

This is the ballet story as published by Angiolini in his original program.

> I have divided the ballet into three acts. The first represents a public street. The Commandeur's house is to one side, Don Juan's to the other. The action begins with a serenade that Don Juan gives to Donna Elvire, his lady, daughter of the Commandeur. He gains entrance into her house, where he is surprised by her father. They fight; the Commandeur is killed and carried off.
>
> In the second act, Don Juan gives a magnificent banquet at his home, preceded by a ball, for his friends and his ladies. After dancing, everyone sits down to eat. At the height of the festivities, the Commandeur, as a statue, knocks loudly at the door. It is opened, and he enters the hall; the guests are frightened and take flight. Don Juan remains alone with the statue. He derisively asks it to eat. It refuses, and, in turn, invites Don Juan to eat at its tomb. Don Juan accepts and leads out the Commandeur. The noise ceases; somewhat reassured, the guests come back into the hall, but they are still afraid and visibly trembling. Don Juan comes back in. He tries to reassure them; they leave him. He remains alone with his servant, gives some orders, and exits.
>
> The third act takes place in an area intended for the burial of persons of distinction. The recently completed mausoleum of the Commandeur is in the middle. He himself is standing before his tomb. Don Juan is somewhat startled to see him. However, he assumes an air of self-assurance and approaches the Commandeur, who seizes him by the arm and exhorts him

to change his life. Don Juan appears obstinate, and, in spite of the Commandeur's threats and the strange events he witnesses, he persists in his impenitence. The center of the earth then opens up, vomiting flames. Out of this volcano come many specters and furies that torment Don Juan. He is chained by them. In frightful despair he is swallowed up with all the monsters, and an earthquake covers the place with a pile of ruins.[26]

Count Zinzendorf recorded in his diary the following brief account of the ballet.

At the theater *Le Joueur* is being played and then a pantomime ballet, *Le Festin de Pierre.* The subject matter is very frightening, lugubrious and gloomy. Don Juan gives a serenade to his lady and enters her home. The Commandeur catches him in the act, fights a duel with him, is mortally wounded and falls on stage. He is carried off. Don Juan enters with some ladies and they dance, then everyone begins to dine; meanwhile the Commandeur arrives in the form of a statue, the guests flee, Don Juan mocks it and imitates all the movements of the specter, it mounts a stone horse on stage, Don Juan mocks it again, the specter leaves, and all of a sudden hell

26. The original French is as follows.

J'ai divisé le ballet en trois actes. Le premier représente une ruë publique. La maison du Commandeur est d'un coté, celle de Don Juan de l'autre. L'action commence par une sérénade que Don Juan donne à Donna Elvire sa maîtresse, fille du Commandeur. Il obtient l'entrée dans la maison, où il est surpris par le pére. Il se bat contre lui; le Commandeur est tué; on l'emporte.

Dans le second acte Don Juan donne chez lui un grand repas, précédé d'un bal, à ses amis & à ses maîtresses. Lorsqu'on a dansé on se met à table. Au plus fort de la joie, le Commandeur, en statue, frappe rudement à la porte. On va ouvrir; il entre dans la sale; les conviés son épouvantés, ils prennent la fuite. Don Juan reste seul avec la statuë. Il la prie, par dérision, de manger. Elle refuse, & convie, à son tour, Don Juan à manger à son tombeau. Don Juan accepte, & reconduit le Commandeur. Le bruit cesse; les conviés, un peu rassurés, reviennent dans la sale, mais la fraïeur les accompagne, ce qui donne lieu à une entrée de trembleurs. Don Juan revient. Il tâche de les rassurer; ils l'abandonnent. Il reste seul avec son laquais, il donne des ordres, & sort.

Le troisième acte se passe dans un endroit destiné à la sépulture de personnes de distinction. Le mausolée du Commandeur nouvellement achevé est au milieu. Il est lui même debout devant son tombeau. Don Juan est un peu étonné en le voiant. Il prend cependant un air assuré, & s'approche du Commandeur. Celui-ci le saisit par le bras, & l'exhorte à changer de vie. Don Juan paroit obstiné, & malgré les menaces du Commandeur & les prodiges dont il est témoin, il persiste dans son impénitence. Alors le centre de la terre s'entrouvre vomissant des flammes. Il sort de ce volcan beaucoup de spectres, & de furies qui tourmentent Don Juan. Il est enchaîné par elles, dans son affreux désespoir il est englouti avec tous les monstres; & un tremblement de terre couvre le lieu d'un monceau de ruines.

appears, furies dance with lighted torches and torment Don Juan; in the background nice fireworks can be seen which represent the fires of hell. One can see devils flying about. The ballet lasts a long time; finally the devils carry off Don Juan and sink with him into a fiery abyss. Everything was very well done, the music quite nice.[27]

It is usually noted that Angiolini turned to Molière's *Dom Juan ou Le festin de Pierre* for the story line of his ballet, but such is absolutely not the case. It is scarcely possible that Angiolini had either seen or read Molière's play (or Thomas Corneille's revision of it), since the two versions are so entirely different. Molière's enigmatic, questioning Don Juan has nothing in common with Angiolini's bold and straightforward hero. Gone, obviously, are Molière's discourses on the nature of love, medicine, religion, and hypocrisy. Gone, too, are most of Molière's characters: the brothers of Done Elvire, the peasants Pierrot, Charlotte, and Mathurine, Dom Juan's father, the pauper, and the amusing M. Dimanche; even Sganarelle has become the pale figure of a nameless servant. Angiolini has completely focused on Don Juan himself. Furthermore, Molière wrote no murder scene or ball scene, which are the material of Angiolini's first act and the first part of his second. Although several other points in the ballet plot may seem similar to Molière's, these points appear in many versions of the legend both before and after his *Le Festin.*[28]

---

27. Karl Zinzendorf, quoted in Engländer, *Don Juan/Semiramis,* xi. The original French is as follows.

> Au spectacle, on donna le joueur et puis un ballet de pantomimes, Le festin de pierre. Le sujet en est extrêmement triste, lugubre et effroyable. Don Juan porte une sérénade à sa maitresse et entre chez elle. Le commandeur le trouve sur le fait, se bat avec lui en duel, est blessé mortellement et tombe sur le théâtre. On l'emporte, Don Juan entre avec des dames et danse un ballet, puis on se met à souper, sur ces entrefaites arrive le commandeur en statue, tous les convives se sauvent, Don Juan s'en moque et imite tous les mouvements du spectre, il monte un cheval molasse sur le théâtre, Don Juan s'en moque encore, le spectre s'en va et tout d'un coup l'enfer paraît, les furies dansent avec des torches allumées et tourmentent Don Juan, dans le fond on voit un beau feu d'artifice, qui représente les feux de l'enfer; on voit voler des diables. Le ballet dure longtemps, enfin les diables emportent Don Juan et se précipitent avec lui dans ce gouffre de feu. Tout cela était très bien executé, la musique fort belle.

28. Only one fact in the ballet can be traced back to Molière alone. In his program, Angiolini refers to "Donna Elvire . . . fille du Commandeur." That name appears in no other version of the Don Juan legend before Molière's. Yet Molière's Done Elvire is not the daughter of the Commander: she is the "femme de Dom Juan" and already cast-off at that. The role Donna Elvire plays in the ballet is the one that is traditionally played by Donna Anna, the legitimate daughter of the Commander, so to speak. This confusion of names is a further indication that Angiolini was not especially familiar with Molière's play.

Most likely, Angiolini was familiar with many different versions of the legend and especially with popular Italian versions. Rather than basing his ballet on a particular and specific source, he evidently put together a story based on the memory of versions that he had seen or read or simply heard about. At the same time, he adapted the well-known legend to the particular demands of the ballet medium and to the demands of a sophisticated public, with results that were extraordinarily original.

Angiolini considerably abbreviated the narrative. In the Italian tradition, Cicognini and the players of the commedia began Don Giovanni's adventures with an attempted seduction of a noblewoman in Naples, followed by his near arrest, an escape by boat, and a shipwreck and rescue by a peasant girl, whom he subsequently seduced. The latter scenes were played for comic effect. Angiolini skipped all that. From the very first he went right to the drama's core by opening his ballet with Don Juan's serenade of Donna Elvire (Anna), his attempted seduction of her, and the murder of her father, a dramatic and highly effective beginning. He brought tragedy immediately to the fore, which must have been a shock to a public waiting for laughs. Angiolini's example was followed by such later choreographers as Vincenzo Galeotti and Domenico Rossi in Italy and Peter Vogt in Germany. Vogt was part of Johannes Böhm's theatrical troupe. Mozart knew Böhm well when the company performed in Salzburg in 1779 and 1780, and he followed Böhm's fortunes with interest, for the troupe had *La finta giardiniera* and other of his works in its repertory. One would presume that Mozart must certainly have attended a Don Juan ballet performance. Angiolini's new and original arrangement was also clearly felt in opera. Giambattista Lorenzi opened his 1783 libretto exactly as Angiolini had. Likewise did Giovanni Bertati in his version of 1787. Bertati even removed the serenade. Da Ponte's opening scene was copied directly from Bertati.

Angiolini's second act is of particular interest. It takes place in Don Juan's home, where he is offering a ball and a magnificent banquet to his friends. The ball with its many guests is an innovation of Angiolini's; no earlier version had it. Traditionally, Don Juan consumed a solitary dinner at home with only a servant or two. It is evident that Angiolini has given Don Juan's guests a new and major role to play because he is shaping the story for the medium of ballet. Their presence rightly allows for dance spectacle without harming the unity of the work. After dancing, the guests sit down to a sumptuous meal in a festive atmosphere. However, at the height of the gaiety there is an abrupt change of mood: a loud knocking is heard, the statue enters, fear grips the guests, and with that the ballet returns to the traditional story.

The new spectacle of the ball and dinner scene of act 2, so right for the musical stage, seems to have impressed itself on later musical versions of the legend. Choreographers used Angiolini's ideas in various ways and to various degrees, as did several opera librettists. The fourth scene of Friedrich Ludwig Schröder's 1769 ballet takes place in a country inn. Don Juan is in the midst of a group of Spanish dancers who, as they prepare to sit at table, are interrupted by the loud knocking of the statue. Peter Vogt situates the fourth scene of his ballet in a large hall with tables set for dinner; Domenico Rossi likewise requires a "large hall illuminated for the party and dinner given by Don Giovanni Tenorio" for his ballet in 1783. Vincenzo Righini's opera specifies a "magnificently decorated table" (II.viii), while in Giovanni Bertati's libretto Don Giovanni orders that a "concerto di stromenti" (xxiii) be performed for him on stage during dinner, surely an echo of Angiolini's ball music.

By the time Lorenzo Da Ponte's Don Giovanni consumes his second-act gourmet meal with the Commendatore, the onstage orchestra has stopped playing dance music and taken up operatic arias. Although no guests but the statue are present at this final dinner, they are present in abundance for the heady feasting and dancing that conclude the first act of Da Ponte's libretto. It is here that Da Ponte's debt to Angiolini is most evident. Early on, Don Giovanni ordered Leporello to invite the local country folk to his home for a celebration. He has his eye on a number of young peasant women and is beginning to prepare his seductions. The means: much rich food, an abundance of wines, and the excitement of furious dancing. The last scene of the first act is set in a "brightly lit hall prepared for a great ball" (I.xx). Plenty of food and drink are available: chocolate, wine, coffee, prosciutti, sorbetti, and confetti. The onstage musicians have just finished playing music for dancing, perhaps the minuet or "alemanna" or "follia" that Don Giovanni had earlier said he wanted to hear, for, as the scene gets under way, the stage directions indicate that Don Giovanni is leading the girls who have just stopped dancing back to their places. The room is crowded with men and women, some of whom have had too much to drink and are more than a little tipsy. Only three persons do not share in the general abandon: the masked figures of Donna Anna, Donna Elvira, and Don Ottavio. Yet even they take part in the dancing, which continues. Don Giovanni dances a stately minuet with Donna Anna. He then turns to Zerlina and dances a contradance with her while Leporello clumsily performs a German dance, a "teitsch," with Masetto. The influence of Angiolini is everywhere. The dancing comes to a conclusion only after Don Giovanni unsuccessfully tries to woo away Zerlina for a private tryst.

It may be that, in Da Ponte's text, the presence at the ball of Donna Anna, masked and frightened, is likewise due to the influence of a ballet tradition.

Angiolini does not specifically indicate that she was there, though of course she may have been (naturally as Donna Elvire). If she was not, she probably appeared not many years later in new stagings of the ballet. In June 1772, in Vienna, Vincenzo Rossi choreographed a four-part version of Gluck's work in which the role of the servant was greatly expanded.[29] The program for that performance no longer exists, but the manuscript program of another four-act version, also with an expanded servant's role, is known to exist. It is entitled "Programm du Ballet de Dom-juan, ou bien, du festin du pierre, pour l'intelligence de la musique, que le Sr. Gluck a faite à Vienne sur ce sujet."[30] Although many details have been added to it, the text is obviously based on Angiolini's, the story of which it follows closely.[31] What is significant is that, during the second-act party scene, this program specifically states that "there is a pas de deux between Dom Juan and the niece of the Commandeur." That is, the Donna Elvire–Anna figure is definitely present at Don Juan's party. It is tempting to think that this *scenario* indicates a tradition that might have been the source for Da Ponte's bringing the maskers to the ball. But it is impossible to be sure, for the manuscript has not been accurately dated.

Two moments of Angiolini's third act are particularly worthy of note. Quite original, and very right for dancing, is Don Juan's mocking imitation of the statue's movements, as mentioned by Count Zinzendorf. The mocking represents a kind of dance equivalent to the customary insults hurled at the statue by the angry and impetuous younger man. After Don Juan's stubborn refusal to recognize his guilt, there is no escaping divine vengeance. The earth gapes open, vomiting flames, and he is swallowed up. As such, this visual effect differs little from most earlier versions in which, to the accompaniment of thunder, lightning, and fire, he sank into the bowels of the earth. Yet again Angiolini made the story particularly his. By tradition, Don Juan and the statue were generally alone on the stage with perhaps only a servant or an occasional extra supernatural creature or offstage voice. Only Shadwell had introduced a full chorus of devils on stage before Don Juan's damnation. Although the legend many times came to a close with his disappearance, some versions included a sort of epilogue in which he was seen in hell, occasionally in the company of hellish creatures. Such

29. Robert Haas, "Der Wiener Bühnentanz von 1740 bis 1767," in *Jahrbuch der Musikbibliothek Peters für 1937* (1937; reprint, Vaduz: Kraus, 1965), 85–86.

30. This handwritten French scenario, Ms. N. 20, is in the Paris Conservatory. For the text, see entry in chap. 4, June 1772.

31. The fact that this manuscript is in four acts indicates no significant departure from Angiolini, whose third act has simply been split into two: first a damnation scene and then one showing Don Juan in hell.

a scene obviously lent itself to further spectacle and also to a bit of pious breast-beating, for at this point Don Juan often spoke out in despair, full of anguish and guilt over his past crimes. Angiolini was not interested in this sort of moralizing, which meant a slackening of the dramatic pace. His story is taut and tragic to the very end, his Don Juan always impenitent. Yet Angiolini did not want to do without the spectacular either. He therefore inserted an inferno scene *before* Don Juan's ultimate damnation. By doing so, he at once maintained the ballet spectacle and the tone of high tragedy. After the Commandeur has returned heavenward but before Don Juan's final descent, a crowd of tormenting specters and furies, some carrying lighted torches, issues from the fissures of the earth. Don Juan is chained and then, "in frightful despair"—again the terrible illumination of truth—he is swallowed up with the monsters, after which an earthquake reduces the stage to a pile of rubble.

Angiolini and Gluck, by accenting the tragic aspects of the legend, took it away from the popular theater; they removed the vulgar adventures, the pratfalls, the jokes, the cheap laughs, the pinched bottoms of peasants and fishergirls, and they created something elegant, heroic, and sublime. Together they turned the legend into a worthy subject for profound music. How sympathetic Da Ponte was to their interpretation is impossible to know, but Mozart, who knew Gluck's score, most surely felt the fascination of it.

Gluck and Angiolini tried new things with great success. With the legend now more widely associated with music, and especially with serious music, it was not long before Don Juan once again appeared on the operatic stage. There was, in fact, following the successes of the ballet, an explosion of enthusiasm for Don Juan operas, the effects of which lasted throughout the remaining years of the century. The Mozart–Da Ponte opera was only one of many.

Don Juan's new operatic appearance, his third after *L'empio punito* and *La pravità castigata,* took place in Prague in 1776 in an opera called *Il convitato di pietra o sia Il dissoluto.* If success is defined by revivals, this opera should be considered more successful than its predecessors. It had six later productions in several different cities of Austria and Germany. Vincenzo Righini was its composer. He was born in Bologna in 1756 and began his career as a singer. After training in his native city, he made his debut as a tenor in Parma in 1775 and joined the opera troupe of Giuseppe Bustelli in Prague in 1776. But his voice seems to have given out rather quickly, so he turned to the teaching of voice, to conducting, and to composition. He wrote several operas for Prague. Then, in 1780, he was called to Vienna by Emperor Joseph II to be singing master to Princess Elisabeth of Württemberg and director of the Italian opera. He remained in Vienna for the next seven years where, because of his intense theatrical activity as director, opera composer, and teacher, he must have early and frequently crossed paths with Mozart and Da Ponte.

It is evident that Mozart did not care for him. He wrote about him with a certain pique in a letter to his father in 1781.

> He makes a good deal of money by teaching, and last Easter he was successful with his cantata [*La sorpresa amorosa*], which was performed twice in succession and had good receipts on both occasions. He composes *very charmingly* and he is not by any means superficial; but he is a monstrous thief. He offers his stolen goods in such superfluity, in such profusion, that people can hardly digest them.[32]

In a slightly earlier letter, speaking of lodging arrangements while in Vienna as a member of Archbishop Colloredo's household, Mozart again mentioned Righini with evident distaste; there is even a bit of nasty innuendo concerning Righini and the lady of the house where he is staying.

> It is true that I might have lodged with Mesmer, the writing-master, but really I prefer to stay with the Webers. Mesmer has Righini (formerly opera buffa singer and now a composer) in his house and is his great friend and protector; but Frau Mesmer is still more so.[33]

According to Michael Kelly, the popular Irish singer who was working in Vienna in this period, who knew Mozart well and who took the part of Don Curzio in the first performance of *Le nozze di Figaro,* Righini "worked like a mole in the dark" to block the production of Mozart's opera in favor of one of his own.[34]

Da Ponte was not fond of Righini either. As official court poet, Da Ponte found himself involved with Righini in a collaborative operation in 1786. The results were a disaster, Da Ponte asserts, due to the composer's ineptitude.

> In spite of my wishes, I was forced to write two librettos for two *maestri di cappella* whom I neither loved nor esteemed very much and the failure of which I was absolutely sure. One of these was Reghini [*sic*]. . . . I therefore wrote a little comic opera that I called *Il filosofo punito* [The Philosopher Punished]; but it would have been better to call it *Il maestro e il poeta puniti*

32. W. A. Mozart, letter to Leopold Mozart, 29 August 1781, in *The Letters of Mozart and his Family,* trans. and ed. Emily Anderson, 3d ed. (New York: Norton, 1985), 762.

33. W. A. Mozart, letter to Leopold Mozart, 13 July 1781, in *Letters of Mozart,* 752.

34. Michael Kelly, *Reminiscences,* ed. Roger Fiske (London: Oxford University Press, 1975), 130.

> *a vicenda* [The Composer and Poet Punished in Turn]. It failed, as it was destined to fail. Reghini's friends blamed the words; I blamed the music and the bad opinion I had of the composer, an opinion which stifled my poetic fancy.[35]

Righini moved on to better things. He left Vienna in 1787 to become *Kapellmeister* at the electoral court in Mainz and then director of Italian opera in Berlin. He wrote a great deal of music for the voice, much chamber music, church music, and about fifteen operas, some of which were rather well known in their time. In spite of Mozart's and Da Ponte's comments, Righini seems to have been a straightforward, unpretentious, and rather likeable person.

Il convitato di pietra was Righini's first opera, composed when he was barely twenty. He wrote it while singing with the Bustelli troupe in Prague, where it was produced in 1776. It was repeated in Prague the following year and also produced in Vienna. Joseph Haydn picked it up a few years later and produced it in 1781 at Esterháza, where he was musical director. He altered some of the music, substituted two of Righini's arias with one by Luigi Bologna and one by Nicolò Jommelli, and inserted a new *scena* or two of his own.[36] Several other performances are on record: in Braunschweig in 1782, in Eisenstadt in 1782, and in Hanover in 1783 or 1784.

Righini's librettist was an obscure laborer in the eighteenth-century musical vineyard by the name of Nunziato Porta. Porta has never made his way into standard musical reference works or encyclopedias.[37] The librettos printed for first performances of Righini's opera in Prague and Vienna do not indicate Porta's authorship, so that the text has often been attributed to an anonymous librettist or to Antonio de' Filistri da Caramondani, who wrote librettos for Righini later in Germany.

Porta met Righini in Prague, where he too was employed by the same impresario, Giuseppe Bustelli. In 1775, he prepared a text for Bustelli for a Prague performance of Pietro Guglielmi's *Orlando paladino.* The following year he prepared *Il convitato di pietra* for Righini. After his Prague experience, he probably spent a year or two in Venice, as attested to by librettos published in that city and generally thought to be his;[38] then, in July 1781, he went to

35. Lorenzo Da Ponte, *Memorie e altri scritti,* ed. Cesare Pagnini (Milan: Longanesi, 1971), 187.

36. See entry in chap. 4, 1781, July through September, for further details.

37. Carlo Schmidl mentions him, but only very briefly, in *Dizionario universale dei musicisti* (Milan: Sonzogno, 1929), 2:305.

38. No list of Porta's work exists. I have come across the following librettos (I include only the earliest known performance of each; dates may not be for first performances): *Orlando paladino,* Pietro Guglielmi, Prague, 1775; *Il convitato di pietra,* Vincenzo Righini, Prague, 1776; *L'americana in*

Esterháza as administrative director of the theater and as chief wardrobe master. His concern was for nonmusical aspects of opera performance. As such, he probably worked closely with Haydn. His salary was rather modest, but he was married to one of the highest paid singers at Esterháza, Matilde Bologna. She sang the role of Donna Anna when Haydn revived Righini's opera. The libretto published for the Esterháza performances is the only *Convitato* libretto with Porta's name printed in it.[39] The following year, in 1782, Porta revived his old Prague text of *Orlando paladino* for Haydn, who used it for what became the most successful of his operas in his lifetime.[40]

Porta remained in Esterháza until September 1790, though he must have made frequent trips to Vienna. There he worked with Righini a second time on an opera entitled *L'incontro inaspettato.* It was in Vienna, too, that Porta came to the notice of Da Ponte. Da Ponte did not care for his work at all. He considered him one of many "ciabattini teatrali" [theatrical cobblers], who had no understanding of poetry.[41] It is hard to disagree in light of the present libretto, which has been cut and pasted out of the past. On the other hand, Porta was simply doing his job; much of his work at Esterháza had to do with the patching and reshaping of used librettos for the needs of his theater and the tastes of his public, not with the creation of new ones. Porta in turn cared little for Da Ponte. When the latter's libretto, *Il ricco d'un giorno,* turned out to be a particularly painful public failure, Porta circulated a satirical poem, the last two lines of which were as follows.

Olanda, Pasquale Anfossi, Venice, 1778; *I contrattempi,* Giuseppe Sarti, Venice, 1778; *Calipso abbandonato,* Luigi Bologna, Vienna, 1783; *L'incontro inaspettato,* Vincenzo Righini, Vienna, 1785.

39. There is some evidence, not entirely conclusive, to suggest that Porta was not the author of the original 1776 libretto, but only of the modified Esterháza version. As Karl Geiringer has pointed out ("From Guglielmi to Haydn: The Transformation of an Opera," *Report of the Eleventh Congress of the International Musicological Society Copenhagen 1972* [Copenhagen: Hansen, 1974], 391–95), when Porta was in Prague, he completely rewrote the text for an opera composed some years earlier by Pietro Guglielmi entitled *Le pazzie di Orlando.* The original libretto was by Carlo Francesco Badini. The revised libretto, now called *Orlando paladino,* bore only Porta's name. Could Porta have done the same thing here, that is, appropriated someone else's libretto? His name appears only on the Esterháza text of 1781. This text is based on a Viennese edition published in 1777, a text that clearly differs in several details from the original Prague text of 1776. If Porta was the author of the original text, why did he not use it as the basis for his Esterháza edition?

40. Details concerning Porta's activities at Esterháza, and many other facts about him as well, are scattered throughout Dénes Bartha and László Somfai, *Haydn als Opernkapellmeister* (Mainz: Schott, 1960) and H. C. Robbins Landon, *Haydn: Chronicle and Works,* 5 vols. (Bloomington: Indiana University Press, 1977–80).

41. Da Ponte, *Memorie,* 124.

Asino tu nascesti ed asino morrai:
per ora dissi poco, col tempo dirò assai.[42]

[A jack-ass you were born, and jack-ass you will die;
so far I've said quite little, with time I'll say much more.]

Da Ponte held his anger at bay until one evening, at a party to celebrate the resounding success of a new opera entitled *Una cosa rara,* Porta loudly praised its lovely but anonymous text and asked who the author of it might be. "Un 'asino tu nascesti,' signor Porta mio," replied Da Ponte and handed him a newly printed copy of the libretto, which now had Lorenzo Da Ponte's name on its cover.[43]

Da Ponte was right when he called Nunziato Porta a cobbler. Porta's three-act *dramma tragicomico* was a patchwork affair, awkwardly stitched together from commedia dell'arte sources for its humor and for its serious elements from Carlo Goldoni, from whom Porta shamelessly borrowed entire scenes and dialogues, sometimes almost word for word. Even the "dissoluto" of his title was lifted from Goldoni (to be later lifted yet again by the hypocritical and none-too-scrupulous master cobbler himself, Da Ponte, as part of his title for Mozart—*Il dissoluto punito o sia Il D. Giovanni*).[44] From Goldoni came, name and all, the grasping, conniving figure of the country girl Elisa; from Goldoni likewise came the headstrong Donna Anna, who is entirely indifferent to the affections of Duke Ottavio (a Duke who never puts in an appearance in this opera) and who resents her father's interference in her amorous affairs, a Donna Anna, though, who is more than a little unsettled by the possessive physical presence and fascination of Don Giovanni, even after he has sought to rape her and has killed her father. Finally, from Goldoni came Porta's strange, contradictory Don Giovanni, who is, on the one hand, lusty, impetuous, and fearless, and, on the other, self-pitying, whining, and, at dinner for the statue, nearly on the verge of a nervous breakdown. Goldoni had tried to present a new, nontraditional figure, but it had not worked. Nor does it here. It is hard to imagine a Don Giovanni who curses women's beauty as he does in this text at the beginning of the second act. It is nearly impossible to accept him as one who is so disturbed by past deeds and so needful of a kind word from somebody, from anybody at all, that, in a desperate bid for friendship, he invites the statue of the man he

42. Nunziato Porta, quoted in Da Ponte, *Memorie,* 154.

43. Da Ponte, *Memorie,* 185.

44. *Indice de' teatrali spettacoli, 1787–88,* 147, lists the title of the Mozart–Da Ponte opera as *Il dissoluto corretto.*

has murdered to dinner. Accustomed as we are to a Don Giovanni of little or no conscience, it is astounding to see him obsessed to such a degree by "grievous thoughts" that he declares death itself his only possible solace (II.viii).

Yet as poor a writer as Nunziato Porta was, he recognized that the popularity and punch of the tale also depended on certain comic elements. So back onto the stage came the slapstick servant and the walking and talking statue, both of whom Porta's model, Goldoni, had contemptuously banished. Here again was a wisecracking Arlecchino, who, stretched out on the ground with sword raised high in the darkness of night, engaged in a mock duel with his master before the house of the Commendatore. This *lazzo,* first used by Cicognini (I.vii), had by now been around for a hundred years or more. Once again there was a final ghastly dinner—toads and snakes were the main course—at which the statue was properly imperious.

These were the sorts of things that Goldoni disliked because he felt they made no logical or psychological sense. What he disliked was the story as legend. In a legend, one need not explain how a statue can walk and talk or how a gentleman can be shipwrecked and washed ashore on the Spanish coast without getting his wig wet. Precisely because the story was legend, no public required logical or rational developments. No one asks how it is that Rip Van Winkle is able to sleep for twenty years or why Paul Bunyan's ox is blue. Porta was not concerned with problems of logic or good taste; he had no theories to uphold; so he put back into the story what he knew his public wanted. If evidence were needed that what was wanted was fun, one need only look at the new second-act ending prepared for Vienna in 1777. In the first edition of 1776, after the statue departed Don Giovanni's house, those who had witnessed the prodigious and terrifying appearance of the stone Commendatore declared that they could scarcely breathe, so rapid was the beating of their fearful hearts, and with that the act came to a conclusion. By the following year, in the new version of 1777, the same witnesses recovered from their fright with extraordinary rapidity and shallowness: "It's time to be happy, there's nothing to be scared of; with horns and flutes, snares and castanets, bassoons and kettledrums, let's laugh and be joyful."[45] This sort of empty frivolity did not find its way into Da Ponte, although it will reappear on occasion in other opera librettos.

The aspects of Porta's libretto that today, when comparing it to other standard eighteenth-century versions, may make it seem unusual and occasionally original, aspects such as Don Giovanni's doubts or Donna Anna's indepen-

45. For the original text, see chap. 3, *Il convitato di pietra o sia Il dissoluto,* Righini and Porta, note 12.

dence, do so only because they never became an intrinsic part of the legend. They violated the basic, widely accepted outline and spirit of the story. Those facets of it that fitted, so to speak, were freely copied and imitated by one writer after another. Those that did not were dropped. In the eighteenth century, it was wrong for a Donna Anna to assert herself too boldly, wrong for a Don Giovanni to be deeply disturbed by self-doubts. Those were erratic male and female patterns of behavior unbecoming to the spirit of the legend; they did not fit and were not retained, at least until reexamined and revised in light of new, nineteenth-century sensibilities.

For these reasons, Porta's libretto left little mark on the legend or on Da Ponte. There is an occasional future echo, as in the verses spoken by Donna Anna's maid as she tries to slip away from the dark room in which Don Giovanni has hidden himself prior to his attack on her mistress.

Pian pianino me ne vo.
Ah, trovassi almen la porta,
per farla un po' più corta,
io di qua me n'anderò.

(I.ix)

[Very quietly I'm going to leave.
If only I can find the door
so as to slip out faster,
I'll get away from here.]

These are verses that easily call to mind Leporello's, as he tries to slip out of the darkened entryway of Donna Anna's palace and out of the clutches of his pursuers.[46] There is an echo in the minuet played at Don Giovanni's dinner, as well as in Arlecchino's halting, confused, and breathless description of the statue's arrival for dinner or of the damnation scene. These examples, however, were not sources for Da Ponte, but standard forms that were by then part of the accepted, ongoing nature of the legend. Yet in retrospect, Porta's libretto did have one true and simple merit. It was the first Don Juan opera of any real success, and

46. Più che cerco, men ritrovo
questa porta sciagurata.
Piano, piano: l'ho trovata.
Ecco il tempo di fuggir.

(II.vii)

its very existence must have suggested to others that the legend was a viable topic for operatic treatment.

In fact, the following year, a new operatic version appeared in the entertainment-hungry city of Venice, where Lorenzo Da Ponte, recently dismissed from his teaching post at a seminary in Treviso, was avidly practicing the arts of seduction, and with such intensity and scandal even for that corrupt city, that he would soon be officially banished from it for fifteen years. One wonders if he went to the San Cassiano theater to see a Don Juan opera that opened during the carnival season of 1777. Like so many others, it too was called *Il convitato di pietra*. It was by Giuseppe Calegari. The author of the libretto is not known. Two names are still frequently cited, but both attributions are obviously erroneous: Pietro Pariati, who was a collaborator of Apostolo Zeno's and who died in 1733, and Giambattista Lorenzi, whose text for *Il convitato di pietra* was set to music not by Calegari but by Giacomo Tritto in 1783.[47]

Giuseppe Calegari—or, as our libretto spells his name, Callegari—was one of many Calegaris, a very large family of musicians from the Veneto region of Northern Italy active in the latter half of the eighteenth century. Indeed, there were so many Calegaris—or Callegaris, or even Caligaris—that it is not always clear today who was related to whom and how. Giuseppe, born in Padua around 1750, was not one of the more successful members of the family. It appears, as an early local biographer noted, that "miserly fortune poorly recompensed the efforts of an industriousness without equal."[48] Relatively little is known about him. His father died at an early age, leaving Giuseppe to raise two younger brothers. All of them studied music. Giuseppe played the cello, evidently with skill, for in 1770 he was appointed first cellist in the orchestra of the Basilica of Sant'Antonio's, where he gave frequent public recitals. During the next fifteen years, he composed, for productions in Padua, Modena, and Venice, the five or so operas that are associated with his name. None seems to have been any great success. Perhaps for that reason, in 1787 and for about ten years thereafter, he assumed the impresarioship of the Teatro Nuovo, one of the two principal theaters of Padua. His job was to make the theater make money, a difficult task that required him to find operas, arrange performances, hire singers, contract for scenery, and so on. Competition from the other local theater was tough and public taste, it seems, not always reliable. While Calegari made a go of it at

47. Of Calegari's other operas, two were set to texts by Metastasio: *L'isola disabitata* (1770) and *La Zenobia in Palmira* (1779); the text for *Artemisia* (1782) was written, cites the libretto, by "Sig. Conte N.N.," while *Il natal d'Apollo* (1783) was by an S. Mattei.

48. Napoleone Pietrucci, *Biografia degli artisti padovani* (1858; reprint, Bologna: Forni, 1970), 57.

first, at the close of the 1796 season his contract was not renewed. He died in Padua in 1812.

Calegari's *Convitato di pietra* lasted only one season in Venice, and there are no indications of later performances elsewhere. Perhaps the music did not please. And yet the libretto is charming, far superior to Nunziato Porta's. It has a unity of tone, style, and spirit that is completely lacking in Porta's. Calegari's sunny, two-act *dramma giocoso* is almost always good comic fun; it is humorous and energetic from start to finish. The opening scene in Naples serves to establish Don Giovanni's rough masculinity, as he pushes away and escapes from Donna Isabella, whom he has just seduced, while she desperately tries to grasp ahold of him and force him to reveal his face. The scene gives a glimpse of the darker side of Don Giovanni's personality; it is evident that, when aroused, he is not a man to be trifled with. In many respects, this opening scene is reminiscent of the opening of Da Ponte's version.[49] However, for the remainder of the libretto, Don Giovanni exhibits a healthy freshness, an *allegria,* that makes him far less threatening and actually quite appealing. He is not disturbed by complexes, as was Porta's Don Giovanni, no doubts or hesitations cloud his mind, nor has he the frenetic and agitated compulsiveness that will drive Da Ponte's Don Giovanni to seducing unattractive old ladies. Calegari's Don Giovanni likes only beautiful women; he enjoys making love. He also likes to eat, likes to laugh, likes to joke, likes to play the spinet, and likes to sing. When he has to face the statue, he does so without doubts or fears, and though he is defeated of course, he faces it with flair and courage.

His antithesis is Duca Ottavio. His effeteness, only hinted at by Da Ponte, is sketched out here in broad, comic strokes. Duca Ottavio is a foolish courtier who remains many morning hours at home each day to primp and powder himself in order to cut the very finest figure at court and who sheds large tears when things do not go as he would like. Donna Anna, too, has none of the health or strength usually associated with her character. She is a wilting, uncertain figure who rejects Duca Ottavio's extravagant expressions of love and concern in order to weep more fully for her lost father.

She weeps excessively, according to her practical friend, Donna Ximena, who remarks that, after all, the deceased was rather elderly. Donna Anna cannot expect him to have lived forever; falling in love will make up for the loss. Donna Ximena has Don Giovanni's vital spirit. So does the peasant girl, Rosalba, whose attraction to Don Giovanni is purely physical, without the touch of greed that

49. Donna Isabella, grasping Don Giovanni's hand: "Non sperar mai ch'io ti lasci, / non sperar mai di fuggire!" (I.i). Donna Anna, grasping Don Giovanni's arm: "Non sperar, se non m'uccidi, / ch'io ti lasci fuggir mai" (I.i).

will be found in Zerlina. Sharing their exuberances is Passarino, Don Giovanni's servant, who scatters his earthy Venetian dialect and wit throughout the comedy. There is no hint of the leering or the envious or the sycophantic in his relationship with Don Giovanni. He brings a smile and an irreverent gaiety to every moment of the libretto. His unintentional parody of the threatening inscription at the base of the Commendatore's statue is a wonderful breath of fresh air to anyone who has seen or read the scene too many times. Sculpted below the statue are the following lines.

> Di chi a torto mi trasse a morte ria,
> dal ciel qui attendo la vendetta mia.
>
> [I await heaven's vengeance on the one
> who wrongfully led me to wicked death.]

Passarino, ordered by his master to read the inscription aloud, is so frightened and flustered that what comes out instead is a garbled parody.

> Da chi le torta fasse in casaria,
> da quel intendo aver la fetta mia.
>
> (II.iv)
>
> [I intend to have my slice
> of homemade pie from the baker.]

After the statue's visit to Don Giovanni's home, Passarino sends him out the door with a muttered epithet that effectively deflates his heavenly dignity: "Che te vegna la tegna e un po' de rogna!" [May you come down with ringworm and a bit of mange!] (II.vii).

Calegari's librettist had clearly read Cicognini's *Convitato,* and he certainly had in mind other spin-offs of the Italian commedia dell'arte tradition. While he had no compunction in borrowing from the former or from any of the other versions that he had at hand, at the same time he created his own bright, healthy, and entertaining form of the legend. His is a classic Don Juan story, the legendary Don Juan as handed down from generation to generation. His libretto reflects no particular authorial personality and his Don Giovanni offers no special peculiarities or variations; he created a shallow Don Giovanni, it is true, but for a general public a Don Juan figure that must have been very attractive to watch and to follow and to think about.

The Don Juan who next appeared in public was perhaps less good-natured but had a more successful operatic career. This one appeared not in Italy, but in Poland. He was taken there by an Italian composer, Gioacchino Albertini, who obtained a notable degree of popularity and critical acclaim for a few years in his lifetime and then fell into oblivion. He was vaguely remembered by most nineteenth-century musical lexicographers as a fine musician and distinguished opera composer, but the facts they offered about him were scant, imprecise, and often contradictory. Nor has his lot improved in this century; discrepancies continue to abound and music historians do not even agree where he was finally laid to rest.

Albertini spent much of his active musical life in Poland. He was born in Pesaro around 1748 or 1749 and probably began his career in Italy; an opera of his, variously listed as *La cacciatrice brillante* or *Il cacciatore brillante,* was produced in Rome in 1772. He then moved to Poland. An entry dated 23 April 1777 in the *Journal littéraire de Varsovie* makes mention of him as an aria composer and young virtuoso. For a few years he was employed as a conductor by Prince Karol Radziwill at his residence at Nieświez. Then, in 1782, he was appointed *maestro di cappella* at the court of King Stanislaw August Poniatowski. He soon rose to become a prominent and applauded figure in Warsaw's theatrical and musical world. He was especially celebrated for his Don Juan opera after its premiere in a Polish translation in 1783. Three other operas followed, but they do not seem to have ever been staged in Warsaw: *Circe ed Ulisse* (Hamburg, 1785), *Virginia* (Rome, 1786, and London, 1788), and *Scipione africano* (Rome, 1789). It is not known for certain if Albertini left Poland to attend their performances. Political events in Poland eventually made it advisable for him to leave the country, and it is thought that he went to Rome in 1796 where he taught singing and worked in the service of the king's nephew and Polish ambassador to Rome, Prince Stanislaw Poniatowski, from whom he received a small pension.[50] The last of his operas performed outside Poland was *La vergine vestale.* It was given in Rome in 1803. Perhaps because his wife was Polish, he once again returned to Warsaw around 1803. He was not able to repeat his earlier good fortune and died in relative penury, probably still in Poland, around 1811 or 1812.

Amid the myriad uncertain facts concerning Albertini, one thing is sure. *Don Juan, albo ukarany libertyn* [Don Juan or the Libertine Punished] was very

50. It should be pointed out that the libretto for *Virginia* (Rome, 1786) states that Albertini was "Maestro di Cappella all'attual Servizio di S. A. il Principe Stanislao Poniatowski Nipote di S. M. il Re di Polonia. . . ." If, as this libretto indicates, he began working for the Prince earlier than 1796, he may also have traveled to Rome earlier, as several biographical sketches suggest. From 1785–86 onward, Albertini's name appears regularly in the *Indice* in its index list of opera composers.

popular in Warsaw. Albertini had evidently completed it by the latter half of 1780, not in a Polish version, but in Italian.[51] It is not known whether the opera was actually performed at that time or not. Even if it was not, it somehow came to the attention of one of the most outstanding men in Polish theatrical life in the latter half of the century. He was Wojciech Bogusławski—actor, opera singer, impresario, playwright, director, translator, and producer of operas and plays from French, German, Italian, and English—whose efforts and energies were fundamental in the creation of a new national Polish theater and opera. Twenty-six years old, Bogusławski translated Albertini's Italian text into Polish and brought a production of it to light on 23 February 1783 at the recently built National Theater of Warsaw. He himself sang the role of Don Juan's servant, Skanarelli, and he is reported to have done so with fine comic skill. The opera proved to be a hit. It was repeated a number of times that year, and three other productions were mounted in Warsaw over the next ten years, even though Mozart's *Don Giovanni* had been staged in the city in 1789. Further productions are on record through the first decades of the nineteenth century.

It is most likely that Albertini's opera never found its way to Italy. Claims of performances in Venice in 1784 and in Florence in 1792 are not well substantiated.[52] Although the libretto for Bogusławski's Polish version of the opera is extant, no Italian libretto has been found either for the supposed Venice or Florence performances or for the possible 1780 performance in Warsaw. What does exist, in the Luigi Cherubini Conservatory of Music in Florence, is a handwritten copy of the full score in two volumes. The title of the work is *Il Don Giovanni,* and Gioacchino Albertini is indicated as its composer. The underlay is in Italian. The manuscript bears no date, only the following notation: "In Roma Presso Gio. Batta Cencetti." Several questions come to mind. Albertini was in Rome between 1796 and 1803. Was this score prepared for a performance in those years? Or was it to be performed in Rome between 1786 and 1789, when two other operas of his were presented there? Or is this the score that Albertini composed for a 1780 performance in Warsaw? I would like to think

51. Zbigniew Raszewski ("Rondo alla Polacca: Operowa dzialalność Wojciecha Bogusławskiego w Latach 1779–83," *Pamiętnik literacki* 61, no. 2 [1970]: 179) indicates that the *General Inventarium* of the Teatr Narodowy lists costumes prepared for a Don Juan opera scheduled to be performed in Warsaw by an Italian troupe. The troupe gave its first Warsaw performance, though not of a Don Juan opera, on 8 May 1780. Raszewski supposes the Don Juan opera in preparation to have been Albertini's.

52. The first (Carlo Schmidl *Dizionario universale* 1:28) probably never took place; the second (Ugo Morini, *La R. Accademia degli Immobili ed il suo Teatro La Pergola* [Pisa: Simoncini, 1926], 84) was probably by Gazzaniga or Fabrizi, not Albertini. See chap. 4, pp. 460 and 478, for further details.

the latter. As for the Italian text, it is irrefutably pre-Dapontian, for in essence it is the same text as the one prepared by Nunziato Porta for Vincenzo Righini's *Il convitato di pietra* in 1776. Whether the Rome volumes were copied out before or after Mozart's version is impossible to establish and is not important within the scope of this study. What I suggest is that the text of the score closely reflects Albertini's first version of the opera, the version that he intended for performance, in Italian, in 1780 in Warsaw. It seems plausible that Albertini's librettist borrowed from the Porta libretto because it had recently had successful runs in Prague and Vienna. It should also be noted that the Italian text in the score is generally similar to Bogusławski's Polish version. The Polish singer prepared his 1783 version of the opera by translating directly from an Italian text. This was the one that he probably used. In other words, even if the Rome manuscript itself was copied out toward the end of the century, its content certainly reflects what Albertini had written around 1780. Indeed, it would be surprising if, in the last decade or so of the century, Albertini had composed a brand new Don Juan opera using Nunziato Porta's old text, by then long gone and forgotten.

When Albertini and his librettist set to work on Porta's libretto, they did not hesitate to manhandle it as they best saw fit. They added new dialogues and new scenes, but they also truncated Porta's third act from seven scenes to two; they modified characterizations at will, and they gave greater emphasis to comic roles, perhaps called upon to do so by the special talents of the Italian company that was to perform the work. Yet for all their changes, their text remained essentially Porta's. Many scenes and dialogues were transcribed almost comma for comma, and the plot line of both remained nearly identical. For that reason, the full text has not been included in the present collection.

Among the libretto's curiosities should be noted the fact that what had been only hinted at in Porta's text and in his source, Goldoni's *Don Giovanni Tenorio,* is now made evident: Donna Anna is in love with Don Giovanni and is impatient to be with him, as she herself breathlessly states in her opening recitative.[53] And Don Giovanni is just as deeply in love with her, as he too clearly states a few

53. Trionfante in Castiglia
rivedrò il genitor; ma da gran tempo
più non vedo colui
che con i sguardi sui
infiammava il mio core.
Ah, dove sei, Don Giovanni mio bene,
sola occulta cagion delle mie pene?

(I.iv)

The equivalent position in Righini is at the opening of I.iii.

pages further on in his first solo aria.[54] Although aching to see her, he suspects that her father, newly returned from the wars in Sicily, may not be sympathetic to their relationship. After what proves to be a luckless encounter for all three, Donna Anna seeks out Don Giovanni in her father's mausoleum, where she intends to kill him. But, as in Righini and Goldoni, she cannot bring herself to do it. Don Giovanni's fascination is too powerful. In fact, Albertini and his librettist added what was intended to be, one supposes, a touching duet for these apparently star-crossed lovers who, realizing that they must part, harmonize their despair together.

D. AN: I am forced to hate my dearly beloved;
it is best that I depart.
D. GIO: How will being faithful
to my dearest love be of help?
D. GIO: Ah, who ever suffered so much cruelty
D. AN: from an angry heaven,
from a wicked and tyrannical destiny,
in such a fierce and cruel situation?[55]

The greatest changes, however, came about in the comic figures. Their roles were so considerably amplified that they, not Don Giovanni, nearly become the center of attention. Certainly, the small Italian company that was preparing this

54. Mentre penso al caro bene,
il mio duol più non rammento,
e una calma in seno io sento,
che mi viene a consolar.
Più non temo il mar turbato,
sprezzo l'onde e la procella,
rivedrò l'amica stella,
che può l'alma rallegrar.

No scene number is indicated in the score, but it immediately follows I.vi. Its equivalent place in Righini is at the beginning of I.vii.

55. D. AN: Deggio odiar l'amato bene,
e partir mi converrà.
D. GIO: D'esser fido al caro bene
cosa mai mi gioverà?
D. GIO: / D. AN: Ah, chi mai del cielo sdegnato,
del destin tiranno e rio,
in sì fiero e crudo stato
provò tanta crudeltà?

(II.iii)

This duet follows the last lines of Righini's II.iii.

opera in Warsaw must have felt itself strong in comic singers. A twist has been added to the usual story. The traditional fishergirl who rescues Don Giovanni from the sea, here called Lisetta, turns out to be Donna Anna's "damigella" as well. The two roles, distinct in Righini, have been joined together and given far greater comic substance. It appears that Donna Anna allows Lisetta to go to the seaside whenever she has nothing better to do at home. There she pulls Don Giovanni out of the waves. Though at first susceptible to his flatteries, she resists temptation and marries him in name only, whereupon he refuses to give her another thought. She enchants Don Giovanni's servant, Ercolino, and a bantering and flirtatious relationship develops between the two that runs throughout the opera. These scenes are Albertini's own. Included in chapter 3 of this volume is the most interesting of their scenes together, one in which the singer who plays Lisetta is given an opportunity to perform a fine piece of bravura comic singing and acting as she gaily makes a fool out of her gullible, love-dulled admirer.

Ercolino is likewise given a fine comic moment in which the stage is his alone. It is dinner time. Don Giovanni is out of sorts and wants an amusing distraction. He asks Ercolino to sing him something. Why not a rondò? Albertini's librettist takes the occasion to make fun of several staples of the contemporary musical world. In Ercolino's opinion, the rondò aria, so popular in opera buffa, is completely lacking in measure and grace; he is shocked at Don Giovanni's poor taste. Such an aria is nothing in comparison to a seria aria, a genre he considers sublime, especially as sung by that great castrato soprano, Don Ciaramella, whom Ercolino then brings to life on stage in all his histrionic glory. The seria aria is so lovely, says Ercolino, that one risks being overcome by a "colica armoniosa," a kind of harmonious loosening of the intestines. However, his attempt to sing a seria aria degenerates into confused nonsense, as Don Giovanni interrupts him with bursts of amused laughter. Ercolino is quite piqued. The text of this *scena* has been included in chapter 3.

When Bogusławski translated Albertini's libretto into Polish, he brought it back closer to Porta's original.[56] He excluded many of the variations that Albertini's librettist had introduced into Porta's text. While he did not remove Ercolino's rondò scene, which he himself sang as Skanarelli, he eliminated the exciting figure of Lisetta. He redivided her into Porta's two original parts: the fishergirl, Eliza, and the uninteresting figure of a confidante of the daughter of the Kommandor. However, the sprightly innkeeper, Karolina, is back once

56. A full text, in Polish, may be found in *Teatr Polski czyli zbior komedyi drammy tragedyi,* vol. 53 (Warsaw: P. Dufour, 1794). No English translation exists.

more from Porta. She had also been subsumed, in Albertini's Italian text, into the fuller figure of Lisetta. Of the minor textual variations of Bogusławski's version, none is of great import. It is curious to see that the Kommandor on horseback is dressed in a Roman toga (II.iv); it is amusing to hear that the fishergirl ranks as number 500 on Skanarelli's list (I.x); and it is truly shocking to imagine the violence with which Don Giovanni is handled by the furies, who, according to the stage directions, tear at his clothes, pull out his hair, beat him with chains, crush his head against rocks, and finally throw him into a cavern (III.ii). This ending is not fun; nothing like it had been seen before. But none of these small differences contributed any significant originality to an otherwise derivative libretto.

While the Don Juan legend was entertaining Warsaw in 1783, it also found favor in Naples during the carnival season of the same year in a one-act version with the usual title, *Il convitato di pietra*. This version was by two local Neapolitan artists, Giambattista Lorenzi and Giacomo Tritto. Tritto (his last name is sometimes given as Tritta) was one of the stalwarts of the Neapolitan school, not one of its most outstanding members, but one of its most reliable and long-lived. For many of his ninety-one years he was a significant part of the local musical culture. Born in 1733 in Altamura, Bari, he began his studies in Naples at the Conservatorio della Pietà dei Turchini at an early age. After graduation, he remained at the conservatory as a teacher and gradually rose in rank and importance until he became its *primo maestro*. When several Neapolitan conservatories merged in 1806 to form the new Collegio Reale di Musica, Tritto was appointed one of three directors. In the last years of his life, he became *maestro* of the Reale Cappella Palatina and of the Reale Camera. He died in Naples in 1824.

Tritto was an amiable man, a good-natured individual who managed to weather the violent political storms of his city without loss of job or prestige. He was a family man, twice married, father of eighteen children. At one moment in his lifetime he had eleven daughters at home for whom to find husbands. He made no lasting impression on the world of music, and history's judgment of him has been harsh. An obituary in the *Giornale delle due Sicilie* admitted that, although he obtained a certain degree of fame in Naples, "his operas never awakened the enthusiasm of those by Jommelli, Paisiello, Cimarosa or Guglielmi."[57] Dennis Libby is more blunt. He calls Tritto "a rather pedestrian

57. *Giornale delle due Sicilie*, no. 230, 27 September 1824, quoted in Giuseppe de Napoli, *La triade melodrammatica altamurana: Giacomo Tritto, Vincenzo Lavigna, Saverio Mercadante* (Milan: n.p., 1931), 40.

composer" of only local significance.[58] In fact, Tritto is remembered today primarily as a distinguished teacher of counterpoint and composition who counted among his students the likes of Gaspare Spontini, Saverio Mercadante, and Vincenzo Bellini.

Prolific as a father, Tritto was even more so as composer. He created about fifty operas, though he did not seriously begin composing for the operatic stage until the age of forty-seven. He began in 1777 by offering to write an opera seria for the San Carlo theater. His request was denied; it was felt that he had neither experience nor reputation in the operatic field. He turned, therefore, to the comic genre and, between 1780 and 1798, composed twenty-four comic operas for various secondary theaters in Naples. He wrote other comic works for Rome, Venice, Vienna, and Madrid. He did not neglect the seria, especially in the latter part of his career. The San Carlo eventually relented and staged a seria work of his in 1784; others followed, not only in Naples but in Rome and Milan as well. None of his operas is ever played today. Tritto wrote *Il convitato di pietra* and its first-act companion piece, *Li due gemelli,* in 1783. According to Carlo Schmidl (on what authority it is not clear), *Il convitato di pietra* "had great success."[59] It is true that five or six additional productions of it are on record, the last in 1809 in Naples. For that performance, Tritto seems to have added new material to the original one-act story, thereby creating a full evening's entertainment. Yet it is hard to think of this small number of productions as an indication of its having been greatly successful.

Tritto's librettist was a fellow Neapolitan, Giambattista Lorenzi. They had much in common. Like Tritto, Lorenzi wrote extensively for the theater; his output, too, was ample, nearly thirty librettos plus four volumes of comedies for the nonmusical stage; like Tritto, Lorenzi was for decades an intimate of the musical and theatrical world of Naples, and, again like the composer, he was extremely long lived. He was born in Naples in 1721 and died there at the age of eighty-six in 1807. As a young man he performed in improvised comedies, many of his own invention, in the homes of the city's most distinguished families. This activity brought him into frequent contact with such notable figures of Neapolitan intellectual life as Napoli-Signorelli. On the strength of his reputation as a performer and writer, he was hired, in 1769, by the King of Naples as an actor and improviser, with the additional task of selecting other actors worthy of performing before the royal family. He was eventually ap-

58. Dennis Libby, "Giacomo Tritto," in *The New Grove Dictionary of Music and Musicians,* ed. Stanley Sadie (London: Macmillan, 1980), 19:157.

59. Schmidl, *Dizionario universale* 2:620.

pointed director of the Teatrino di Corte with responsibilities that included writing new comedies for it. In the latter years of his life, he was appointed *regio revisore,* that is, official censor of theatrical works, a position he is said to have filled with great scrupulousness.

Lorenzi was a highly educated man whose output, in the opinion of Ariella Lanfranchi in "La librettistica italiana del Settecento," "best represents the period of greatest splendor of the Neapolitan opera buffa."[60] Lorenzi prepared his librettos with fine theatrical acumen and technical skill, ably integrating recitative and aria. Though his texts were never more than pure entertainment, never particularly profound either in idea or characterization, in his hands the opera buffa text became less coarse, less vulgar, less biting and satiric; he made it more refined, literary, and musical in its verse. With Lorenzi, Neapolitan opera buffa ceased to be a "spettacolo popolare" as it had been for nearly fifty years and became a "spettacolo borghese."[61] Lorenzi was the first in Naples to make this sort of libretto respectable. The coming of age took place in 1768 with a performance of *L'idolo cinese.* Lorenzi's was the text, Giovanni Paisiello's the music. It was performed with unexpected success, not in a popular theater as was the tradition, but in the Teatrino di Corte of the royal palace at Caserta. Opera buffa now had an official seal of approval. In fact, Lorenzi was the only writer for the Neapolitan musical theater whose works were collected and published while the author was still living.

Lorenzi worked with the best composers of his city. He collaborated a second time with Tritto on a very popular *La scuffiara* in 1784. He also worked with Nicola Piccinni, Domenico Cimarosa, and Pietro Guglielmi, but most especially with his dear friend Paisiello, who set many of his texts. Among their most notable efforts was *Il Socrate immaginario* in 1775 and *Nina o sia La pazza per amore* in 1789. The libretto for the former satirized the mania for Greek studies then rampant in Naples. In it, the provincial aspirant to Socrates-hood, Don Tammaro Promontorio, demands that even his dog wag its tail Greek-style. Lorenzi never thought of himself as a social or political critic, but this libretto nearly got him into trouble. A distinguished local intellectual thought he recognized himself under the guise of Promontorio, and the opera was closed down after five performances.

Lorenzo Da Ponte was familiar with Lorenzi's work. In 1790 in Vienna he reworked *Nina o sia La pazza per amore* for Joseph Weigl, a protégé of Salieri's.

60. Ariella Lanfranchi, "La librettistica italiana del Settecento," in *Storia dell'opera* (Turin: UTET, 1977), 3, pt. 2:103.

61. Vanda Monaco, *Giambattista Lorenzi e la commedia per musica* (Naples: Berisio, 1968), 40.

There is also an oblique reference to Lorenzi in Da Ponte's text for *Don Giovanni.* When, during the last dinner scene, Leporello recognizes a popular melody played by the onstage orchestra and sings out "Evvivano *I litiganti,*" he is referring to one of Lorenzi's very earliest librettos, *Fra i due litiganti il terzo gode,* written in 1766. It was put to music in 1782 by Giuseppe Sarti, whose music Mozart is quoting. Lorenzi likewise knew of Da Ponte's work, or at least of his libretto for *Le nozze di Figaro.* In 1792, he made a shortened version of it, entitled *La serva onorata,* for Piccinni.

There is nothing to indicate that Da Ponte had ever seen or read Lorenzi's *Convitato.* Nonetheless, in some respects his libretto easily calls to mind Da Ponte's. It is clear that both shared the same tradition, that both felt the shaping influence of the Gluck-Angiolini ballet of twenty-five years before. Like Da Ponte's story, Lorenzi's begins neither in Naples, as Calegari's, nor along the Spanish shore, as Righini's and Albertini's; there are no rescues from the ocean waves and no fishergirls appear, while Donna Isabella, seduced and abandoned sometime before in Naples, shows up only briefly in Spain for the purpose of healing her injured honor.[62] Both Lorenzi and Da Ponte set all actions in Seville. Like the ballet, their librettos open in front of the house of Commendatore Ulloa and his daughter Anna. In Lorenzi's version, Don Giovanni, disguised as Duca Ottavio, has prepared a serenade, after which he slips into her apartment. It is not long before the Commendatore is dead. What Lorenzi has been the first to do in a Don Juan text for opera is to shorten or eliminate all parts of the story that take place before the seduction of Donna Anna and to increase the number of events that take place afterwards. Hence, he gives major importance to the role of the country folk. Pulcinella, Don Giovanni's servant, is preparing to wed Lesbina, to the great delight of her father, Bastiano. There is singing and dancing, a celebration of love, just as there will be later in Da Ponte.

Viva, viva sempre ammore,
che li zite a core a core
fa co gusto e co priezza,
co allegrezza grellejà.

(v)

62. Although seeking justice from the Spanish king, Donna Isabella's demeanor betrays a still-vibrant love for Don Giovanni. Thus does the personality and story of this traditional figure begin to blend with that of Molière's abandoned Done Elvire; from their conjunction in Giovanni Bertati's libretto will eventually derive the magnificent figure of Da Ponte's Donna Elvira.

[Long live love forever.
It intoxicates the hearts
of youth with pleasure,
joy, and happiness.]

But the good times are brief. Don Giovanni enters, and Lesbina is overcome by his presence and his promises. At heart, she is a grasping soul. Nor is her father displeased at the new turn of events and its social implications. The truly angry one is Pulcinella, who swears to Bastiano that when Don Giovanni has finished with his daughter she will be good only for a "robbevecchia" [a junk dealer] (viii). At this moment, Pulcinella is clearly a future unhappy Masetto.

There are other aspects of Lorenzi's libretto that are not reflected in Da Ponte's. They indicate a partial shift in direction that the legend was taking. We have come a good distance from Porta and Righini. Their Don Giovanni was essentially a serious figure. Lorenzi's, too, has his serious side: he is unmoved by the divine, unafraid of the statue, and, as the opera draws to a close, uninterested in repentance: "What I was, such am I still" (xix). But, like Calegari's protagonist, he has also assumed a lighter, gayer quality as well. He loves chasing women and confesses that he does so impelled by a kind of innate "bizzarria" (i). Yet the question that then arises, whether this young adventurer is a tragic or a comic figure, soon proves to be irrelevant, for Don Giovanni turns out to be no figure at all. Lorenzi has not made him the central actor of the story, nor are his social equals, Donna Anna and Donna Isabella and their respective ordeals, central in any way. Porta called his libretto a *dramma tragicomico,* Calegari defined his as a *dramma giocoso.* Lorenzi's is simply a *commedia,* and the central figures of his comedy are the low-class folk: a wisecracking, edgy, put-upon, vociferous Pulcinella, and two ignorant country yokels, Lesbina and Bastiano. These three figures and their many scenes together form the comedy's heart and soul:[63] Lesbina and her father Bastiano with their foolish aspirations to be other

63. When Lorenzi revised the libretto for publication in his collected works, he gave even more prominence to the figure of Pulcinella, Lesbina, and her father. At the same time, he entirely removed the character of Donna Isabella and of the Marchese Dorasquez. The revised version is almost totally comic. Lorenzi even excised the final inferno scene. He defined the revision as a *farsa.* This is the version published by Vanda Monaco; hers cannot be the original libretto. Although she does not so state, I assume that she has taken her text from Lorenzi's *Opere teatrali,* published in Naples in four volumes between 1806 and 1820. The title page of the text as published by Monaco (*Giambattista Lorenzi,* 463) speaks of the work as something from the past: "Farsa per musica rappresentata nel Teatro dei Fiorentini nell'anno 1783." The original libretto (see chap. 3) speaks of *Il convitato di pietra* and its companion piece as two one-act comedies still to be given: "Da rappresentarle [*sic*] nel nuovo Teatro de' Fiorentini."

than country peasants, dressed in rented garb of the nobility, clothing they believe befits their rank now that Lesbina has "wed" the noble Don Giovanni, two awkward and greedy country people in search of justice in the big city of Seville; and Pulcinella, the little fellow with a tough and demanding master, the perpetual underdog, whose comic and sentimental personality dominates the work. All he wants is a good wife and a good plate of macaroni; all he gets is betrayal: from Lesbina, from Bastiano, and even from his own employer. Just so, Leporello will find that Don Giovanni tried to make love to his girl friend and would not have cared in the least had she been his wife. Though Pulcinella and Don Giovanni share a bantering sort of camaraderie, for Pulcinella their relationship is hardly much fun; there is no genuine affection between the two, and Pulcinella is often treated rather shabbily: "These guys are bastards with us servants. They skin us alive for two bits a month" (iii). Like Leporello, he recognizes that he should try to break free; maybe he will give it a try tomorrow, but come tomorrow he can never quite bring it off.[64]

Perhaps the problem lies with Naples itself. Maybe it is in the system. Perhaps that is just the way things work there. For this is a libretto that lives and breathes Naples, not Venice or northern Italy and certainly not Spain. Bastiano and his daughter may be living in Seville, but they have not given up their heritage. Lesbina's wedding is "alla napoletana," she is dressed "da luciana," like a young woman from the Santa Lucia section of Naples, and everyone dances the tarantella (v). Pulcinella and Chiarella, Donna Anna's servant, speak the thick dialect of Naples, their speeches peppered with proverbs, witticisms, and references to local names and places. Even Pulcinella's arias are sung in dialect. The appeal of the libretto is the appeal of the warm, wry, sad-sack Neapolitan servant, bent but never broken, an ignorant but good-natured goof resigned to a system he cannot fathom or avoid. However, just this once, true justice does prevail, even in Naples. Don Giovanni is sent to hell, and, at the opera's conclusion, all rejoice together, Pulcinella included.

> Ecco il fin di chi mal opra,
> ecco il cielo che sa far.
>
> (xxi)
>
> [Behold the end of one who works evil;
> see what heaven is able to do.]

64. In Lorenzi's revised version, Pulcinella actually achieves a kind of revenge: he gives Don Giovanni two swift kicks in the pants.

These celebratory words are later echoed by another liberated servant, Leporello: "Questo è il fin di chi fa mal. . . ."

Lorenzi's libretto was a libretto for southern Italy, and it was performed in Naples, Palermo, and Catania. When a brilliant young Neapolitan composer, Vincenzo Fabrizi, set it to music a few years later, he eliminated from it what made it particularly southern. His new opera had far greater diffusion, but the libretto lost a certain glow of truth. Fabrizi's *Il convitato di pietra* premiered during the fall season of 1787 in Rome. Because he did not use an original text but adopted Lorenzi's, his version is of less interest to us now. One wonders, nonetheless, whether it was not of interest to Mozart or Da Ponte after their own premiere, for no other reason than that Fabrizi's opera had a more immediate burst of popularity than theirs. Or might it be that Da Ponte, through the musical grapevine, heard of its coming production in Rome and became further convinced that the legend of Don Juan was indeed a marketable product?

The case of Vincenzo Fabrizi is a curious one. He was born in Naples in 1764. He began to compose operas at the age of eighteen or nineteen and completed fourteen within the next six years. His first was given in Naples in 1783. He then prepared works for theaters in northern Italy that were often picked up by theaters abroad. For more than three years he was musical director of the Teatro Capronica in Rome, and, in 1786, he was employed at the University of Rome as a *maestro di cappella.* His operas produced in Rome were highly successful; flattering things were written about his youth, his talents, and his work. Then he disappeared. Nothing is known about him after 1788; there is no word, no record, only the fact that he seems to have been still alive in 1812.

There is another curious thing. Fabrizi was a pupil of Giacomo Tritto's, whose *Convitato di pietra* debuted at the Teatro de' Fiorentini in Naples in the carnival season of 1783. Fabrizi's first theatrical work, an intermezzo called *I tre gobbi rivali,* was also first performed in the same year and season and in the same city and theater—and perhaps even with another one-act opera by Tritto. Fabrizi had every opportunity to observe his teacher's work. Four years later he exhibited his own score, and it was quite well received. He had made a number of changes and additions to the story. He increased the length of Lorenzi's original one-act version (in fact Fabrizi's new version was sometimes given in two acts), and he somewhat augmented the standard roles of Donna Isabella and Donna Anna. But the most telling change he made was to translate the talk of Lorenzi's servants into Italian. He avoided Tritto's limitation of setting to music a libretto tailored, in many respects, to a Neapolitan audience. Thus, Pulcinella and his earthy dialect became a more sophisticated and linguistically refined Ficcanaso who could be understood throughout the Italian peninsula and even abroad.[65] Tritto's version had only five other productions before the end of the century. Fabrizi's had more than twenty-five, mostly in Italy, but also in Madrid, Barcelona, and Lisbon. It is not known who made the text changes for him.

The year 1787 was a remarkable one for the legend. Fabrizi's opera debuted in the fall; Mozart's at the end of October. Earlier in the year, on 5 February, two versions appeared in Venice. At the Teatro Giustiniani di San Moisè, two well-established artists, Giuseppe Gazzaniga and Giovanni Bertati, presented their latest collaborative effort. They already had a long list of solid theatrical successes to their credit and had no reason to fear a competing Don Juan opera opening that same evening at the Teatro San Samuele. It was called *Il nuovo convitato di pietra* and was by two young men in their late twenties, Francesco Gardi and Giuseppe Maria Foppa. The *nuovo* of their title was intended as a curiosity-raising ploy, directed toward a public that by then had certainly had its fill of the legend, and as a youthful challenge to the solid reputation of their older rivals across the way.

Francesco Gardi, a Venetian, was the composer. Like Giuseppe Calegari, whose *Il convitato di pietra* Venice had seen ten years earlier, Gardi came and went without leaving much trace of himself. He spent most of his life in and around the city. He was born most likely between 1760 and 1765 and died about 1810. For a time, he served as director of the choir and orchestra of the Ospizio dei Derelitti in Venice and for some years he was *maestro di cappella* with the Conservatorio dei Mendicanti. Although he composed sacred oratorios and public cantatas, his real vocation was the theater. He made his operatic debut in Modena in 1786 with an opera seria, *Enea nel Lazio,* and most of the operas that immediately followed were likewise very serious. Perhaps he was under the influence, as he was certainly in the employ, of an eccentric and rather irresponsible Venetian nobleman by the name of Alessandro Pepoli, whose energies and wealth were consumed by the theater. Pepoli loved tragedies and published six volumes of his own. It was his intention to emulate and, he hoped, to obfuscate a more famous contemporary playwright, Vittorio Alfieri. Pepoli felt he was capable of everything. From Gardi he commissioned the music for several of his texts for performances to be held in his own private theater. Gardi was not free to compose as he pleased. In the introduction of the printed libretto of their opera *Tancredi,* Pepoli affirmed that the music for it was arranged according to his particular wishes.[66] In addition, he organized the performance, acted in it,

65. These comments are based on a review of three librettos: Bologna, 1791; Venice, 1792; and Lucca, 1792. I have not seen the libretto for the 1787 production in Rome.

66. Libretto, Library of Congress, Schatz 3542.

and sang. The libretto was even published by the Tipografia Pepoliana. Sometime around the time of Pepoli's death (he died penniless in 1796 at the age of thirty-nine), Gardi seems to have thrown aside the tragic and the heroic. He teamed up with Giuseppe Maria Foppa, a prominent local librettist. Together, for roughly fifteen years (up to 1805), they wrote more than a dozen one-act farces for local performance. These works seem to have truly delighted the Venetian theatergoing public. As noted, Gardi and Foppa had briefly collaborated ten years or so earlier on *Il nuovo convitato di pietra*.[67] The opera was Gardi's second and was very farcical, obviously written before he had been "Pepolized."

Like Gardi, Giuseppe Maria Foppa was Venetian through and through. He was born in Venice in 1760 and died there in 1845. As a young man, he was hired as archivist by many leading Venetian families; later he was employed as secretary for a number of years by the Venetian state. He seems to have left Venice only briefly, between 1797 and 1798, when engaged as poet and director of the San Carlos Theater in Lisbon. Foppa was apparently a hearty, boisterous, and energetic individual. Like another Venetian, Lorenzo Da Ponte, he was very fond of women. Foppa, too, published his memoirs in later life, and in them confessed that he early on began "to flit about the dangerous island of Cytherea. Many butterflies attracted me."[68] He married in 1788, but his wife died only seven years later. He sired six daughters; they, too, had all died by the time he wrote his little book of recollections. In it he sadly noted his regret at not having been faithful to the memory of his wife.

Foppa began his literary career as a writer of sentimental adventure novels. He next wrote oratorio texts for the Conservatorio dei Mendicanti and then, his principal literary activity, opera librettos. His first was *Armida abbandonata* in 1781 for Ferdinando Bertoni. He wrote more than eighty. Most were comic, although he did not entirely shun the serious. He was a competent craftsman who drew on well-established themes, styles, and sources, especially the commedia dell'arte, without adding anything particularly new or original of his own. His text for Gardi was among the earliest of his works.[69] In his never modest

67. Thus the title on the 1787 libretto. All following versions were titled simply *Il convitato di pietra*. Stefan Kunze (*Don Giovanni vor Mozart* [Munich: Wilhelm Fink, 1972], 84) reports that the extant score reads "Il Convitato /in S. Samuele / del Sig. Francesco Gardi / 1787."

68. Giuseppe Maria Foppa, *Memorie storiche della vita di Giuseppe M.a Foppa viniziano scritte da lui medesimo* (Venice: Molinari, 1840), 54.

69. It should be pointed out that, although the text of *Il nuovo convitato di pietra* is generally attributed to Foppa, it is not entirely certain that it is his. No author's name appears on the original libretto or on any other except the one published for the last known production of the opera in Venice in 1802. That text reads: "Il / Convitato di pietra / Ridotto in Farsa per musica / dal Sig. Giuseppe Foppa. . . . La Musica tutta nuova è del Sig. Maestro F. Gardi Accademico Filarmonico" (see Kunze,

memoirs he claims that his librettos were responsible for the early successes of such composers as Simone Mayr, Stefano Pavesi, and Gioacchino Rossini.[70] Certainly, Foppa was a complete and knowledgeable man of the theater. A friend of Carlo Gozzi's, he was well versed in the happenings and developments of Italian theatrical life, especially familiar with the works of his Neapolitan contemporaries and of Goldoni, and very well read in modern French theater. He spent much of his free time at the theater, where one evening backstage a burning sponge, used to create the illusion of a forest in flames, fell on his head and ignited his wig. He was saved by a nimble actor.[71] Foppa collaborated with some of the best and most popular composers of his day and with many of them many times: Giuseppe Farinelli, Marco Portogallo, and Ferdinando Paer, to name just a few. His most renowned libretto was *Giulietta e Romeo*—he was among the first to introduce Shakespeare onto the operatic stage—for Nicola Zingarelli in 1796. Toward the end of his career, he teamed up with a very young Rossini on four operas, though not always with as great a measure of success as he liked to claim: *L'inganno felice* (1812), *La scala di seta* (1812), *Il signor Bruschino* (1813), and *Sigismondo* (1814).[72] He retired from the theater a few years later. In 1840, as his life was coming to a close, he published his memoirs. They are brief, pleasant, and somewhat informative, but lack the strong personality of a Da Ponte.

Il nuovo convitato di pietra was indeed new; that much can be said of it. Foppa and Gardi ruthlessly altered the old story for laughs. They opened their version far into the traditional tale: Isabella has been seduced, Tisbea likewise, and the Commendatore is long dead. Lip service is paid to Don Giovanni's three traditional meetings with the statue, but Gardi and Foppa are not much interested in these scenes. Four ladies are the focus of their new plot, four lovesick ladies and their machinations to make Don Giovanni theirs, while he, for his part, attempts to give them the slip and pursue fresh prey. Also new are the personalities of some old acquaintances. The noble and self-possessed Donna Anna has turned mean and catty. She speaks to the fishergirl Tisbea, a strong rival for Don

Don Giovanni vor Mozart, 84). In this period, Foppa was doing many farces with Gardi in Venice. It may well be that he did not write the 1787 version and that his name is associated with it only because he prepared the 1802 version from it. In 1989, Kunze ("Su alcune farse di Giuseppe Foppa musicate da Francesco Gardi," in *I vicini di Mozart* [Florence: Olschki, 1989], 2:484) speaks of *Il nuovo convitato di pietra* as being by a "librettista ignoto."

70. Foppa, *Memorie storiche,* 22–25.

71. Foppa, *Memorie storiche,* 47–48.

72. *Sigismondo* was a total failure. Herbert Weinstock (*Rossini: A Biography* [New York: Knopf, 1968], 42) considers that "Foppa's libretto very probably was the worst that Rossini ever was cornered into composing."

Giovanni's attentions, with patronizing scorn. Does she know how to walk with grace, to bow before a king, manage a fan, dance the minuet or play cards (I.ix)? Donna Anna is obstinately set on marrying the libertine who murdered her father; if she is not able to, she will either (1) kill herself or (2) poison him. (Duke Ottavio is neither seen nor heard from.) Even her dead father considers her behavior questionable. Finding her at Don Giovanni's dinner, he informs her that she is no daughter of his and waves her away (I.xvii). Donna Isabella is a parody of her former self, a languid and perpetually weeping lover who has been searching for her lost love for four years and two months and who, up to the last moment of Don Giovanni's earthly existence, never ceases to hope that he will choose her again and never ceases to mouth vapid verses of love as if she were performing in a Metastasian opera seria: "Mio cor, sospiri? Ah, scordati d'un empio, d'un mancator di fè" (II.xvi). As for Don Giovanni's traditional servant, on the theory that more is better, his role has been doubled. There are now two: a secretary, Don Masone, who suffers from an uncomfortable hernia and is not able easily to keep apace with Don Giovanni as he flees his pursuers, and Zuccasecca, who except for his name, Pumpkinhead, really has no distinguishing features at all. It soon becomes clear that more is not better.

New, too, is the depth of silliness reached by this work. In no previous opera libretto had the story been trivialized as it has been here. Foppa and Gardi claimed that their opera was a *dramma tragicomico*. What it was, was a farce, a vehicle for arias, ensembles, and show pieces that often had little to do with the story itself but that gave performers a chance to exhibit their comic singing and acting abilities: thus Donna Anna explains to Don Masone and Zuccasecca how to be a successful highway robber (I.xiv); thus she participates in a quintet with Donna Isabella, Don Giovanni, and his two attendants in which they all imitate musical instruments (II.xiii). The spirit of the work is that of the pantomime entertainments now appearing in London in which the legend was only an excuse for amusing songs and skits.

What is not new in this opera is the figure of Don Giovanni himself. He remains the usual restless womanizer, but with a gay and sunny disposition, flashing good looks, and a kind of adolescent instability. He is undisturbed by moral, ethical, or theological doubts, impelled only by a rather intense but essentially innocent horniness. He fearlessly faces the statue, unrepentant to the end. One can fault him only for a certain lack of gentlemanly decorum when, to escape from several nagging ladies, he roughly binds them to a tree and abandons them in the forest.

With Foppa, the legend hit rock bottom. It had become a vehicle for simple amusements. The librettist offered nothing to think about, nor had he any intention of doing so. Nunziato Porta did not have the talent to craft a serious libretto; Foppa had no interest in crafting a serious one. It was of no concern to him—perhaps he did not sense—that behind these remarkable characters and their tale, now in public view for more than 150 years, lay a profusion of rich and challenging ideas, complex questions, and unsettling suggestions having to do with the right and wrong uses of man's sexual, creative energies, with his role and responsibilities in this world, and finally with his relationship to what is eternal. For that reason, of all the librettos on the Don Juan theme, this one least of all suggests Da Ponte's.

Il nuovo convitato di pietra was only moderately successful. It had four later productions, the last in 1802. It had none of the quick popularity of the competing version by Giovanni Gazzaniga and Giuseppe Bertati that, although its early good fortune was limited mainly to Italy, was the most immediately successful of all Don Juan operas, Mozart's included.

Giuseppe Gazzaniga is regarded today as a facile composer, an easy inventor of pleasant melodies and of pleasant operas who left little mark on those who followed. Like his operas, many details of his life have been forgotten by history. He was born in Verona in 1743. He studied first in Venice under the guidance of Nicola Porpora and then in Naples with Nicola Piccinni. He debuted as an opera composer in Naples in 1768 with a comic intermezzo, *Il barone di Trocchia,* based on a text by Neapolitan playwright Francesco Cerlone. In 1770, he returned to Venice, where he was befriended and advised by Antonio Sacchini. From then on, for nearly twenty years, his life was a succession of one opera production after another in nearly all the principal cities of Italy and many abroad. In 1791, he settled in Crema as *maestro di cappella* at the Crema cathedral. Little is known of his final years except that he amassed a fine private music library that included works by Handel. He died in Crema in 1818.

Gazzaniga wrote more than forty operas, most in the buffa tradition. His Don Juan opera was the work of a mature composer who had had years of operatic experience. His librettist, Giovanni Bertati, was an equally experienced man of the theater with many successes to his credit. The two of them had been working together on and off since 1771, so that it is not surprising that they were successful once again. For the Teatro Giustiniani they planned a rather amusing evening's entertainment in two acts entitled *Il capriccio drammatico.*[73] The first act deals with an Italian opera troupe touring in Germany. Unsuccessful with high-quality opera seria performances, the troupe's impresario decides to put on

73. It is occasionally reported that the first performance was in Venice at the Teatro Sant'Angelo in the spring of 1782. There is no evidence to support this statement.

something of a more popular nature. What the troupe presents is presented by Gazzaniga and Bertati in their second act, subtitled *Don Giovanni o sia Il convitato di pietra.* Although the text of the first act was Bertati's, the music was not Gazzaniga's. The libretto does not mention the name of a composer, but it was probably Giovanni Valentini, a minor Neapolitan opera composer.[74] Later on, Valentini's first act was frequently set aside in favor of Cimarosa's one-act comedy *L'impresario in angustie.*

In his letters, Mozart never mentions Gazzaniga, and how familiar he was with Gazzaniga's Don Juan score is not entirely certain.[75] Da Ponte, who probably knew Gazzaniga rather better, regarded him somewhat condescendingly as a "composer of some merit, but with a no longer modern style."[76] They had had a brief, unhappy collaboration in Vienna in 1786 on an opera titled *Il finto cieco.* Da Ponte had just enjoyed his first real triumph as a librettist with his book for Martín y Soler's *Il burbero di buon core.* Immediately afterward, he noted with self-complacence in his memoirs, "various composers looked to me for librettos."[77] He felt that only two were worthy of his esteem: Martín y Soler and Mozart. While contemplating a libretto for the popular Spanish composer and one for Mozart, he was interrupted by an order from the Viennese theatrical administration, by whom he was employed, to prepare a text for Gazzaniga. He was very annoyed; he would have preferred to think about librettos for his "two dear friends."

> In order to get it over with quickly, I chose a French comedy called *L'Aveugle clairvoyant,* and in a very few days I scribbled out [*schiccherai*] a play which pleased practically no one, both for the words and the music. An infatuation for a fifty-year-old woman that disturbed the mind of that good fellow [Gazzaniga] kept him from finishing the opera within the time he had been given. Therefore, I had to stick into the second act some pieces done twenty years before, make use of various scenes from other operas, both his and by other composers, in a word, create a pastiche, a jumble,

74. Even though many later librettos attribute the music to *maestri vari,* several give the single name Valenti, several others Valentini, and one or two Giovanni Valentini. The *Indice* occasionally links this opera to Valentini's name.

75. It is interesting to note that Antonio Baglione sang the tenor role of Don Giovanni in the first performance of the Gazzaniga opera and the tenor role of Duca Ottavio in the first performance of Mozart's opera.

76. Da Ponte, *Memorie,* 163.

77. Da Ponte, *Memorie,* 161.

that had neither beginning nor end and that was played three times and then put to sleep.[78]

Da Ponte's readers are meant to see that he performed heroically in the face of adversity, although one can also read into the verb *schiccherai* a very rarely confessed sense of guilt. What is more, Da Ponte usually heaped greater quantities of contempt on those who involved him in failure than he does here. At any rate, with the unfortunate interruption of *Il finto cieco* out of the way, he was able to get back to his contemplations. A few months later he completed *Le nozze di Figaro.*

Da Ponte was not so gentle with Giovanni Bertati. Of all the Italian librettists he disliked, he disliked Bertati more than most. It may be that Bertati was not very likeable. His biographer, Ulderico Rolandi, speaks of his "harshness of temperament" and quotes a fellow Venetian whom we have already met, Giuseppe Maria Foppa, who accuses Bertati of "zelotypia," that is, burning jealousy, toward his fellow writers. Although Foppa adds that "his conduct in general was never blameworthy," one is curious to know what thought lay behind the qualifying expression "in general."[79] Bertati never married. He was not a physically attractive man. A colleague described him as short of stature but of voluminous size, with a fleshy, oval face, tiny black shiny eyes, and quick, lively movements that were quite unsuitable to his stocky figure.[80] To be fair, this description is of an elderly Bertati, who, in the later years of his life, having given up the theater, worked in Venice as a civil servant from 1798 until his death in 1815.

Bertati was born in 1735 in Martellago, Treviso, a small country town near Venice. Because his family was poor, he was sent to study at a seminary in Treviso, the same school in which some years later Lorenzo Da Ponte would begin his career as a teacher. Bertati was evidently not cut out for the priesthood, for the next notice of him regards the opening in Venice in 1763 of an opera for which he had written the text and Antonio Tozzi the music: *La morte di Dimone.* He spent the following decades in Venice, where he turned out libretto after libretto, sometimes at the rate of three or four per year.

It was during this long period of Venetian residency that he wrote *Il capriccio drammatico* with its second act entitled *Don Giovanni o sia Il convitato di pietra. Il capriccio drammatico* was based on a libretto Bertati had prepared for Venetian

78. Da Ponte, *Memorie,* 163.

79. Ulderico Rolandi, *Il librettista del "Matrimonio segreto" Giovanni Bertati* (Tricase: Raeli, 1926), 18, 19. No source is given for Foppa's remark.

80. Giovanni Casoni, quoted in Rolandi, *Il librettista,* 19 (no source given).

performance twelve years earlier, in 1775. That opera was called *La novità*. Its second act, however, was not a one-act Don Juan story but a one-act "farsa all'uso francese" entitled *L'italiano a Parigi*. The music for both acts was by Felice Alessandri.[81] All in all Bertati wrote more than seventy librettos, most of them for the comic theater. Though his librettos were often prepared in haste and were sometimes rough, he always infused them with a strong sense of theatricality. For that reason, he was much sought after by the most prestigious composers of his day: Baldassarre Galuppi, Pasquale Anfossi, Giovanni Paisiello, Antonio Salieri, and Nicola Zingarelli, not to mention Gazzaniga, for whom he prepared eleven librettos.

Bertati was eventually invited to Vienna. In July 1791, he was offered Da Ponte's position as court poet after the latter's sudden and undignified exit from the court and the city for certain questionable activities and behavior that brought upon him the disfavor of well-placed court officials. It was as Viennese court poet that Bertati created his most popular libretto, the one for which he is still remembered today, *Il matrimonio segreto*. Domenico Cimarosa set it to music. It was given in 1792 and was a stunning success. Bertati retained his court post until 1794 but then went back to Venice where, a few years later, he gave up writing altogether. He said he was tired and preferred to earn his livelihood as an employee of the state.

In his letters, Mozart was as silent about Bertati as about his partner Gazzaniga. Da Ponte was another matter. He never missed a chance to slander him. In his memoirs, he listed Bertati among the "theatrical cobblers" (Nunziato Porta was there, too) who did not know how

> to write a play that could be tolerated, let alone considered worthy of being read or seen on stage, . . . who never knew the first thing about poetry, let alone the infinite number of rules, laws and notions that are necessary for the creation of a good play.[82]

He heaped scorn on Bertati's text for *Il matrimonio segreto*. He cites an on-again, off-again friend and fellow librettist, Giambattista Casti, who remarks that Bertati is "a poor old dimwit. He is preparing an opera for Cimarosa; he doesn't

81. *La novità* and *Il capriccio drammatico* have the same cast of characters and basically the same plot. However, *La novità* is much shorter and does not contain the remarks on *Il convitato di pietra* found in the revised libretto. A copy of the libretto at the Casa Goldoni indicates Bertati's authorship. *Indice*, 1775–76, 32, notes the fall 1775 performance and states: "Musica nuova del Sig. Maestro Alessandri."

82. Da Ponte, *Memorie*, 124. On p. 357 he again refers to Bertati as a "povero ciabattino drammatico."

deserve so much honor."[83] Because Da Ponte was not in Vienna for the opera's premiere, Casti wrote to him about it. Da Ponte quotes the letter.

> Yesterday evening *Il matrimonio segreto* was given for the first time. The music is marvelously beautiful, but the words turned out to be far less than expected, and everyone is unhappy with them, especially the singers. Everyone says: "Da Ponte won't leave this arrogant fellow unpunished." I'm sending you the libretto so that you can see and learn how to write beautiful poetry![84]

Da Ponte was delighted by Bertati's failure. After perusing his libretto, he spitefully replied to Casti that the verses were exactly what everyone should have expected. Vienna had gotten what it paid for.[85]

The difficulty with many musicians, complained Da Ponte at a later date, is that they are incapable of properly judging a libretto, they do not know "how much difference there is between the verses of Metastasio and those of Bertati or of Nunziato Porta."[86] Of course, the perceptive Mozart knew. "Why," asks Da Ponte with rhetoric ablaze, this time writing directly in English and with slight regard for historical fact,

> why did Mozart refuse to set to music the *Don Giovanni* (of evil memory) by Bertatti [*sic*], and offered to him by one Guardassoni, (non adhibeo testes dormientes) manager of the Italian theatre of Prague? Why did he insist upon having a book written by Da Ponte on the same subject, *and not by any other dramatist*? Shall I tell you why? Because Mozart knew very well that the success of an opera depends, FIRST OF ALL, ON THE POET.[87]

Bertati could hardly be called a poet. In Da Ponte's estimation, he was a hack, a drudge who depended on grammar books, rhyming dictionaries, and other playwrights' plots. That is the implication of the following passage from Da Ponte's memoirs, in which he recounts his only face-to-face meeting with his rival. Da Ponte had just fallen out of the good graces of the Viennese court and decided to pay a surprise visit on his successor.

---

83. Da Ponte, *Memorie,* 240.

84. Da Ponte, *Memorie,* 241.

85. Da Ponte, *Memorie,* 241.

86. Da Ponte, *Memorie,* 466.

87. Lorenzo da Ponte, *An Extract from the Life of Lorenzo Da Ponte* (New York: Grey, 1819), 17–18. Actually, Mozart did write something on a text by Bertati: two *scene* in 1785 inserted into Francesco Bianchi's *La villanella rapita* for which Bertati had written the libretto.

> More than anyone else, the new theater poet was anxious to know if I intended to leave Vienna or to take up residency there again. I knew his work, but not him. He had written an infinite number of things and by dint of writing had somewhat learned the art of producing theatrical effects. But unfortunately for him, he was not a born poet and did not know Italian. As a consequence, it was easier to put up with his works on stage rather than to read them. I took it into my head to meet him. I went to visit him in high spirits. When I reached his residence, he was talking with one of the singers at the door of his room. I approached him. He asked me my name; I told him that I had had the honor of being his predecessor and that my name was Da Ponte. He seemed struck by a bolt of lightning. Looking very embarrassed and confused, he asked me how he could be of service, but always remaining in the doorway. When I told him that I had something to communicate to him, he found himself obliged to have me enter his room, which he did with some reluctance. He offered me a seat in the middle of the room. Without any ulterior motive, I sat down near a table where, as I gathered from its appearance, he was accustomed to do his writing. Seeing me seated, he too sat down in an armchair and rapidly began to close up a number of messy note pads and books which completely covered the table. Nonetheless, I had a chance to see what books they were for the most part. A tome of French plays, a dictionary, a rhymer and Corticelli's grammar were all to the right of our Mr. Poet. I could not see the ones that he had to the left. I then believed I understood the reason why he did not want to let me enter. He asked me again how he could help me, and I, having no other ready excuse, said that I had come to visit him for the pleasure of meeting a man of such great merit and to ask him to give me a copy of my work that, at my departure from Vienna, I had forgotten to take with me. Looking at me with disparagement, he said that he had nothing to do with my books, which were being sold for the management by the custodian of the theater boxes. After remaining another ten minutes with him and after having recognized in every possible way that Mr. Bertati the poet was nothing more than a windbag, I took my leave.[88]

After leaving Vienna in disgrace, Da Ponte went to London where he was hired as poet in residence at the King's Theater, Haymarket. There he clashed with another poet, a certain Carlo Badini. Writing to Giacomo Casanova in January 1793, Da Ponte sought to say of Badini the worst that he could think of: As far

88. Da Ponte, *Memorie,* 238–39.

as concerns the theater, he wrote venomously, Badini knows even "less than Bertati's shoes."[89]

Why all this anger? Perhaps Bertati was truly irascible and combative. But perhaps Da Ponte was jealous—jealous of the other librettist's successes, angry at his own failures. For in his *Memorie,* Da Ponte never tells all. He does not tell us that his first libretto in Vienna—the one for Vincenzo Righini entitled *Il ricco di un giorno*—had been adapted from one by Bertati. Da Ponte's adaptation was a failure. He does not tell us that a great deal of his *Don Giovanni* libretto for Mozart was closely copied from Bertati's Don Juan text. Nor does he tell us that, as his first assignment in London, he made a new arrangement of Bertati's most famous text, the one he and Giambattista Casti had so sharply criticized, *Il matrimonio segreto.* He does mention that two months later, in March 1794, his theater presented the Bertati-Gazzaniga one-act *Don Giovanni,* but he presents the information in such a way as to downgrade the Bertati-Gazzaniga work and bolster his own good image.

> It was at the performance of Gazzaniga's *Don Giovanni,* an opera proposed by Federici [music director of the King's Theater] and offered to the public on his advice, a bestial preference over Mozart's *Don Giovanni* brought to London and proposed by me, that Taylor [managing director] . . . found himself running the risk of seeing his theater dismantled and himself ruined forever.[90]

If only Taylor had entrusted himself to Da Ponte's superior tastes! Once again Da Ponte "proved" that Bertati was a failure. But what he does not mention once again is that he had tried to pass the work off as his own. The libretto reads: "The words are new, by L. da Ponte, poet of this theater, except those that are not marked with inverted commas."[91] The text, in fact, is a mishmash of Bertati and Da Ponte, the music a mishmash of Gazzaniga, Sarti, Federici, and Guglielmi, with Mozart's catalog song thrown in for good measure. The production was withdrawn after two performances. Was Da Ponte pleased that it had such a limited run? It is hard to have it both ways.[92]

---

89. P. Molmenti, *Carteggi casanoviani: Lettere di Giacomo Casanova e di altri a lui* (Naples: Sandron, 1916), 273.

90. Da Ponte, *Memorie,* 264. Da Ponte also ignores the fact that this London *Don Giovanni* was the second act of a full evening's performance that bore Bertati's comprehensive title of *Il capriccio drammatico,* just as it had in Venice.

91. Lorenzo Da Ponte, quoted in Kunze, *Don Giovanni vor Mozart,* 137.

92. Some years before he published his *Memorie,* Da Ponte made a similar criticism of this production. In his *Extract* (17), published in 1819, he wrote:

As already indicated, not all of *Il capriccio drammatico* had to do with the Don Juan legend. Indeed, the first act concerns a company of Italian opera singers performing in an unnamed German city. The Germans, "either deaf or without taste" (iii), do not seem to appreciate high-class Italian opera and are staying away from the theater in droves, so that the company is undergoing very stressful financial difficulties. The company's impresario, Policastro, desperate because he sees his financial reserves dwindling away, is convinced that his singers must prepare an opera more attractive to low-class German taste. The opera he suggests is *Il convitato di pietra.* The assembled troupe of virtuosos is horrified and refuses to perform such trash. They are *artistes,* not comedians. But when Policastro threatens to withhold their pay, they give in. The second act of *Il capriccio drammatico* is, then, their version of the Don Juan legend.

While the first act of *Il capriccio drammatico* is entertaining as a backstage look at the difficulties of eighteenth-century opera production, it would be of

---

> In the year 1796 [1794], the manager of the Haymarket Theatre wanted an opera. I proposed to him the Don Giovanni of Mozart, and obtained the Spartito from Vienna. Federici, who was at that time one of the theatrical rulers, opposed its performance, insisting that the music was not fit for the English taste. The Don Giovanni of Bertatti, with the music of Gazziniga [*sic*] was then performed: and the opera house was in the most imminent danger of being pulled down by the subscribers.

Sheila Hodges (*Lorenzo Da Ponte: The Life and Times of Mozart's Librettist* [New York: Universe Books, 1985], 139) cites a review from the *Times* of 10 March 1794 that states that the opera "was throughout disapproved. So determined an opposition to this kind of entertainment we have never witnessed." Yet contemporary comments reported by William C. Smith (*The Italian Opera and Contemporary Ballet in London 1789–1820* [London: Society for Theater Research, 1955], 28–29) do not corroborate the opinion of Da Ponte or the *Times.* From the *Morning Chronicle,* 3 March 1794: "Negri sang with fine taste and feeling." From the *Oracle,* 3 March: "The Italian gentry must *pantomime* it more—they really stand as dull as some of our own actors, with one eye upon the Prompter, and the other upon the Leader of the Band, beating time with both hand and foot like children in the science." Again from the *Morning Chronicle,* 3 March:

> The decorations were admirable—particularly what M. Noverre calls his *practicable hell,* in which Marinari has displayed very fine talents. It is wonderful what an effect of fire he has produced by the power of transparencies. . . . The House was in all parts crowded, and by the blaze of torches with a red reflection from the scene, threw flashes of light into the boxes, which had a most superb effect, in the way of spectacle.

It seems that the "imminent danger" Da Ponte spoke of and the risk run by Taylor of seeing his theater "dismantled" were hardly due to the Bertati text, as Da Ponte would like his readers to believe, but either to the use of backstage fire or, much more likely, to problems with the ballet in which, as Deryck Lynham writes in *The Chevalier Noverre: Father of Modern Ballet* (London: Sylvan Press 1950), 112, "a funeral procession of over one hundred persons, attired in Spanish period costumes, had to cross the stage but, on the first night, the press of uninvited mourners was such that the artists could barely move and, at subsequent performances, the ban on members of the audience coming on to the stage had to be enforced."

little interest now were it not for a kind of subtext running throughout it. When Policastro orders his singers to prepare a Don Juan opera, they do not hesitate to give him their frank opinions of the tale. The first act of this opera is not only an insider's view of backstage opera life, it is also an angry discussion of the Don Juan legend. The collective views of the company represent an up-to-the-minute view of the way in which the legend was generally regarded in 1787. What emerges from the singers' comments is a tale so without worth or value that one wonders how or why Mozart or Da Ponte would have chosen it. It is the troupe's opinion that the story best befits the comic actors of the commedia dell'arte, who had been giving rowdy performances of it for an ignorant, low-class public for two centuries.[93] A leading lady huffs: "The action is improbable and the libretto ignores all the proper rules" (ii). Another character bluntly predicts that the new opera will turn out to be "a stupendous piece of hogwash" (vi). Policastro is a knowledgeable man of the theater; he is aware that, from an artistic point of view, his singers are not entirely wrong. He recognizes that their criticisms differ little from those voiced earlier by Goldoni and his predecessors. He admits that the work he has proposed, even though descended from Tirso and Molière, is full of awkwardnesses and defects, but, like so many writers and producers before him, he promises to make up for its weaknesses with good music, interesting scenery, and exciting showstoppers. Therefore, astute and practical impresario that he is, he insists.

I imagine that Mozart and Da Ponte settled on the legend for fundamentally the same reason that Policastro did, and for that matter for the same reason that Bertati and Gazzaniga did too, and not they alone, but Lorenzi and Tritto, Porta and Righini, Le Tellier, Shadwell, Villiers, Cicognini, and even Molière. They chose it because bad taste pays. Policastro defends himself in the following way.

Si bada a quel che piace, e spesse volte
si fanno più denari
con delle strampalate
di quello che con cose
studiate, regolate e giudiziose.

(ii)

93. La fanno i commedianti
da due secoli in qua con del schiamazzo,
ma solamente per il popolazzo.

(xi)

> [We pay attention to what people like,
> and we often make more money
> with nonsense,
> than with careful,
> well-put-together, sensible things.]

Yet I also suspect that some who chose to work with the story also had another reason as well. They sensed that if the legend had had a vigorous existence for 30, 50, 100, or 150 years, it must have also possessed an undeniable validity. The legend of Don Juan could not have endured had it not reflected a need, had it not spoken to the needs and desires of those who watched it: the pleasures of being wicked and the pleasures of being good, the satisfactions of sexuality and the satisfactions of justice. For quiet people, the legend expressed unspoken longings and desires. For them it held meanings that transcended an awkward story and improbable actions. By many people, the essence of the legend was understood quite well indeed. In Bertati and Gazzaniga it did not find artists capable of clearly illustrating those meanings. But often in Da Ponte and always in Mozart, it found a voice able to transcend all awkwardnesses and all improbabilities so as to express with clarity and simplicity its truest and profoundest messages.

Bertati, in spite of his criticisms of the legend in the first act of *Il capriccio drammatico,* still tried to put together as good a Don Juan libretto as he knew how, and his efforts were rewarded by more than fifty productions of the opera between 1787 and the end of the century. He prepared a standard, no-frills tale with a standard, no-frills Don Giovanni; he recreated the usual, attractive, fearless, and unrepentant figure that publics expected. He did not twist the story out of shape as Foppa did or demean the Don Juan figure as Lorenzi had. There is nothing out of the ordinary about his version. Compared to the many that preceded it, nothing in his version stands forth as particularly innovative or insightful. His libretto was simply a competent theatrical job that, when fitted out with Gazzaniga's music, more than adequately met the expectations and approbations of a general public that probably wanted nothing less, but certainly expected nothing more.

Nonetheless, the libretto is lacking. Not that Bertati lacked technical know-how, seriousness of purpose, or artistic integrity. What he lacked, at least as far as concerns this libretto, was even the smallest touch of genius. Not always, but every now and then, Da Ponte was brushed by its wing. Bertati's libretto is competent, but it is pedestrian in a way that Da Ponte's never is. Da Ponte was right. Bertati was a cobbler. He stitched together scenes without giving much thought to such things as character development or overall artistic unity: a good number of scenes from Molière, something from the commedia dell'arte, perhaps an idea or two from Tirso, and, to be fair, something now and then from his own imagination. But his was not a creative imagination that could penetrate deeply into the mind and soul of his characters, it could not grapple with the true problems they faced. His characters are shallow and dull, and their tale lacks unifying force and conviction. The cobbler created a good pair of walking shoes, sturdy but not very attractive.

These defects did not hinder Da Ponte from borrowing from Bertati and from borrowing extensively. Da Ponte shamelessly dipped his pen into Bertati's inkwell, for shame and embarrassment were never among Da Ponte's strongest virtues. To read Bertati's version is to read much of Da Ponte's *in nuce.* There are extenuating circumstances. The art of borrowing was nothing out of the ordinary, a practice long sanctioned by tradition and exercised not only by lesser artists but by the very best. The legend of Don Juan was in the public domain and a borrower's paradise. There was also a more personal reason. Da Ponte was under pressure. He was working on three librettos at the same time: *Tarare* for Salieri, *L'arbore di Diana* for Martín y Soler, and this one for Mozart. In his *Memorie,* he claims that, by the end of the first day of work, he had completed two scenes of *L'arbore,* more than half of the first act of *Tarare,* and the first two scenes of *Don Giovanni.*[94] What he does not mention is the fact that he had a copy of Bertati's libretto at his elbow. The first two scenes of the libretto for Mozart were directly structured on Bertati's text.

Da Ponte's borrowings from Bertati throughout his libretto are many and generally quite evident. The most important include the startling opening scene—Don Giovanni's postentry flight, Donna Anna's pursuit, and the murder of her father (of course Bertati himself owes serious debts to Gasparo Angiolini)—as well as a fully developed country wedding episode with detailed seduction of the bride and humiliating harassment of the groom; an abandoned Donna Elvira (whose name appears in operatic literature for the first time in Bertati's text), first angry and vengeful, then loving and piteous (big debts must obviously be paid to Molière); Duca Ottavio back onstage again in all his weakness imploring Donna Anna to marry him; a list of conquests not just in name but also in song (what we have in Bertati is, indeed, the first true catalog aria); Don Giovanni dragged to hell at his own dinner party, not, as usually happened, at a return meal served by the statue in his mausoleum—the three meetings of tradition with the statue have been shortened by Bertati to two.

94. Da Ponte, *Memorie,* 190.

But there are things that Da Ponte did not borrow. He did not borrow Bertati's pedestrian rhymes.

> Un'alma nobile, no, in te non v'è.
> Per dove fuggasi non so più affè.
>
> (ii)
>
> [No noble soul's in you, it's clear.
> I don't know where to flee, oh dear.]

Da Ponte's rhymes are richer, less predictable. He did not borrow Bertati's generic verse, such as the colorless lines between Don Giovanni and his servant Pasquariello following the Commendatore's murder. Pasquariello is asking what happened.

PAS: E il vecchio? Se n'è ito?
D. GIO: È morto, o mortalmente io l'ho ferito.
PAS: Bravo! Due azioni eroiche:
Donn'Anna violentata
e al padre una stoccata.
D. GIO: Ehi, te l'ho detto ancora
che non vo' rimostranze.
Seguimi e taci. Andiamo.
PAS: Sì, signore.
(Simular mi convien perchè ho timore.)

(ii)

[PAS: And the old man? Has he left?
D. GIO: He's dead, or I wounded him mortally.
PAS: Good for you! Two heroic actions:
Donna Anna violated
and a sword-thrust at her father.
D. GIO: Listen, I've told you before
that I don't want your criticisms.
Follow me and keep quiet. Let's go.
PAS: Yes, sir.
(I'd best put on a good front, because I'm scared.)]

Da Ponte appropriated the scene, but he rewrote it so that a tough Don Giovanni and a leering and equivocal Leporello sprang to life.

LEP: Chi è morto, voi o il vecchio?
D. GIO: Che domanda da bestia! Il vecchio.
LEP: Bravo!
Due imprese leggiadre:
sforzar la figlia, ed ammazzar il padre.
D. GIO: L'ha voluto: suo danno.
LEP: Ma Donn'Anna
cosa ha voluto?
D. GIO: Taci,
non mi seccar! Vien meco, se non vuoi
qualche cosa ancor tu.
LEP: Non vo' nulla, signor: non parlo più.

(I ii)

[LEP: Who's dead, you or the old man?
D. GIO: What a stupid question! The old man.
LEP: Good for you.
Two fine undertakings;
violating the daughter and killing her father.
D. GIO: He asked for it: so much the worse for him.
LEP: And Donna Anna,
what did she ask for?
D. GIO: Keep quiet;
you get on my nerves. Follow me,
unless you're asking for something too.
LEP: I don't want anything, sir; I won't say another word.]

Da Ponte never created a trivial scene or a trivial character. Bertati trivialized both. In Da Ponte, Donna Elvira, in her clumsy but generous, warm-blooded, and embracing way, tries to save Zerlina from Don Giovanni and from moral ruin: "Get away from this treacherous man. . . . You must learn from my pain" (I.x). Bertati, at the equivalent moment between Donna Elvira and Maturina, lets the scene slip toward the farce of female jealousies and the language of housemaids.

D. Elv: Vanne via, va', pazzarella,
ch'ei non ama una sardella.
Mat: Via pur voi, correte in fretta,
ch'ei non ama una polpetta.

(xviii)

[D. Elv: Get out of here, you daffy dish,
do you think he can love a skinny fish?
Mat: *You* get out fast! You've got real gall;
do you think he can love a fat meat ball?]

Bertati's figures lack the sharpness of insight and precision of character definition that Da Ponte will give them. Donna Anna, after the death of her father, completely disappears from the story. Donna Ximena remains, but she drifts in and out, one is really not ever quite sure why. Maturina, although she does many of the things that Zerlina will do, is *not* Zerlina: she is not yet sufficiently grasping and ambitious and duplicitous; she is not yet in focus. Fascinated by Don Giovanni and anxious to run off with him and be rid of her awkward husband-to-be, she asks Biagio to leave them alone a moment, but her words are flat, they lack conviction of character: "Go, Biagio, be patient" (xii). In the same circumstance, Zerlina speaks with infinitely greater craftiness and wickedness to her about-to-be-discarded husband: "Go, don't be afraid, I'm in the hands of a gentleman" (I.viii). Pasquariello, too, is for the most part the pale figure of a servant whose personality and actions lack a clearly defined profile, dictated as they are by essentially a single negative factor, fear, used by Bertati as a tiring leitmotif throughout the text. Missing in Pasquariello is the ambivalence of a Leporello, his twisting and turning under the moral light of conscience, his voyeuristic admiration and envy of Don Giovanni's social position and sexual conquests, his sentimental pity for Don Giovanni's victims, and his spontaneous though plebian understanding of spiritual matters.

Da Ponte eschewed one-dimensionality, the easy laugh, the facile, entertaining solution. Right or wrong, successful or not, he pushed things to their extremes. His characters have no limitations. If sometimes not completely comprehensible, he always made his figures grand. Bertati did not. There are many indications, small but telling, of their divergent methods: Bertati the cobbler, Da Ponte the risk taker. Da Ponte's betrayed Donna Elvira has a grandeur of spirit that, tempered by love and suffering, embraces all humanity; Bertati's betrayed Donna Elvira sings a humorous but trivial antimale aria (vi). Bertati's Don Giovanni is not immediately certain if he has killed the Commendatore outright or not (ii). In Da Ponte's text, the killing efficiency of Don Giovanni's sword is never in doubt. Bertati's Don Giovanni refuses to sleep with old women; Da Ponte's suffers no restrictions. In Da Ponte's libretto, three times and more the statue commands Don Giovanni to repent; in Bertati's, he does so only twice.

Da Ponte recognizes that the consequence of pushing outward, pushing to extremes, requires the inevitable death of his hero, a death that he accepts as right and just and the meaning of which he does not attempt to ignore or hide. He concludes his story with jubilation, with a celebration of the triumph of justice over wickedness: he and his onstage players have been witness to the proper and fitting end of an evildoer, of a dissolute who had upset the harmony of their lives, and they rejoice. Not so Bertati. He has not been able to stretch himself; he has not fully grasped the deeper significances of the legend; he seems, therefore, unable to speak of what has happened within his libretto. At the end of his tale, he falls backward, away from extremes, away from words and thoughts, into pathetic vaudeville comedy, untouched by or unable to comprehend the vision that he has had. He and his characters refuse to recognize the meaning of the fearful event they have witnessed. Let's not say another word about it, they sing; let's think only about having fun. And so they choose to end their opera with a simple entertainment from the past. As the final curtain descends, they sing and dance a lively but mindless chorus in which Passarino imitates the sounds of a bassoon and Duca Ottavio pretends to be a guitar. Don Giovanni's death has taught them nothing.

In Da Ponte's text it has. In his text, the very same figures rejoice, following the death of sin, that their world has been cleansed, renewed, and reordered. All persons touched by Don Giovanni's bright flame unite to celebrate his damnation in words and music that breathe out a heady, ferocious joy: this prodigious event we have witnessed is the just reward of those who do evil; the death of wicked men is always a reflection of their lives.

> Questo è il fin di chi fa mal:
> e de' perfidi la morte
> alla vita è sempre ugual!

Da Ponte recognized that his Don Giovanni was too grand a figure to be shunted aside in Bertati's trivial manner. No public could escape the demonic force of his disordering presence unscathed. They had seen him grasp avidly at self-fulfillment, at beauty, at creation, at time and eternity, regardless of the consequences. They had seen him offer up his very being. It did not matter that he had lost; the boldness, the fearlessness, the grandeur of his gesture moved and disturbed. Da Ponte recognized the dangerous consequences of Don Giovanni's heroic single-mindedness. He had to be punished, publicly and unequivocally.

As for Wolfgang Amadeus Mozart, the quiet man whose soul, like Dante's or Shakespeare's, embraced all men and whose own small, confined life must have seen in the figure of Don Juan an image of freedom, an image of freedom of the imagination, he may not have been quite so certain that Don Giovanni had to be condemned; by Da Ponte in his libretto, perhaps, but not by Mozart in his music. One cannot condemn one's own genius. And so, as the statue knocked upon Don Juan's door and Don Juan began to walk his downward path toward hell, Mozart undertook his apotheosis. The harsher and more insistent the statue's demands for repentance and justice, the more glorious the music that Mozart prepared; the closer Don Juan approached the fire, the more Mozart's music raised him up; the more wicked the man, the more heavenly the music. When at last Don Juan ended his life in time, he began it again in eternity through Mozart's music. For Mozart, Da Ponte's text served to open the way; through it he saw in the legend, more brightly than anyone before, what for 150 years had attracted and compelled. He seized Da Ponte's libretto, and with it he reignited the imagination of the world.

3

Don Juan Librettos

A Note on the Texts

The texts of the present collection have been prepared from original librettos located as follows: *La pravità castigata* (Bambini), Brno, Czechoslovakia; *Il convitato di pietra o sia Il dissoluto* (Righini and Porta), Křimice, Czechoslovakia; *Il convitato di pietra* (Calegari), Library of Congress, Washington, D.C.; *Il convitato di pietra* (Tritto and Lorenzi), Fondazione Cini, Venice; *Il nuovo convitato di pietra* (Gardi and Foppa), Library of Congress; *Il capriccio drammatico* and *Don Giovanni o sia Il convitato di pietra* (Valentini, Gazzaniga and Bertati), Library of Congress. The text of *Il Don Giovanni* (Albertini) has been taken from a manuscript score in two volumes in the Conservatorio Luigi Cherubini, Florence.

In preparing these texts, punctuation, capitalization, and apostrophes have been made to conform to modern usage, although the original librettos have always served as a basis and as little as possible has been altered. In general, orthography has not been modified or modernized except in those few cases in which the spelling of a word used only once did not seem characteristic of the libretto as a whole. For example, in Righini, *soppiato* has been changed to *soppiatto*. Words repeated within a single libretto with variant spellings have been left as in the original: *Arlecchino* / *Arlechino, Commendatore* / *Comendatore.* Obvious mistakes or typographical errors have been corrected: *sospenderci* changed to *sorprenderci* (Calegari), *salatio* to *salario* (Bambini). For the passages in Neapolitan dialect in the Tritto and Lorenzi libretto, Vanda Monaco's *Giambattista Lorenzi e la commedia per musica* proved to be an indispensable guide.

In all texts, the verse scansion of the recitatives, *settenari* and *endecasillabi* almost without exception, has been restored as much as possible and put into evidence typographically. In this regard, some of the original librettos were very carefully printed, others far less so; the Righini and Porta libretto was particularly poorly done. Arias have been set apart, with the first line of each stanza indented several spaces. Ensembles have likewise been set apart and every change in meter marked by an indentation.

Notes have been kept to a minimum. Odd words or obscure references have been briefly explained when possible. No modern edition of these texts exists except for Bertati's *Capriccio* and *Don Giovanni,* which can be found in Stefan Kunze, *Don Giovanni vor Mozart.* The Lorenzi comedy published by Monaco is a revised version of the 1783 original libretto, from which it differs considerably.

La pravità castigata

EUSTACHIO BAMBINI

1734

LA PRAVITÀ CASTIGATA
drama per musica
da rappresentarsi
nel Teatro Novissimo della Taverna
Consecrato
agl'Illustrissimi & Eccellentissimi Signori da S.M.C. e Catt. Nominati Regolatori nell'Economico della Reggia Città di Bruna Cive
Illustrissimo & Eccellentissimo Sig.
FRANCESCO MICHELE
Schubürz, Libero Barone di Chobinie, Signore di Jaromeritz, Consigliere Intimo di S.M.C. e Catt. e Supremo Giudice Provinciale del Marchesato di Moravia
Ed
Illustrissimo Signore, Signore
FRANCESCO CASIMIRO,
Libero Barone di Moravetz, Signore di Moravetz e Mitrou, Consigliere di S.M.C. e Catt., Giudice Accessore Provinciale e Regio Capitano del Distretto di Bruna nel Marchesato di Moravia
Ed
Illustrissimo Signore
FRIDERICO GIORGIO ZIALKOVSKY
de' Zialkovitz, Signore di Hosolitz e Feudo Oben Moschtienitz, Consigliere di S.M.C. e Catt., Giudice Accessore Provinciale, e Regio Cameriere nel Marchesato di Moravia
Nel Carnevale dell'Anno M DCC XXXIV
In Bruna nella Stamperia di Giacomo Massimiliano Swoboda

Illustrissimi
et
Eccellentissimi
SSig.ri SSig.ri e Pat.ni Col.mi

L'aver le SS.e VV.e Ill.e & Ecc.e, con atto della loro ingenita virtù e propensione al virtuoso ricreo della musica, effetuata l'idea per la continuazione d'un così nobile trattenimento nell'erezzione del nuovo sontuoso teatro in questa reggia città, incoraggisce presentemente il mio rispetto a consacrare alle SSig.e VV.e Ill.e & Ecc.e la PRAVITÀ CASTIGATA, eroicomica rappresentazione di singolare piacere. Mi vo speranzando con tal mezzo di veder che ne venga impedito l'attentato d'un qualche zoilo contro la medema sul riflesso all'alto patrocinio, che fortunatamente viene a godere delle SS. VV. Ill. & Ecc., & in gualche parte resti consolato il mio cuore, che altro non ambisce che l'occasione di manifestarle l'umile e riverente sua servitù. Accettino per tanto le SSig. VV. Ill. & Ecc. questo picciolo tributo in segno di quella venerazione con la quale mi do l'onore, e presentemente e in avvenire, di potermi soscrivere con profondissimo osseguio

Delle SSig.e VV.e Ill.e & Ecc.e
Bruna, 20 Febraro 1734
Umil. Dev. & Obb. Servitore
Angelo Mingotti

Lettore Discreto

Non essendovi il minimo antefatto che porti delucidazione all'intreccio, ti risparmio la lettura dell'argomento, il quale sentirai molto chiaro in bocca dei personaggi, se averai l'attenzion d'ascoltarli, in una favella studiatamente assai bassa.

Il motivo principal che m'indusse a scegliere questo non nuovo soggetto è a punto il saperlo invecchiato su tutte le scene d'Europa e che però non lascia di fare annualmente la sua reiterata comparsa, sempre in quella figura che fa la sposa novella fra un folto stuolo di venerande matrone, tutto che sempre senza quel grande equipaggio ch'ora (cred'io poter giustamente vantarmi) per la prima volta lo adorna, senza punto alterarlo nella sua degna sostanza.

Egli non può essere più esemplare, perchè si vede punita dell'ultima pena la scelleratezza dal cielo; non più mirabile, perchè ciò segue con raro e duplicato prodigio; e non finalmente più ameno, perchè la foggia varia de' vestimenti, la frequente mutazion del teatro, la misura (qual ella siasi) del verso e la musica delle arie (avventurosamente ottenuta) d'un autore di cui si compiace frequentemente il primo monarca del mondo, li danno una estraordinaria vaghezza.

Questi sono i motivi che m'hanno incoraggito ad esporlo, li quali aduco non già ai bene affetti al teatro, ma solo a chi preocupato già fosse dai soliti falsi rapporti di chi dovrebbe, per strettissimo debito, tacerne anche i veri.

Vieni, vedi, e gradisci, almen per instinto della tua gentilezza.

ATTORI

Manfredi, re di Napoli
La sig. Laura Bambini di Pesaro
Don Alvaro, comendatore di Sant'Iago, e ministro del re
Il sig. Giuseppe Alberti di Padova
Donna Isabella, di lui figliola promessa in moglie al duca
La sig. Teresa Peruzzi detta Denzia di Venezia
Don Garzia, gonsigliero del re
N.N.
Donna Beatrice, dama di corte
La sig. Chiara Orlandi di Mantova
Don Ottavio, duca di Chiarenza, sposo di Donna Isabella
Il sig. Domenico Battaglini
Don Giovanni, forastiero in Napoli
La sig. Rosa Cardini di Venezia
Rosalba, pescatrice, abitante la spiaggia vicina a Napoli
La sig. Cecilia Monti
Malorco, servo di Don Giovanni
Il sig. Bartolomeo Caio

La musica è del sig. Eustachio Bambini di Pesaro a riserva d'alcune arie. La scena è in Napoli.

MUTAZIONI DI SCENA

Nell'atto primo

I Spiaggia di mare con veduta della città di Napoli in lontano e capanna sul lido. Filuca che approda a quello.

II Gabinetti reali nella reggia di Napoli.

III Sala regia illuminata di notte per la conversazione di corte.

Nell'atto secondo

IV Atrio superiore nella reggia.

V Veduta esterna del reale palazzo, con scale corrispondenti da quello a magnifica loggia inferiore.

Nell'atto terzo

VI Tempio alla gottica con statoa equestre e sepolcro dell'ucciso Comendatore, istoriato con varie statoe e militari trofei.

VII Appartamenti di Donna Isabella.

VIII Sala vastissima con aparato di lauta mensa.

IX Stanze del re.

X Bosco fuori di Napoli, che si cangia in

XI orribil caverna con aparato di mensa logubre.

XII Gabinetto reale.

XIII Prigione infernale per supplicio dei reprobi.

Duplicato volo del Comendatore.

Voragine che inabissa Don Giovanni e la mensa.

ATTO PRIMO

Scena i

Spiaggia di mare con veduta della città di Napoli in lontano; povera capanna di pescatrice sulla spiaggia sudetta.

Don Giovanni e Malorco, mezzi spogliati, a nuoto per l'onde, e dalla capanna a soccorerli la pescatrice Rosalba

D. GIO: Aita!
MAL: Aiu . . . to!
D. GIO: O cielo,
pietà; mi pento.
MAL: Aiu . . .
ROSA: Ah! Due meschini
che si affogano in mar.
D. GIO: Cielo clemente,
salvami!
MAL: Aiu . . .
ROSA: Coraggio. *(entra)*
Presto, una fune.
D. GIO: O Dio,
prometto emenda; non sarò più infido.
ROSA: Eccomi: questa fune
stringete. *(li getta una fune a Don Giovanni)*
MAL: Aiu . . . to!
ROSA: Or via, già siete al lido.
D. GIO: Barbaro cielo.
MAL: Aiu . . .
D. GIO: *(uscendo dal mare)* Ninfa gentile,
siete pur bella!
MAL: *(uscendo anch'esso dal mare)*
O caro il mio barile,
mi tenesti sul mar sì ben sospeso
che in memoria del fatto
ti voglio ognor portare al collo appeso. *(se lo appende)*
ROSA: Allegramente, mio signor, dal mare
siete, grazia del ciel, già preservato.
D. GIO: Che cielo? A voi, mio ben, sono obligato.

MAL: Eh, ehi, patron, è questo
"Cielo, pietà, mi pento?"
Nel periglio
parlai senza consiglio.
MAL: Bravo, bravo;
parlate pur così.
D. GIO: Quanto vezzosa
voi siete.
ROSA: Lei mi burla.
D. GIO: Non burlo, no; dovete esser mia sposa.
ROSA: Che sento!
MAL: (E ottantasette!)
D. GIO: Il vostro nome?
ROSA: Rosalba.
MAL: Et io Malorco.
D. GIO: Io Don Giovanni,
per voto fatto in mar, vostro consorte.
ROSA: Son poverella ed orfana.
D. GIO: Tal sorte
per ciò vi tocca.
MAL: (E grande!)
ROSA: Ho certi panni
che portò, giorni sono,
al lido in una cassa irato il mare;
meco venite, ch'io ve li vuo' dare
da rivestirvi, già che promettete
d'essermi sposo; ma non mi burlate.
D. GIO: Io burlarvi?
MAL: Eh, pensate.
D. GIO: Ecco la destra.
ROSA: Et ecco, (oh gran fortuna),
Rosalba avventurata,
che fra le braccia sue sposa vi accoglie.
D. GIO: Vi prendo per mia moglie.
MAL: (Ah, turco bianco!)
ROSA: Mi sarete poi fido?
D. GIO: Sempre al fianco
m'avrete.
ROSA: O me felice!

MAL: (E non posso parlar, ch'è troppo bestia
costui.) *(facendo moto di no a Rosalba)*

ROSA: Se non giurate, io non vi credo.

D. GIO: Scellerato, ti vedo. *(a Malorco, vedutolo a far cenni)*

MAL: Sì a me? Non parlo.

D. GIO: Udite:
Prego il ciel che mi faccia,
se mai da sue promesse il cor s'arretra,
uccidere da un uom, (ma sia di pietra). *(a Malorco)*

Se un bell'ardire può innamorarti,
non arrossire nè vergognarti
di quello strale che ti piagò;
a chi fu chiaro per grandi imprese,
amor dal paro di quel mi rese,
e della sorte mi riderò.

Scena ii

Donna Isabella, Donna Beatrice ed il Duca con seguito di paggi e servi; e nobil filuca che approda al lido.

D. ISA: Eccoci al lido. Basta,
Duca Ottavio, fin qui. Voi l'improvisa
mia partenza vi prego d'iscusare
con le amiche.

DUCA: Mancare
sanno ben che non può Donna Isabella.

D. BEA: E poi, cagion sì bella
abbastanza v'iscusa.

DUCA: Il genitore
andate a riveder nel suo ritorno
da Lusitania, già gran tempo atteso.

D. BEA: Or s'avvicina il giorno
in cui veder di vostre nozze io spero
stretto il nodo felice.

DUCA: Sì, sì, Donna Beatrice,
de' nostri cari dì questi è il foriero.

D. ISA: Tanto piacere in petto
non più, mia cara, aspetto *(a Donna Beatrice)*
quant'è questo piacer;
perchè del genitore
non dovrà più il mio core,
lontan così, temer.

Scena iii

Don Giovanni in osservazione con Malorco, e Donna Beatrice col Duca, che tornano indietro doppo imbarcata nella filuca Donna Isabella, cercando un cinto gemmato perduto da Donna Beatrice e raccolto da Malorco furtivamente.

D. BEA: O sventura. Ho perduto
il mio cinto gemmato.
DUCA: E dove mai?
D. BEA: Non so.
MAL: (Io l'ho trovato,
ma non lo rendo già.)
D. GIO: Che vaga dama!
Senti, Malorco.
MAL: Ho grandi affari.
D. GIO: Ascolta.
(Malorco fugge seguito da Don Giovanni)
MAL: Sentirò un'altra volta.
DUCA: Olà, servi; cercate
di questa dama il cinto.
D. BEA: Per trovarlo
torniam sui nostri passi.
(entrano con li servi cercando)
D. GIO: Fermati.
MAL: Che fracassi!
D. GIO: *(uscendo di nuovo)* Impertinente,
vien qua.
MAL: La vostra parte
se pretendete, non vuo' darvi niente.
D. GIO: Bramo la dama e non il cinto. Lascia *(togliendolo il cinto)*
ch'io te lo serbi. In tanto
pensa a bene esequir. Vedi la bella,

che sta pronta all'imbarco
per Napoli?

MAL: Gnor sì.

D. GIO: Devi a quel molo
giunger prima di lei, ed indi, cauto,
seguirla in fin che vedi
qual fia l'albergo suo.

MAL: Sto male in piedi
per far presto un tal viaggio.

D. GIO: Olà! *(minacciandolo)*

MAL: Bel bello. Vuol vossignoria
ch'io vada a far la spia?

D. GIO: Sempre onorata
quando serve ad amor.

MAL: Bel sentimento
da cavaglier! Lasciate
una volta gli amori ed ascoltate
d'un fido servo il buon consiglio.

D. GIO: Taci,
e vanne ad esequir.

MAL: Nol farò mai.

D. GIO: E tu 'l cinto da me più non avrai.

MAL: Come? Quello è già mio. Saria ben bella.
Non voglio, non lo devo, e far nol posso.
Ma lei non venga rosso [*sic*]
che queste azzioni son disonorate?

D. GIO: E cento bastonate, *(in atto di bastonarlo)*
cosa saranno? Di'!

MAL: Non fate il bravo.

D. GIO: Dunque, esequisci.

MAL: Subito.
Baston, cinto e salario, io vi son schiavo.

(Malorco parte per Napoli, e Don Giovanni torna nella capanna)

Scena iv

Donna Beatrice, Duca e servi.

DUCA: Ricercato l'abbiam fin ora in vano.
D. BEA: Pazienza. Vada il cinto,
lieve perdita al fine,
e sia de' mali miei questo il confine.

Nel ritorno che fa al nido
non trovando i cari figli,
sta piangendo la rondinella;
tiene in moto l'ali e il piede;
ma se riede e non li vede,
più non piange e non gl'appella.
(Donna Beatrice entra nella filuca, e Duca Ottavio ritorna a dietro)

Scena v

Rosalba e Don Giovanni

ROSA: Come, signor, volete *(trattenendolo)*
partir senza di me?
D. GIO: Rosalba, adio.
ROSA: Con voi ne vengo anch'io.
D. GIO: Resta, che stanco
io sono omai di te; mi sei noiosa.
ROSA: Annoiarvi la sposa? Ingrato! Infido!
D. GIO: Mia sposa? Me ne rido.
ROSA: Non mi daste
di marito la fede?
D. GIO: Pazza e ben in amor ad uomo crede.
ROSA: Dunque, son le promesse? . . .
D. GIO: Di queste io ne fo spesse.
ROSA: E il vostro voto?
D. GIO: Vada cogli altri a vuoto.
ROSA: Il giuramento?
D. GIO: Seco portollo il vento.
ROSA: Et il mio onore?

D. GIO: Le compiacenze mie lo fer maggiore.
Adio.

ROSA: Ferma, spietato, e i miei sospiri
ascolta per pietà.

D. GIO: Va' che deliri. *(la respinge e parte)*

ROSA: Tal mi schernisci, o perfido,
e nell'onor già lacera
sola mi lasci e misera?
Vattene pure, e piombino
sovra il tuo capo scellere
del giusto cielo i fulmini.
Sì; dell'inferno i demoni
ti strazino, o sacrilego,
l'empie ferine viscere,
indegne di goder l'aure di vita.
Vendetta, o giusto ciel; sono tradita.
(entra disperata)

Scena vi
Gabinetti reali nella reggia di Napoli.

Manfredi con guardie, ed indi Don Alvaro Comendatore

MAN: Abbia il Comendatore
da noi privata udienza.
Questi è un degno ministro,
specchio di fedeltà, zelo e prudenza.
Sedie. Commendatore.

COM: Umil vassallo
della vostra maestade a piè mi prostro.

MAN: Cuoprite, o amico. Il giubilo
abbonda in noi per il ritorno vostro.
Cuoprite, dissi.

COM: Alta bontà.

MAN: Siedete.

COM: Anzi che genuflesso, *(si prostra)*
dovrei . . .

MAN: Men complimenti, ed esponete.

COM: Ubbidisco. Volai, Sire insignito,
vostra mercè, col titolo glorioso
di Regio Ambasciator, in Lusitania.
Indicibili sono
da quella maestà gli alti favori
a me impartiti. Al fine,
all'armi de' fedeli in lega uniti
per fiaccar, dove oprossi
la nostra redenzione,[1] il turco orgoglio,
egli aggiunger promette
venti mila guerrieri in questo foglio. *(li porge una carta)*

MAN: Della vostra facondia
e del zelo regal non nuovi effetti.
Ai vassalli diletti, in la noturna
già solita assemblea, con noi sarete
a pubblicarli.

COM: Ubbidirò.

MAN: Basta, o amico. Al riposo
è omai tempo che andate,
e del vostro ritorno
goder l'unica figlia anche lasciate.

COM: Sarà fino alle ceneri
mia cura e mia ventura
preporre a tutti il re.
Tal è di buon vassallo
il debito e l'affetto;
precetto è della fè.

Scena vii
Manfredi solo.

Giubila, o cor; seconda il giusto cielo
de' suoi fedeli il zelo,
poichè gli ausili ancor del Lusitano

1. I.e., Jerusalem.

averemo all'impresa
contro il barbaro ardir dell'ottomano.

Pargoletto con mano innocente
lieto scherza con l'aspide algente,
ma s'il morde, languendo sen va.
Si diletta a quei vaghi colori
onde appar tutto adorno di fuori,
ma il velen che racchiude nol sa.

Scena viii
Strada magnifica in Napoli.

Donna Isabella e Donna Beatrice con servi, e Malorco in disparte.

D. ISA: Donna Beatrice, adio. Se fino in corte
non vi accompagno, condonate.
D. BEA: In vero
io doverei seguirvi
alle paterne case, ma sospendo
per non turbar con mia presenza, o amica,
li rissalti del core
che averete l'un l'altro in rivedervi,
figlia amorosa e amante genitore.

Scena ix
Duca, Donna Isabella, servi, e poi Don Giovanni

DUCA: Madama, s'io non erro,
giunsi (dopo adempito a' vostri cenni)
col mio legno veloce
in Napoli con voi nel tempo stesso.
D. ISA: Appunto; ora m'appresso
alle mura paterne . . .
D. GIO: (O che bel volto!)
D. ISA: . . . trattenuta però così per via,
sul ritorno del padre in complimenti,
da qualche amica mia.

D. GIO: (Voglio accostarmi.)
Cavagliero, madama, d'iscusarmi
pregovi, se vi sturbo. Io certo altrove
ebbi onor di vedervi.

DUCA: Non mi sovvien, ma pure, ovunqu'io possa,
bramo quel d'obbedirvi ed ora e poi.

D. GIO: Gentilezza obligante.

DUCA: Cavagliero,
breve spazio attendete, e sono a voi.
(va da Donna Isabella, che li fa cenno)

D. ISA: Duca, dello straniero
il volto, oh Dio, no, non mi piace;
e nel vederlo un non so che d'ignoto
conturba la mia gioia e la mia pace.

Scena x
Don Giovanni ed il Duca

D. GIO: Più che osservo la dama,
più ne ravviso i lineamenti.

DUCA: È questa
Donna Isabella Oliola,
del buon Comendatore unica figlia,
a me promessa in sposa.

D. GIO: Di quella a cui somiglia è più vezzosa.
Ben impiegaste il vostro genio.

DUCA: Altero
troppo della mia scelta fa ch'io vada
la vostra approvazione, o Cavagliero.

D. GIO: Io già d'autorizarla
il merito non ho.

DUCA: Tutto l'avete,
caro amico; vi parla
il duca di Chiarenza innamorato
della vostra bell'indole, e vi dice
che in quanto può di lui l'arbitro siete.

D. GIO: Io mi chiamo felice, ed a gran sorte

m'ascriverò non men che a sommo onore,
se un tanto prence produrrami in corte.

DUCA: Scherza quest'alma mia
col tuo gradito amor,
come con l'aura il fior
sul verde prato.
Ma, oh Dio, che tirania
a me faria il destin,
se non ha lieto fin
l'alto attentato.

Scena xi
Malorco e Don Giovanni

MAL: O padrone; su, presto,
torni a bottega il cinto.
D. GIO: Sai dove sta la dama?
MAL: Il punto è questo,
ch'io dirlo non vorrei, se si potesse;
ma mi fa mal oprare
il vostro minacciare e l'interesse.
D. GIO: Il cinto è pronto. Su, palesa.
MAL: In corte,
nell'atrio superiore a mano destra
ha il suo quarto la dama, e sul giardino
ha più d'una finestra. Il cinto.
D. GIO: Aspetta.
MAL: Ehi, sì burliam, padrone?
Questo, forse
assai mi servirà d'introduzione.
Maledetta la scuola
dove apprendeste tal cavaleria!
O che bel cavaglier che tien parola!
Cavagliero, il malan che il ciel vi dia!
D. GIO: Non t'adirar, e senti un mio pensiero:
ho veduta una dama,
bella fra quante viddi a' giorni miei;

voglio al padre di lei
finger del Duca Alfonso un scritto foglio,
che a lui m'indrizzi; ed indi
la figlia a' miei desir piegare io voglio.

MAL: Volete ch'io vi dica?
Minacciate, gridate, andate in colera,
trattenetemi il cinto e bastonatemi;
vi dico ch'è prodigio, se vi tollera
la terra e non v'ingoia,
perchè molti di voi men scellerati
a finir sono andati in man del boia.
Che diavolo! Protesto, in vita mia,
di non aver veduto
un simile guidon be . . . stiale astuto,
che sol nel bene oprar fa l'ignorante,
ma ch'è dottor nell'arte del birbante.
Orsù, prendo congedo; *(partendo)*
preparatemi pur il mio salario,
per ch'io temo perire un dì con voi.

D. GIO: Sentimi, temerario;
io ti bastonerò come un giumento.
Coreggi i pari tuoi.

MAL: Così la sento.

Oggidì, va così. Chi non sa
adular non può campar,
perchè rari san patir
di sentir le correzioni.

Chi lasciasse ai servitori
sputar fuori il lor concetto,
ora questo e quel difetto
fuggirebbero i padroni.

Scena xii

Sala regia illuminata di notte per l'ordinaria assemblea.

Manfredi e Donna Isabella, Duca e Donna Beatrice, Comendatore con altra dama, tutti sedenti al gioco, con altri cavaglieri e dame che stanno giocando.

Doppo breve sinfonia comparisce un cavagliero, il quale, poichè ha parlato all'orecchio del Duca, siede nel di lui posto a giocare; e levatosi il Duca, esce dalla sala, indi ritorna con Don Giovanni e Malorco.

DUCA: *(a Don Giovanni, accostandosi al Comendatore)*
Or al Comendatore
dirò che da recarli avete un foglio.
D. GIO: Tu pur sei qui?
MAL: Vi sono.
D. GIO: Parti.
MAL: Partite voi,
che siete, più di me, poco di buono.
D. GIO: Sei mordace.
MAL: Mi duole
che nulla fan con voi le mie parole.
Ehi, quella finta lettera
non date!
D. GIO: Che? Ti do . . .
MAL: (Gran bestia et cetera.)
(qui Malorco va poi tentando di giocar con qualche d'uno)
COM: Voi siete, o Cavaglier, che il Duca Alfonso
indrizza a me? *(andandoli appresso)*
D. GIO: Eccone il foglio.
DUCA: *(a Don Giovanni)* Amico,
qual è la condizione
del straniero faceto?
D. GIO: È un mio buffone.
DUCA: Carattere che luogo
apre in ogni adunanza.
COM: O non mai abbastanza *(doppo letta la lettera)*
preggiato cavaglier, poi che godete
del duca l'amistà. Devo gloriarmi
che a me siate indrizzato,

e l'onor d'impiegarmi
ad ogni vostro cenno a me fia grato.

D. GIO: Somma finezza.

COM: Il duca,
già mio genero eletto,
della canizie mia potrà suplire
al forzato difetto.
Ed in tanto servire
lasciatevi in mia casa.

DUCA: Il re si leva.

COM: È giusto il presentarvi
a sua maestà.

MAL: Nè posso, no, avisarvi
che abbracciate un autor di frodi e inganni.

COM: Sire, al piè Don Giovanni,
del bel ceppo Tenorio illustre tralcio,
vi si umiglia.

MAN: Sorgete. *(a Don Giovanni prostrato)*

MAL: (Che ben presto ne avrete
per le accoglienze un calcio. E tacer devo?)

D. GIO: Agli onor che ricevo
dal benigno e gentil Comendatore,
ei ne aggiunge un maggiore,
col far che a' vostri piè, Sire, mi prostri.

MAN: Li complimenti vostri
nel miglior grado riceviamo, e caro
ci sarà nel vedervi
in corte a frequentar l'unione e il gioco.

D. GIO: Quest'ultimo non mai.

COM: Lice per poco
ad ogni mente e ad ogni grado.

D. GIO: È vero.

MAN: Commendatore, andiamo.

COM: Duca, restate voi col cavaliero.
(parte Manfredi col Comendatore,
servendo Donna Beatrice)

DUCA: Sarà molto avvanzata *(prendendo fuori l'oriuolo)*
la notte.

D. GIO: Io non lo so. *(a Malorco)* (O che bel colpo

machina il mio pensier.) Di Londra è forse
il bel lavoro?

DUCA: A punto.

D. GIO: Ove un simile
acquistarne potrei?

DUCA: Pronto l'avete
in vostra mano.

D. GIO: *(rendendolo)* No; troppo gentile,
caro Duca, voi siete.

DUCA: *(ricusandolo)* Riponetelo
in segno che mi amate.

D. GIO: (Il colpo è fatto.)
(una dama fa cenno al Duca d'accostarsele)

DUCA: Amico, perdonate; or a voi torno.

D. GIO: No, servitevi pure;
parto anch'io. Ci vedremo al nuovo giorno.
(si leva tutto il resto della assemblea)
Vien qui! Vanne e provedi
una lanterna.

MAL: E poi?

D. GIO: Ritorna in corte.
Io resto, la mia sorte
a tentar con la bella che qui alberga;
e sul duca, rival già in altro amore,
spero far, col suo dono,
cader tutto il sospetto. O bel pensiero,
vo ad esequirlo e tosto.

MAL: Non ne andate sì altero,
che doppo i pasti al fin si paga l'oste.

D. GIO: Sì, cavalier io sono,
vanto corraggio e onore;
e questo core in dono,
t'ho dedicato, amor.
Tu per mercede almeno,
per compensarmi appieno,
mi presta il tuo favor.

fine dell'atto primo

ATTO SECONDO

Scena i

Continua la notte. Atrio in corte contiguo agli appartamenti reali.

Malorco con lanterna, e poi Don Garzia

MAL: Mo', che vita è mai questa?
La notte caminar coi pipistrelli,
mangiar poco e alla presta,
gli occhi tener aperti coi puntelli
per gran sonno, nè mai veder salario
in quanti giorni segna il calendario.
Ma vi sono, e costretto
dalla necessità convien star saldo
con questa razza porca,
e un giorno, a mio dispetto, qual ribaldo
far la strada al padron giù da una forca.
Ma qui vien gente. *(Malorco oscura la lanterna)*
D. GAR: Al buio
son pigri i passi miei.
MAL: (Fosse il padrone.
Voglio vedere.) *(scuopre la detta)*
D. GAR: Olà!
MAL: Alto!
D. GAR: Che azzione
incivile è cotesta? Ma la spada
di Don Garzia la punirà.
MAL: *(se li amorza il lume)* Es nada.
D. GAR: Nada un tal atto? Olà, chi sei? Rispondi.
MAL: (Che devo dire?) Un uom di questi mondi.
D. GAR: Allo scherno ti estendi,
o mal nato? Da' il nome o ti difendi.
(porta colpi all'oscuro)
MAL: Piano pian. Siete voi?
D. GAR: Chi?
MAL: Don . . . Non so.
D. GAR: Ti burli anche di me?

MAL: Fermatevi, il norsino[2] io son del re.
D. GAR: Temerario! Deridi
la regia maestà? Cedi.
MAL: (È imbrogliata.
Testa ci vuole.) Olà, miei camerata. *(poi con altra voce)*
Che c'è? Che c'è? *(con voce propria)* Chiamate
quell'altre due brigate. *(altra voce)* Herr Walckersdorff.
Ja, bald, ich komme. Monsieur la Margautiere.
Ouy, je vien tout alleur.
Eh, Alajù, lama todos los chiamarros
y vengan con alfanjes,
luego. Anche voi, Don Gioan Piccone.
D. GAR: Questa è una ribellione;
ma foste mille, io non pavento. Ahimè!
(urta in Malorco, che sta corco a terra, e cade; indi si leva)
MAL: (È caduto.)
D. GAR: *(rizzatosi)* Non è
prudenza andar contro di tanti un solo. *(parte a tentone)*
Mi ritiro in difesa.
MAL: Al calpestio
sento ch'ei parte, e me ne vado anch'io. *(entra carpone)*

Scena ii

Don Giovanni afferrato da Donna Beatrice in abito da notte, ed indi Manfredi con lume alla mano.

D. GIO: Lasciami, o donna.
D. BEA: Temerario! In vano
tenti fuggir; palesa
l'iniquo nome.
D. GIO: Lascierai la mano
alle mie vesti appesa,
se a trattenermi tu persisti, o ardita.
D. BEA: Vi lascierò la vita,
pria che lasciarti.
D. GIO: Cedi omai.

2. Castrator of pigs or of young boys.

D. BEA: Discuopri
chi tu sei.
D. GIO: Nol vuo' dire.
Venni incognito, e tale
voglio di qui partire.
D. BEA: Olà, di corte;
gente, soccorso!
D. GIO: Taci.
D. BEA: Olà, di corte . . .
D. GIO: Taci, dissi, o muori.
(ponendole la mano alla bocca)
MAN: Quali strida? Quai voci? Ah, traditori.
(Don Giovanni, vedendosi scoperto dal lume di Manfredi, con la spada glielo getta di mano)
Guardie, guardie, accorrete!
Lumi.
D. BEA: Ah, Sire . . .
MAN: Chi siete?
D. BEA: Son Beatrice. Salvatevi.
MAN: Di corte,
olà.
D. BEA: Monarca invitto,
non vi esponete.
MAN: Olà, di corte.
D. GIO: (Questo
il duca accusi reo del mio delitto.) *(gettato a terra l'orologio dal duca già regalatoli, parte)*

Scena iii

Don Garzia con guardie e lumi, Manfredi e Donna Beatrice

MAN: Guardie.
D. GAR: Sire.
MAN: Cercate
nella reggia. Ma chi?
D. BEA: Dell'onor mio
l'iniquo assalitor.
MAN: Come? Narrate.

D. GAR: Affrettiamci. *(parte Don Garzia con guardie)*
MAN: Chi fu?
D. BEA: M'è ignoto.
MAN: Il fio
l'audace pagherà. Dite . . . Ma proprio
qui non è il trattenervi così spoglia.
Al vostro quarto fate pur ritorno,
e deporrete il fatto al nuovo giorno.

D. BEA: Del rapito onor mio,
vendetta sol da te, signor, vogl'io.

Scena iv

Don Garzia, che ritorna, ritrovando l'orologio gittato da Don Giovanni.
Manfredi e guardie con lumi.

D. GAR: Sire, già i rei, che molti
di crederli ho ragione,
con la fugga al supplizio si son tolti;
ma forse cognizione
d'essi darà quest'orologio a terra
qui trovato.
MAN: Vediamolo. Se non erra
lo sguardo, un reo ci è noto,
et è il duca.
D. GAR: Esser può?
MAN: Chiaro si vede.
D. GAR: Il duca?
MAN: Niegar fede
come a un tal testimon? Pur si proceda
taciti e cauti. Andate;
la colpa a voi sol nota egli si creda;
al dover lo guidate,
o di punirlo troveremo il modo.
D. GAR: Ad ubbidir mi accingo,
e la vostra saviezza ammiro e lodo. *(parte)*

MAN: Non speri perdono
quel core ribelle;
qual padre ti sono,
qual figlia mi sei.
Saprò col rigore
punire quel core,
saranno i suoi danni
mia gioia e trofei.

Scena v

Principia l'alba. Parte esteriore della reggia di Napoli, con scale che corispondono sopra le loggie d'un regio cortile.

Don Giovanni, che si cala da una finestra, e poi Malorco

D. GIO: All'audace, nemica
la sorte non fu mai; con gran fatica,
è ver, ma pur sottrato
m'ho dal periglio, e ne son pago assai.
MAN: (Sento il padrone.) Chi va là?
D. GIO: Son io,
Malorco.
MAL: (Lo so ben. Vuo' fare il bravo.)
Io non conosco. Olà, cospetto mio,
avvanza il nome, o che la spada io cavo
furibonda a' tuoi danni.
D. GIO: Ferma, son Don Giovanni.
MAL: Un altro poco
se stavi a palesarvi,
finiva questo gioco in amazzarvi.
D. GIO: Bravo, così mi piaci.
MAL: Va ben così?
D. GIO: Benissimo, e più bene
io pure la passai.
Sentimi; con quel cinto penetrai
da Beatrice, fingendo che rubbato
io gliel'abbia e pentito
render volerlo in tutta secretezza

e però mascherato;
lei, colma d'allegrezza,
li domestici apparta; al tergo loro
le porte io chiudo presto;
lei fugge.

MAL: Basta, basta.

D. GIO: Senti il resto.
Una secreta uscita
s'apre, io l'arresto, e lei d'ira ne sviene;
indi, parto; scuoprirmi
lei tenta, e giunge il re . . .

MAL: Qui un altro viene.

Scena vi

Comendatore con servi e detti.

COM: Così di gran mattino
siete già, o Cavalier, fuori del letto?

D. GIO: Sol per farvi un inchino
e tutto rassegnarvi il mio rispetto.

COM: Se cotanto mi amate,
perchè non accettate
l'ospizio di mia casa, in cui goderci
noi potrem con frequenza?

D. GIO: Non so far ressistenza
più al lungo a tanto onor.

COM: Così è ben fatto,
caro amico. Fra tanto, (ehi, tu, ad un tratto *(ad un servo)*
vanne col di lui servo), permettete
ch'oggi passi in mia casa
tutto il vostro equipaggio.

D. GIO: Facciasi.

MAL: Non sapete
che l'abbiamo perduto nel naufraggio? *(a Don Giovanni)*

D. GIO: Appunto.

COM: Me ne duole. Amico, adio.
Parto per fretta; da quest'ora in poi

dipenderan da voi
me stesso e tutta la servil famiglia.

D. GIO: Siete troppo gentil. (Basta la figlia.)

COM: Fortunato, allor, io spero
che sarò, se voi da vero
disporrete in libertà.
Ma se poi non siete accorto
nell'usarne, fate un torto
a voi stesso e all'amistà.

Scena vii
Duca e detti.

DUCA: Don Giovanni, la mostra
ieri a voi regalata . . .

D. GIO: A punto, amico, già mi fu rubbata.

DUCA: Possibile?

D. GIO: È così.

DUCA: Gran caso strano!
La stessa in altra mano
passata, non so come, oggi m'accusa
d'un enorme attentato.

D. GIO: In corte io produrrò la vostra scusa,
(ben è riuscito il colpo), o Duca amato.

DUCA: Come la cerva al fonte
per isfogar sua sete
corre dal prato al monte,
nè mai presta sen riede
finchè estinta l'ha;
tal degl'eroi il core,
pieno di zelo e ardore;
ogni lor cura prende
l'amore e la pietà.

Scena viii

Don Giovanni, Malorco, e poi Rosalba

D. GIO: Malorco, che ti par? Non ti sorprende
la perspicaccia mia?
MAL: È grande! Ma però chi ben intende
non la chiama così, ma furbaria.
ROSA: Passi e sospiri in vano
nel cercarvi, o spergiuro, io non gettai.
Pur vi trovo, inumano,
barbaro, senza fè.
MAL: Qui c'è dei guai.
D. GIO: Parli tu meco?
ROSA: Non mi conosciete?
So che mal mi vedete
e che vi son molesta,
ma il giusto ciel . . .
MAL: Sbrigatevi da questa.
D. GIO: O povera figliola,
pazza tu sei, se pur meco favelli.
ROSA: Pazza, o crudel?
D. GIO: Guidare
ti farò per pietà nei pazzarelli. *(vuol partire)*

Scena ix

Manfredi, che discende dalla reggia con seguito di guardie, e detti.

ROSA: Ferma, che dileggiare *(lo trattiene)*
sempre non mi potrai. Sire, a' tuoi piedi *(si prostra)*
prostrasi un'infelice,
empiamente tradita e deflorata
dal cavalier che vedi,
implorando giustizia umilmente.
MAN: Sorgi.
D. GIO: Sire, costei vaneggia o mente.
ROSA: Io mentir? Dica il servo
chi son, che feci, e s'io tolsi dal mare
naufragante il protervo.

MAN: Favella. È vero?
MAL: Non lo so niegare.
D. GIO: Sin qui d'accordo anch'io.
ROSA: Non sono queste
le donatevi spoglie?
D. GIO: Pur questo è vero.
ROSA: Non mi prometteste
di prendermi per moglie?
D. GIO: Oh, questo poi . . .
ROSA: Dillo tu.
MAL: Qui non c'entro;
v'intendeste fra voi.
MAN: Pure . . .
MAL: Qualch'ombra
ebbi del fatto . . .
D. GIO: Sire, omai disgombra
ogni sospetto. È vero, io le giurai
prenderla per mia moglie; e quando mai
moglie prendessi, anch'ella
con altre, sceglierò sua damigella.
MAN: Con più maturo esame
si tenterà meglio scuoprire il vero;
se giuste son tue brame,
io so che appagherale il cavaliero. *(parte)*

D. GIO: Per dolce tuo riposo
pensa che non hai sposo;
è vano il tuo dolore,
il rege è a mio favore,
e paventar non so.
In vano tu sospiri,
lagnandoti deliri,
chè un fallo aventuroso
farmi terror non può.

Scena x
Rosalba e Malorco

ROSA: S'egli di me si ride, io nel sovrano
le mie speranze affido,
che risarcir farà di quell'infido
l'onor mio dalla mano.
MAL: Eh, non sapete
quante di queste ei n'abbia;
che mi venga la rabbia,
guardate, se in un giorno le leggete.
(le mostra la lista e parte)

ROSA: Dovevi prima il cor
togliermi, o traditor, ma non partire.
Questa è la data fè?
È questa la mercè, crudel consorte?
Va' pur, spietato e rio
cagion del pianto mio, della mia morte.

Scena xi
Stanze di Donna Isabella.

Donna Isabella, Donna Beatrice, e poi Malorco

D. ISA: Dolce amica, il confesso
che, quanto mi cagiona di cordoglio
l'accadutovi mal, grave all'accesso,
altrettanto stupore
mi cagiona l'udir sospetto il duca
di complice o d'autore; ma guardate
che poi non v'ingannate.
D. BEA: Don Garzia
n'ha incontrastabil prova.
D. ISA: (O gelosia!)
Non piangete.
MAL: Signora,
vorrebbe il mio padron con sua licenza

farle umil riverenza.

D. Isa: (O cielo!) Venga.
Io tal visita accetto
per civiltà, ma vi repugna il core.

D. Bea: Sarà del sangue effetto,
per lo più indifferente.

D. Isa: Un grand'orrore
per tanto lo funesta.

Scena xii

Don Giovanni e dette.

D. Gio: Madama, non è questa
ora opportuna, il so, ma si permetta
ad un ospite e servo
cotesta libertà.

D. Isa: M'è sempre accetta
la vostra cortesia.

D. Gio: *(vedendo Donna Beatrice)*
Sol ora osservo
questa dama, a cui devo
di condoglianza un atto per il caso
accadutole, son poch'ore scorse.

D. Bea: (O mio rossor!) Che se ne parla forse?

D. Gio: V'ha dubbio? Persuaso
dagli indizi è però ciascun di corte
che il duca ne sia reo.

D. Isa: (Crudo consorte!)

D. Bea: (Amica, perdonate;
la verecondia vuol ch'io mi nasconda.

D. Isa: Deh, non mi abbandonate.

D. Bea: Restar non posso. Adio. Già il pianto abbonda.)

Tra due fiamme e tra due venti
son facella, navicella.
Per idea de' miei spaventi
mi sovrasta, ov'io mi volga,
o l'incendio o la procella.

Scena xiii
Don Giovanni e Donna Isabella

D. GIO: Voi, madama, abitate
stanze molto remote.
D. ISA: Perchè del sol, quest'ore più infocate,
l'ardor non le percuote.
D. GIO: D'altro ardore
voi forse avvamperete.
D. ISA: Come a dire?
D. GIO: Di quello che per voi mi fa morire.
D. ISA: (Qual favellar!)
D. GIO: *(andando a chiuder la porta della stanza al di dentro)*
Soffrite
che senza testimoni del mio foco
vi trattenga per poco.
Chiudiam l'ingresso.
D. ISA: Olà!
D. GIO: Già è chiuso. Udite.
D. ISA: Cavalier, io mi credo
che voi così per bizarria scherzate,
ma però il mio congedo
ricevete e sgombrate; io non ascolto
espressioni in secreto,
che se dite da vero, osate molto,
o s'è pur scherzo, egli è troppo indiscreto.
D. GIO: Ah, mia cara . . .
D. ISA: Intendete?
D. GIO: Con tal sdegno, o mio ben, più m'accendete.
D. ISA: Temeraria baldanza! *(va per aprire la porta)*
Or schiuderò . . .
D. GIO: No, cara, della stanza
non s'aprirà l'ingresso
prima che il vostro amor mi sia concesso.
D. ISA: Mal cavaliero! Padre, servi, aita!
Soccorso, io son tradita!
Servi, padre, venite . . .
D. GIO: Omai tacete!
D. ISA: Domestici, accorete!

D. GIO: A chi v'ama, così?
D. ISA: Genti, famiglia . . .
COM: Che c'è? *(di dentro)*
D. GIO: Crudele.
COM: Che vi accade, o figlia!
D. ISA: Padre, venite armato
del mio onore in difesa.
COM: O Dio.
D. ISA: M'assale un traditor mal nato.
COM: Dessisti dall'impresa,
o fellon, che se ardisci
d'insultar il mio sangue,
io ben ti punirò.
D. GIO: *(aprendo la porta)* Dunque esequisci,
ma guarda ben che qui non resti esangue.

Scena xiv

Commendatore, che entra in veste di camera con spada alla mano, assalendo Don Giovanni, e Donna Isabella fugge a chiamar servi in soccorso.

COM: Don Giovanni! Tu qui? Osi assalire
in tal guisa il mio onore, ospite infido?
Ah, perfido! Vendetta. *(attacandolo)*
D. GIO: Vuoi morire?
Contendimi l'uscita, ed io t'uccido.
COM: Ben quel tuo sangue ardito
dell'onor mio risarcirà il tesoro.
D. GIO: Eh, vecchio rimbambito,
stanco di viver sei. To', cadi.
(Don Giovanni fugge, ed il Commendatore cade)
COM: Io muoro.
Servi, figlia! Oh Dio,
manco. Perdon d'ogni commesso errore,
deh, tu mi dona, ed io,
per amor tuo, perdono all'uccisore.
Più non reggo . . . La vita
esposi, lo sai tu, solo in difesa
dell'onestà, cotanto a te gradita.

All'uccisor l'offesa
perdona, qual io fo, nume verace.
Muoro . . . Spiro . . . Signor, donami pace. *(muore)*

Scena xv

Donna Isabella, che ritorna con servi per soccorrere il padre e, trovandolo morto, immobile resta.

O ciel! Che miro? O Dio,
ucciso il padre mio?

Scena xvi

Manfredi e Donna Isabella piangente.

MAN: Donna Isabella, se non ero, parmi
vedervi in volto innusitato orrore.
D. ISA: Ve lo dica il mio pianto.
Don Giovanni m'ha ucciso il genitore.
MAN: Che? Don Alvaro? O Dio! Ma come? E quando?
Ah, scellerato brando!
D. ISA: Nell'onore, dal perfido assalita,
chiedo soccorso; il padre accorre armato,
e vi lascia, o mio duol, la cara vita
per mano dell'iniquo ospite ingrato.
MAN: Alvaro, tu sei morto?
Ma se ha poter Manfredi,
vendicherà sull'uccisore il torto. *(parte risoluto)*

D. ISA: Risvegliata da più venti,
freme irata la tempesta,
ed inalza or alle sponde,
or precipita nell'onde
combattuta navicella.
Fra lo sdegno e fra l'amore
grido: stragi all'uccisore.
Piango poscia il genitore,
sempre in grembo alla procella.

fine dell'atto secondo

ATTO TERZO

Scena i

Gran tempio alla gottica con magnifico monumento adorno di marmoree figure, fra le quali la statoa equestre del Comendatore defunto.

Malorco e Don Giovanni, che corrono a ricovrarsi per timore di ministri della giustizia.

MAL: Scappa, scappa!
D. GIO: Vigliacco,
qual timor? Questo tempio ne assicura.
MAL: Sì? Adesso mi distracco.
D. GIO: Alla campagna,
sull'imbrunire, andrem giù per le mura.
MAL: Via, dunque; le calcagna
meniam veloci più che lepri o ghirri,
chè se qui noi restiamo,
a giunger ci vediamo adosso i sbirri.
D. GIO: Qui non ponno arrestarci.
MAL: Oh buon! Vedete.
D. GIO: Che ben scolpiti marmi!
Che mausoleo superbo!
MAL: Conoscete
quel a cavallo?
D. GIO: Parmi
quasi raffigurarlo.
MAL: Ahimè! Padrone,
egli è il Comendator che avete ucciso.
D. GIO: Lo dirà l'iscrizione.
MAL: Mal augurio.
D. GIO: Di che? Mi muovi al riso.
"Qui del Comendator posa la salma, *(legge)*
che un empio traditor privò dell'alma."
Io traditor? Indegno! I colpi miei
non fur da traditore,
e tornassi tu vivo, ch'io saprei
passarti ancor, standoti a fronte, il core.

MAL: Patron, non irritate
il ciel, scherzando coi defunti. Oprare
egli sa gran miracoli, e guardate
ben bene il fatto vostro.
D. GIO: Or vuo' provare
se questo cielo o i morti
hanno poter di vendicare i torti.
MAL: Andiamo, andiamo.
D. GIO: Aspetta.
Ecco, o vecchio ribaldo, chi t'uccise;
scendi a farne vendetta.
Che dici? Non si muove. In altre guise
guardami a provocarlo.
MAL: Andiamo via.
D. GIO: No, no, fermati. In faccia. *(il getta un guanto)*
Prendi, la spoglia della destra mia
ti getto. Or la minaccia
che mi facesti non succede?
MAL: Adagio.
D. GIO: O stolto che tu sei!
MAL: (O che malvagio!)
D. GIO: Vuoi di meglio? Proviamo.
Ti sprezzo, ti detesto;
un mentitore infame e vil ti chiamo.
Non ti resenti ancor nè meno a questo?
Eh, sì. Via, quel marmoreo tuo colosso
mi precipiti adosso; ecco, l'aspetto;
stare immobil prometto.
Eh! Malorco!
MAL: Andiam via, ch'io sono in pena.
D. GIO: Tu, de' morti sì amico,
invitalo con noi oggi alla cena.
MAL: In questo io non m'intrico.
D. GIO: Et io lo voglio, o ti bastonerò.
MAL: Che venga un marmo a cena esser non può.
D. GIO: Vedi se ti ho convinto?
Chi questo non può far, null'altro puole.
MAL: Può farlo anche dipinto,
quando che il ciel lo vuole.

D. GIO: Or via, l'invita.
MAL: Lo farò perchè sia
quest'istoria finita.
Prega, vossignoria,
il mio padron che siate a cena seco.
(la statoa china il capo)
Ahimè! Bassò la testa e guarda bieco.
D. GIO: Travedere ti fe' la tua credenza.
MAL: Fate voi l'esperienza,
invitatelo voi. O che terrore!
D. GIO: Proviam. Comendatore,
meco a cena t'invito.
Verrai?
STATOA: Verrò.
MAL: Mi scappa l'appetito.

D. GIO: Timido il cor, o folle,
già non mi batte in petto;
egli non è ricetto
di tema o di terror.
Ad ogni strano evento
son di coraggio armato,
nè può l'avverso fato
scemare il mio valor.

Scena ii
Stanza di Donna Isabella.

Donna Beatrice e Donna Isabella

D. BEA: Di consolarci, o amica,
pari il bisogno abbiam, pari 'l dolore;
ma scambievol fatica
ambo averemo in dar la pace al core.
D. ISA: Pur troppo è vero; ma voi, cara, al fine,
delle perdite vostre nel mio caro
averete il riparo;
non così delle mie, senza confine—
perduti, già per sempre, padre e sposo.

D. BEA: No, datevi riposo.
Resta appieno provato
ch'egli innocente sia,
e colui che vi uccise il padre amato,
che assalì, noto è ancora, l'onestà mia.

D. ISA: Io t'impegno
a scagliar, dell'empio indegno
sull'iniqua orribil testa,
la tempesta
del tuo sdegno, o cielo irato.
Ei l'onore
a lei tolse; il genitore
a me uccise inferocito.
L'ha tradito
infedel ospite ingrato.

Scena iii
Donna Beatrice sola.

Se del mal che a noi viene
li ministri noi siamo,
tal or, che fu un bene,
per secreti del cielo, al fin proviamo.

Lo stimolo, così
tal or, il cavalier
adopra col destrier,
che a sdegno il sente.
Ma con quel tormentar
lo giunge ad involar,
in fine, del leon
al fiero dente.

Scena iv

Sala in un palazzo fuori di Napoli, con aparato di lauta cena da Don Giovanni ordinata.

Don Giovanni pensoso e Malorco

MAL: Olà, servi, su, presto,
prepparate la mensa.
Signor padron, perchè state sì mesto?
S'aprino le cantine e la dispensa.
Via, sedete.
D. GIO: Sediamo. *(portano in tavola)*
MAL: Che avete?
D. GIO: Io son, nè so perchè, turbato.
MAL: State allegro, e mangiamo. *(siede alla tavola)*
D. GIO: Olà! *(respingendolo)*
MAL: Via, ch'ho burlato.
D. GIO: Leva questa vivanda;
non piace al gusto mio.
MAL: Quando all'incontro lei non mi comanda,
la mangerò ben io.
D. GIO: Ah, mal creato.
MAL: È lei molto ben nata.
D. GIO: Recate l'insalata.
Fammi qualche racconto
per divertirmi.
MAL: L'oste vuol far conto.
D. GIO: Eh, finiscila. Di'.
MAL: Vi sovvien quante
favorite che aveste per il mondo?
D. GIO: Oh, son state pur tante!
Che fai?
MAL: Vi cambio il tondo.
D. GIO: Non fa bisogno.
MAL: Ma quella signora
che ritrovammo in Francia? . . .
D. GIO: Che fai?
MAL: Lo cambio ancora.
D. GIO: Insolente.

MAL: Io non già, ma la mia pancia.
Orsù, quella che in mare
ci diede aiuto? . . .

D. GIO: Eh, non mi parlare
delle gioie passate;
soddisfatto il desio, non son più grate.

MAL: Che? Non vi dà contento
il rammentarle? Non ne andate lieto?
Vedete? Il fin è un tardo pentimento.

D. GIO: Prendi l'oglio e l'aceto;
gira quest'insalata. Non voltarla!
Che fai, bestia? Sossopra?
Ferma!

MAL: Voglio salarla.

D. GIO: Prima va l'oglio sopra, che non c'è.

MAL: Lasciate fare a me.

D. GIO: Che? Quel della lucerna,
sordido, vi si pone?
O siete pur co . . .

MAL: . . . ntento. La cisterna
farà provigione
dell'oglio ch'è gettato. *(corrono alcuni servi spaventati)*

D. GIO: Guardisi chi ha bussato. Cos'è questo?
Va' a veder. Cos'è mai tal confusione?
Che fia? Stupido resto! *(Malorco prende un lume e va)*

MAL: Ahimè, signor padrone. Oh, che terrore! *(ritorna spaventato)*
Barabàn . . . Biribìo . . .

D. GIO: Che c'è? Parla.

MAL: È già qui il Comendatore.

D. GIO: Pazzo, da' qui; a vedere anderò io.

Scena v

Statoa del Commendatore, Don Giovanni, che la precede col lume; indi si pongono a tavola, e Malorco spaventato.

D. GIO: Se avessi, o convitato,
creduto il tuo venir, la terra e il mare
avrei ordinato

che si dovesser del miglior spogliare,
con quant'arte che in oggi il lusso insegna,
per imbandire a te cena condegna.
Tu dunque al desir mio
generoso supplisci,
e per instinto nobile natio
ciò che trovi gradisci.
Non mangi? Che vorresti? A me lo addita.

STATOA: Cibo non prende più chi è fuor di vita.

MAL: O poveretti noi!

D. GIO: Vuoi che si canti? Di'!

STATOA: Fa' ciò che vuoi.

D. GIO: Suonisi, e tu, Malorco,
canta qualch'aria.

MAL: Ohimè! Son tutto sporco!

A comparsa così strana,
voglia avete ch'io vi canti?
Tempo è questo più di pianti,
che di star in allegria.
Fa tremar l'anima mia
quel bamboccio là impietrito.
Ho già perso l'appetito,
e mi va l'angoscia al cor.
Licenziatelo, vi prego;
sufficiente già la prova
del coraggio mio n'avete.
Se lo guardo, mi rinova
lo spavento ed il terror.

D. GIO: Olà, servi; recate
da mangiare a Malorco.

MAL: Eh, mi perdoni,
non ho fame.

D. GIO: Portate.

MAL: Niente, no.

D. GIO: I maccheroni. *(li servi glieli portano)*

MAL: Date. Li mangio per non farli torto, *(intanto si suona)*
che son di quei che dan la vita a un morto.

D. GIO: Or bevi alla salute
della dama che a te parve più bella.
MAL: Alla salute di Donna Isabella.
(beve, e la statoa s'alza con impeto)
STATOA: Giovanni, a cena teco
m'invitasti, ed io venni; con il servo
t'invito a cena meco.
Verrai?
MAL: Per me, sicuro, non vi servo,
nè voi pur.
D. GIO: Sì, verrò da cavaliero.
Servi il Comendatore.
STATOA: Un'altra luce
miglior della terrena ho per mio duce. *(vola via per aria)*
MAL: To', to'! Dalla finestra in aria vola.
D. GIO: Son cavalier, e manterò parola.

Sorpreso, confuso,
che dissi, che penso?
Ma pieno d'orgoglio
non cedo al timor;
Non può farmi senso,
nè il voglio deluso,
quel spetro di scoglio,
ch'intrepido ho il cor.
Non temo il morire,
nè larve pavento;
l'impegno ho già assunto,
nè punto mi pento.
Chi può del mio ardir
vantarne un maggior?

Scena vi
Gabinetti reali.

Manfredi et il Duca

MAN: Sì, caro Duca, sono,
senza le vostre scuse
convinte a piè del trono,
di mendaci le accuse.
DUCA: Fu Don Giovanni il reo.
MAN: Degno di morte.
DUCA: Gioisco; già sparì l'atra procella.
MAN: Et Isabella vi sarà consorte. *(parte)*

Scena vii
Duca solo.

Piombino pur dagli astri
con maligna influenza
mille e mille disastri,
che nulla posson mai dov'è innocenza.

Un caro e dolce sguardo
nell'intimo del petto
mi va cercando il cor;
io lo diffendo e guardo,
e pure a mio dispetto
sa ritrovarlo amor.

Scena viii
Bosco fuori di Napoli.

Malorco e Don Giovanni

MAL: Voi vi mettete in pena
perchè il Comendator non disse dove
preparerà la cena?

D. GIO: E lo cerco impaziente; andiamo altrove.
MAL: O padron mio garbato,
io dubito che voi siate da vero
o pazzo o disperato.
Perchè cercate il mal?
D. GIO: Son . . .
Promisi, nè giammai saprò mancare
per ragione o pretesto.
MAL: Ve ne posso in coscienza dispensare,
perchè avete mancato altro che in questo.
D. GIO: In che cosa?
MAL: In migliaia.
La pescatrice è vostra moglie?
D. GIO: Quella?
MAL: Giuraste.
D. GIO: E bene?
MAL: È baia
mancare al ciel, tradire una donzella?
Patron, patron . . .
D. GIO: Olà; taci o m'adiro.

Scena ix

Si cambia all'improviso la scena in una orrida, montuosa con uno speco nel mezzo in cui vedesi statoa del Comendatore sedente ad una mensa logubre.

Malorco e Don Giovanni attoniti.

MAL: Non parlo . . . Dove siamo? Ahimè!
D. GIO: Che miro!
STATOA: T'accosta.
D. GIO: Eccomi.
STATOA: Mangia.
D. GIO: Sono questi
li cibi che tu appresti
ad un mio pari?
MAL: (E in volto non si cangia!)
D. GIO: Crudel! Così mi tratti? Dimmi.
STATOA: Mangia.

D. GIO: Sì, fossero serpenti, *(ne prende e morde)*
pure ne mangierò. Malorco, prendi.
MAL: Eh, mi fan male i denti.
D. GIO: Che amarezza! Tai cibi a me tu rendi?
STATOA: Vuoi che si canti?
D. GIO: Sì.
STATOA: Suonisi ancora.
(qui sentesi orribile suono di catene)
D. GIO: Che orribil suono è questo! Ahi, che mi accora?
VOCE: Ecco il punto fatal, protervo ed empio,
in cui già stanco d'aspettarti è Dio.
D'empietade finor se fosti esempio,
un istante ti avvanza a farti pio.
La clemenza ti chiama; orribil scempio
dalla giustizia avrai, se ancor restio.
Vola il tempo. Tu scegli: o sempiterno
gaudio nel cielo o crucio nell'inferno.
STATOA: Dammi la mano.
D. GIO: Prendi.
STATOA: Pentiti, o Don Giovanni.
D. GIO: Ahimè, che gelo!
STATOA: Chiedi perdono al cielo.
D. GIO: Lasciami.
STATOA: Don Giovanni,
pentiti.
D. GIO: Ahimè! Non vale. Oh che spavento!
STATOA: Da Dio clemenza impetra.
Pentiti.
D. GIO: No.
STATOA: Il momento è traboccato.
T'uccide l'uom di pietra, e sei dannato.
(con orribile scossa di terremoto precipita Don Giovanni all'inferno, la statoa vola per l'aria, e Malorco parte stordito e senza favella)

Scena x
Gabinetti reali.

Manfredi, Donna Isabella, Donna Beatrice et il Duca

MAN: Voi restate, o Beatrice,
già destinata in sposa a Don Garzia.
D. ISA: Giorno per noi felice. *(a Donna Beatrice)*
MAN: Piacevi?
D. BEA: Quando lui pago ne sia,
io contento ne sono.
MAN: Il vostro re
per lui vi dà la fè. Duca, porgete
la destra ad Isabella.
DUCA: Eccola. Ricevete
con essa il core.
D. ISA: Ancella
più che moglie il dovere a voi m'annoda.
DUCA: / D. ISA: O contento! O piacere!
MAN: / D. BEA: Due cori in un sol core ognor lo goda.

MAN: Generoso risveglia il tuo cuore;
serva pure quei lacci d'amore,
che ti strinse amorosa beltà.
Ma t'affretta a quel talamo amato
per godere quel bene adorato,
che sì dolce morire ti fa.

Scena ultima
Inferno orribile, eterna prigione de' reprobi.

Don Giovanni cinto di catene fra demoni.

D. GIO: O demoni crudeli,
che le viscere mie qui lacerate,
e quando terminate

saran mie pene atroci e mesti lai?
Rispondetemi.

DEMONI: Mai!

D. GIO: Tormentosa risposta!
Tremendi troppo e troppo fieri accenti!
Senza fine i tormenti
sono de' quali, stolto, io mi burlai?
Mai cesseranno?

DEMONI: Mai!

D. GIO: Maledetti peccati!
Maledetti sien pur quelli che meco
vi commiser. Da cieco
col lume di ragion nel male oprai.
Nè v'è perdono?

DEMONI: Mai!

D. GIO: Maledetto sia il giorno
che generato fui, che nacqui al mondo.
Sia maledetto il pondo
di queste carni ree per cui peccai.
E non posso morir?

DEMONI: No, mai, mai, mai!

D. GIO: Ah, per pietà, sbranatemi!
Eh! Questi è un luogo di pietà già privo.
Da me apprenda chi è vivo
ad ascoltar gli inviti a penitenza,
o meco avrà l'orribile sentenza.

il fine

Il convitato di pietra o sia Il dissoluto

Vincenzo Righini
Nunziato Porta

1776

IL CONVITATO DI PIETRA o sia IL DISSOLUTO

dramma
tragicomico

da rappresentarsi
nel reggio teatro di
Praga
sotto
l'impresa e direzione
di
Giuseppe Bustelli

Praga, l'anno 1776

ATTORI

Don Giovanni Tenorio, cavaliere napolitano
Don Alfonso, ministro del re di Castiglia
Il Commendatore di Loioa, castigliano
Donn'Anna, figlia del Commendatore
Donn'Isabella, figlia del duca d'Altomonte
Elisa, pescatrice
Ombrino, pescatore
Corallina, ostessa
Tiburzio, garzone d'osteria
Lisetta, cameriera di Donn'Anna
Arlechino, servo di Don Giovanni

Comparse

Pescatori
Servitori
Garzoni d'osteria
Guardie

Coro di furie

MUTAZIONI DI SCENE

Nell'atto primo

Spiaggia di mare con capanne pescareccie.
Appartamenti di Donn'Anna.
Spiaggia di mare come sopra.
Appartamenti di Don Alfonso.
Strada con veduta del palazzo del Commendatore.
Appartamenti di Donn'Anna.

Nell'atto secondo

Strada con veduta del palazzo del Commendatore.
Appartamenti di Don Alfonso.
Atrio con vari mausolei fra' quali la statua del Commendatore.
Camera di locanda.
Sala con tavola imbandita.

Nell'atto terzo

Camera apparata a lutto per la cena del Commendatore.
Appartamenti di Don Alfonso.

La scena si rappresenta in Castiglia.

La musica è del sig. Vincenzo Righini.

ATTO PRIMO

Scena i

Spiaggia di mare con capanne pescareccie.

Elisa, Ombrino; poi Don Giovanni, indi Arlechino

ELISA: Pescatori, dove siete?
Soccoriamo l'infelice,
che del mare fra gl'orrori,
fra li vortici sonori,
la sua vita perde già.
OMB: Presto, presto, buona gente,
una fune od un battello,
che si perde il meschinello,
se di lui non s'ha pietà.

D. GIO: Soccorso, oimè, che moro!

A 3:
OMB: ELISA: Già l'impeto dell'onde
gli vieta a queste sponde
potersi approssimar.
D. GIO: Già l'impeto dell'onde
mi vieta a queste sponde
potervi ora approdar.

ELISA: Cieli! Chi mai sarà? Huom d'alto affare
mi rassembra all'aspetto.
OMB: Facciamol riposar su questo sasso.
ELISA: Puole appena il meschin muovere il passo.
ARL: Aiuto!
OMB: Un'altra voce
mi parve di sentire.
ELISA: Forse sarà qualch'altro sventurato
dall'impeto dell'onde qui gettato.
OMB: Ad aiutarlo andiamo.
ELISA: Coraggio, galantuomo.
OMB: Prendete un po' di fiato.

ELISA: Lasciate di nuotare;
non v'è dubbio v'abbiate ad affogare.
OMB: Riposate.
ELISA: Sedete.
OMB: Diteci almen chi siete?
ARL: Un cavaliere.
OMB: In questi arnesi?
ARL: Veston tutti così ne' miei paesi.
ELISA: Conoscerebbe forse
quest'altro sventurato?
ARL: (Oh diavolo, il padron!)
OMB: Che cosa è stato?
ARL: Quest'è il nostro fratello mascolino.
ELISA: Fratello?
ARL: Sì, signora, fratello.
OMB: Ma se voi siete brutto e questo è bello?
ARL: Sono brunetto un poco
per una voglia ch'ebbe la mia madre
di ber la cioccolata,
e sul viso la macchia è a me restata.
D. GIO: Infelice, ove son?
OMB: I vostri casi
a noi già son palesi.
D. GIO: E chi v'ha mai informato?
ELISA: Il fratel vostro qui da noi salvato.
D. GIO: Arlechino?
ARL: Signor?
D. GIO: Quest'è il mio servo.
OMB: Ma se costui ci disse
esser vostro germano!
D. GIO: Quest'è un buffone.
ARL: Ma come, sior padrone,
mi fate sputrefare?
Non vi volle nemen prendere il mare!
ELISA: Signore, v'offerisco
tutto quello che posso.
D. GIO: Son grato al vostro amore.
ARL: Vi ringrazio ancor io di tutto core,
ma intanto si potrebbe riposare.

D. GIO: Precedimi.
ELISA: Conducilo tu, Ombrino,
entro la mia capanna.
ARL: Non sempre la fortuna fu tiranna. *(parte con Ombrino)*

Scena ii
Don Giovanni ed Elisa

D. GIO: (Atta costei mi sembra a compensare
tutto quel che mi tolse a un tratto il mare.)
ELISA: Che parlate fra voi;
forse sdegnate i miei poveri doni?
D. GIO: Ah, no, gl'apprezzo, o cara, ma vorrei . . .
ELISA: Cosa, signor?
D. GIO: Quel vostro core . . .
ELISA: Eh, non è tempo di parlar d'amore.
D. GIO: Al primo balenar de' vostri sguardi
io rimasi ferito.
ELISA: Se creder vi potessi . . .
D. GIO: A voi prometto un'eterna costanza.
ELISA: Impunemente
manchereste di fede a un'infelice?
D. GIO: Non sa tradir chi ha nobil sangue in seno.
ELISA: Siete voi cavaliero?
D. GIO: Io nacqui tale, e tale morirò.
ELISA: Il nome vostro?
D. GIO: Don Giovanni Tenorio.
ELISA: I vostri passi
dove or sono indirizzati?
D. GIO: Per inchinarmi al trono
del vostro re, ch'alla Castiglia impera.
ELISA: Ah, Don Giovanni,
se non temessi
rimanere delusa . . .
D. GIO: Io non saprei
come meglio accertarvi. Ecco la mano.
ELISA: Giurate.
D. GIO: Giuro al nume ch'al cielo e al mondo impera:

voi sarete mia sposa.

ELISA: E se mancate?

D. GIO: Cada un fulmin dal ciel, e l'alma infida
precipiti agl'abissi.

ELISA: Ora vi credo. Ecco la destra mia.

D. GIO: (Amor pietoso, quanto ti deggio mai!)

ELISA: Che pensate fra voi?

D. GIO: Vo meditando le mie felicità.

ELISA: S'un cuor fedele
potrà farvi felice, in me l'avrete.
(Ama donna ciascuna
più dell'amante suo la sua fortuna.)

Se voi, mio caro,
fedel sarete,
sempre m'avrete
costante ognor.
Non mi tradite,
non m'ingannate;
se mi lasciate,
che mai farò?
No, che quel volto
non è mendace.
Quel ch'a voi piace
farà il mio cor. *(parte con Don Giovanni)*

Scena iii
Appartamenti di Donn'Anna.

Donn'Anna, Don Alfonso; indi il Commendatore

D. ALF: State lieta, Donn'Anna, ch'a momenti
il genitor s'appressa.

D. AN: Signor, tal volta il nostro cuor presago
è co' palpiti suoi di sue sventure.

D. ALF: Tempo or non è di meditar sciagure.

COM: Figlia, ti stringo al seno.
Oh, come lieto quivi voi rimiro!

Signor, de' siciliani il fiero orgoglio . . .
D. ALF: Lo so, fiaccaste, e ad impetrar perdono
de' lor commessi errori
in Castiglia verranno i promotori.
Il nostro re desia che pertanto
pensiate a custodirvi
per sicurezza della sua corona.
COM: Questa è troppa bontà.
D. ALF: Ei v'amò sempre,
ed or s'accresce in lui vieppiù l'amore,
perchè s'aumenta in voi merto e valore.
Per eternare il vostro nome,
del tempo edace ad onta,
equestre statua erigere vi fece,
e rese immune
l'atrio onorato dell'illustre marmo.
A vostra figlia scelse
uno sposo real
degno di voi, di lei.
La dote ei stesso le farà;
solo per me vi chiede
il paterno volere.
COM: Puole il sovran disporre a suo piacere.
Donn'Anna, udiste?
Della reggia bontà del signor nostro
che vi par? Rispondete.
D. AN: Io lieta incontro il reale favore;
può sempre il re disporre del mio core.
COM: Chi fia lo sposo?
D. ALF: Il Duca Ottavio,
del sovrano nipote,
vostro sposo sarà. Ma impallidite!
Fissate a terra i lumi!
COM: Simula per modestia, e il lieto annunzio,
ch'altrui fora caggion di vano orgoglio,
rende il suo cor per riverenza umile.
D. ALF: Con voi sen resti; il suo desire al padre
può la figlia spiegar senza rossore.
D. AN: Per me parlò abbastanza il genitore.

COM: Signore, al mio sovrano
favellate per me; disporre ei puote
come del sangue mio del mio volere.
D. ALF: Tutto il sovran saprà con suo piacere. *(parte)*

Scena iv
Commendatore e Donn'Anna

COM: Eh, che s'oppone alla vostra letizia?
D. AN: Ah, non so dirlo.
COM: Aprite il vostro interno.
D. AN: Staccarmi non saprei dal fianco vostro
senza un aspro dolore.
COM: Conosco, amata figlia, il vostro amore,
ma è necessario
al destin inchinar umil la fronte.
D. AN: Il destin nostro
da noi stessi facciamo;
non è tiranno il cielo, e de' mortali
non usa mai l'arbitrio violentare.
COM: Col genitor non s'ha da contrastare.
Del Duca Ottavio
la sposa voi sarete.
Se il vostro cor non acconsente al nodo,
il padre vostro faravvi acconsentir,
se in fiero sdegno e in odio aspro e spietato
non vorrete veder l'amor cangiato.

Tutta dal mio volere
la sorte tua dipende,
e chi meco contende
più figlia mia non è. *(parte)*

D. AN: Faccia mio padre tutto quello che può,
faccia il re stesso tutto quello che sa,
non vuo', nè il dico in vano,
all'odiato imeneo porger la mano. *(parte)*

Scena v
Spiaggia di mare come sopra.

Elisa, D. Giovanni; indi Arlechino

D. GIO: Ninfa cortese, son grato al vostro amor.
ELISA: Perchè non darmi il bel nome di sposa?
D. GIO: Tale ancora non siete.
ELISA: E che vi manca il nodo a stabilire?
D. GIO: Ciò che conviene:
le cerimonie, il rito
e le pompe nuzziali.
ELISA: Andiam dunque a compir codesti riti.
D. GIO: Ma non conviene, o cara,
ch'ora meco venghiate.
ELISA: Dunque quivi soletta mi lasciate?
D. GIO: Fra pochi giorni v'attendo alla città,
e il mio servo Arlecchin vi condurrà.
ELISA: Ingannarmi volete?
D. GIO: Non son capace di tanta iniquità;
il mio servo di ciò v'accerterà.
ARL: Il mio padrone
è costante, fedele e fedelone.
ELISA: I numi stessi
vi puniran, se me tradir pensate.
D. GIO: Di ciò, bell'idol mio, non dubitate.
ELISA: Posso spervarvi, o caro,
nell'amarmi costante?
D. GIO: Un'altra volta
giurerò, se bramate.
ELISA: Ite felice;
anch'io vi seguirò.
ARL: Aspettate, che presto io tornerò.
ELISA: Ed io frattanto resto
addolorata e trista.
ARL: (Scriveremo anche questa su la lista.)
D. GIO: (Invano speri rivedermi
mai più.) Mia cara, addio.
ELISA: Tutto tutto con te porti il cor mio. *(si dividono)*

Scena vi
Appartamenti di Don Alfonso.

Don Alfonso solo con foglio in mano.

D. Alf: "Don Giovanni Tenorio, il cui sfrenato
perfido cuor di mille colpe è reo,
s'involò dalla patria, e seco il cuore
l'empio portò d'una donzella illustre.
Donn'Isabella, unica figlia e cara
del duca d'Altomonte, è quella
che tradita rimase.
Or l'infelice sola siegue l'indegno,
che, sperando trovar scampo al delitto,
ver Castiglia fuggì.
S'ambi in poter del vostro re son giunti,
dateci pronto avviso.
L'infelice donzella abbiate a cuore;
fra' lacci a noi spedite il traditore."

Come in un nobil petto
può darsi un cor sì fiero,
e come un cavaliero
di fede può mancar!
La vilipesa dama,
ch'è per amor fuggita,
da me restituita
al genitor sarà!
Tremi però l'indegno,
vigliacco, mancatore,
nè speri il traditore
di ritrovar pietà. *(parte)*

Scena vii
Strada con veduta della casa del Commendatore.

Arlechino, indi Don Giovanni

ARL: Conservati fedele;
pensa ch'io sto al sereno,
ch'un raffreddore almeno
mi prenderò per te.

Che bella discrezzione
è quella del padrone,
voler che fermo stia
a far la sentinella
fintanto che non viene. Oh, questa è bella!
Il moccolo è finito,
e più non ci si vede.
Me n'anderò bel bello . . .
E se il padrone viene e non mi trova?
Bisognerà ch'aspetti.
Mi ricordo che disse:
"Aspettami colà fino ch'io vengo,
e se qualcuno volesse contrastare,
uccidilo." Mi voglio ora provare.

Per esempio se il nemico
mi tirasse una stoccata?
Ecco qua l'ho riparata
senz'avermi a incommodar.[1]

D. GIO: Chi va la!
ARL: (Quest'è il padrone,
zitto zitto voglio star.)
D. GIO: Se non parli, mascalzone,
qui svenato hai da restar.
Fuori il ferro, ah, eh, ih, ah!
E non cedi! Il braccio mio
più resistere non sa.

1. Arlecchino is probably stretched out on the ground with his sword extended upward.

ARL: (Che grand'homo che son io,
un eguale non si dà).
D. GIO: (Costui in vero ha gran valore,
e invincibile mi par.)
ARL: Sono il vostro servitore,
che vi stava ad aspettar.
D. GIO: Ed osasti, o vil poltrone,
di volermi trucidar!
A 2:
ARL: Lei mi scusi, mio padrone,
che l'ho fatto per burlar.

D. GIO: Orsù, della tua fede
vuo' fare esperimento.
Ascolta ben.
ARL: Parlate, che ci sento.
[D. GIO: Entra costì.][2]
ARL: All'oscuro?
D. GIO: Non paventar; le scale
tu salirai bel bello,
e quando giunto
nella sala maggiore tu sarai,
se vegliano li servi osserverai
da lungi, e di soppiatto
seguirò i passi tuoi;
un cenno sol mi basta,
una parola sola,
che al lato tuo sarò.
Intendesti, Arlechino?
ARL: Signore, no.
D. GIO: Non mi fare inquietare.
ARL: E se venisse qualche bastonata?
D. GIO: Non v'è dubbio: cammina.
ARL: Oh sorte ingrata! *(entra)*
D. GIO: Occasione più bella
sperar mai non potea
per vagheggiar di nuovo
di Donna Anna i bei lumi.
Il genitor austero,

2. From the Vienna edition, 1777.

allor che fui in Castiglia un'altra volta,
m'impediva sovente
il raggionar con lei.
La sua modestia era scopo a' miei sguardi,
argine a' miei desiri.
Ora ch'assente è il genitor severo,
ridurla a' miei desiri io non dispero.

ARL: Eh! Eh!

D. GIO: Sei tu? Il cenno è questo.

ARL: Non si sente nessuno.

D. GIO: Eccomi lesto. *(entrano)*

Scena viii
Appartamenti di Donn'Anna.

Donn'Anna e Lisetta

D. AN: Lasciami in pace.

LIS: E perchè mai, signora?

D. AN: Ho una smania nel sen che mi divora.
Vanne tu a riposar, lasciami sola.

LIS: E non volete che vi venga a spogliar?

D. AN: Da me stessa il farò.
Non so trovar più pace;
qualcosa di funesto
presagisce il mio core.

LIS: Eh, lasciate, signora, ogni timore.

D. AN: Dammi il lume, Lisetta;
di te per ora più bisogno non ho;
puoi andare a riposar. *(parte)*

LIS: Obbedirò.

Scena ix
Don Giovanni, Arlechino e detto.

LIS: Povera mia padrona,
oh quanto mi dispiace!

Perduta ha la sua pace,
che, sì che l'indovino,
la tormenta un pochin qualche amorino.

ARL: No che non c'è nessuno.

LIS: Aiuto!

D. GIO: Ignorantaccio, non parlare.

LIS: Oh poveretta me, gente è qui in sala!
Chi saranno? Ah, potessi
qualcheduno chiamar! Certo una voce
mi parve di sentir in quel cantone.
Inganna qualche volta l'apprensione.

Mi sento venir meno,
mi sento inorridir,
mi batte il cor nel seno,
mi sento già languir.
Pian pianino me ne vo.
Ah, trovassi almen la porta,
per farla un po' più corta,
io di qua me n'anderò. *(parte)*

Scena x
Don Giovanni e Arlechino[3]

D. GIO: No, non m'inganno. È questo
di Donn'Anna l'adorato soggiorno.
Che più si tarda?
Si rapisca e si fugga.
A qual periglio mai
mi strascina l'amore!
Riflettere che giova?
Amor mi sprona, amor m'assisterà.
Tutto è in silenzio,
coraggio non mi manca;
del bene che mi porge or la fortuna

3. At this point, the libretto prepared by Porta for Joseph Haydn (Esterháza, 1781) adds the following interesting stage direction: "*Magnifico giardino del Commendatore con cancellate che servono di fortezza al palazzo, diversi sedili erbosi e due urne. Luna che risplende.*"

abusarmi non vuo'. Più miglior tempo
di questo non si trova;
del mio spirto or vuo' far l'ultima prova.

Dell'onda sdegnata
non teme l'orgoglio
quel sasso, quel scoglio
che sorge nel mar.
Gl'insulti non teme
di vento nemico
quel tronco ch'antico
gli sa contrastar. *(entra)*

ARL: Giudizio, sior padrone. Se non foss'io,
che con la mia prudenza
regolassi quel strano umor bestiale,
sarebbe di già andato allo spedale.
Oh che fracasso!
La guaglia è nella rete.
Se posso, vo' bel bello
far per l'istessa strada il ritornello. *(parte)*

Scena xi

Donn'Anna, Don Giovanni; indi il Commendatore

D. AN: Lasciami, traditore;
con quale ardire penetrasti fin qui?
D. GIO: Taci.
D. AN: Non lo sperare.
D. GIO: Vieni tosto con me.
D. AN: Dove e in qual parte?
D. GIO: Raggion non rendo a te del voler mio.
D. AN: Padre! Servi! Lisetta! Un lume! Oh Dio!
D. GIO: E il padre e i servi
e i numi stessi or tu li chiami in vano.
Arrenditi.
D. AN: Non voglio.
D. GIO: Con questo ferro . . .

D. AN: Che violenze son queste! Ah, scellerato!
D. GIO: (Sono scoperto.) Vieni.
D. AN: Ah, padre amato!
COM: Don Giovanni! Voi qui? Figlia, ch'avvenne?
D. AN: Ah, padre, è questi un empio, un traditore;
col ferro in mano
giunsemi a minacciare.
Il perfido volea
all'inique sue voglie . . .
COM: Uscite, indegno, fuor di queste soglie.
D. GIO: (Pronto riparo adoperar conviene.)
D. AN: I servi desterò. Stelle! Ove sono? *(parte)*
COM: Malnato cavalier, onta simile
vuol vendetta, vuol sangue.
Oimè! Spengesti il lume!
Fra le tenebre ancora
saprò passarti il core. Vieni pure.
D. GIO: Son teco. *(si battono)*
COM: Ah, son ferito.
Torna, barbaro, torna. Ah, non mi reggo . . .
Vieni, vieni, ritorna a me d'appresso.
D. GIO: Chi è caggion del suo mal, pianga se stesso.

COM: Dalle squarciate vene
scorre in più parte il sangue;
il piè non mi sostiene,
cado . . . vacillo esangue . . .
Figlia . . . più non m'ascolta.
Servi . . . li chiamo invano.
Ah, che crudel martoro!
Barbaro . . . figlia . . . io moro. *(cade morto)*

Scena xii
Donn'Anna sola.

D. AN: Eccoci, o genitor . . . Cieli! Che miro?
Non respira! È già morto! Ah, dov'è l'empio,

barbaro feritor? Crudo spietato,
che ti fe' l'infelice? Ah, padre amato,
questo tenero pianto il primo uffizio
sia della mia pietà, ma da me attendi
la più giusta vendetta.
Su questa man invitta
l'infelice tua figlia a te lo giura.
Ah, padre, amato padre! Oh, che sciagura!

Tutte le furie unite
dentro il mio petto io sento,
che stan, per mio tormento,
a lacerarmi il cor.
Vittima del mio sdegno
fra poco tu sarai,
illeso non andrai
dal giusto mio furor. *(parte)*[4]

fine dell'atto primo

---

4. In the equivalent scene xi in the Esterháza edition, immediately following Donn'Anna's aria, Arlecchino enters and says: "Salva, salva. Meschin, che brutto caso! / Spero d'esser sicuro in questo vaso." The act then concludes as follows.

Scena xii

Donn'Anna, Don Alfonso, Lisetta, servi e serve del Commendatore con torcie ed armi, che sortono dal palazzo e s'avanzano.

LIS: Ch'è successo?
TUTTI: Ch'è accaduto?
D. AN: Deh, venite, soccorrete!
TUTTI: Giusto ciel, cos'ho veduto?
Non ho forza da parlar.
Sento che il sangue s'agita,
e per le vene circola
un fuoco, un certo gelo,
e un tenebroso velo
toglie la luce al dì.
Ah, non ho più ritegno,
predomina lo sdegno,
m'accende già il furor.
D. GIO: E sento in tal momento
già lacerarmi il cor.
ARL: E ticche, ticche, tocche,
mi va facendo il cor.

ATTO SECONDO

Scena i

Strada.

Don Giovanni, Arlecchino

D. Gio: Ah, destino crudele,
a qual periglio mai tu mi guidasti!
Oh donne all'huom funeste
per la vostra beltà!
Reso omicida già mi sono per voi.
Donn'Anna irata vendetta chiederà;
vorrà vedermi oppresso il re sdegnato.
Crudo perverso amor! Barbaro fato!
Arl: L'avete fatta bella.
Oh che rumor! Che caso! Che spavento!
D. Gio: Perciò tu ti sgomenti!
Risoluzion ci vuole.
Vanne al mio albergo,
e se qualcun colà di me cercasse,
rispondi che partito
all'istante son io.
Arl: Senza pranzare?
D. Gio: No, il mio pranzo colà fa' preparare.
Arl: Ottimamente.
D. Gio: Indi ritorna a me, che qualche tempo
vuo' nell'atrio celarmi,
immune a' delinquenti.
Arl: Io per me vi direi, signor padrone,
doppo aver fatto una buona mangiata
di battere ben presto ritirata.
D. Gio: Lascia far, partirem; ma è necessario
qualche tempo aspettar. Vanne di volo,
non mi lasciar colà gran tempo solo. *(parte)*
Arl: Va', torna, resta!
Non mi ricordo niente
di quello che m'ha detto.
Sono scarso un pochino d'intelletto. *(parte)*

Scena ii
Appartamenti di Don Alfonso.

Donn'Isabella e Don Alfonso

D. ISA: Signor, Donn'Isabella, unico germe
de' duchi d'Altomonte, a voi s'inchina,
e il favor vostro in suo soccorso implora.

D. ALF: Già tutto m'è palese, o mia signora.
Cura s'avrà di voi,
l'empio punito fra momenti sarà.
Ad ogni costo il monarca sdegnato
vuole che paghi il fio
dell'enorme delitto,
perchè al Commendator ha il sen trafitto.

D. ISA: Di tutto è ben capace
un mostro di perfidia.
Di quanto che a mio pro farete ognora,
vi renderà mercede il cielo ancora.

D. ALF: Olà, del reo si cerchi
da per tutte le parti; il re l'impone,
che brama dare al mondo un giusto esempio
come punisca un traditore, un empio. *(parte)*

D. ISA: Chi mai in quel core
figurare potea
tanta malvagità! Ah, se dal volto
si deve argomentar qual sia l'interno,
ingannata ciascuna io ben discerno.

È folle chi crede
costanza in amore,
è stolta chi fede
figura in un core
avezzo a ingannar. *(parte)*

Scena iii

Atrio con vari mausolei fra' quali la statua del Commendatore.

Don Giovanni, indi Donn'Anna

D. GIO: Sì, questo luogo
mi servirà d'asilo, e quest'orrori
mi celeranno almeno
dalle ricerche altrui. Ma più non posso
in piedi sostenermi.
Almen per poco, miei funesti pensieri,
in pace mi lasciate,
e tregua a questo core un poco date.

D. AN: Giacchè non m'è vietato
che le lacrime mie versare possa
su quest'illustre e venerato avello,
ombra del padre mio . . . Stelle, che miro?
Qui Don Giovanni? Ah, non a caso i numi
mel fecer ritrovare.
E come quel crudele
può ritrovar riposo?
Come il rimorso non trafigge il core
a questo mostro d'Averno, traditore?
Con questo ferro passerà il fellone
dal letargo alla morte . . .
Ma sarà grata
vittima così indegna al padre mio?
L'uccido o no? Oimè, che far degg'io?

Ombra del padre amato,
dimmi che vuoi da me?
Vuoi l'empio trucidato
vedere alli tuoi piè?
Parla. T'intendo appieno;
all'omicida il seno
a trappassare andrò.

Ombra del padre mio che qui t'aggiri,
vedi l'empio morir.

D. GIO: Ferma, che fai?
Estinto tu mi brami? Ecco il mio seno.
Meglio l'ira saziar così potrai.
Ecco il petto, ecco il sen, che tardi omai?
Morrò senza lo sfregio
d'una publica pena; ma rammenta
che la fiamma d'amor cieco mi rese,
e in quelli tuoi begl'occhi amor m'accese.
A un disperato per le tue ripulse
chi poteva porger freno o consiglio?
Venne in mal punto allora il padre armato,
e senza udir discolpe
al cimento m'indusse. Io, provocato,
colpi vibrai dal mio voler non retti.
Fra le tenebre il ferro chi diriger potea?
Ah, Donn'Anna, pietade; ti sia a cuore
d'un sventurato amante e vita e onore.

D. AN: Perfido, l'onor tuo a me tu chiedi?
E il mio chi mai difendere potrà
dall'ombra indegna?

D. GIO: Risarcir si potrebbe,
s'a te la destra . . .

D. AN: Scellerato! A tanto
così meco t'avanzi, e ancor ti soffro?

D. GIO: Al genitore, oh cara, il crudo sdegno
sacrificar tu dei,
non il sangue d'un reo che pietà chiede.
Del pentimento mio ti faccian fede
queste lacrime mie dal duol spremute.

D. AN: Al re tu dei,
non di femmina vil, gittarti ai piedi.

D. GIO: Da' labbri tuoi il mio destin dipende.
Deh, pronunzia, crudel, la mia sentenza,
condannami tu stessa.

D. AN: Sorgi, ti dico. (Ahimè, qual dolce incanto
è per me di costui la smania e il pianto!)

D. GIO: (Comincia a impietosire.)
Rivolgi a me uno sguardo,

per un momento soffri i mesti lumi
d'un che languisce e more solo per te.

D. AN: Un sguardo vuoi da me?
Forse tu speri con mentiti sospiri
d'ottenerne perdono?
(Ah, che in mirarlo
in atto umil con sì bel pianto agl'occhi
si calma il mio furore.)

D. GIO: Ah, Donn'Anna, pietà.

D. AN: Perfido cuore!
Volgiti a quella imago,
chiedi a quella pietà,
a quella spetta darti morte o perdono.

D. GIO: Ah, Donn'Anna, pietade del mio errore.

D. AN: Non merita pietade un traditore. *(parte)*

Scena iv

Don Giovanni e Arlecchino

D. GIO: Perfide stelle, finito ho di sperar!

ARL: È preparato . . .

D. GIO: È la pietade terminata per me.
Un fulmine non v'è? V'è una saetta?

ARL: Andiamo, sior padron, ch'il cuoco aspetta.

D. GIO: E perchè da quel marmo,
Commendator, non vieni a subissarmi?
Forse meno crudele
della figlia tu sei;
l'amoroso trasporto
forse perdoni a un infelice amante?
Per contrasegno almeno
d'un benigno perdono a me favella.

ARL: Oh, questa sì ch'è bella.

D. GIO: Arlecchino.

ARL: Signor?

D. GIO: Colà t'appressa, e da mia parte dille
che meco a pranzo il bramo.

ARL: Chi bramate con voi?

D. GIO: Il Commendator.
ARL: La statua?
D. GIO: Sì.
ARL: Eh, via!
(Per certo il mio padron dato ha in pazzia.)
D. GIO: Vanne, non replicare.
ARL: E cosa gl'ho da dir? Come ho da fare?
D. GIO: Manco ciarle, fa' presto.
ARL: Signor Commendatore stimatissimo,
padrone colendissimo,
il mio padron v'invita a desinare.
Verrete sì o no?
Sì! Oh poveretto me!
D. GIO: Che cosa è stato?
ARL: Con il capo l'invito ha già accettato.
D. GIO: Dille che dal suo labbro
intendere lo bramo.
ARL: Caro padron, scusate;
non m'accosto più là, se m'accoppate.
D. GIO: Commendatore, d'amistade in segno,
alla mensa t'invito.
Dal labbro tuo sapere ora lo vuo';
rispondi se t'aggrada.
COM: Sì, verrò.
ARL: Ah, mamma mia!
D. GIO: Zitto, all'albergo torna,
e fa' che raddoppiata
tosto la mensa sia;
a ognun celato
fa' che sia il convitato.
Io fra momenti colà mi porterò.
Hai tu capito?
ARL: Con tante cose sono già stordito. *(parte)*

Scena v
Don Giovanni solo

Don Giovanni, che fai?
A qual funesto passo
ti trasporta l'ardir? Osi alla mensa
passar il tempo in riso,
e quello da te ucciso
brami teco a mangiar? Sogno? Vaneggio?
Ah, che quel più non sono
ch'una volta già fui.
Sono un serpente, un demone, una furia.
Oh Dio, il suol traballa,
e una terra caligine
offusca gl'occhi miei;
imagini d'orrore
mi van girando intorno.
Ah, che del mio morir è giunto il giorno!

Par che dal cielo un fulmine
sul capo mi precipiti,
turba di neri spiriti
qua parmi di veder.
Di qua Donn'Isabella
mi sgrida e mi minaccia,
Elisa mi martella,
Donn'Anna mi rinfaccia
la sua tradita fè.
Di là il Commendatore
mi mostra il sen trafitto.
Astrea[5] col suo rigore
rimprovera il delitto.
Ah, che nel mio cervello
ho un foco, un Mongibello,[6]
un aspide, un serpente,
che con l'acuto dente
va lacerando il cor. *(parte)*

5. Greek goddess of justice.
6. Mount Etna.

Scena vi
Camera nella locanda.

Arlechino e Corallina

ARL: Ebbene, Corallina,
il pranzo sarà lesto?
COR: Fra una mezz'oretta
all'ordine sarà.
ARL: Bada che non vi sia nessun disordine.
COR: Magnifico sarà, non dubitare.
ARL: (Mi voglio con costei un po' spiegare.)
Parlare ti dovrei.
COR: Per parte di chi?
ARL: D'un galantuomo.
COR: Costui chi è? È bello, spiritoso?
ARL: Oh, l'è un bell'omo,
bassoto, spiritoso, traccagnoto,
che veste a tutta moda,
civile, creanzato,
bello di viso e nel parlar garbato.
COR: Non lo conosco.
ARL: E pur lui vi conosce;
è innammorato cotto.
COR: Oh, mi burlate!
ARL: E se sperar potesse
grata corrispondenza,
a voi si scoprirebbe.
COR: Dirò: se mi piacesse,
io forse l'amerei.
ARL: Oh cosa dice lei!
Lo vuol veder adesso?
COR: Volentier lo vedrò.
ARL: Aspetti un pochettin, lo chiamerò.
COR: (Ingannata mi son, di lui non parla.)
Che istoria è questa mai!
ARL: Ha visto?
COR: Chi?
ARL: Quel che per lei sospira.

COR: (Costui certo delira.)
Io non viddi che voi.
ARL: Ma . . .
COR: Siete voi quello?
ARL: Son io . . .
COR: Perchè prima d'adesso
non avete parlato?
ARL: Sono un po' vergognoso.
COR: (Oh quanto mai è grazioso!)
ARL: E così cosa dite?
COR: Dico . . .
ARL: Via, su, parlate.
COR: Anch'io son vergognosa.
ARL: Oh, che gran bella cosa.
COR: . . . in verità, che mi date nel genio.
ARL: Siete fanciulla?
COR: Certo.
ARL: Ed io son putto ancora.
COR: Non mi son maritata,
perchè non ho trovato
chi nel genio mi dia.
ARL: Posso sperar d'urtar la simpatia?
COR: In verità . . . Basta . . . Non vuo' parlare.
ARL: Dunque, cosa farò?
COR: Si può sperare.

In quel tuo visetto
leggiadro, furbetto,
ci veggo un so che.
Intendi, carino,
mio caro Arlechino,
tu sai che cos'è. *(partono insieme)*

Scena vii
Appartamenti di Don Alfonso.

Donn'Anna e Don Alfonso

D. AN: Ah, signor, se pietade in voi s'annida,
castigate e punite l'omicida.
D. ALF: Figlia, che con tal nome io vuo' chiamarvi,
per quel tenero amor ch'a voi mi lega,
vendicata sarete.
D. AN: Ah, non lo spero.
D. ALF: Per ogni dove dalle guardie del re
è il reo cercato.
D. AN: Lo viddi or or ne' mausolei celato,
che prendeva riposo.
D. ALF: Ne' mausolei l'indegno!
E tanto osò quel scelerato core?
D. AN: Volea l'iniquo
procurar di placarmi,
inventando più scuse al suo delitto.
Ma sen fugge il ribaldo se tardate.
D. ALF: Di ciò non dubitate.
D. AN: Vado frattanto
a sfogar da me sola il rio dolore.
Oh perdita crudel! Ah, genitore! *(parte)*
D. ALF: No, non andrà alla patria in lacci avvinto.
Colà dovrà morire. All'atrio intorno
vegli un stuolo di guardie notte e giorno.
Fame l'ucciderà se non un ferro,
e non vi sia alimentarlo ardisca;
e se ardisse qualcuno mai per sorte
contradir al comando, è reo di morte.

Talora la clemenza
giova d'appresso al trono,
ed il negar perdono
tal volta è crudeltà.
Ma a quello ch'ostinato
del fallo non si pente

è l'essere clemente
un segno di viltà. *(parte)*[7]

Scena viii
Sala con tavola magnificamente addobata.

Don Giovanni e Arlecchino

ARL: Signor padrone, è in tavola.
D. GIO: Ah, più che penso
scacciar dalla mia mente
i funesti pensieri,
più s'affacciano al cor, lugubri, neri.
ARL: La minestra patisce.
D. GIO: Il mangiare m'annoia,
disperato son io,

7. Porta added this additional scene, for which Haydn wrote the music.

Scena viii
Donn'Isabella sola.

Mora l'infido, sì, mora . . . Ma, oh dei!
Par che vacilli in ria tempesta il core.
Del mio funesto amore
la crudel rimembranza
già mi torna in mente.
Vorrei vederlo estinto;
salvo pure lo bramo,
e sento nel mio sen ch'ancor io l'amo.
Misero me, che dissi!
S'asconda nel mio seno
l'abborrita mia fiamma,
e sol s'accenda il core
d'odio, vendetta e d'un crudel furore.
Ah sì, vedrammi estinta
il mio destin, non avvilita mai.
Andrò sola, raminga,
fuggitiva infelice in tanti affanni.
Ah, che più mi serbate, astri tiranni?

Mi sento nel seno
dal duolo tiranno
che pieno d'affanno
mi palpita il cor. *(parte)*

la morte è il mio sollievo.
ARL: Un bel morir tutta la vita onora,
ma un bel mangiar salva la vita ancora.
D. GIO: Divertimi, Arlecchino,
solleva il tuo padrone.
ARL: Non faccio già il buffone.
D. GIO: Canta.
ARL: Prima di mangiare
è difficil che possa ben cantare.
D. GIO: Canta e poi mangerai.
ARL: Cosa devo cantar?
D. GIO: Quel che tu vuoi.
ARL: Qual cosa canterò.
D. GIO: Sì, come puoi.
ARL: "Padre, figlia, Siface,
adorato mio re. Cara Mandane,
ah, genitor, t'accheta.
Numi! Stelle! Comete!
Marzia, Fulvia, Ezio, Berenice!
E lei, signor Siface, che ne dice?
È morto e più non vive il gran Catone . . ."[8]
Io non ne so di più, signor padrone.
D. GIO: T'accheta, che son stanco
di soffrirti di più.
Si porti in tavola.
ARL: Subitamente.
D. GIO: È folle chi dà mente
ai spiriti, alle larve,
sebbene pur mi parve
che favellasse a me. Con queste orecchie
sentii le sue parole . . .
Eh, talvolta succede
ch'a noi la fantasia fa travedere.

8. The persons mentioned by Arlecchino are characters from various melodramas by Metastasio.

Scena ix

Arlecchino, Tiburzio, Corallina e Don Giovanni

COR: È all'ordine, signor.
TIB: Vada a sedere. *(siegue minuetto)*
D. GIO: Arlecchino.
ARL: Signore?
D. GIO: Da ber. Almen potessi
nel dolce umor di Bacco
ammorzar la passion e il fier cordoglio.
Un brindisi qui adesso fare io voglio.
"Dame gentili, illustri cavalieri,
del boemico suol pregio ed onore,
vi doni il ciel propizio
di Nestore l'età; regni fra voi
l'amicizia, la pace, onore e fede,
e nelli vostri petti abbian la sede.
Prodi guerrier, che del feroce Marte
veri seguaci e imitator ne siete,
che per virtù, per senno e per valore
fate scordare a noi
gl'antichi valorosi e grand'eroi,
sian mura i vostri petti,
fulmini i vostri ferri,
e il solo aspetto delle vostre bandiere
fugga e disperda l'inimiche schiere.
Gente benigna, publico clemente,
astro maligno a voi
minacciar mai non possa influssi rei,
ma facciano gli dei
ch'illeso questo suolo sempre sia,
nè mai di Giove l'ira qui sia volta.
Evviva Praga, evviva chi m'ascolta."
ARL: Adesso tocca a me. Care ragazze,
del povero Arlecchino
scusate l'ignoranza,
ch'un brindisi farà ma alla sua usanza.

Euch bleibe ich stets ergeben,
Mägdchen, die schön und herzig seyd;
Ihr solt leben, Ihr solt schweben
In Anmuth und Zufriedenheit.[9]

D. GIO: Spiritoso davvero.
Ma il tempo passa, più differir non vuo'.
Oltrepassata è l'ora,
ed il Commendator non giunge ancora?
Ah, sempre più confermo l'opinione
che fu sogno, chimera ed illusione.

FINALE

D. GIO: Venga il restante in tavola,
che voglio sortir subito.
(Mentre assai forte dubito
d'esser sorpreso qua.)
ARL: Animo, Corallina,
portate da mangiar.
COR: Prendete sta gallina.
TIB: La salsa eccola qua.
ARL: Ecco, signor padrone,
la madre d'un cappone.
D. GIO: Trinciala come va.
ARL: La trincio alla mia usanza,
che meglio assai mi par.
TIB: Eccovi qui il bodino.
ARL: Cos'è questo bodino?
Odora e par polenta.
No, che non è polenta,
ma li somiglia un poco.
Oh ch'eccellente cuoco,
degno d'addottorar.
D. GIO: Ardisci tu, animale,
mangiar prima di me!

9. And I shall always be devoted to you, / maidens, you who are beautiful and warm-hearted. / You shall live, you shall float / in grace and satisfaction.

ARL: Potrebbe farvi male,
se non l'assaggio affè.
TIB: Prendete, ecco, l'arrosto,
e questo è il fricandò.
ARL: Ariosto e Fracastoro.[10]
COR: Eccoti i maccheroni.
ARL: Oh cari, vengo meno.
Oh, come sono buoni;
mi sento liquefar.
D. GIO: Pare che sia battuto,
guardate voi chi è.
ARL: Cari, aspettate un poco.
TIB: Nessuno abbiam veduto.
COR: Nessuno là non c'è.
D. GIO: Può darsi; avrò sbagliato.
Un piatto.
ARL: È preparato.
D. GIO: Resta tu qui per or.
TIB: Mi pare da lontano
sentir qualche rumor.
COR: S'avanza piano piano.
Oimè, che batticuor!
D. GIO: No, che non m'ingannai,
qualcuno vuol passar.
ARL: Oh, cosa dite mai!
D. GIO: Tornate un po' a guardar.
TIB: Me infelice, ch'ho veduto!
COR: Una larva! Aiuto! Aiuto!
TIB: Un demonio che camina.
A 2: Che scompiglio! Che ruina!
Siam perduti in verità.
ARL: Sior padron?
D. GIO: Che cos'è stato?
ARL: Presto, presto, ch'è arrivato
quel signore molinaro
tutto quanto incipriato;
voglio dir quel del cavallo,

10. Ariosto was a Renaissance epic poet, author of *Orlando furioso;* Fracastoro was a Renaissance poet and physician, author of *Syphilis sive Moribus Gallicus.*

quel che sopra il piedestallo,
ch'è di marmo, l'iscrizzione,
col cimiero e col bastone,
tutto quanto intirizzito,
per la cena, per l'invito,
vuol passare, vuol entrare . . .
Ah, m'ha fatto spiritare,
e più fiato in sen non ho.

D. GIO: Sciocchi, vili quanti siete;
ritiratevi e vedrete
se lo vado a far passar.
Prendi il lume.

ARL: Per che fare?

D. GIO: Devi andarlo ad incontrare.

ARL: Oh, mi scusi, non son buono.

D. GIO: Prendi il lume, o ti bastono.

ARL: Lei mi vuol troppo onorar.

TIB: Ecco che s'avvicina.

A 2: Andiamoci a salvar.

COR: Andiamcene in cantina
ben presto a rinserrar. *(si ritirano)*

Scena x

Commendatore, D. Giovanni e Arlecchino

D. GIO: Siedi, Commendatore.

COM: Io siedo.

D. GIO: Scusa ti chiedo
s'annoiato dal gran lungo aspettare
la mensa cominciai . . .
Ma tu non mangi!
Quanto di raro
di cibi e di liquori
puol provedere Castiglia è a te presente.
Domanda ciò che vuoi.

COM: Non voglio niente.

D. GIO: Dunque tu sdegni un simile convito?

COM: Sono pago ora.
M'invitasti alla mensa, io non mancai.
T'invito a cenar meco, tu verrai?
D. GIO: A cenar teco, e dove?
COM: Vieni da me, che ti sarà palese.
D. GIO: (Che fo? Vado . . . Ma, oh Dio! . . .
Vada lungi il timore!)
Tel prometto, verrò.
COM: Teco il servo conduci.
D. GIO: Il condurrò.
ARL: Eh, eh, signor padron.
D. GIO: Taci, importuno.
ARL: Diteli da mia parte che digiuno.

Scena xi

Tiburzio, Corallina, Arlecchino; indi Don Giovanni

COR: È partito?
TIB: Se n'è andato?
A 2: Posso appena prender fiato
che m'ha fatto spiritar.
COR: Parmi ancor vederlo adesso.
TIB: A me pur sembra lo stesso.
A 2: Ah, fuggiamo via di qua.
D. GIO: È già vano ogni timore,
perchè mai di qua partir?
A 2: Per pietade, mio signore,
non ci fate intimorir.
ARL: Esco fuori,[11] son sicuro.
Se n'è andato a far squartar?[12]

11. Probably from under a table.

12. At this point, the Vienna libretto of 1777 and the Esterháza libretto substitute the following lines.

D. GIO: Non temete, ve lo giuro;
non ci è più da paventar.
TIB., COR., ARL., D. GIO: Vada lungi ogni timore;
cominciamo a respirar.

COR: Ah, signore, v'assicuro . . .
TIB: . . . c'ho creduto di crepar.
TUTTI: Oh che imbroglio! Oh ch'accidente!
Dal spavento, dal timore
va balzando in petto il core,
posso appena respirar.
D. GIO: Non vi turbi l'accidente,
è viltà l'aver timore;
imparate dal mio core
ogni incontro a superar.

fine dell'atto secondo

ATTO TERZO

Scena i

Luogo remoto

Don Giovanni, il Commendatore e Arlechino

D. GIO: Eccomi a mantenerti
la parola già data.
Qual luogo è questo mai?
E questa mensa ti par degna di me?
COM: Sì, questa mensa ben si conviene a te.
Approssimati.
D. GIO: Perchè?
COM: Ti bramo a me vicino.
D. GIO: Ed a che fare?
COM: A sedere, a mangiare.

TUTTI: Allegramente
qui s'ha da stare,
nè più si deve
qui paventare;
con trombe e flauti,
tamburri e nacchere,
fagotti e timpani,
in festa e giubilo
qui s'ha da star.

D. Gio: Sì che verrò.
Prendi qua la mia spada ed il cappello.
Arl: Non v'accostate là, padron mio bello.
D. Gio: Eccomi a te d'appresso.
Quai cibi sono questi?
Rospi, serpenti, aspidi!
E chi credi ch'io sia,
forse d'Averno la crudel Megera[13]
o il trifauce custode[14] dell'abbisso?
Com: Mangia, s'hai cuore.
Impallidisci e tremi?
D. Gio: Su questo volto
mai non si vide a comparir timore.
T'inganni se credi . . .
Com: Mangia, s'hai cuore.
D. Gio: Per fare a te vedere
che timore non ho,
rospi, serpenti, cicute io mangerò.
Arl: Badate, sior padrone,
che vi faranno dell'indigestione.
Com: Ascolta, Don Giovanni.
D. Gio: Cosa dirmi tu vuoi?
Com: I tuoi enormi delitti
è stanco il cielo di soffrire di più.
In te stesso ritorna;
da' numi implora un benigno perdono.
Pentiti.
D. Gio: No. Io così vil non sono.
Com: Volgi agli dei
con umil cor le calde preci e i voti,
e il perdono verrà.
D. Gio: Son nomi ignoti
i numi a me; già per lunga staggione
perduto ho l'uso
di favellar con essi.
Com: Pentiti.
D. Gio: Ch'io mi penta?

13. One of the three Furies.
14. Cerberus, a three-headed dog.

COM: La tua sfrenata vita ora detesta,
invoca l'alto potere de' numi.
D. GIO: Ah, che più tosto invocherò d'Averno
le terribili furie;
esse verranno a lacerarmi il seno.
Numi spietati, deità menzognere,
il vostro braccio ora sfido a vendetta.
COM: L'ultima volta è questa che tel dico.
Pentiti.
D. GIO: Ch'io mi penta?
COM: Il ciel per me ti parla.
D. GIO: Se fia vero che in cielo
sovra l'huomo mortal vi sia potere,
s'è giustizia lassù,
nelle viscere sue m'ascondi il suolo.
COM: Precipita all'abbisso, anima rea.
ARL: Oh, questo in verità non lo credea. *(fugge)*

Scena ii
Appartamenti di Don Alfonso.

Don Alfonso, Donn'Anna; indi Arlechino

D. ALF: Vane finora
son state le ricerche;
dall'atrio già l'indegno fuggì.
Forse ch'ascoso
si sarà in qualche bosco.
Ma a lungo non potrà restar celato,
troppo il reo dalle guardie è ricercato.
D. AN: Voglia il ciel che si trovi.
D. ALF: O presto o tardi l'empio si troverà.
Troppo al re cale
aver in mano l'omicida indegno . . .
D. AN: Ma qual rumor io sento!
ARL: Oh che caso! Oh che nuova! Oh che spavento!
D. ALF: Che rechi?
ARL: Il mio padrone . . .

D. ALF: Palesa, ove è celato?
ARL: Il diavolo, signor, se l'ha portato.
D. AN: Possibile sarà?
D. ALF: E pensi tu, buffone,
con tai fole salvare il tuo padrone?
Olà, sia custodito.
ARL: Per carità, sentite.
D. AN: Sentiamo.
D. ALF: Ebben, favella.
ARL: Quel signor del cimiero,
cioè che sta a cavallo . . .
perchè . . . come . . . quando . . . allora che venne . . .
non mangiò niente . . .
con li serpenti per via della mano . . .
pentiti, e lui non voleva . . .
in somma andiede giù,
nè mai più si vederà ritornar su.
D. ALF: Da' detti di costui
niente si può capire.
D. AN: Un qualche caso strano
sembra che sia successo!
ARL: Troppo chiaro ho parlato,
ma se non intendete,
chiamate Corallina e lo saprete.
D. ALF: Chi è costei?
ARL: Quella che in casa alloggiò il mio padrone.
D. ALF: Venga dunque costei, e tu ritirati,
ma nol fate sortir da questo loco.
ARL: Ma io sono innocente.
D. ALF: Lo vedremo.
ARL: Oh poveretto me, io sudo, io tremo.
D. ALF: Il prestar fede a' detti di costui
or prudenza non è; forse al confronto
facile pur sarà scoprir l'arcano.
Donn'Anna, per un poco m'allontano. *(parte)*

Scena iii
Donn'Anna sola.

Se fosse ver che il cielo
punito avesse l'indegno traditore,
tornerebbe la quiete a questo core.
Doppo tante sciagure,
doppo tanti disastri
necessaria è la calma
per tornare la quiete e pace all'alma.

Geme la tortorella
nel caro nido amato,
se sente là sul prato
il serpe a sibilar.
Ma poi s'altrove il mira
volger l'acuto dente,
nuovo piacer risente
e torna a respirar. *(parte)*

Scena iv
Corallina e Arlechino; indi Don Alfonso

ARL: Corallina, sei qua?
COR: Qua fui chiamata
dal ministro del re,
che saper volle il fatto della cena.
Tutto a lui raccontai.
Don Giovanni dov'è?
ARL: Lontano assai il diavol l'ha portato.
COR: D'esser sua sposa pur mi [ha] lusingato,
ed io da pazza
prestai fede a' suoi detti; or che farò?
ARL: In questa lista te pur scriverò.
COR: Hai raggion di burlarmi.
Il ministro s'appressa.
D. ALF: È ver pur troppo quello che narrasti.
Donn'Anna non è qua?

ARL: Noi non l'abbiam veduta.
D. ALF: Vadasi a lei il tutto a raccontar.
Alla sua patria torni Donn'Isabella.
La giustizia del cielo ha prevenuto
il tardo colpo di giustizia umana.
Il terribile caso omai c'insegni
che l'huom muore qual visse, e il giusto cielo
dimostra adesso a noi con quest'esempi
come punisca i dissoluti e gl'empi. *(parte)*

Scena v
Corallina ed Arlechino

ARL: Corallina!
COR: Arlechino!
ARL: E noi cosa faremo?
COR: Se vuoi, ci sposeremo.
ARL: La cosa del padrone
mi dà qualch'apprensione.
COR: Sei tanto delicato?
ARL: Son un huomo onorato.
COR: Dunque non mi vuoi più?
ARL: Non dico questo . . .
COR: Non vuo' difficoltà; dimmi sì o no.
ARL: Ebben, quand'è così, ti sposerò.
COR: Andiamo a celebrar le nostre nozze.
ARL: Andiamo, andiamo pure.
COR: Tempo non è di rammentar sciagure. *(parte)*

Scena ultima
Infernale.

Don Giovanni solo; coro di furie.

CORO: Fra nere furie orribbili
per sempre hai da penar.

D. GIO: Spietati dei dell'Erebo,
mi sento lacerar!
CORO: Fra nere furie orribbili
per sempre hai da penar.
D. GIO: Chi dunque mi condanna?
CORO: Sovvengati Donn'Anna.
D. GIO: Che smania! Che dolore!
CORO: Peggio il Commendatore
soffrì per tua caggion.
D. GIO: Ah sorte iniqua e fella!
CORO: Sovvengati Isabella.
D. GIO: Pietà d'un infelice!
CORO: Tu con la pescatrice
usasti crudeltà.
D. GIO: Ma quando cesseranno
tanti tormenti e guai?
CORO: Non cesseranno mai,
per sempre hai da penar.
D. GIO: Ahi che pena! Che dolore!
Oh, che affanno, che brucciore!
Più non [posso] sopportar!
CORO: Fra nere furie orribbili
per sempre hai da penar.

fine del dramma

Il convitato di pietra

Giuseppe Calegari

1777

IL
CONVITATO DI PIETRA

dramma giocoso
per musica
da rappresentarsi
nel nobile
Teatro Tron
di San Cassiano
nel carnovale
dell'anno 1777

In Venezia, MDCCLXXVII

Presso Gio. Battista Casali
Con licenza de' superiori

ATTORI

Prima buffa
Donna Isabella, Rosalba, Donn'Anna—La signora Geltruda Flavis

Primo buffo mezzo carattere
D. Giovanni—Il signor Domenico Madrigali

Primo buffo caricato
Passarino, servo di D. Giovanni—Il signor Virginio Bondicchi

Seconda buffa
D. Ximena—La sig. Rosa Pallerini

Don Pietro, Don Sancio, barigello—Il signor Alessandro Giovanola

Duca Ottavio—Il signor N. N.

Ines, cameriera di D. Anna—La signora Marianna Bindi

Commendatore d'Oiola—Il sig. Lorenzo Conobio

La scena si finge in Napoli ed in Castiglia.
La musica è del sig. maestro Giuseppe Callegari.

MUTAZIONI DI SCENA

Atto primo

Notte. Sala reale.

Notte. Strada.

Appartamento di D. Isabella in abito da camera e tavolino con lumi.

Spiaggia con tempesta di mare.

Anticamera in corte di Castiglia.

Notte. Camera di D. Anna con lumi.

Strada con porta grande di casa laterale.

Atto secondo

Notte. Anticamera suddetta in corte con lumi.

Tempio illuminato colla statua del Comendatore.

Solita anticamera in corte.

Strada diversa dalle prime.

Camera di D. Giovanni con credenza e lumi.

Camera di D. Anna con lumi.

Strada.

Tempio lugubre. Statua nel mezzo ad una tavola imbandita.

Infernale.

ATTO PRIMO

Scena prima
Notte. Sala reale.

D. Isabella in farsetto e D. Giovanni involto in un lungo mantello alla spagnola col cappello sugl'occhi.

D. Isa: Non sperar mai ch'io ti lasci, *(tenendo D. Giovanni per la mano)*
non sperar mai di fuggire!
No, spietato, il mio martire
desti almeno in te pietà!
D. Gio: Sì, che alfin mi lascierai;
stanco son di più soffrire.
Già saranno i sdegni e l'ire
qual si fu la crudeltà.
D. Isa: Ah, tiranno menzognero!
D. Gio: Ma tu sai ch'io dico il vero.
D. Isa: Ah, crudel, oltre l'oltraggio,
d'insultarmi hai tu coraggio?
D. Isa: Il tuo ardire
a 2: orror mi fa.
D. Gio: Il tuo affanno
D. Gio: Eh, lasciami alfine. *(tentando liberarsi)*
D. Isa: No, fin ch'io potrò. *(afferrando il mantello)*
Indegno, spietato,
qual barbaro fato
a te mi serbò?
D. Gio: Quel fato che vuole
sì poche parole
e un sì più che un no.
D. Isa: Almen ti palesa.
D. Gio: È inutil pretesa.
D. Isa: Ed io griderò
soccorso, pietà. *(alzando la voce)*
D. Gio: Deh! Taci una volta!
Che femina stolta!
D. Isa: Soccorso, pietà! *(più forte; si ritira)*

Scena ii

D. Pietro con lume e D. Giovanni in disparte.

D. PIE: Chi mai chiede soccorso?
Chi mai osa turbar le reggie stanze
in quest'ore notturne?
Il re che qui m'invia intese e disse
che voce feminil pietà chiedea;
ma quivi alcun non vedo,
se agl'occhi miei pur credo. *(cerca intorno col lume dalla parte opposta ove sta ritirato D. Giovanni, che in questo fratempo si porrà in ginocchio presso D. Pietro senza che se ne accorga)*

D. GIO: Ah, mio zio, ah, per pietà!
Deh, perdon, se pur m'amate.
Fu l'amore e la mia età:
colpe umane e colpe usate.
Da voi spero libertà.

D. PIE: Sorgete, mio nipote! Io son sì oppresso, *(D. Giovanni s'alza)*
sì confuso son io,
che non so che pensar. Come! In quest'ora
che fu? Qual donna? Orsù, schietto parlate.
D. GIO: Sì, lo dirò; ma deh, non mi sgridate. *(facendo il timido)*
Amai Donna Isabella, all'amor mio
sempre ingrata, crudel, perchè pietosa
al Duca Ottavio. In van nol sospettai;
sconosciuto qui venni e ne trionfai.
D. PIE: Malnato cavaliero! Ove apprendeste
il genio a violentar? E che poss'io
contro l'ira del re quando a lui nota
sia la vostra perfidia?
D. GIO: Ignora il violator Donn'Isabella.
D. PIE: L'ignora?
D. GIO: Sì, e forse essa sospetta
il Duca, e col gridar sperò vendetta.
D. PIE: Sia però che si voglia:
di qui partir conviene. Unito a un servo,
portatevi in Castiglia; ivi denaro

e mie lettere insiem non mancheranno.
Io qui reggerò il resto,
ma il mal oprar, sappiate, io lo detesto. *(sostenuto)*

D. GIO: Ma voi, mio zio, presso il re sì potente,
m'obligate a partir? Io non credea . . .

D. PIE: Gioventù sconsigliata!
Vi par lieve delitto
una dama oltraggiar nel regio tetto?
Il semplice sospetto
la libertà potria costarvi e poi,
avverata la colpa,
con mia pena infinita,
o il forzato imeneo o pur la vita.
Andiamo. Il re m'attende e fors'è stanco
di tanto induggio mio. Forse alcun altro
sorprenderci potria.
Seguitemi; lo scampo
io vi procurerò da questa reggia.
Partite, e il nuovo sol qui non vi veggia.

D. GIO: Partirò; voi l'imponete.
Spiega il pianto il mio dolor. *(fingendo)*

D. PIE: Ricordatevi che siete,
rispettate il vostro onor.

D. GIO: Sì, mio zio. *(come sopra)*

D. PIE: Partite; addio,
e v'accompagni il ciel.

D. GIO: Parto da questo ciel. *(partono)*

Scena iii
Strada e notte.

Passarino, poi D. Giovanni

PASS: Povero Passarin, gran vita è questa!
Ma quel becco cornù del mo patron
no vien più via dalla conversazion.
E mi tutta la notte,

come fusse un allocco, un barbagian,
per lu me tocca andar a zirondon!
Ma zitto, che me par . . . l'è lu . . . al so passo.
Voi vendicarme e torme un po' de spasso.

D. GIO: Sento gente. Chi va là?
Passarin, forse sei tu?
PASS: Son Don Slosa Baccalà,
buon da porvi in un ragout. *(contrafacendo la voce)*
D. GIO: Sicuro al ciel, Cavaliero . . .
PASS: Non ti stimo un corno intiero.
D. GIO: Mezzo all'armi. [Mezzo all'armi.] *(impugna la spada)*
PASS: Via, ti prova di tirarmi! *(si stende in terra con la spada in alto)*
D. GIO: Ah . . . ah . . . ah! . . .
PASS: Eh . . . eh . . . eh! . . .
Bravo. Ahi! Son morto! Oimè!

D. GIO: I pari tuoi finiscono così.
PASS: Oh novo Don Chisiot dei nostri dì!
Ve seu mo ben sfogà?
Se cerchè Passarin, eccolo qua. *(s'alza)*
D. GIO: Ah! Briccone, birbante . . .
PASS: No me fe' l'arrogante,
che ritorno Don Slosa, e a' numi il giuro
dal mio fettor più non sarai sicuro.
D. GIO: Buffone! Or basta, si finiscan gli scherzi.
Parliam sul serio. In somma,
da Napoli convien tosto partire.
PASS: Disiu da bon?
D. GIO: E prima che il sol nasca.
PASS: Vu avì donca passà qualche burasca.
Don Zuan, abbiè giudizi,
perchè el mal far condus al precipizi.
D. GIO: Eh, non seccarmi. Orsù, convien partire.
Seguimi, andiam.
PASS: Troveve un servitor;
pagheme prima e andè, se gavì cuor.
D. GIO: E tu l'hai di lasciarmi?
PASS: Se volì, me despias; ma, sior patron,

a Napoli lassar i maccaron
a l'è un gran pas.

D. GIO: Ma se vieni in Castiglia,
vi son fiumi di latte,
colline di formaggio,
e di bottiro fatta ogni montagna.

PASS: Se disì el ver, quest'è una gran cucagna.

D. GIO: Io dico il ver; ma tu venir non vuoi?
Resta pur, resta in libertà.

PASS: Disime: *(tenendolo pel tabarro)*
col latte, col bottiro e col formaggio,
se ghe farina e fogo,
ne farà i maccaroni un qualche cogo?

D. GIO: Questo facil sarà.

PASS: Co l'è cussì, mi vegno in verità.
Andemio adess'. Aspettè, caro vu,
no go onti i stivali.

D. GIO: Questo è il minor dei mali;
già per acqua si va.

PASS: Oimè, oimè! Questo l'è un altro intoppo.

D. GIO: Ma perchè mai?

PASS: Perchè
dove xe l'acqua no ghe vin.

D. GIO: Di tutto vi sarà.

PASS: Oh, fortunato sior Don Passarin.

Andem pur, andem de trotto!
Vin, formaggio e maccaron
dal gran gusto adess'inghiotto;
un drio l'altro sti boccon
e me par de devorar.
Gran fortuna, se ghe arrivo!
Quando andemio? Via, fe' presto!
E appena zonto,
mi ve protesto,
che onto e bisonto
voi ben magnar. *(parte)*

Scena iv

Appartamento di D. Isabella in abito da camera, e tavolino con lumi.

D. Isabella e D. Pietro

D. Pie: Donna Isabella, il re da me informato
dell'indegno attentato
a voi m'invia sollecito d'udire
dal vostro labro il caso strano. Dite
chi fu l'ardito pronto ad insultarvi,
e il re non sarà tardo a vendicarvi.

D. Isa: Per la dama d'onor che fui finora,
Don Pietro, ignoro il traditor, l'indegno.
So ben ch'ardo di sdegno;
e il mio giusto rossore,
quando giungeste voi, non mi ha permesso
di sostenergli in faccia il suo processo.

D. Pie: Erraste; era assai meglio
convincerlo sul fatto.

D. Isa: Non ressi in faccia vostra e mi nascosi.
A me bastò che fosse noto a voi,
che siete di giustizia infra gli eroi.

D. Pie: Ma pur agl'atti, ai modi ed alla voce
come nol ravvisaste?

D. Isa: La voce era artefatta, ed all'oscuro,
forse il minor dei mali,
uomini e donne sono tutti eguali.

D. Pie: Ma quando giunsi con quel lume in mano?

D. Isa: Allor nol ravvisai che di lontano,
nè ardii più ritornar.

D. Pie: Donna Isabella,
tai casi sono rari;
ma ogn'altra incauta dall'esempio impari.

D. Isa: Voi mi fate arrossir, ma mi conforta
che voi sapete il reo.

D. Pie: Il so; ma tocca a voi
di palesarlo al re.

D. Isa: Egli è quel tale
da voi riconosciuto ed a me ignoto.

D. PIE: Ignoto? Il Duca Ottavio
non v'ama forse?

D. ISA: E ben; e che per questo?

D. PIE: Voi facilmente indovinate il resto.

D. ISA: Fia ver? Come? È possibile? . . .

D. PIE: Calmate
quell'ira intempestiva; ora si tratta
di confermarlo al re, onde vi ottenga
co' dovuti sponsali
pronto rimedio ai trascurati mali.

D. ISA: Sì, lo farò, e l'onor mio richiede
che ottenga il fallo suo giusta mercede.

Sì, spietato, sì, tiranno,
mi vedrai al reggio piede
ragion chieder dell'inganno
che un cor perfido tramò.
Forse allor ti pentirai,
ma fia tardo il pentimento;
io farò per tuo tormento
qual la colpa il meritò. *(parte)*

Scena v
Don Pietro solo.

Da questa parte intanto
buona piega l'affar prende. L'aurora
è già vicina, e il Duca Ottavio ormai
forse desto sarà. Suol di buon'ora
lisciarsi, imbellettarsi e polverarsi
per esser primo in corte a far figura.
Sì, vada lui; con arte e con ingegno
si compisca il dissegno. *(incaminandosi)*
Oh sorte! Eccolo qui, che sì opportuno
in questo quartier viene
sull'alba ad adorar le sue catene.

Scena vi

Duca Ottavio con caricatura e detto.

D. Ott: Oh! Qual sorte propizia e qual mai stella
fortunata per me, Don Pietro, onore
della tenoria prole,
fa che vi vegga qui sull'alba appena?
Se foste altro che voi, sarei geloso;
ma in voi fondo più tosto il mio riposo.
D. Pie: Mi fate onor, ma troppo
voi sollecito siete in queste stanze.
So che amor vi condusse,
ma troppo ancor talora
rende ciechi i vassalli al par del duce.
D. Ott: Come? Non vi comprendo.
D. Pie: Mi spiegherò. Donna Isabella amate,
ma in certe ore indiscrete
non s'assedian le donne.
D. Ott: Io son di sasso!
Che volete voi dir?
D. Pie: Ove passaste
la scorsa notte?
D. Ott: In buona compagnia:
Don Lopez, Don Gil Blas ponno far fede.
D. Pie: Eppur ciò non si crede.
Donna Isabella amate, e questo è noto.
Essa forzata fu poch'ore innanzi,
e vi vuol reo del perfido delitto;
v'accusa in faccia al re. Il re sdegnato
vi vuole vivo o morto in suo potere,
e veggo il vostro caso assai funesto.
D. Ott: Santi numi del ciel! Che colpo è questo?
D. Pie: Ogni apparenza intanto
v'accusa e vi condanna.
D. Ott: Lo veggo anch'io, ma l'apparenza inganna.
Innocente son'io. Ma come, oh dei,
l'empia m'accusa? Or vado
a scolparmi al suo piè; forse sedotta
s'inganna e inganna il re. *(incaminandosi)*

D. PIE: Duca, lasciate
a me la cura di giustificarvi
a miglior tempo, se innocente siete.
Ora sarebbe un periglioso azzardo.
Io col re parlerò. Donna Isabella
conoscerà l'error.

D. OTT: Sia che si voglia, *(sospeso)*
penso però . . . Sia qual si voglia il caso,
sia stata o no forzata,
vedo che sempre a torto io l'avrò amata.

D. PIE: Sano consiglio; e intanto
che risolvete voi
contro l'ira del re?

D. OTT: Di ritirarmi
presso il re di Castiglia, il cui favore
posso sperare al par degli avi miei,
e dal seno strapparmi alfin colei.

D. PIE: Tal partito è il miglior. Io vi prometto,
lontan che siate, ogni migliore effetto.

D. OTT: Parto, vado, e in voi confido;
abbandono ad altri il lido
dove amavo d'approdar.
Già lascio la sponda,
chè il flusso dell'onda
mi spinse in un banco
e in porto franco
mi fe' naufragar. *(parte)*

Scena vii
D. Pietro solo.

Lodato il ciel, salvo sarà il nipote;
il Duca Ottavio, già creduto il reo,
si salva col partir. Il tempo alfine
tutto il resto farà. Donna Isabella,
che sempre è un buon partito,
troverà non ostante anco il marito.

Di trovarlo io non dispero,
ve ne son di tanti buoni!
Ognun sa s'io dico il vero;
mia mercè lo troverà.
E di più, Donna Isabella,
col passar per buona e bella,
un rimbrotto non avrà. *(parte)*

Scena viii
Spiaggia con tempesta di mare. Giorno.

Don Giovanni e Passarino escono dal mare vestiti con caricatura; poi Rosalba vestita da ninfa.

D. Gio: Oh, oh, oh!
Pass: Ih, ih, ih!
O poveretto mi!
D. Gio: Mai più per mare.
A 2: Mai più, oibò. *(uscendo dal mare)*
D. Gio: Che spavento!
Pass: Un pignoletto no me va più drento.
D. Gio: Scorsi abbiam coll'Italia altri paesi
e fatto tanti viaggi in terra, in mare,
pria che in Castiglia amasti d'approdare;
ma tra tutti fu questo
l'unico mio viaggio il più funesto.
Pass: Saver perchè? Perchè vel dirò io:
perchè gavè burlà sior barba zio,
e per goder de donne ogni cuccagna
dopo sie mesi alfin l'è vegnù in Spagna.
D. Gio: Miseri! Che farem così grondanti?
Va', cerca, trova alcun che ci soccorra.
Pass: Oh, oh, oh, oh, zente, ghe qua nissun *(gridando per la scena)*
che soccorra do grami ch'è a dezun?
D. Gio: Taci, che di lontano
parmi veder venire una donzella. *(verso la scena)*
Pass: A vu ve basterà che la sia bella.
D. Gio: Ecco che vien correndo.

PASS: Soccorso, per pietà; carne, polame,
polenta, pan, perchè go la gran fame.
D. GIO: Ed a me il freddo dà maggior tormento.
PASS: E mi quando go fame no lo sento.

Scena ix
Rosalba e detti.

ROSA: Oimè! Non ho più fiato, *(ansante e frettolosa)*
tanto ho corso per voi, miseri grami;
da lungi vi ho veduto
uscir dal mar e corsi a darvi aiuto.
D. GIO: Che gentil pastorella!
Osserva, Passarin, com'è mai bella!
ROSA: Pastorella non son. Son pescatrice.
PASS: E quanto prima, donna assai infelice.
ROSA: Ma voi stanchi sarete e così molli
che del foco vi occor per asciuttarvi.
PASS: E da magnar, ghe ne sarà?
ROSA: Lo spero;
non avrete a patir.
PASS: E i maccaroni
saveu mo farli?
ROSA: E come i faccio buoni!
PASS: E vin ghe ne sarà?
ROSA: Ve n'ho della migliore qualità.
D. GIO: Taci, importun; non finiresti mai.
PASS: Ma caro sior, se tratta alfin d'assai.
ROSA: Ma, deh, chi siete voi? E qual destino? . . . *(a Passarino)*
PASS: Lu è Don Giovanni, e mi Don Gioannino.
Ve diremo po' el resto.
D. GIO: Che vai dicendo?
PASS: Che go moggio il cesto.
ROSA: Miseri! Chiunque siate, il vostro caso
pietà mi desta; andiamo
tosto alla mia capanna. Ivi avrò il modo
da restorarvi e da vestirvi ancora,
e superba sarò di chi mi onora. *(verso D. Giovanni)*

D. Gio: Quanto siete gentile e quanto umana!
Pass: A lu tanto ghe basta una villana.
D. Gio: Andiam, che troppo il freddo mi molesta.
Rosa: Andiam, signore, che la strada è questa. *(accennandola)*

All'aspetto, al portamento,
voi sembrate un gran signor. *(a D. Giovanni)*
Ma se a dirvi, oh, quel che sento,
voi sembrate un pescator. *(a Passarino)*
Egli è bello e sì ben fatto; *(a D. Giovanni)*
ma voi brutto e contrafatto, *(a Passarino)*
secco secco, lungo lungo,
e più giallo assai del fungo
che dispetto fate e orror.
Andiam, ma costui
lontano mi stia.
Io sento per lui *(a Passarino)*
cos'è antipatia,
per voi cos'è ardor. *(a D. Giovanni)*
(partono tutti tre)

Scena x

D. Ottavio e D. Sancio vestito alla vecchia.

D. Ott: Don Sancio, oh qual mai stella fortunata
mi trasportò in Villena, ove la corte
ora soggiorna e dove il re comparte,
merto degl'avi miei, grazie sì eccelse
al brevissimo merito d'un tale
che quasi si scordò d'esser mortale?
D. San: Il gran re di Castiglia a onor concede
a chiunque meritar la tal mercede.
D. Ott: Io me conosco indegno,
ma la grandezza sua
forma ovunque la gloria del suo regno.
D. San: Egli alla spiaggia d'Illice,
sol sei leghe discosta da Villena,
ci manda a rintracciar se la tempesta

abbia gettato nella scorsa notte
qualche infelice a questa sponda infida,
perchè desia fin sotto al regal tetto
agli infelici di donar ricetto.

D. OTT: Qual bontà d'un monarca!
Certo la lena mia non è mai stanca
di segnar il suo nome in pietra bianca.
Gran sovrano! Gran re! Felice il mondo
se ogn'altro re l'imita!
L'umanità gli rende eterna vita.
Ma . . . che veggo? . . . Mi par . . . no, non m'inganno;
certo . . . è quel Don Giovanni . . . e il servo ancora.
(s'incamina e s'incontra in Don Giovanni)

Scena xi

D. Giovanni e Passarino vestiti miseramente e detti.

D. OTT: Qual fortuna! *(s'abbracciano)*

D. GIO: Qual sorte, Duca Ottavio,
fa che in voi mi riscontri? In me vedete
della scorsa tempesta un tristo avanzo
quasi lacero e spoglio, e se non era
il soccorso assai pronto ed il conforto,
stanco, molle dal freddo, sarei morto.

PASS: E mi, sior, dalla fame.

D. OTT: Io son di sasso!

PASS: Che dretto! Oh, veh, che scuro!
Cussì dalla mia fame, oh, se' al sicuro.

D. OTT: V'offro tutto me stesso. *(a D. Giovanni)*

PASS: El sasso no xe bon rosto nè lesso.

D. GIO: Taci, sciocco, importun.

PASS: Chi è sto martuffo? *(si volta e guarda D. Sancio)*

D. OTT: Ma voi, come in Castiglia?

D. GIO: Per veder questa corte e un re sì grande.
E voi per quale oggetto?

D. OTT: Anch'io sì venni per l'istesso affetto.
E grazie al mio bell'astro fortunato,

dal re mi vedo amato;
Don Sancio il dica.

PASS: Oh bello! *(guardando D. Sancio caricatamente)*
Via mo che senta!

D. SAN: È vero,
ma il duca qui non ferma il suo pensiero.

PASS: El parla anca costù. *(con sorpresa)*
Mi nol credeva mai! Tal gente ignota
sembrava agl'occhi nostri una marmota.

Col gaban del cinquecento,
del siesento la velada,
camisiola recamada
e braghesse col galon:
flon, flon, che l'è pur bello,
flon, flon, che l'è pur bon.

D. GIO: Vuoi tacer, importuno, o ti bastono! *(minacciandolo)*

PASS: Se parlo più, signor, non son chi sono.

D. GIO: Ma qual sorte maggiore il Duca Ottavio
della grazia del re aver può mai? *(a D. Sancio)*

D. SAN: Basta. Non so; vel dica egli, se vuole.

D. OTT: Siamo amici, e vel dico in due parole.
Amo Donn'Anna. È questa unica figlia
di Don Alvar, Commendator d'Oliola,
che tra poco l'attende da Lisbona,
ove il re l'inviò. Mi corrisponde
l'amabile figliola.

PASS: Sior patron, poss'io dir una parola? *(tirandolo a parte)*

D. GIO: Taci, o t'ammazzo, indegno.

PASS: Oh fazzo assae, se posso star a segno. *(da sè)*

D. GIO: Sarà gentile e bella. *(a D. Ottavio)*

D. OTT: Quanto nel ciel seren lucida stella;
Don Sancio il dica.

D. SAN: È vero.

PASS: Ci giuri ustè da nobil cavaliero.

D. SAN: Lo giuro, sì signor. *(con gravità)*

PASS: Bene; e mi ghe farò da protettor.

D. GIO: Perdonate; è buffone, *(a D. Sancio)*
e voi lo conoscete. *(a D. Ottavio)*

D. OTT: Orsù, venite in corte e la vedrete.
Io guida vi farò. In questa notte,
benchè scarso al suo merto,
le ho preparato un musical concerto.

D. GIO: Ma dove? In casa?

D. OTT: No, alla spagnola,
sulla pubblica strada.
Via, venite a Villena.

D. GIO: Oimè! Non posso!
Arrossirei con questi cenci indosso.

D. OTT: Eccovi i miei. Cambiamo
la cappa ed il cappello. Io parto intanto, *(si cambiano i panni)*
perchè un posto non ho che vi convenga,
ma tra brev'ora a quel lontano albergo
(accennando la parte opposta a quella di Rosalba)
troverete, onde la via sicura,
quella ch'io manderò pronta vettura.

D. GIO: Quante grazie vi rendo. Io son confuso . . .

D. OTT: Eh! Via, tacete; siamo
amici e tanto basta.
Addio; tra poco a rivederci.

D. SAN: Io spero
che me stesso onorar vorrete ancora
dell'amicizia vostra, e v'offro in tanto
la mia.

D. GIO: Grazie vi rendo, e vi prometto
amicizia del par. *(partono D. Sancio e D. Ottavio)*

PASS: Gran cosse belle!
E molto più, se 'l gaverà sorelle.

D. GIO: Che vai dicendo, pazzo contrafatto?

PASS: Eh, diseva gnau, gnau, co dise el gatto.

D. GIO: Buffone! Orsù, andiam tosto all'albergo
che il duca m'additò e da me prima
ignorato perchè si vede appena.

PASS: Andem, ma de Rosalba
cossa sarà?

D. GIO: Sarà come dell'altre.

PASS: Bravo! Viva el buon cuor;
burlarle tutte col zurarghe amor.
D. GIO: Non mi seccare! Andiam. Vo meditando
un certo pero morto . . . [1]
PASS: Pero morto? E cussì?
Cosa vorlo mai dir, caro el mio storto?
D. GIO: Andiam; te lo dirò. *(incamminandosi)*
PASS: No se' più a tempo;
xe qua l'amiga.

Scena xii
Rosalba e detti.

ROSA: Stanca di aspettarvi
io son venuta a voi; ma D. Giovanni
è pur quello? *(osservandolo in abito cambiato)*
PASS: L'è lu.
ROSA: Con quel mantello?
D. GIO: Sì, son'io, che ho cambiati i vostri cenci
in questi assai migliori.
PASS: Evviva el grato cuor dei gran signori!
D. GIO: Addio, Rosalba. Ho fretta
di rendermi alla corte
da dove attendo un treno a me dovuto.
Forse si rivedrem.[2]
ROSA: Come? Che forse?
Non hai promesso di sposarmi?
D. GIO: È vero,
e t'ho sposata ancor, ma col pensiero.
ROSA: E in premio di mia fede
non ricevesti forse la mercede?
D. GIO: Tutto è vero, e perciò?
ROSA: Perciò pretendo
d'esser tua sposa.
D. GIO: Il fosti;
nessun te lo contrasta.

1. A slang expression, also found in other Don Juan versions, indicating an encounter, a meeting.
2. Ci rivedremo.

PASS: Saveu mo che 'l vol dir, che fe' ch' el basta!
D. GIO: Sciocca villana! Ti fei troppo onore;
altre fur le mie amanti!
PASS: E de sta marcanzia, tra bona e trista,
se nol credessi mai, questa è la lista. *(getta il rottolo)*
ROSA: Oimè, che sento! Oh mia
già perduta innocenza!
PASS: Sorella cara, armeve de pacienza.
No se' sola in sto stato.
ROSA: E sarà dunque ver, perfido, ingrato,
che tu fia sì crudel con chi t'adora,
che tradita tu m'abbia e m'abbandoni?
I giuramenti, i tuoi falsi deliri,
empio, m'avran sedotta e i tuoi sospiri.

D. GIO: I sospiri degl'amanti,
vel dirò se nol sapete,
sono stati intemperanti
che amor dona alla beltà.
Sciocche voi, se ci credete,
o, fingendo crudeltà,
finalmente per pietà
sdrucciolate nella rete;
ed il danno ben vi sta.
"Io moro e spasimo,"
"mie care viscere,"
"vado in deliquio:"
son tutte frottole,
e sciocche siete,
se mai credete
tai falsità. *(parte con Passarino)*

ROSA: Così l'indegno m'abbandona! Io sono
tradita e disprezzata!
Ah, ch'io son disperata!
Ho già rissolto. Io voglio,
sì, voglio alfin punirmi *(rivolgiendosi al mare)*
d'aver amato il perfido, e ormai fia
quel mar che lo salvò la tomba mia. *(si getta in mare)*

Scena xiii
Anticamera in corte di Castiglia.

D. Ottavio e D. Sancio, poi D. Ximena

D. OTT: Gran sospetti ho nel cor. Son già molt'ore
che Don Giovanni è giunto
in Villena, nè ancora
ei da me fu veduto.
La cappa ed il cappello
nè meno mi mandò.
D. SAN: Sarà, credete,
qual gli conviene a porsi in degno arnese
onde non arrossir dei panni altrui,
nè in faccia vostra o in corte.
D. OTT: Sarà . . . basta . . . non so; mi dice il core
quello che di sognar non oso appena.
D. SAN: Ma pur . . .
D. OTT: Ecco a noi vien Donna Ximena.
Signora. *(s'inchinano)*
D. XIM: Oh, Duca Ottavio. Il re poc'anzi
mi parlava di voi. Sa che dovete
regalar a Donn'Anna
questa notte un concerto
e ne mostrò piacer. Io sperar voglio,
tornato che sarà il suo genitore,
di goder queste nozze.
D. OTT: Il voglia amore!
Se un tal dì giungerà, io sarò al colmo
d'ogni umano desio.
D. XIM: Io da lei vado intanto
per goder del concerto. Imbruna ormai;
non vi fate bramar.
D. OTT: Dal re dipendo,
sua mercè, lo sapete.
D. XIM: Sì, ma vecchio è quel detto:
non sollecito amante è ognor sospetto.

Se amore v'accende,
non fate languir;
la bella v'attende;
non date martir.
L'indugio sovente
fa danno all'amante,
che in vano si pente
del prospero istante
che vede finir. *(parte)*

D. SAN: Donna Ximena è vaga.
D. OTT: Essa è d'un lieto umor, sempre gioconda.
Essa stimoli aggiunge all'amor mio;
ma tu sai che dipendo, o cieco Dio! . . .
D. SAN: Ecco il Commendator, che a noi sen viene.
D. OTT: Oh qual piacer! Ma pur novello inciampo
per induggiar dal re; Donna Ximena
mi condanni, se può.

Scena xiv
Commendatore e detti.

COM: Amici, alfine
m'è dato il rivedervi.
D. OTT: Oh qual contento!
D. SAN: Qual piacere, signor! *(s'abbracciano)*
COM: Io nol credea;
la mia canuta età ed il viaggio
rendean quasi impotente il mio coraggio.
D. OTT: Lodo al ciel, voi tornate
sì vegeto, signor, con gioia nostra,
che non sembrate mai dell'età vostra.
COM: Ma vi son però gl'anni.
D. SAN: Per chi è sano è il minor degl'altri affanni.
COM: Oh, gran Lisbona! Oh qual mai re cortese!
Morta [*sic*] che sia palese
a tutto il mondo il suo regal splendore!
Ricolmo d'ogni onore,

ritorno alfin del nostro
sempre augusto monarca,
e prezzo di mia fede
sarà l'ulivo offerto al reggio piede.
Ma ormai si vada a lui, prima che il sole
giunga all'occaso. Qui troppo indugiai;
impaziente sono
di prostrarmi dinanzi al regio trono.

D. OTT: Giusto è il vostro desio; io vi precedo
per annunziarvi. *(incamminandosi)*

COM: Andiamo,
andiamo a un tanto re, che onoro ed amo. *(a D. Sancio; e partono tutti tre)*

Scena xv

Camera di D. Anna con lumi. Notte.

D. Anna, D. Ximena ed Ines

D. AN: Cara Donna Ximena,
quanto grata mi siete.

D. XIM: Il Duca Ottavio
sollecito sarà col suo concerto,
se pur mi presta fè.

D. AN: Voi sempre siete
di lieto umor, ed io mi meraviglio;
tutt'oggi ho [il] pianto quasi sempre al ciglio.

D. XIM: Donneschi effetti.

INES: Anch'io gliel'ho pur detto.

D. XIM: Tornò il Commendator, voi siete amata.
Ah, volete di più la serenata?

FINALE

INES: Mie signore, certo certo
di lontan sento il concerto.

D. XIM: Sì, mi pare, in fede mia.

Che contento! Che allegria!
Il suon dice: Amo e bramo;
via, Donn'Anna, presto, andiamo.

D. AN: Vengo sì, ma per mia fè,
l'allegria non fa per me.

D. XIM: Che pazzie! [Che pazzie!]

INES:
D. XIM: Che mai strane fantasie!

INES: Non sentite?

D. XIM: Via, venite!

INES: Che piacer! Qual armonia!

D. XIM: Che contento! Che allegria!

D. AN: Che crudel malinconia!

D. XIM: Via, venite e passerà.

INES: Oh, sì, certo in fede mia.

D. AN: No, nol credo in verità.
(la prendono sotto il braccio e partono tutti tre)

Scena xvi

Strada con porta grande di casa laterale.

Don Giovanni e Passarino

D. GIO: Amor m'assista
con questo inganno.

PASS: E se succede
qualche malanno?

D. GIO: Ci pensi allora
chi ha da pensar.

PASS: E creppa ancora
chi ha da creppar.

D. GIO: Sorte propizia,
la porta è aperta,
e la vittoria
mi sembra certa.
Senz'altro indugio
conviene entrar. *(entra e chiude la porta)*

PASS: E mi, gramazzo,

za son seguro
che qua de fora
mi solo a scuro
almanco un'ora
me tocca a star. *(va in disparte)*

Scena xvii

Duca Ottavio, D. Sancio e detto.

D. Ott: Allegri, suonate. *(all'orchestra)*
D. San: Amico, non fate.
La porta è serrata,
v'è da dubitar.
a 2: Zi, zi, tacete. *(ai suonatori)*
D. San: Sento romore.
Pass: Che serenata
delle polpette!
D. Ott: Mi batte il core.
D. San: Via, non temete.
D. Ott: Tacete, sentite?
D. San: Sì, sento, ma dite . . .
a 2: . . . che abbiamo da far?
D. Xim: Aiuto, fermate! *(si sente entro la scena)*
Ines: Ribaldo, lasciate!
D. An: Soccorso, pietà!
a 2: Aiuto, pietà!
D. Ott: Ahi, qual caso, oh Dio, funesto! *(in strada)*
Pass: Coss'è mai, che imbrogio è questo?
D. San: Già si battono.
Pass: I se dà. *(si sente entro la scena romor di spada)*
D. Ott: Ah! Don Sancio in voi confido.
D. San: Sì, ma oimè, siamo all'oscuro. *(mettono mano alla spada)*
Pass: Oh, dasseno che no rido,
e la schena puzo al muro.

Scena xviii

Commendatore, D. Giovanni e detti; poi D. Anna, D. Ximena ed Ines

COM: Fuor di qua, indegno. *(incalzando D. Giovanni fuori dalla porta con spada)*
D. GIO: Vecchio, sta a segno. *(D. Giovanni con l'altro mantello; si battono in strada)*
A 2: Ah, ah, eh, eh.
COM: Ahi, crudel, son morto, oimè! *(cade)*
D. SAN: Ferma.
D. OTT: Dagli.
A 2: Ah, ah, eh, eh.
(battendosi all'azzardo con D. Giovanni)
D. GIO: Sì, son buon anco per tre. *(si diffende dalle due spade)*
D. AN: Teme il cor qualche sventura.
D. XIM: Non temete, non sarà.
D. AN: Tremo, oimè, dalla paura.
PASS: Deve pur, e mi son qua.
D. OTT: Traditore, cederai.
D. SAN: Vieni, indegno, e proverai . . . *(battendosi di tratto in tratto contro*
A 2: . . . della destra il mio furor. *D. Giovanni)*
D. GIO: Questo no, non sarà mai,
finchè regge il mio vigor.
D. XIM: Per pietà, non vi battete.
INES: Palesate almen chi siete.
D. AN: Che mai fu del genitor?
TUTTI: Qual confusione orribile!
Qual notte, oh Dio, funesta,
che uscir sembra dal Tartaro
e chiaro manifesta
dal ciel la man terribile
armata di rigor!

fine dell'atto primo

ATTO SECONDO

Scena prima

Anticamera suddetta in corte con lumi. Notte.

Duca Ottavio e Don Sancio

D. Ott: Il caso è atroce, e la real vendetta
piomberà sopra il reo. *(mestamente)*

D. San: L'indegno Don Giovanni,
perfido amico, è già scoperto autore
dell'iniquo attentato, e son già dati
gl'ordini necessari onde non fugga
da Villena. Io men vado,
quanto al nome del re voi m'imponete
sollecito a compire.
E voi, frenate intanto
quel che il ciglio v'inonda amaro pianto.

Che mai giova un pianto amaro?
Di follia parmi un eccesso,
sia che il mal abbia un riparo
e più allor che non si dà.
Delle lacrime il conforto
lascio agl'occhi del bel sesso,
che per giunger salvo in porto
miglior astro alfin non ha.
Ma ancor piangete?
Fissate ancor? . . .
Voi mi volete
far arrabbiar. *(parte)*

D. Ott: Infelice Donna Anna,
io penso al suo dolor. Qual duro caso!
Ma, oh Dio! Di tutta notte, in nero amanto
sollecita sen viene *(guardando tra le scene)*
per implorar dolente al regio piede
contro l'iniquo reo giusta mercede.

Scena ii
D. Anna, D. Ximena e detto.

D. AN: Col pianto al ciglio oppressa e dal dolore
chiede audienza, signor, dal re clemente
una figlia dolente,
cui rapì mano ardita il genitore.

D. OTT: Troppo è ormai noto il caso, oh Dio, funesto,
e il vostro giusto affanno
ciascun risente. Il re, che veglia ancora
desto al romor dell'attentato enorme,
brama di vendicarvi.
Amerà di vedervi e consolarvi.

D. XIM: Dunque non più s'induggi. Ite, D. Anna,
al reggio piede; io seguirovvi, e fia
il duca vostra scorta.

D. AN: Misera, dal dolor son quasi morta! *(piange)*

Parto . . . sì . . . ma il piè vacilla,
dell'orror mi reggo appena.
L'alma oppressa in van raffrena
i trasporti del dolor.
Voi che pietà sentite, *(al D. Ottavio e D. Ximena)*
i passi miei seguite,
conforti del mio cor.
(parte col D. Ottavio, che le dà mano)

Scena iii
D. Ximena sola.

D. XIM: Misera! Io la compiango e il suo dolore
risento, è ver, ma sono stanca alfine
di lagrimar. Ho pianto per quattr'ore,
nè di pianger mi vanto,
e se piango di più, mi sciolgo in pianto.
Alfin perduto ha un vecchio genitore.
Riparerà l'amore
la dolorosa perdita, e tra poco

l'acqua del pianto amor cangerà in foco.
Il pianto delle donne,
se devo dire il vero,
quando l'asciuga amor, poco è sincero.
Ma mettiansi[3] sul serio un'altra volta.
Seguir devo l'amica:
a dover contrafarsi, oh, qual fatica!

Il dover piangere
e amar di ridere
è penosissima
fatalità.
Ditelo, femmine
d'allegro umore,
se ammazza il core
la serietà.

Scena iv

Tempio illuminato colla statua del Comendatore.
(Una comparsa finge incidere la iscrizione, avendo una lanterna.)

D. Giovanni e Passarino

PASS: Oe! L'avè fatta, amigo,
e semo adess' in tun gran brutto intrigo!
D. GIO: Eh, non temer, che teco è D. Giovanni. *(col secondo mantello)*
PASS: E pur mi temo, sior, mille malanni.
D. GIO: In questo tempio intanto, a sorte aperto
e sì vicin al nostro albergo, siamo
al sicuro per ora. Io son chi sono.
Sono un principe alfin: l'oro fa tutto,
la sorte ride in faccia nostra e mai
non si dimostra a noi crudele e ria.
PASS: E se la ve mandasse in Piccardia?[4]
Basta, penseghe vu.

3. Mettiamoci.
4. To the gallows.

D. GIO: Ci ho bel pensato.
PASS: E 'l me salari?
D. GIO: Sì, ti sarà dato.
PASS: Basta cussì; demel pur, che lo vogio,
che voi scampar, se nasce qualche imbrogio.
D. GIO: Vedesti con qual arte
e per diverse strade
fuggii e mi diffesi da due spade?
PASS: Gerimo a scuro, nè mi ho visto gnente.
So ben che dalla zente
ho sentio a dir in tel vegnir a casa,
prima che v'incontrasse,
che gera morto el sior Commandaor
e Don Zuan accusà per l'uccisor.
D. GIO: Udisti il nome mio?
PASS: Sì ben e come schietto l'ho sentio!
D. GIO: Ciò merita riflesso. Il Duca Ottavio
e D. Sancio mi han dunque conosciuto.
PASS: No i v'ha fatto gran torto.
In summa, xe andà sbuso el pero morto.
D. GIO: Orsù, dimani all'alba
convien partire.
PASS: Eh ben! Principe mio,
un pignoletto no ve va da drio.
D. GIO: Senti per ora ciò che far conviene
per giungere sicuri al nostro albergo.
Benchè il cammin sia breve,
quivi ancor noi siam noti.
Cambiam mantello, e se la corte incontri,
tu non sei D. Giovanni, e sei sicuro;
io sembrerò livrea co' panni tuoi,
così ciascun andrà pe' fatti suoi.
PASS: V'hoi da imprestar mo ancora el me mustazzo?
D. GIO: Eh, non occor. Sei pazzo?
PASS: Ah, digo ben. Parlessimo pur schietto:
tutto sì, ma no impresto el mio musetto. *(accar.)*
Ma disim, caro vu, no xe za questo,
al color, el tabarro dell'amigo?

D. GIO: Quello era sopra questo, e lo lasciai
col mio gran fine in casa di Donna Anna.
PASS: Bravo! Cussì se tenta che i se inganna.
D. GIO: L'ho fatto a questo fin.
PASS: Bona la moda
per far che 'l duca sorba su la broda.
D. GIO: Andiamo nel vicin atrio, che conduce
più presto al nostro albergo. Ivi faremo
il divisato cambiamento. Alcuno
potria qui {sorprenderci}. La cena
pronta sarà; dopo farem fardello,
lesti a partir appena spunta il giorno.
PASS: Un certo gavè el cuor fatto de corno.
D. GIO: Perchè?
PASS: Perchè con tante iniquità
v'arecordè de non aver cenà;
e mi, che son el pare della fame,
sta sera no gho gnente de appetito.
D. GIO: Sai tu perchè? Perchè sei scimunito!
Alfine son chi sono.
PASS: El mal far no è sicuro gnanca in trono.
D. GIO: In somma, andiam . . . che vedo? *(incaminat.)*
Qual monumento pria non osservato!
PASS: Oh! L'è mo vera! Gnanca mi segura *(sorpreso)*
no l'aveva osservà. Altro per testa
gavevimo co semo entrai qua drento.
D. GIO: Superbo monumento,
opra che si può dir quasi divina!
PASS: Certo. Che 'l {sembra} fatto de puina!
D. GIO: Ma mi par di conoscerlo.
PASS: Anca mi.
D. GIO: Chi ti sembra che sia?
PASS: L'è lu, oe, l'è el barbon, in fede mia.
D. GIO: Chi, il Commendator?
PASS: Bravo per dia.
D. GIO: I merti suoi gl'avranno meritato
d'una statua l'onore ancor vivente,
e l'iscrizione lo dirà. Leggiamo:
"Di chi a torto mi trasse a morte ria,

dal ciel qui attendo la vendetta mia."
Oh vecchio stolto, che vendetta attendi?
Passarin, vedi ciò che è scritto e leggi.

PASS: Da chi le torta fasse in casaria,
da quel intendo aver la fetta mia.

D. GIO: Ardo di sdegno, e se follia non fosse
l'imperversar contro quel muto marmo,
l'offenderei di nuovo. Io son furente!
To', vecchio stolto, intanto
para il colpo, se puoi, di questo guanto.
(lo getta contro la statua)

PASS: Siu matto, sior paron! Almanco i morti
no ste' a insultar, no ghe fi' mai sti torti.

D. GIO: Io non li temo; io non li stimo un zero.
Chi è morto è morto, e vuoi veder s'è vero?
Meco invitalo a cena, e se può, venga.

PASS: Oh, questa l'è una grossa stramberia.

D. GIO: Invitalo, ti dico, a casa mia.

PASS: Nol vegnirà, ma se 'l vegnisse mai . . .

D. GIO: Noi gli darem da cena.

PASS: Per mi v'impianto, che no vogio guai.

D. GIO: Orsù, vo' che l'inviti. *(con calore)*

PASS: Basta, penseghe vu.
Or sior Comandaor,
la sa che ambassador no porta pena;
vorla dal mio paron vegnir a cena?
(qui la statua dice di sì; Passarino casca in terra)

D. GIO: Cos'hai? Dimmi, cos'hai?

PASS: Oh, poveretto mi. Sior, ghe dei guai;
el m'ha dito di sì.

D. GIO: Eh, che sei pazzo,
sono tutte fantasie; torna di nuovo
ad invitarlo.

PASS: Andemo
via de qua, sior paron, infin che posso,
perchè da senno me l'ho fatta adosso.

D. GIO: Eh, che i morti son morti, e i duri sassi
non si muovon da sè; son tue pazzie.
Torna, torna a invitarlo, e lascial fare,
ch'io stesso son qui pronto ad osservare.

PASS: Vardè ben donca. Oe, sior Comandaor,
ghe dise el mio paron con bona ciera
se a cena el vol vegnir da lu sta sera.
(la statua torna dir di sì)
Oh, poveretto mi! Co levo su *(casca)*
la triaca[5] in ti bragon no ghe sta più!

D. GIO: Andiam, coraggio, e venga pur se ha core.
Per me non ho timore;
da cena gli darò.

PASS: E mi sì, ben che gnente vogio darghe;
cammino in tanto colle gambe larghe. *(con caricatura e partono)*

Scena v

Solita anticamera in corte.

D. Anna, D. Ximena e Duca Ottavio

D. OTT: Rasserenate, amabile D. Anna,
il mesto ciglio. Voi del re sapete
che il reo non fuggirà. Ordine espresso
ogni uscita interdice
da queste mura, e solo il dì s'aspetta
per dar principio alla fatal vendetta.
Del reo si cerca intanto in ogni parte,
nè ascondersi potrà. Veglia Don Sancio.
Un comune interesse
tutti ci chiama pronti a vendicarvi
d'opra sì indegna e ria.

D. AN: Lieve compenso alla sventura mia. *(mesta)*

D. XIM: Dice però la gente:
qualche cosa è miglior sempre del niente.
Andiamo al vostro albergo;

5. Theriac, a molasseslike medicinal substance.

vibrato è il colpo appena,
ma il tempo suol cangiar qualunque scena.

D. AN: Forse fia ver, ma intanto
oppresso il cor non sa frenare il pianto. *(piange)*
Misera, qual destino!
Del mio gran genitore
a sì funesta idea non regge il core;
troppo presago fu di sue sventure,
troppo vel dissi, oh Dio. *(a D. Ximena)*

D. XIM: Sì, ma dovete ormai porle in oblio.

D. OTT: È il più sano consiglio.

D. AN: Facile è il consigliar fuor di periglio. *(al D. Ottavio)*

Alme sensibili
al mio dolor,
deh, compiangetemi,
se avete un cor,
chè pietà merito
e non rigor. *(parte con D. Ximena)*

D. OTT: Qual mai destino è il mio!
Donna Isabella a Napoli m'è tolta,
e ignoro il traditor. Vengo in Castiglia,
ed un perfido amico
vuol rapirmi Donna Anna,
il genitor le uccide, e tenta ardito,
cieco dal suo destin, colla mia cappa,
con quella che gli fu pegno d'affetto,
che sopra me ricada ogni sospetto!
Chi vide in questo stato
uomo al mondo di me più sventurato?
Ma qualunque pensier cede a D. Anna,
misera! Quanto peno al suo dolore,
ditelo voi che conoscete amore.

Cogl'occhi io la divoro,
il cor la segue appresso,
e son fuor di me stesso
ai rai di sua beltà.

Faccia pietoso amore
che un dì sereno splenda
e dal suo labbro intenda
cangiato il suo dolore
per mia felicità. *(parte)*

Scena vi
Strada diversa dalle prime.

Don Giovanni, Passarino e la corte.

D. Gio: Siam vicini all'albergo; affretta il passo.
Pass: Son qua, son qua; non son miga de sasso.
D. Gio: Ma la corte incontriam. *(verso Passarino)*
Corte: Ferma, la corte! *(fermano D. Giovanni)*
D. Gio: Son fermo. Non vedete? Io son livrea.
Corte: Va pur, che per un altro ti prendea. *(D. Giovanni parte)*
E voi, signor, chi siete? *(fermando Passarino)*
Pass: Guardeme in tel musaz. Mi son Marenas.
Corte: E l'altro era con voi?
Pass: Gnor sì.
Corte: Ma chi è?
Pass: Sotto a quella livrea l'è un fiol del re. *(in confidenza)*
Oh, che gusto! I è scampà; ghe l'ho ficada, *({la} corte si ritira)*
e ho burlà l'onorata peverada. *(con allegria, e parte)*

Scena vii
Camera di D. Giovanni con credenza e lumi.

D. Giovanni, Passarino; poi il convitato.

D. Gio: Costui non viene ancora. Io non vorrei,
sciocco com'è, che dato avesse in rete,
incontrando la corte, e palesato
avesse tutto allor che fu fermato.
Pass: Oh, son qua. Rido e rido; oh, l'è gustosa
d'averghela ficada a maravegia

al baresello e a tutta la famegia!
Oe, vu se fio del re,
e mi fursi credù vostro lacchè.

D. GIO: Bravo, gran Passarino, per mia fè!

PASS: Cossa diseu! Songio un gran omo mi.

D. GIO: L'ho sempre detto e replico di sì.
Finiamo la commedia.
Prendi il tuo ferraiuolo e va' a vedere *(Passarino prende il ferraiuolo)*
come stiamo in cucina.

PASS: Metto zo el vostro, e po' vago dal cogo
a far che sotto al rosto el metta el fogo.

D. GIO: Tanto ci vuole ancor!

PASS: Mezz'ora almanco;
ho visto in tel passar che lu dormiva
e intanto el naso ghe fasea da piva.

D. GIO: Uh, sveglialo in malora, e di' che tosto
voglio cenar e pronto aver l'arrosto.

PASS: Uh, uh, furia francese, e no xe ancora
sonada mezza notte e xe a bon'ora
al par delle altre sere.

D. GIO: Ben, ma non sai che aspetto . . .

PASS: Oe, se 'l vien, mi me ficco sotto al letto.
Credeu che 'l vegnirà?

D. GIO: Nol credo, ma se vuol mangiar, potrà.
Intanto per passar men male il tempo
di queste eterne notti dell'inverno,
finchè la cena è pronta,
fammi portar il cembalo, che voglio
un'arietta provar di data nova.

PASS: Un più bel matto al mondo no se trova. *(da sè)*
(ordina, e due livree portano una spinetta; D. Giovanni siede e finge di suonare e cantare)

D. GIO: Or va', ordina e tosto a me ritorna.

PASS: No ho visto al mondo testa la più storna. *(da sè)*

D. GIO: Oh, vediamo; va bene. *(finge tasteggiare la spinetta e canta)*
Eh, ehm. *(si schiarisce)*

Le donne che affettano *(intanto si prepara la tavola per la cena)*
austero contegno,

facendo le burbare,
mostrando ira e sdegno
se un nomina amor;
  appena esse incontrano
chi scaltro seconda
l'umor che le domina,
senz'argine o sponda
si trova il rigor.
  Le donne belle, finchè son giovani,
  donne o donzelle, son tutte simili:
  basta conoscere il loro umor.

PASS: Evviva! Allegramente
fin che se canta, no se pensa a gnente.
D. GIO: E cosa ho da pensar? *(si leva e si pone a tavola)*
PASS: Metteve a tola,
che anca mi go da dirve una parola.
D. GIO: Che hai tu da dirmi mai?
PASS: Che vu magnè da bon
e che mi per vu ingiotto ogni boccon.
D. GIO: Se non avevi fame!
PASS: Ve dirò:
l'è vegnuda, io ho visto i maccaron.
D. GIO: Ben, dunque; siedi e mangia.
Dammi da bere in pria,
che un brindisi vo' far, già che conviene
di qua partir. Domani in sull'aurora
verso Venezia indrizzerem la prora.
(si leva e col bicchiere alla mano fa il brindisi)

Viva il genio sì cortese
che ogni secolo ammirò;
viva eterno il bel paese
che nell'Adria il ciel formò. *(beve, e suonano le trombe)*

PASS: Animo, bevè presto,
che me preme pagarme anca sul resto. *(ripone la tazza)*
Oe, da seder, canagia! *(ai servitori)*
A mi quei maccaroni e la fortaggia! *(mangia)*

Presto, da bever. Senti che creanza! *(trombe scordate)*
I fasioli ghe scampa dalla panza.
Orsù, da bever, che anco mi voi far *(lo serv.)*
un brindese al paese che sta in mar.
(si leva e fa come D. Giovanni)

Veneziani da ben, mi dir vorria;
poco no ve convien, donca mi taso;
viva quanti che se', sana pagnia,
e con tutto il cuor ve trago un baso.

D. GIO: Bravo, e che viva! Oh qui ci fosse almeno
qualche donneta in nostra compagnia.
PASS: Certo saria più granda l'allegria.
Ma disim, caro vu, no se' mai stuffo
de donne d'ogni sorte?
Za v'ho da veder colle gambe storte.
(battono dentro; un servo spaventato torna e fa la cascada con la candela)
D. GIO: Cos'hai? *(al servo)*
PASS: Colù l'è ispirità. Me par *(ribatte)*
che sia poca creanza
a st'ora de vegnirne a incomodar.
D. GIO: Va' tu, Passarin; vedi
chi mai fia a quest'ora.
PASS: Sia chi se sia, lo mando alla malora. *(ribatte più forte)*
D. GIO: Senti, batton più forte.
PASS: Adess' adess' i butta zo le porte.
(va a vedere e ritorna spaventato)
D. GIO: Non so mai chi esser possa.
Crederei, se temessi . . . O che la corte . . .
PASS: Oh, poveretto mi! Oh sior patron!
L'è lu!
D. GIO: Ma chi?
PASS: L'è giusto quel barbon.
(D. Giovanni si leva, prende dalla tavola un lume; va incontro al convitato e lo conduce a tavola; mentre viene, Passarino si nasconde sotto ad essa)
D. GIO: Se mai creduto avessi, o convitato,

che fosti di venir tanto cortese,
la terra d'ogni dono avrei spogliato
onde ti fosse il mio desir palese.
Per tua grandezza accetta ciò che puoi,
gradisci il cuor, e mangia pur se vuoi.

CON: Non abbisogna un vil cibo terreno
a chi passò da questo al ciel sereno.

D. GIO: Passarin, dove sei?

PASS: Son in cantina,
nè vegno fora fin a domattina.

D. GIO: Vuoi che si canti? *(al convitato)*

CON: Fa' pur ciò che vuoi.

D. GIO: Cantagli, Passarin.

PASS: Se canto, canto sotto a sto taolin.
Mandelo in sepoltura,
che la ose me trema da paura.

D. GIO: Orsù canta, coraggio.

PASS: Lassè almen che fenissa el mio formaggio.

Za che me fe' sto torto
de far che canta a un morto,
cossa voi far, sentì.
So che co sponta el dì
i morti più no tira;
i scampa, i se ritira.
El come lo so mi
per far che 'l scampa via;
so ben cossa ho da far.
Sentì la furbaria:
da gallo voi cantar
col fa chi chi ri chi.

CON: Don Giovanni, invitato a cena io venni,
e tu, pria di partir, da me verrai?

PASS: El fa tutto colù.

D. GIO: Verrò.

CON: Conduci
teco il servo.

PASS: Cu, cu,
mi go tutti i bauli da far su.
CON: *(parte)*
PASS: Oe, el va, se no fallo;
l'ha bu paura del cantar da gallo.
D. GIO: Vuoi lume?
CON: No. Lume non m'abbisogna. *(parte)*
PASS: Che te vegna la tegna e un po' de rogna!
(esce da sotto la tavola)
Oimè! L'è andà. Orsù, sior paron caro,
poche parole e bone.
El me salari, che voggio andar via.
D. GIO: Perchè mai, Passarino?
PASS: Perchè ai morti no fazzo compagnia.
D. GIO: Ho promesso d'andar. Son cavaliero,
di parola non manco, ed è ragione
che tu venga con me pria di partire.
Fosti invitato e ti convien venire.
PASS: Ma mi da pover'omo a go paura
che andem incontro a qualche scontraura.
D. GIO: Eh, non temer; sei meco, e tanto basta.
Seguimi.
PASS: Andemi' adess'?
D. GIO: No, ma ben tosto,
quando al partir sarà tutto disposto.
PASS: Basta, mi vegnirò perchè a si' vu;
ma tutto sta che no ghe pensa su.
In ogni caso, se 'l me tocca mi,
oh, ghe torno a cantar chi chi ri chi. *(partono)*

Scena viii
Camera di D. Anna con lumi.

D. Anna, D. Ximena; poi Ines

D. XIM: L'ora è assai tarda, e dal dolore oppressa
vi occor qualche riposo.
D. AN: Per me sarebbe vana impresa. Io bramo

pria di sapere il reo fermato, e poi
penserò a me. Se peno, egli è per voi.

D. XIM: Deh, non pensate a me; non vi abbandono
in sì funesto caso ad onta ancora
di riuscirvi importuna.

D. AN: Mi siete anzi più cara.

INES: Signora, il Duca Ottavio con premura *(frettol.)*
chiede essere introdotto, e il re l'invia.

D. AN: Passi. Che mai sarà? Come, in quest'ora?

D. XIM: Agli amanti è propizia anzi l'aurora.

Scena ix

Duca Ottavio, Ines, che lo precede, D. Sancio e dette.

D. OTT: Signore, ogni riguardo il caso strano
sorpassa, e vuole il re che vi sia noto;
a voi m'invia, Donn'Anna, acciò sappiate
che il vostro genitor, quell'alma eccelsa,
per decreto del ciel forse intraprende
contro del reo terribile vendetta.
Ardì di nuovo l'empio
insultarlo nel tempio,
e giunse l'ardir suo, non vi dia pena,
fin per disprezzo d'invitarlo a cena.
V'andò il Commendator.

D. AN: Come?

D. XIM: Che sento?

INES: Che freddo orror!

D. SAN: Nè ha qui fine il portento.
Il vostro genitor, pria di partire,
invitò Don Giovanni, ed ei promise
prima che spunti il dì, pieno d'ardire,
di portarsi nel tempio. Il fatto è certo.
I servi l'han deposto, ed il re vuole
vedere il fin di così strana scena,
che sul teatro reggerebbe appena.
Per me si veglia intanto,
acciò non fugga il reo, che in ogni canto

da nascose milizie è circondato,
ond'egli è ormai vicino
a compir da ogni parte il suo destino.

D. XIM: Il caso è strano, ma se Don Giovanni
mantien la fè, vogl'io
veder cogl'occhi miei
ciò che udendol narrar non crederei.

INES: E tal coraggio avrete?

D. XIM: Sola non sarò; già Donn'Anna stessa
deve meco venir, cui tanto spetta
veder del genitor la gran vendetta.

D. OTT: Il re lo bramò almen; con questa speme
di scortarla m'impose,
quando le regga il cor.

D. XIM: Io non dispero.

D. AN: Non so; tra i dubbi ondeggia il mio pensiero. *(parte)*

Scena x

D. Ximena, D. Ottavio ed Ines

D. OTT: Orsù, Donna Ximena,
voi che potete sul suo cuor, tentate
che al re compiaccia, e venga
Donn'Anna, ormai deposto ogni timore,
la vendetta a veder del genitore.
Non mancherà Don Sancio il pronto avviso
d'inviarmi, se il reo ardito ed empio,
cieco dal suo destin, si porta al tempio.

D. XIM: Coraggio io le farò, ma so che suole
d'un uom valer più assai sol due parole.

D. OTT: Si segua dunque, e tentisi a vicenda
d'indurla.

D. XIM: Intendo assai questa facenda.
Capisco già ciò che vi può piacere,
ma è presto ancor per far un tal mestiere.
(D. Ottavio e D. Ximena partono)

INES: Che mai farà la povera padrona?
Certo nol so; ma s'ella si fa core,
voglio anch'io superare il mio timore.

Potrò farlo? Non lo so;
la paura or dice no.
Tremo tutta al sol pensiero,
e se il fatto fosse vero,
temerei già di morir.
Ma la gran curiosità,
mal comun del nostro sesso,
il portento far potrà
che, ogni spasimo dimesso,
il timor divenga ardir. *(parte)*

Scena xi
Strada.

D. Giovanni e Passarino

D. GIO: Presto, t'affretta, andiam; è ormai vicino
il nuovo dì, ed il Commendatore
forse m'attende e di viltà m'accusa;
ormai mancano al tempio pochi passi.
PASS: Ohi! Me fa mal i sassi;
i xe cussì ineguali,
che vago zotto dal dolor dei cali. *(zoppicando)*
D. GIO: Spicciati in tua malora!
PASS: Vegno, ma vardè ben,
che non fus mei andar al magazen? *(partono)*

Scena xii
Tempio lugubre. Statua seduta nel mezzo ad una tavola imbandita.

Commendatore, D. Giovanni e Passarino

FINALE

D. GIO: Ahi! Qual orrore, *(sorpresa)*
qual nero aspetto!

PASS: Sia maledetto
co son vegnù!

D. GIO: Tutto è lugubre,
tutto spaventa.

PASS: Ah, che polenta
no magno più!

D. GIO: Voglio accostarmi;
tien la mia spada. *(dà la spada)*
Ho assai coraggio
per vendicarmi. *(si accosta alla tavola)*

PASS: Addio formaggio,
dove sei tu?

D. GIO: Qual lutto orribile,
indegno vecchio,
larva terribile,
qual apparecchio
s'appresta a me?

PASS: Robba da nottole,
che no fa se'. *(allungando il collo verso la tavola)*

COM: Mangia, mangia, Don Giovanni.

PASS: Magnè pur, se gavè denti.

D. GIO: Mangerò, sì, non t'inganni,
(spezzandone uno e fingendo mangiarne)
s'anco fossero serpenti.
Passarin, to', prendine uno. *(ne getta uno a Passarino)*

PASS: Oh, da senno,
e l'è un pezzo che savè.

COM: Vuoi tu canti, Don Giovanni?

D. GIO: Sì, fa' pur ciò che tu vuoi. *(s'ode suono di catene)*
(dentro la scena, con musica lugubre, si cantino questi versi senza ritornelli)

Nel fior degl'anni
i falli tuoi
dal cielo attendono
giusta mercè.

Scena xiii

D. Sancio, Duca Ottavio, D. Anna e D. Ximena, Ines e detti.

D. San: Venite a vedere
spettacolo orrendo. *(alla compagnia che viene)*
D. Ott: Non v'è da temere, *(a Donna Anna, dandole mano)*
già siete con me.
D. San: Coraggio, venite. *(alla stessa, dall'altra parte)*
D. An: Ah, voi non sentite
l'orror, lo spavento,
il fiero tormento,
che prova il mio cor.
Ines: Anch'io pur rissento
l'istesso terror.
Pass: Vardè quanta zente
ch'è corsa qua drento!
Quei do li cognosso;
le donne mo gnente.
Ma intanto mi addosso
me sento el fettor.
Com: Don Giovanni, la tua mano. *(si leva in piedi)*
D. Gio: Ecco; a me nol chiedi in vano . . . *(glie la dà)*
Ahi, che freddo! Ahi, qual dolore!
Ahi, che smania! Traditore!
Prendi, indegno! *(con un stilo lo ferisce nel petto)*
Com: Vano sdegno
ed inutile furor.
D. An: Ferma, spietato, oh Dio,
rispetta il mio dolore!
Qual crudo affanno è il mio!
Misero genitore!
Per togliermi di vita
rinovi la ferita,
barbaro, indegno core;
mi sento, oimè, mancar. *(sviene)*
D. San: Pronte, assistitela,
per carità.
Pass: Vorle acqua nanfa?[6]

6. Water distilled from the flower of the orange tree.

Eccola qua. *(mostrando un fialetto)*

D. XIM: Via, consolatevi,
che già principia
a respirar.

PASS: Gran acqua nanfa!
Basta nasar.

D. GIO: Lasciami, barbaro. *(facendo sforzi per liberarsi)*

COM: Non lo sperar.
Pentiti, Don Giovanni.

D. GIO: Ahi! Mi moro, astri tiranni!

COM: Pentiti, Don Giovanni.

D. GIO: Ahi! Pietà non v'ha per me. *(D. Giovanni si sprofonda)*

PASS: Oi, dov'el? Oi, più nol ghe! *(guardando dove si è sprofondato)*

D. OTT: / D. SAN: Oh spettacolo tremendo!

D. XIM: / INES: Oh del ciel giusto rigore!

(segue la trasformazione dell'inferno)

D. AN: Oh vendetta! Oh caso orrendo!

A 5: Ahi! Non regge in seno il core,
e sorpresi dall'orrore
tutti, oh Dio, fremer ci fa.

Scena xiv

Don Giovanni nell'inferno.

D. GIO: Mostri d'Averno—che lacerate
queste mie viscere—deh, pietà usate,
se nell'inferno—vive pietà.
Quando avran termine—sì crudi guai?
V'intendo, barbari,—risponder mai. *(coro col suon di catene)*
Sento l'orribile—suon di catene;
so che mi annunziano—eterne pene.
Oh, qual eccesso—di crudeltà!

COM: Da questo esempio—ogni empio impari
il funestissimo—fine che avrà.

PASS: E mi gramazzo,—patroni cari,
del me salari—cossa sarà?

TUTTI: Sorge ormai nel ciel l'aurora,
e rivolta a noi tremando
all'aspetto si scolora
dell'Averno, e palpitando
mostra forse il nuovo dì.
Ma da notte sì terribile
chiaro resta a noi visibile
come un empio il ciel punì.

fine del dramma

Il Don Giovanni

Gioacchino Albertini

1780

IL DON GIOVANNI

musica

del signore Gioacchino Albertini

[ACT ONE]

Scena viii[1]

Lisetta, indi Ercolino; poi Tiburzio

LIS: Povera mia padrona,
è innamorata morta
d'un buon nobil davvero.
Oh, se sapesse ch'or si trova in Castiglia,
che dall'onde il salvai . . . Ma chi mi fece
capitar su quel lido?
Buon per me che all'infido
non diedi retta.
Oh quante quante ne ho sapute
di quel briccone, ma . . . Bel bel chi viene?
Il servo di colui. Faccio rumore,
chiamo . . . no, ritiriamoci per poco;
vo' veder cosa cerca in questo loco.

ERC: Oh che notte di guai, che gran disgrazia
è il servire un padrone innamorato.
Pian piano s'è celato
non so dove aspettando
come fa il gatto furbo l'occasione
di divorarsi il sorce in un boccone.

LIS: Costui è un servo sciocco;
non mi fa gran paura.

ERC: Ah, son scoperto!
Ercoletto ci sei . . .
Or chiama i servi e mi fa disossare.
Sarà meglio che me la faccia amica,
che le parli spagnuolo.
Ostè, che chiere?

LIS: Anzi, che chiere, ostè?
Abla, abla, le dico.

ERC: Ma che abla! Chi vi capisce?

LIS: Picaro.

---

1. This scene is an expansion of Porta's I.ix. Tiburzio serves in the Commendatore's house with Lisetta, with whom he is in love.

ERC: Io non mi chiamo picaro,
sono Ercolino; ma pian piano, oh dei,
non siete voi colei
che sposaste colui,
ciò è lo sposator della città? . . .
Già m'intendete.

LIS: Sì, son io, son io,
servo birbante.

ERC: Il titolo
è da mio par.

LIS: In queste stanze adesso
che vieni a fare? Cuerpo de mi vida.

ERC: Non alzate le grida,
parlate italiano per carità.
V'ho visto qualche volta,
patriotta mia cara,
in Italia, e volevo
discorrerla con voi.

TIB: Ci è gran rumore
per la casa. Oh che vedo!
In quest'ore notturne
costor che hanno a fare?

LIS: Vi vo' per questa volta perdonare,
ma partite, e se mai vi viene in testa
di far meco il vezzoso,
povero voi.

TIB: Povero voi davero.
Dentro d'un fazzoletto
vi pongo l'ossa e ve le mando a casa.

ERC: Troppa bontà.

LIS: Se poi
foste un uomo di garbo
come dich'io, cioè cortese, onesto,
che non fa nè mentir nè trappolare,
allora allor se ne potria parlare.

ERC: Parliamo dunque. Picarone, udisti?,
un notturno congresso
dobbiam tener fra noi;
alor, vaici!

LIS: Tiburzio,
sta' attento se qualcuno qui capitasse.
TIB: Per la rabbia io fremo.
Il mezzano ho da far; ci parleremo.

Scena [ix]
Ercolino e Lisetta

ERC: Cara madamigella,
discorriamola ora che siamo soli.
LIS: Mi vien voglia di burlar questo sciocco.
In brevi note io vi dirò;
lo sposo ch'ho da prendere
voglio ch'abbia buon core,
che sia pieno d'onore
fin sul cappello.
ERC: Male
quando l'onore arriva
fin sul cappello.
LIS: Perchè io sono onesta
come furono tutti gli avi miei,
e per salvar l'onor m'ucciderei.
ERC: Eh, lo credo, lo credo,
si conosce alla fronte.
LIS: Ho un cor sì bello, ho un core così buono
che per core non la cedo a nessuno.
ERC: Già lo vedo ch'avete un cor d'agnella.
LIS: Son cortese, son bella,
civil, bene educata,
amo chi mi vuol ben, nè sono ingrata.

Quante volte alla finestra
ho veduto un giovinetto,
che facendomi l'occhietto
mi guardava con amor.
Che credete ch'io facessi
a quel vezzo, a quell'occhiata?
ERC: Vi sarete ritirata

per salvare il vostro onor.
LIS: No, che son bene educata,
non conviene, no signor.
Poverino, ripassava,
alla fin mi salutava.
ERC: E voi forte a disprezzarlo
senza mai risalutarlo.
LIS: No, il buon cor non permettea,
dite male, no signor.
Io modesta piano piano
con la tenera manina
gli faceva un baciamano
tutta piena di rossor.
ERC: Oh, vedete, poverina,
che ragazza di buon cuor.
LIS: Qualch'un altro mi voleva
regalare uno struccetto,
un ventaglio, un anelletto,
un ventaglio, uno struccetto.
ERC: Già l'avrete ricusato,
che l'onore vuol così.
LIS: Non ho un core così ingrato,
l'ho accettato, signor sì.
ERC: Ma che onore, ma che onore!
LIS: Ma che sciocco, ma che sciocco!
ERC: Che ragazza di buon core.
LIS: Che ridicolo, che alocco,
LIS: ma che sciocco, ma che alocco,
oh che gusto che mi dà!
ERC: Che ragazza, che modestia,
che buon core;
no, l'eguale non si dà!
LIS: Poverino, ripassava,
alla fin mi salutava.
ERC: E voi forte a disprezzarlo
senza mai risalutarlo.

Scena [x]
Ercolino, poi Tiburzio

ERC: Oh che brava fanciulla,
semplice, buona, onesta e senza inganni.
Oh che lega faria con D. Giovanni.
TIB: Come, non sei partito?
Sei forse qualche ladro
che a quest'ora . . .
ERC: Che ladro!
Guardami in faccia e vedi che bel Giove
scolpito ho in fronte.
TIB: Non alzar la voce
o ti taglio un orecchio.
ERC: A chi? Non sai
che io son quell'Ercolino
che tagliò mezz'orecchio ad un rabino.
TIB: Ah, se non fossi in corte . . . Vieni, vieni sulla strada!
ERC: Domattina all'alba o a mezzogiorno . . .
verrò . . . sì, sì, verrò, t'aspetto in piazza,
son galantuom. L'ho detto e l'ho promesso.
TIB: Intanto parti adesso;
non vo' gente per casa.
ERC: Non m'è comodo.
Dormo qui questa notte.
TIB: Che birbante!
ERC: Guardame dios. [*sic*] Birbante a me,
a me birbante? (Così non fossi!)
TIB: Avverti che se alla mia Lisetta
volgi uno sguardo benchè lusco or storto,
da giovane onorato tu sei morto.

Di te non vo' che resti
neppure un osso sano.
Vedeste mai sul piano
un orso inferocito,
un toro ch'è bandito,
un cane scatenato?—
così, di stizza armato

contro di te verrò.
Fa' a modo mio, figliolo,
non farti strapazzare;
torna colà sul mare,
se no, tu mi vedrai
così di stizza armato
che con un sguardo solo
t'anichilo, ti fulmino,
ti lacero, ti stritolo,
e in polve minutissima
per aria andar ti fo.

ERC: Paratelo, paratelo! Per dirla,
ho un tantin di paura;
in qualche stanza oscura
potessi intanto il mio padron trovare.
Ah, domani [mi] voglio licenziare.

[ACT TWO]

[Scena ix][2]

Ercolino e D. Giovanni

D. GIO: Più penso, più procuro
di scacciar dalla mente
i funesti pensieri,
più s'affacciano al cor, funesti e neri.
Divertimi, Ercolino,
solleva il tuo padrone.
ERC: Non faccio già il buffone.
D. GIO: Canta.
ERC: Pria di mangiare
come volete ch'io possa ben cantare?
D. GIO: Canta, e poi mangerai.
ERC: Che cosa canterò?

2. No scene number is indicated in the text. This scene takes the place of Porta's II.viii.

D. GIO: Cantami, per esempio, un bel rondò.
ERC: Un rondò, male male;
si vede che buon gusto non avete
e di musica giudice non siete.
D. GIO: Per qual ragione?
ERC: Adesso
vi narrerò quel che m'accadde un giorno
nel teatro di Palo,
teatro di dieci ordini che poi
cadde e si rovinò. Salute a noi.
D. GIO: Sbrigati.
ERC: Venne fuora con gran plauso
un buffo caricato
e una scena cantò,
che mi diè gran piacer, contro rondò.
D. GIO: E così?
ERC: Colla fretta
non si fa niente. Io mi ricordo tutta
la musica e l'azione
di questo buffo. State dunque attento
senza batter un occhio,
che tal qual ve la dico e ve la scrocchio.
"Animo, fate presto,
sbrigatevi in malora;
sapete pur che questa sera debbo
cantare in Accademia e che gli astanti
m'attendan per udire
quell'aria che cantai
nel teatro d'Aleppo
ove una dama (ma che dama, che dama!),
quando sentì quel passo che facea
(*8ª sopra*) 'tai, tai, la la la la la la la'
(*voce naturale*)
incominciò a gridare, 'Oh bravo, oh bravo!,'
e presale una colica armoniosa;
dalle tante espressioni
le vennero alla fin le convulsioni.
Sì, sì, quest'è quell'aria,
che insegnata mi fu dal mio maestro

Don Ciaramella,[3] celebre castrato.
Mi ricordo che a lato
standomi un dì mi disse,
(*8ª sopra*) 'Figlio, figlio mio,
canta ciò che tu vuoi, purchè non canti
la gioia[4] dei rondò,
perchè da quelli non ne risulta mai
un genere sublime e ben digesto
come sarebbe questo:' (*siegue subito {an instrumental piece}*)
Questo chiamar possiamo un stil sublime
e non i rondò vostri,
in cui non v'è nè grazia nè decoro,
e tutti tutti tutti tutti tutti s'assomiglian fra di loro;
e che sia vero, in tutte le cadenze
si sente la medesma cantilena.
Per esempio:
   Idol mio quest'alma amante
   sempre fida a te sarà.
                    Simili seccature
son stucchevoli inezie e son freddure.
Ma per farvi veder ch'ho gran raggione,
senza darmi più vanto,
osservate l'azione
del dotto Ciaramella e udite il canto.
   'Per quel paterno amplesso,
   per questo estremo addio,
   conservami, conser . . . '"
Cospetto, voi ridete;
lasciatemi finir,
lasciatemi finir.
"'Conservami te stesso;
placami l'idol mio;
difendimi il mio re;
placami, difendimi,
difendimi il mio re;
padre, prence, signor;
barbara, ah, tu non sai . . . '"

3. The ciaramella is a reedy sort of Italian bagpipe.

4. The text reads *joia*.

Voi non capite niente!
Questa si chiama musica;
voi non capite niente,
e un gener più sublime
di questo non si dà.

Il convitato di pietra

Giacomo Tritto
Giambattista Lorenzi

1783

LI
DUE GEMELLI
ed
IL CONVITATO DI PIETRA

commedie di un atto
per musica
di
Giambattista Lorenzi P.A.
da rappresentarle
nel nuovo Teatro de' Fiorentini
nel carnevale del corrente
anno 1783

In Napoli MDCCLXXXIII
Con licenza de' superiori

MUTAZIONI DI SCENE

per *Il convitato di pietra*

Piazza colla casa del Commendatore e balcone pratticabile.
Campagna con rustiche abitazioni.
Camera.
Piazza.
Tempio colla statua del Commendatore.
Atrio del tempio.
Camera.
Tempio alluttato colla cena della statua. Da un fulmine percosso, precipita detto tempio, e comparisce una bocca dell'inferno.

La musica è del sig. D. Giacomo Tritta,
maestro di cappella, napoletano.

Inventore, dipintore ed architetto delle scene
il sig. D. Giuseppe Baldi, napoletano.

Inventore e sartore degli abiti
il sig. Francesco Marescotti.

ATTORI

Lesbina, contadina, promessa sposa di Pulcinella
La sig. Celeste Coltellini, prima buffa toscana

La Marchesa Isabella da Pellegrina, ingannata da D. Giovanni
La sig. Lucia Celeste Trabalza

Chiarella, serva in casa di D. Anna Ulloa
La sig. Maria Giuseppa Migliozzi

D. Anna di Ulloa, figlia del Commendatore
La sig. Anna Coltellini

Pulcinella, promesso sposo di Lesbina e servo di D. Giovanni Tenorio
Il sig. Gennaro Luzio, primo buffo caricato

Bastiano, contadino, padre di Lesbina
Il sig. Francesco Marchese, primo buffo toscano

D. Giovanni Tenorio
Il sig. Giovanni Bernucci

Il Marchese Dorasquez, ministro del re
Il sig. Giovanni Beltrani

Il Commendatore Ulloa
Il sig. Giuseppe Trabalza

La scena è in Siviglia.

Scena prima

Città col palazzo del Commendatore da un lato e terrazzo praticabile.

D. Giovanni con cappa e Pulcinella con lanterna e spada sotto il braccio, suonatori, e poi Chiarella sul terrazzo.

D. GIO: Chiudi presto la lanterna,
ch'io non voglio esser veduto.
Tu ci senti?
PUL: Aggio sentuto,
ma lo manco na lucerna
famme primmo procurà.
D. GIO: Perchè mai?
PUL: Oh, chesta è bella!
Stuto chesta e allummo chella
pe bederce a cammenà.
D. GIO: Chiudi, bestia.
PUL: È chiusa già.
D. GIO: Pulcinella?
PUL: Che bolite?
D. GIO: Sono pronti i suonatori? *(Pulcinella, senza rispondere, cala la testa.)*
Pulcinella?
PUL: Gnò? Decite.
D. GIO: Sono pronti? *(come sopra)* Presto, di'.
PUL: E non bide ca da n'ora
co la capo dico sì?
D. GIO: Ma che sciocco! Via, poltrone,
fa' suonare. Che si fa?
PUL: Priesto, a buje, ca lo patrone
ave voglia d'arraglià. *(si suona, e D. Giovanni canta)*
D. GIO: Ombre amiche, amici orrori,
fide scorte degli amanti,
qui per voi tra poch'istanti
il mio sol vagheggerò.
PUL: Scope amiche, amiche mazze,
fide scorte dei birbanti,
il padron fra poch'istanti

	zoppicar per voi vedrò.[1]
D. GIO:	Che mai dici, temerario?
	Che mai brontoli, si sa?
PUL:	Ca stanotte il calannario
	mette secce in quantità.
	(*Chiarella e detti*)
CHIA:	Lo Duca Attavio chisto sarrà.
	La serenata ch'ave portata
	justo è lo signo che nc'ha da dà.
D. GIO:	Di là una voce mi par d'udire.
PUL:	Vì comme 'ncoccia! Non buò fuire?
CHIA:	Pis, pis. Vuje site?
D. GIO:	Pis, pis. Io sono.
PUL:	Vì ca lo cielo t'agghiusta buono.
CHIA:	Pecchè tardastevo?
D. GIO:	Si ruppe il cocchio.
PUL:	Vì ca lo cielo te rompe n'uocchio.
CHIA:	Mo scenno abbascio, ca la signora
	che cuollo ha fatto pe v'aspettà! *(entra dentro)*
D. GIO:	Vicino è il sole, se uscì l'aurora;
	ah, che il mio core brillando sta.
PUL:	Vì, lo pennone s'è asciuto fora;
	lo 'mpiso appriesso non pò mancà.

D. GIO:	Ei tu, da' quattro pezze a' sonatori,
	e fa' che vadan via.
PUL:	Quatto pezze? Addò site?
	Vedimmoce dimane a lo spetale,
	ca ve do quanta pezze . . .
D. GIO:	Oh che animale!
	Pezzi duri, io ti dico.
PUL:	Ah, piezze dure?
	E parla chiaro! È fatto. Ma n'è meglio,

1. Perhaps a parody of an aria from *La costanza in amore vince l'inganno* by Antonio Caldara, librettist unknown.

> Selve amiche, ombrose piante,
> fido albergo del mio core,
> chiede a voi quest'alma amante
> qualche pace al suo dolore.

'mmece de piezze dure,
dare pizze e panelle a sti signure?

D. GIO: Eh, non più buffonate.
Prendete e andate via. *(dà monete a' suonatori, e questi vanno via)*

PUL: 'Nzomma ccà che facimmo?

D. GIO: Già sai che il Duca Ottavio sposar deve
Donn'Anna, figlia del Commendatore.
Per un biglietto intercettato, io seppi
che questa notte insieme
ritrovar si dovean da solo a sola.
Io, spinto dalla mia
solita bizzarria . . .

PUL: De spate 'ncuorpo . . .

D. GIO: . . . ho fatto il Duca Ottavio
ingolfare nel gioco, e innosservato
mi ho preso il suo cappello e la sua cappa,
e, fingendomi or quegli,
voglio introdurmi in casa di Donn'Anna.

PUL: E si chella arvolea la mezacanna?

D. GIO: Eh!

PUL: Vide ca la maneca
tante vote va dinto a la lancella,
nfi a tanto che lo puzzo po nce resta.

D. GIO: Eh!

PUL: E fa "eh!" Tu a Napole 'ngannaste
Donna Sabbella, e si non allippave,
avea Pontannecchino[2]
l'onor de t'appuntare il crovattino.

D. GIO: Eh!

PUL: Eh? 'Nfaccia a Majorca
jammo a sbattere, e 'nganne
Tisbea, la pescatrice; e si non fuje,
nce guastano la pelle a tutte duje.

D. GIO: Eh!

PUL: Eh? Viene a Seviglia, e fuss'accisa
chella jornata che sì stato ciunco.
Vì ca chil' "eh" no juorno

2. A famous executioner; see Vanda Monaco, *Giambattista Lorenzi e la commedia per musica* (Naples: Berisio, 1968), 471.

n'arreventa no "ih" che t'arrecetta.
Vì ca lo cielo è ghiusto e te la jetta.

D. Gio: Che cielo e ciel? Del cielo e degli numi
io non temo e non curo, e se di questi
più mi parli, birbone,
io ti farò spirar sotto un bastone.

Scena ii

Chiarella e detti.

Chia: Donn'Attavio . . .
D. Gio: Son qui.
Pul: (È fatto il caso.)
Chia: Venite, ma Donn'Anna
ha paura che po' no la tradissevo.
D. Gio: Io tradirla?
Pul: (Accossì t'ascesse n'uocchio!)
D. Gio: Se il mio voler dal suo voler si arretra,
che mi dia morte un uom, (ma sia di pietra.)
Pul: (Te pozza cadè 'ncapo!)
D. Gio: Ehi tu, qui aspetta.
Pul: (Vì ca lo cielo è ghiusto e te la jetta.)

Scena iii

Pulcinella, e poi dentro voce del Commendatore confusa con altri gridi; indi D. Giovanni, che si getta da un balcone.

Pul: Aibò, non è chiù cosa de tenerlo
a patrone co mmico. Craje matina
voglio aggiustà li cunte:
si m'ha da dà, mme paga; e si ha d'avere,
non 'nce ne parlo affatto e ne lo manno.
Io già stongo appuntato
de mme sposà Lesbina,
ch'è meza meza pajesana mia.
Essa ha no buono terretorio, e io
pozzo a sciore campà 'ncopp'a lo mmio.

Aguà. *(sbadiglia)* Lo suonno già mme va zucanno.
Non c'è che dì: so cane li patrune
co nuje settepanelle.
Nce levono la pelle
pe dì rana lo mese,
ma l'agghiustammo nuje ncopp'a le spese.
(gridi di dentro e voce del Commendatore)

[COM:] Ferma, empio ladron dell'onor mio!
PUL: Cancaro! Dinto nc'è tropea. Che sfizio!
D. GIO: Donami l'ale, amor, nel precipizio. *(si getta dal balcone)*
PUL: (Aimè! Ch'è stato? A nnuje cagnammo lengua.)
Arrietos. Chi va glià?
D. GIO: Chiunque sei,
dammi libero il passo.
PUL: Los passos? Vaja ostè dal potecaros.
D. GIO: Dammi il passo o ti uccido.
PUL: Ah, porcagliones,
toma ostè la cocciglia, ch'io t'attiennos.
(Lassame mette 'nguardia.) *(si difende a terra colla spada in alto)*
Ba . . . Ih . . .
D. GIO: Cotanto ardire
vedrai s'io so punire.
PUL: Ih . . . ah . . . ba . . . scì. *(si battono)*
D. GIO: Chi resister può tanto al braccio mio?
PUL: Cavaleros?
D. GIO: Che vuoi?
PUL: È ostè ammattado?
D. GIO: No.
PUL: Cuorpo de Pilado!
E ba, votta le mmescoles. Ba . . . scì . . .
D. GIO: Ma chi argin può fare a Don Giovanni?
PUL: Si patrò, site vuje?
D. GIO: Sei Pulcinella?
PUL: Gnossì, ma vide buono, sì feruto?
D. GIO: No, grazie al cielo.
PUL: E appiennete pe buto.
D. GIO: Ma tu combatti a terra?
PUL: E che so llocco?

	Co sta guardia non trova lo 'nnemmico
	nè spalle nè lo pietto. Ma ch'è stato?
D. Gio:	Appena di Donn'Anna
	entrai nel gabinetto,
	che il vecchio padre ci sorprese, ond'io,
	acciocchè non mi avesse conosciuto,
	il lume gli ho smorzato,
	e da quel balconcin mi son gittato.
Pul:	E te pare mo azione . . .
Com:	Perfido, ah, dove sei? *(da dentro)*
	L'oltraggiato onor mio vendetta chiede.
Pul:	Ah, ca mo vene. Si patrò, fuimmo.
D. Gio:	Che? Se ardisce venir, gli passo il core.
Pul:	E fa lo fatto tujo,
	ca pe n'essere acciso io mme ne fujo. *(parte)*

Scena iv

Commendatore spogliato con spada nuda e lume, indi D. Anna, Chiarella, servi e D. Giovanni

Com:	Dove sei traditor? Vieni al cimento.
D. Gio:	Son qui, vecchio insensato.
	Provi l'audacia tua l'ultimo fato.
	(si battono, ed il Commendatore resta ferito a morte, e D. Giovanni parte)
Com:	Ahi colpo! Dove sei? Barbaro, ferma,
	che se ben semivivo, col mio ferro
	saprò passarti il seno.
	Ecco, eccomi pronto. Ahi! Vengo meno. *(cade)*
Chia:	Si patrone mio bello!
D. An:	Ah caro padre mio!
Chia:	Uh, che feruta!
D. An:	In piè non reggo, oh Dio!
Chia:	So addebboluta!
Com:	Figlia, mia cara figlia. *(li servi lo sollevano)*
D. An:	Mio genitore amato.
Com:	Ascolta. Non ho fiato.
	Della mia vita è questo
	l'ultimo istante. Il cielo . . . il cielo . . . oh Dio! . . .

il ciel ti serbi, oimè . . . già muoio . . . addio.
(muore e li servi lo conducono dentro)

D. AN: Ah, padre, ah, padre mio. Più non risponde.

CHIA: Salute a buje: ha fatto marco sfila. *(entra)*

D. AN: Perfida! Io dunque sono
la barbara cagion della sua morte?
Ah, quale il mio delitto, eterni dei,
apre orribile scena agli occhi miei!

Ove lo sguardo giro,
orride larve io veggo;
in ogni oggetto io leggo
del fallo mio l'orror!
Ah se un acciar dal seno
l'alma non trasse ancor,
fatelo voi almeno,
rimorsi del mio cor. *(parte)*

Scena v

Campagna con rustiche abitazioni.

Lesbina, Pulcinella e Bastiano ballando e cantando al suono di colascione, tamburo e di altri istromenti popolari.

LES: / PUL: Viva, viva sempe ammore,
che li zite a core a core
fa co gusto e co priezza,
co allegrezza grellejà.

BAS: Oh che gioja, che piacere
proverò, quando a dozzine
e nepoti e nepotine
questa coppia mi darà.

A 3: Mo nce vò na tarantella. *(cantano e ballano la tarantella)*
Votta, mena, gioja bella,
schiatta 'mmidia e tozza llà.

PUL: Fata mia, co st'abballo
e co le parolelle che mm'haje ditto

a ll'uso del Mantracchio[3] mm'haje sanato.
A te, dinne quatt'aute.
LES: Io no nne saccio chiune.
BAS: La mia figlia
nacque in Napoli, è ver, ma ragazzina
qui la condussi meco,
e acciò che le sue nozze si facessero
alla napoletana,
te l'ho vestita ancor da luciana.[4]
PUL: Ho capisciuto. Orzù, vamme mollanno
l'amata palajozza
della tua man.
LES: (Vo' divertirmi un poco.)
PUL: Via, molla.
LES: Adaggio . . . piano . . .
io tremo, tremo.
PUL: E che lo matremmonio
fosse qua cannonata?
BAS: Poverina,
bisogna compatirla; è semplicina.
PUL: Via, molla mo.
LES: Ma io
sono ragazza ancora, ed ho paura
di star vicino a un uom da solo a sola.
Almeno in casa mia
vorrei star con tre altri in compagnia.
PUL: No, sta semprecetà no mme despiace.
Gnopà, bommespre.
BAS: Dove vai? Ascolta.
PUL: Bommespre.
LES: Adaggio, piano,
io finora scherzai. Questa è la mano.

A 3: Mo nce vò na tarantella.
Votta, mena, gioja bella.

3. The name is intended to indicate a physician of renown (Monaco, *Giambattista Lorenzi*, 476).
4. Like a young woman from the Santa Lucia section of Naples (Monaco, *Giambattista Lorenzi*, 477).

Scena vi

D. Giovanni, che s'intriga nel ballo, e detti.

PUL: Chià, chià, levate suono, ch'è benuto
lo cane corzo. *(si cessa di suonare e cantare)*

D. GIO: Come!
Così meco si tratta?
(Quanto sei cara.)

LES: (Dite a me?)

D. GIO: (Sì, bella.)

LES: (Costui mi piace più di Pulcinella.)

PUL: Tu 'nzomma te nne vaje? *(a D. Giovanni)*

BAS: Ma chi è lei, che fra noi
viene a ficcarsi?

D. GIO: Io sono
un cavalier ben conosciuto.

PUL: E ghiusto
pecchè sì canosciuto, voca fora.
Vì ch'uosemo che tene sto mmalora.

BAS: Ehi, parla con rispetto. I cavalieri
si tengon sopra, capite.

PUL: Nce lo puo' portà tu, ca pe mme 'ntanto
sto piso no lo voglio.

D. GIO: (Quanto mi piaci! E se tu vuoi, ti sposo.)

LES: (E se voi mi sposate,
mi chiameranno poi Donna Lesbina?)

D. GIO: (Anzi il titolo avrai di contessina.)

LES: (Uh che piacere!)

PUL: Ma vì chella comme
vò ire 'ncann'all'urzo. Io mo lo sciacco.

BAS: (Zitto, ch'è cavalier. Prendi tabbacco.)

PUL: (Oh zi viecchio de st'arma, t'arremmiedje
chesta gioja de faccia,
e no la vinne p'asso de carrozza?)

LES: (Io Pulcinella adesso
discaccerò.)

D. GIO: (Non discacciarlo ancora;
fingi di amarlo, e verrai meco or ora.)

PUL: Ora su, si patrone, abbreviammo.

Chesta ccà m'è mogliera.
D. Gio: Che? Tua moglie?
Pul: Pe servirve. Azoè 'nzervizio mio.
E pecchè nce sapimmo,
o nce ne jammo nuje o vota rimmo.
D. Gio: Non temer. Vado via.
E per darti una prova
della fedeltà mia, voglio abbracciarti. *(abbraccia Pulcinella e da dietro le spalle sue dà la mano a Lesbina)*
Pul: Mille grazie.
Bas: Che amabile signore!
D. Gio: Non mi distaccherei
mai più da te.
Pul: No nce vò auto. Avasta!
D. Gio: Ah qual momento è questo!
Pul: Ma vì ch'affetto! Lassa, ca so stracco.
D. Gio: Ci siamo intesi. *(Pulcinella si avvede che stavano per la mano insieme, e D. Giovanni senz'altro dire parte)*
Pul: Gnò?
Bas: Prendi tabbacco.

Scena vii
Lesbina, Pulcinella e Bastiano

Pul: Ah, guitta perchiepetola, e comme
nfra nuje nc'era lo patto
ch'io aveva da vennere
schitto 'nzalata, e mo 'ncagno de chesta
vago vennenno fasulille e aresta?
Bas: Eh via, che tu sei matto.
Les: Meschina me, che ho fatto?
Pul: Comme? Chillo
fegneva d'abbracciarme, e buje facivevo
ncopp'a le spalle meje strangolaprievete.
Les: Io? Che buggia!
Bas: Non farti
sentir per queste baje.
Pul: Che baja?

BAS: Ragazzate! Via, via.
Venite, amici, a bere, *(alli suonatori)*
che dopo qualche piccolo intervallo
vuol Pulcinella ripigliare il ballo. *(via colli sonatori)*
PUL: Io ballar? Se chiù ballo, de la luna,
con mia pena molesta,
pozza cadermi il primo quarto in testa.
LES: (Lo prenderei a schiaffi,
ma il mio nobile sposo
vuole ch'io finga tuttavia di amarlo.)
PUL: (Pulcinella, risolvi. Alfin si fugga
questa cajonza imbelle.)
Mappina, addio.
LES: (Mi friggono le mani.)
PUL: (Vì comme campanea.) Proterva, udisti
del mio tradito piede
l'ultima volontà?
LES: Cioè?
PUL: Rivolgo
lungi da teco l'orme fuggitive.
LES: E puoi lasciarmi?
PUL: Sì.
LES: Nè per placarti
basta il mio pianto?
PUL: No. Troppo son'io
de' tuoi falli satollo.
LES: Dunque mi lasci?
PUL: Sì.
LES: Rotta di collo.
PUL: Mannaggia ll'ora che non muore 'mpesa.
LES: Perdonami, carino. Fu l'affanno
che fece dirmi quella brutta cosa.
PUL: Taci, infida zellosa,
o sul tuo capo di ficozze io gioco.
LES: (Soffri, Donna Lesbina, un altro poco.)

Se dal tuo cor Lesbina,
crudel, da te si scaccia,
mira la poverina,

vedila almen spirar.
PUL: Taci, infedel ciaferra;
se chiù ti guardo in faccia,
mi fulmini la terra,
m'incenerisca il mar.
LES: Dunque è finita?
PUL: Sì.
LES: Nè vi è speranza?
PUL: No.
Il cor mi s'indurì,
l'alma mi s'intostò.
LES: Ah, non mi dir così,
ch'io qui mi ucciderò.
(Fa l'uomo il birbone,
ma quando Lesbina
sarà contessina,
punir lo saprà.)
PUL: (Mio core cafone,
mantiene a la scesa,
ca già da sta 'impesa
te sento vottà.)
LES: Che smanie, che pene,
che caso spietato!
PUL: (Mio core, mantiene,
ca già t'ha vottato.)
LES: *(guardando verso la scena d'onde viene D. Giovanni col quale va via, senza che Pulcinella se n'avvegga)*
Ma quando il mio bene
si muove a pietà?
PUL: (Lo chianto mme vene;
che nce aggio da fà?)

Scena viii

Pulcinella solo, indi Bastiano con bocale e bicchiero.

Via, Pulcinella,
fa' core d'aruojo.
Consola la bella,

che more pe tte.
Mia cara . . . *(si volta e non trova più Lesbina, ma gli viene in faccia Bastiano)*

BAS: Un bicchieretto
ci vuole anche allo sposo. Bevi, bevi.
PUL: E la sposa addov'è?
BAS: Tu la tenevi.
Io da dentro ho veduto
che or ora stava qui. Corpo di Pluto!
Dov'è mia figlia?
PUL: Se n'è ghiuta 'nfummo.
BAS: Cacciala adesso. Caccia, caccia, caccia . . .
PUL: Ora vì c'auto guajo!
BAS: A te l'ho consegnata.
E che stava con te l'avrà veduto
anche il padrone tuo, che poco prima
stava fermato lì.
PUL: Chillo nce steva lì? E quanno torna
figlieta, gioja bella,
chiamma no robbevecchia e binnencella.
BAS: Venderla? Quell'ha d'essere tua moglie.
PUL: Moglie? Minime quaqueram.
BAS: Lo vedremo. Correte, amici, andate;
cercatela, trovatela,
e di nuovo allo sposo consegnatela.
PUL: Tu che dice? Sì pazzo.
Io sempre fui saccon, non matarazzo.

BAS: Lo vedremo, animalaccio,
quel nequaqueram cos'è?
Tu l'onor del mio mostaccio
non lo sporchi per mia fè.
Sul decoro feminino
della razza mia lucente,
senza dir del mascolino,
qualche pezzo più recente
sopra sopra ti dirò.
Fu mia nonna impegnatrice,

ed ognun racconta e dice
quanto grata si mostrò.
Fu mia madre locandiera,
e con grazia e con maniera
mille nobili trattò.
Fu mia moglie . . . Ma che giova
ch'io mi sfiati più con te?
Basta dirti, animalaccio,
che l'onor del mio mostaccio
non lo sporchi per mia fè.
(parte e si strascina appresso Pulcinella)

Scena ix
Camera.

Il Marchese Dorasquez, la Duchessa Isabella, e poi D. Anna e Chiarella

M. Do: E capace il Tenorio
sarà di un tradimento così enorme?

D. Isa: Ah, signor, se v'inganno,
che mi fulmini il cielo. Ei mi sedusse;
alle lusinghe sue sacrificai
credula l'onor mio,
ed allor ch'io credea col sacro rito
toglier l'orrore al mio commesso fallo,
fugge l'empio e mi lascia
de' miei parenti alla vendetta esposta.
Fuggo ancor'io da Napoli, e seguendo
del traditor le tracce,
qui lo ritrovo alfine. A voi ricorro,
e da voi, gran ministro,
non il mio folle amore,
giustizia implora il mio ferito onore.

M. Do: Intesi quanto basta. Don Giovanni
da me chiamato qui verrà tra poco.
La ragion, non temete, avrà il suo loco.
(ad un servo che viene coll'imbasciata)
Chi è, Donn'Anna? Venga.

D. AN: Signor, ecco di nuovo a' piedi vostri
l'orfana figlia di Consalvo Ulloa,
che da voi la vendetta
del suo trafitto genitore aspetta.

CHIA: Signò, justizia. Trova chillo birbo
ch'accise lo patrone.
Mpiennelo, azzellentissemo,
e si tu stisso co le proprie mano
da la scala lo jette,
sa' che corona 'ncapo tu te miette?

M. DO: Ma finora in sospetto
vi cadde alcun ch'esser potesse il reo?

D. AN: Dirò: con questo foglio il Duca Ottavio
mi avverte che al ridotto,
mentre ch'egli giocava, un certo tale
Don Giovanni Tenorio fu veduto,
che si prese la cappa e il suo cappello.

CHIA: E chesta robba appunto
'ncuollo a chillo frabbutto io la vedette,
e 'imperrò Donn'Attavio lo credette.

D. ISA: Ah, che del mio tiranno è questo ancora
un altro tradimento.

M. DO: Chi? Don Giovanni? Venga. *(ad un altro servitore)*
Ritiratevi voi per un momento.
(le donne si ritirano in disparte)

Scena x

D. Giovanni, il Marchese; e le donne in disparte.

D. GIO: Al Marchese Dorasquez
il Tenorio s'inchina.

M. DO: Ed al Tenorio
fa l'istesso il Dorasquez.
Sedete. (Ei sta perplesso.)

D. GIO: (Franchezza mia, non mi tradire adesso.)

M. DO: Ditemi un poco: nella scorsa notte
voi dove foste?

D. GIO: A caccia.
M. DO: Di notte?
D. GIO: Sissignore,
e ammazzai un coniglio.
M. DO: (Principiamo assai male.) Il Duca Ottavio
dacchè voi nol vedete?
D. GIO: Sarà un mese.
M. DO: Un mese?
D. GIO: Più o meno.
M. DO: Ah Tenorio, Tenorio, il vostro genio
troppo mal vi consiglia.
D. GIO: (Se s'imbroglian le carte, addio Siviglia.)
Ma non intendo . . .
M. DO: Ora passiamo ad altro.
In Napoli da voi fu conosciuta
la Duchessa Isabella?
D. GIO: Sì, l'intesi
nominar qualche volta, ma veduta
io non l'ho mai.
D. ISA: Ah, mentitor, spergiuro. *(facendosi avanti)*
Guardami in volto, e poi
il tradimento tuo niega, se puoi.
D. GIO: (Oh diavolo!)
D. AN: Assassino!
D. GIO: (Oimè, Donn'Anna!)
D. AN: Se questa notte fosti a caccia, come
nel ridotto rubasti al Duca Ottavio
la cappa ed il cappello? Scellerato,
tu con queste divise
proccurasti ingannarmi, e poi, oh Dio!,
barbaro, mi svenasti il padre mio.
M. DO: (Si smarrì.)
CHIA: (Poveriello, non è brutto,
e si maje è stat'isso,
che bello 'mpiso ha da parè, marisso!)
D. AN: Signor, è questo il reo. Vendetta chiede
l'ucciso genitore.
D. ISA: Voi, vendicate il mio tradito onore!
D. GIO: (Coraggio.) Delle vostre

nere calunnie mi darete conto.
Ci rivedrem . . . *(va per partire)*

M. DO: Fermate.
Per ora, Don Giovanni,
sia carcer vostro questo albergo mio.
Saprò la verità trovar ben io.

D. GIO: Come! Un arresto ad un par mio?

M. DO: Tacete.
Sul labbro mio severo
così comanda il re.

D. GIO: Cedo all'impero.

Cedo. Il comando impresso
nel cor mi resterà. *(resta pensieroso)*

M. DO: (Lo vedo assai perplesso,
segno di reità.)

D. ISA: (In quel suo volto espresso
veggo il rimorso già.)

D. AN: (Il suo delitto istesso
già lo tormenterà.)

CHIA: (Va trova. A lo prociesso
chillo mo penzarrà.)

M. DO: (Non parla.)

D. ISA: (Non ha fiato.)

D. AN: (È un tronco.)

CHIA: (S'è agghiajato.)

D. ISA:, D. AN:, M. DO:, CHIA: (La colpa atroce e nera
lo deve lacerar.)

D. GIO: (No, quella cameriera *(guardando Chiarella)*
non è da disprezzar.)

M. DO:, D. ISA:, D. AN:, CHIA: Comprendi il fallo enorme?
Tremi all'error commesso?
Ma la clemenza dorme.
Ma è morta la pietà.

D. GIO: Trema chi è delinquente,
chi dalla colpa è oppresso,

ma un'anima innocente
tremar giammai non sa. *(partono)*

Scena xi
Città.

Pulcinella solo.

Oh ca mme vedo scapolo
da chillo vessicante de gnopatre,
e lo patrone mio,
senza portà respetto a la livrea,
pure ha voluto stennere la mano
dinto a lo piatto mio! Diavolo, affocalo!
Ma che? Si llascio, mare l'ossa soja,
nce ne voglio dì quatto co lo pepe.
Isso che mme pò fà? Na schiaffiata?
Isso schiaffea, e io carreco.
Me sbatte 'nterra? E io carreco.
Mme smossa? Me stravisa?
Ma le faccio sudare na cammisa.

Scena xii
Lesbina vestita in adriè,[5] Bastiano con giamberga ricca ed ombrellina, ed alcuni villani vestiti da servitori e detto.

LES: Contino padre?
MAS: Contessina figlia?
LES: Dite da parte mia
al sole che se n'entri. Io non vorrei
che il mio nobil marito
mi trovasse col volto abbrustolito.
BAS: No, contessina figlia, non va bene.
Può darsi il caso che qualch'altra dama
abbia fatto il bucato e le bisogni
ancora il sol per rasciugare i panni.

5. Lorenzi's revised version reads: "Lesbina vestita da signora ma goffamente." See Monaco, *Giambattista Lorenzi,* 486.

Ci vuole, abbi pazienza,
tra dame e dame qualche convenienza.

PUL: (Occhi miei, quid maloram videbimini!
So lloro o non so lloro?)

LES: Contino padre?

BAS: Contessina figlia?

LES: E il conte sposo non si vede ancora
col tiro per tirarci?

BAS: Veramente,
or che siamo chi siamo,
il farci andar per terra entro Siviglia
è un taglia faccia, contessina figlia.

LES: Non sia mai, e incontrassi
qualche duchessa e mi vedesse, oh dei,
camminar colli piedi, io vi giuro
per l'ombra di mia madre
morirei di rossor, contino padre.

PUL: (Conte, contessa. Chiste so 'impazzute.)
Nè, si conte rapesta, vaje co figlieta
cantanno Annuccia mia?

LES: Olà, facchino,
bada ben come parli con un conte.

PUL: Conte de dò? De le colonne a Napole?

LES: Ah, birbantaccio! Olà, contino padre,
dite al mio maggiordomo
che gli tiri due pietre.

BAS: No, contessina figlia, con il manico
della zappa facciamolo
più presto dissossare
dal nostro segretario, che ti pare?

PUL: No, benedica, avite
na corte proprio scelta. Tale quale
ne tene una lo Conte Tarcenale.[6]

BAS: Ora tu gracchia e crepa; il tuo padrone
ha fatt'a tuo dispetto contessina
la mia cara Lesbina.

PUL: Oh bella cosa!

6. A two-bit count (Monaco, *Giambattista Lorenzi,* 488).

LES: E noi,
per venire in città da pari nostri,
questi vestiti abbiamo presi a nolo.

BAS: Ma or ora dal mercante
collo sposo anderemo
ed avrem quanti tagli noi vorremo.

PUL: Addò? 'Nfaccia? Che riso, bene mio. *(ride forte)*
Si conte, ah, ah!

LES: Tu ridi?
Io farò cacciar l'albero
della nostra prosapina, e vedrai
se il titolo di conte gli sta bene.

PUL: E l'arvolo a che serve?
So denare jettate. Lo si conte
l'arvolo sujo già lo porta 'nfronte.

LES: Come a dir?

BAS: Parla chiaro!

PUL: Bene mio,
e comme lo si conte
ha da ire strellanno n'auta vota:
cecorie, sarvaggiole, ah, le cecorie!

LES: Olà, melenso.

PUL: E la siè contessina
comm'ha da parè bella
quanno torna a strellare:
purchiacchielle e arucole, purchiacchielle!

LES: Birbo, così si parla
con una dama errante,
che marcia colla coda e il guardinfante?

PUL: Uh, de ste damme lo patrone mio
sa quante n'ave fatte? Terra tienete!
Tè, smicciate, schiarateve la vista,
contatevelle vuje, chesta è la lista. *(spiega una lunga nota)*

LES: Contino padre!

BAS: Contessina figlia!

LES: E sarà vero?

PUL: Purchiacchielle e arucole . . . *(tra sè, ripiegando la lista)*

BAS: Io divento di stucco.

PUL: Cecorie, sarvaggiole, ah, le cecorie! *(come sopra)*
LES: E sarà tanto birba la mia stella!

Scena xiii
D. Giovanni e detti.

D. GIO: A tempo ti ritrovo, Pulcinella.
Su, presto, vieni meco.
LES: Caro sposo . . .
BAS: Signore . . .
D. GIO: Andate al diavolo!
Cammina.
PUL: Addove jammo?
D. GIO: Nel tempio qui vicino a pormi in salvo.
PUL: Zoè?
D. GIO: Cammina. Parleremo or ora.
LES: Senti, contino mio . . .
D. GIO: E va' in malora! *(parte con Pulcinella)*
LES: Così mi scaccia! Ah barbaro!
Povera contessina!
PUL: Purchiacchielle e arucole, purchiacchielle . . .
(viene di carriera e ritorna dentro)
BAS: Ed io ho da restare
con questo smacco in faccia!
Oh sangue d'una rapa!
PUL: Cecorie, sarvaggiole, ah, le cecorie. *(come sopra; ed intanto quelli che facevano da servitori si levano le livree e le buttono a' piedi della Lesbina e di Bastiano e vanno via)*
BAS: Fuori di me son'io!
LES: Addio, mia coda, guardinfante, addio.

Dov'è più la contessina?
Dove andò la nobiltà?
Della povera Lesbina
chi mai sente, oh Dio, pietà?
Ma qui ferma, disleale;
non fuggirmi, traditore;

o trafiggi questo core
o ritornami ad amar.
  Ma pentito il caro bene
già mi viene a consolar.
Già si fanno le mie nozze.
Che fracasso d'istromenti,
che rumore di carrozze,
ma lo sposo mio dov'è?
  Uh, che pianto, che singhiozzo!
Io mi affoco, io mi strozzo;
non vi son più giuramenti,
no, non v'è più fedeltà.
(Bastiano raccoglie le livree e parte colla Lesbina)

Scena xiv
Il Marchese Dorasquez, D. Anna e poi D. Isabella

M. Do: D'ordine del sovrano
eretta è già nel tempio
la statua equestre del Commendatore,
l'istessa che in sua vita
fu per voto comune a lui scolpita.
D. An: Signore, alla pietosa
real munificenza del monarca
sensibile son'io,
ma vendicato io chiedo il padre mio.
M. Do: Donn'Anna, non temete.
Il Tenorio è arrestato, e dalle prove
se convinto egli resta,
al carnefice infame
sopra di un palco egli darà la testa.
D. Isa: Ah, signore, accorrete.
Il traditor Tenorio, da un balcone
del vostro albergo, ardito
si gittò disperato ed è fuggito.
D. An: Come!
M. Do: È fuggito! Ah, quanto è ver che sempre

il malvaggio da un fallo
passa a fallo maggiore.

D. ISA: Barbaro, traditore . . . *(piange)*

D. AN: Anima rea! Povero padre mio! *(come sopra)*

M. DO: No, non temete. Il troverò ben'io. *(parte con D. Anna)*

Scena xv
D. Isabella sola

Infelice Isabella, in qual sepolto
angolo della terra
celerai il rossore
del tuo facile amore? Oh Dio! Mi sento
mancar l'anima in sen! Semplici donne,
dal mio caso apprendete
quanto caute in amor esser dovete.

Di un amatore al pianto,
che fedeltà promette,
non vi fidate tanto,
anime semplicette;
sempre non son le lagrime
figlie di un vero amor.
Lo sa pur troppo il misero
mio sventurato cor.

Scena xvi
Tempio colla statua equestre del Commendatore.

D. Giovanni e Pulcinella

PUL: Oh, ca jammo fujenno n'auta vota,
che te pare? Quann'io te commerteva,
mme responnive sempe:
"Taci, olà, mascalzone,
o ti sfonno coi piedi quel calzone."
E mo? Sbruffe, sospire, e te jastimme
n'uocchio deritto.

D. GIO: Ah, caro Pulcinella,
son morto.

PUL: Te lo credo. Mo canusce
le tue prescite infamità proterve.

D. GIO: Ah, dimmi, hai tu veduta
la moglie del trattore qui vicino?
Quanto è bella! È un boccone da svogliato!

PUL: Uh che mannaggia chi te n'ha terato!
Tu staje p'essere 'mpiso
e manco t'arremiette? A quanto vedo,
ncopp'a lo core tujo
lo vizio puorco nc'ha vattuto l'asteco.
Vi ca lo cielo . . .

D. GIO: Eh, taci in tua malora,
linguaccia indemoniata.

PUL: Ninche sente dì cielo, ha na vrecciata.
(Via via è cravonella
de la vrasera addò se scarfa Pruto.)
E mutammo trascurzo. Nè, se magna?

D. GIO: Oh vedi, Pulcinella,
che bella statua è quella!

PUL: Oh bella, bella, bella! Nè, se magna?

D. GIO: Parmi l'effigie del Commendatore.

PUL: Oh cancaro! È lo vero. Nè, se magna?

D. GIO: Vo' legger l'iscrizione.

PUL: (Vì comme vota fuoglio lo briccone.)

D. GIO: "Di colui che mi trasse a morte ria, *(legge il marmo sepolcrale)*
dal cielo attendo la vendetta mia."
Vecchio stolto, e dal ciel vendetta speri?
Ridicola speranza!
A far la tua vendetta
scendi e vieni tu stesso,
che colla spada in mano
Don Giovanni ti aspetta. *(caccia la spada e finge di attendere la statua)*

PUL: È pazzo, è pazzo!

D. GIO: Che dici?

PUL: Io? Niente affatto.

D. GIO: Ti maravigli forse ch'io favello
con un marmo insensato?

Io nell'effigie il morto originale
intendo di beffare.

PUL: 'Nzomma porzì li muorte aje da zucare?
E fa' lo fatto tujo. Or abbreviammo:
magnammo o no magnammo?

D. GIO: Ho già parlato
al trattor che portasse
qualche cosa nell'atrio.

PUL: Quacche cosa?
Io stongo de na vena
che mo me magnarria na vacca prena.

D. GIO: Silenzio olà, che col Commendatore
voglio pacificarmi. Egli è vecchietto,
invitalo a mangiar meco una zuppa.

PUL: A chi mo?

D. GIO: Alla statua.

PUL: Ah, ah, oh bella! *(ride fortemente)*
Benemio, mo lo sgorgio . . .

D. GIO: Animo, via!

PUL: 'Mmita masto Giorgio.[7]

D. GIO: Va', ti dico, o per Bacco . . .

PUL: Senza collera,
mo vago. Nè, volite . . . *(alla statua, che apre gli occhi)*
Miserecordia . . .

D. GIO: Cosa fu?

PUL: Ah, ch'ave
apierte tanto d'uocchio, lo mariuolo.
Benemio, ca mo moro.

D. GIO: Eh, che sei matto!
Apprensione, apprensione . . . [8]

PUL: Che apprenzione?
Ogn'uocchio 'nzanetà parea lampione.

D. GIO: Non più parole; invitalo.

PUL: Ma chillo . . .

D. GIO: Avanti, o che ti passo il core.

7. Monaco (*Giambattista Lorenzi,* 504) explains that a male attendant was popularly referred to as Mastro Giorgio in Neapolitan asylums.

8. Illusion.

PUL: Chià, chià, mo jammo. Si Commennatore,
volite favorire de magnare
nziemme co nnuje na papparella molla? *(la statua cala la testa accenando di sì)*
Mamma mia . . .

D. GIO: Cosa fu?

PUL: Ha calata la capo la cepolla.

Bene mio! E che paura,
uh, che triemmolo m'afferra.
Chià, mantiè, mo vago 'nterra.
Chi mme votta a cammenà?
Mo te conto, mo te dico,
chillo gioja, chill'amico,
la carcioffola ha calata;
uh che freve m'è sparata!
No mme fido de parlà.
È apprenzione? Non è niente?
Chesta tanfa che tu siente
te pò dì la verità.
Ma frabbutto, marranchino,
tu nce curpe a chesto ccà,
e na funa, no vorpino
pe te 'impiso non ce sta? *(fugge, tremando)*

D. GIO: Che imbecille! Vedrò se moto e voce
quel marmo avrà con me. Commendatore,
t'invito a cenar meco e di trattarti
da par tuo ti prometto.
Dimmi, verrai?

STA: Verrò.

D. GIO: Ed io ti aspetto. *(via)*

Scena xvii
Atrio del tempio.

Pulcinella scappando, indi D. Giovanni

PUL: Pulecenella, sì bivo ancora?
Ma si sì bivo, n'auta mezora,
salute a nuje, tu puo' campà. *(va per partire)*
D. GIO: Dove tu fuggi, vigliacco core?
PUL: Vago a chiammarme no 'nzagnatore.
D. GIO: Ferma, ti dico, quel timor vano.
PUL: Voglio appuntare mo co Patano.[9]
D. GIO: I maccheroni per quest'intoppo
dunque non serve portarli qui.
PUL: Va' chià, magnammo, ca moro doppo.
Pozzo tirare, falle venì. *(D. Giovanni accenna verso la scena, e vien la tavola preparata ed un bacile di maccheroni)*
D. GIO: Ecco, servito sei.
Mangia, ch'io mangio ancor.
PUL: Diletti maccabei,
sopponte del mio cor . . . *(volendo principiare a mangiare, si sente bussare da dentro)*
D. GIO: Si bussa.
PUL: Cannonata!
Noce de cuollo 'nterra,
po dice ca uno sferra.
Manco se pò magnà!
D. GIO: Prendi quel lume e va'. *(Pulcinella va a vedere chi è)*
Ah fosse questa almeno
qualche gentil beltà.
PUL: Ah, mamma, chi m'aiuta?
D. GIO: Che avvenne?
PUL: Ah, ch'è benuta
la statua a lo commito
e mo se 'mpizza ccà.
D. GIO: Che cavalier compito!
PUL: Ch'arma de baccalà!

9. A famous gravedigger (Monaco, *Giambattista Lorenzi,* 506).

D. GIO: Io stesso incontrerollo.
Lo vuol la civiltà. *(prende un lume e va per incontrare la statua)*
PUL: Auh, le cadesse 'ncuollo
co scusa de sciulià. *(Pulcinella in veder la statua si nasconde sotto la tavola)*

(statua del Commendatore e detti)

STA: Don Giovanni, ravvisi
quell'onorato cavalier che a cena
teco invitasti?
D. GIO: Sì.
STA: La mia promessa
ecco adempita. Venni a cenar teco;
or ancor'io t'invito a cenar meco.
Verrai?
D. GIO: Verrò.
STA: Ed io ti attendo.
D. GIO: Intanto
qui prendi qualche cibo.
STA: I cibi miei
non son terreni. Io vado.
D. GIO: Or ci vedremo.
Vuoi lume?
STA: No.
D. GIO: E al bujo
puoi girne così solo?
STA: L'oscurità non m'impedisce il volo. *(si alza a volo e a mezz'aria invita Pulcinella)*
Conduci ancora il servo Pulcinella.
PUL: Non signore, io diuno, gioja bella.

Gnò, comme va sta cosa?
Tè, vide, comm'assomma!
Mme pare na palomma
che nn'aria se nne va.
D. GIO: Crede atterrirmi il cielo
con questo suo portento,
ma non mi dà spavento,
timore il cor non ha.

Andiamo.
PUL: Addò?
D. GIO: A cenare.
PUL: Eh, ca vuò pazziare.
D. GIO: Cammina, o che ti ammazzo.
PUL: Mmalora, chisto è pazzo!
D. GIO: Alma al coraggio avvezza,
no, che timor non ha.
PUL: (Che arma de monnezza!
Chisto mme fa tremmà.) *(partono)*

[Scena xviii]
Camera in casa del Marchese.

Lesbina, Bastiano ed il Marchese

M. DO: Ma chi siete? Ma che dite?
Chi venite a querelar?
LES: / BAS: Ma se voi non ci capite,
che ci abbiamo noi da far?
M. DO: (Oh che due medaglie care!)
LES: E così, per seguitare,
esso venne, cioè quello,
piglia e para, il bricconcello,
poi mi pianta e se ne va.
BAS: Questo è il fatto come sta.
M. DO: Io v'intendo a discrezione.
Ma chi mai fu questo tale?
LES: Fu quel tale che ora voglio.
M. DO: Ma chi fu?
LES: Fu lui.
M. DO: Che imbroglio!
Ma chi lui?
BAS: Quello, il quale.
M. DO: Vi spiegate molto male,
nè v'intendo in verità.
LES: (Oh che giudice animale!

BAS: Disperar costui ci fa.)
(D. Isabella, D. Anna, Chiarella e detti)

M. DO: Venite voi. Già l'ordine
si diede dal sovrano
ch'estratto sia il Tenorio
dal tempio ov' egli sta.
E vuol che a voi la mano *(a D. Isabella)*
di sposo prima ei dia,
e poi di sè spettacolo
al popolo farà.

D. ISA: / D. AN: / CHIA: / M. DO: Oh di giustizia esempio!
Oh grande, oh saggio re!

LES: / BAS: Si nominò Tenorio;
diteci voi perchè.

D. ISA: / M. DO: Perchè Tenorio è un barbaro.

LES: È mio marito, cattera!

D. AN: / CHIA: Perchè Tenorio è un perfido.

BAS: Cospetto! Egli è mio genero.

D. ISA: / D. AN: / CHIA: / M. DO: In mano del carnefice
la vita ei lascerà.

LES: / BAS: Non la farà certissimo
questa bestialità. *(partono)*

[Scena xix]

Tempio con tavola coverta di lutto con candelieri e candele nere e seminata di serpi, rospi e di altri animali venenosi.

Statua, D. Giovanni e Pulcinella

D. GIO: Su, cammina, avanti, dico,
che già il fumo mi salì.

PUL:	Che te 'nzurfe a fà co mmico? A le gamme ll'haje da dì.
D. GIO:	Oh, che orribil cena è questa d'atro sangue e di ceraste!
PUL:	Da st'amico belli paste! Va', t'assetta e mena priesto.
D. GIO:	Vieni, mangia.
PUL:	Sto 'ndigesto.
D. GIO:	Vieni, o il capo ti fracasso.
PUL:	Faccio passo, faccio passo.
D. GIO:	Serpi e rospi io mangerò. *(si accosta alla tavola e prende un rospo)*
PUL:	Fuss'acciso chi nne vò.
STA:	Don Giovanni.
D. GIO:	Che pretendi?
STA:	La tua mano.
D. GIO:	Eccola, prendi. *(la statua stringe la mano di D. Giovanni e questi fa forza per ritirarla a sè, ma non può)*
PUL:	Ah, canaglia, no la dà.
D. GIO:	Ahi, che foco, ahi, che pena! Io mi sento incenerire.
STA:	Tarda il ciel, ma sa punire; se ti penti, avrai perdono.
PUL:	Di' ca sì.
D. GIO:	Qual fui, tal sono.
PUL:	Di' ca sì.
STA:	Detesta il fallo.
PUL:	Che nce spienne quacche callo? Di' ca sì.
D. GIO:	No, no, ridico.
STA:	Don Giovanni.
D. GIO:	Maledico.
PUL:	Zitto, bestia, non dì appriesso, ca Mamozio[10] te la fa.
D. GIO:	Non mi pento, son l'istesso, nè timore il ciel mi dà.

10. A well-known and very time-worn statue at Pozzuoli (Monaco, *Giambattista Lorenzi,* 511).

STA: Mori pur da' falli oppresso,
più soffrirti il ciel non sa. *(D. Giovanni sprofonda, la statua vola e Pulcinella cade a terra pel timore)*

PUL: Mamma mia! Che a li sprofunne
lo patrone se n'è ghiuto!
E l'assequia lo quernuto
s'ha voluta sparagnà. *(va per partire tremando)*

[Scena xx]

Lesbina, D. Isabella, D. Anna, Chiarella, Marchese, guardie, Bastiano e Pulcinella

M. DO: Soldati, olà, si arresti
or ora D. Giovanni.

D. ISA: / D. AN: / CHIA: Il servo suo è questi;
esso può dir dov'è. *(li soldati circondano Pulcinella)*

PUL: Mena, fortuna porca,
refunne chiù cafè.

LES: Briccone, ti ci ho colto.
Caccia lo sposo mio,
o con quest'ugne il volto
ti lacero così.

PUL: Lo sposo tuo sparì.

BAS: Olà, poche parole,
caccialo adesso qui.

PUL: Cecorie, sarvaggiole,
manco la vuò fenì!

M. DO: Legate quel birbante. *(a' soldati)*

PUL: Signò, mo dico tutto.
La statola mo nnante
le fece fà no butto,
e io sto pe sconocchià.

D. ISA:
D. AN:
LES: Legatelo. Al carnefice
CHIA: dirà la verità.
BAS:
M. DO:

PUL: Cielo, addò sta Mamozio?
Fallo venì mo ccà. *(scoppia un fulmine e, diroccando il tempio, scopre una bocca dell'inferno)*

[Scena xxi]
Inferno

Larva rappresentante D. Giovanni dannato e detti.

LARVA: Dove sono! Ahi, dove caddi!
Son dannato! Oimè, che pene!
Per un breve e falso bene
in eterno ho da penar!

TUTTI: Che terrore! Che spavento!
Che funesta orribil scena!
Per l'orrore in sen mi sento
ogni fibra palpitar.

LARVA: Ahi, che sono, me infelice,
da' miei falli atroci e immondi
negli abbissi più profondi
strascinato a lagrimar.

TUTTI: Ah, che il cor mi trema in petto!
Ahi, qual giel mi cadde sopra!
Ecco il fin di chi mal opra,
ecco il cielo che sa far.

fine

Il nuovo convitato di pietra

Francesco Gardi
Giuseppe Maria Foppa

1787

IL NUOVO
CONVITATO DI PIETRA

dramma tragicomico
da rappresentarsi
nel nobile teatro
di San Samuele
il carnovale dell'anno
MDCCLXXXVII

In Venezia
MDCCLXXXVII

Appresso Modesto Fenzo
Con le debite permissioni

ATTORI

Prime buffe a parti eguali

Donn'Anna, figlia del Commendatore Oloa
La sig. Maddalena de Masi

Donna Isabella, signora napolitana
La sig. Susanna Contini

Primo mezzo carattere
Don Giovanni Tenorio, napolitano
Il sig. Francesco Morella

Primo buffo caricato
Don Masone, secretario di Don Giovanni
Il sig. Girolamo Vedova

Altro primo buffo mezzo carattere
Zuccasecca, servo di D. Giovanni
Il sig. Fausto Borselli

Seconde buffe

Tisbea, pescatrice
La sig. Maria Zacchielli

Donna Betta, locandiera
La sig. Camila Bollini

Altro buffo
Comino, servo di Donna Isabella
Il sig. Ignazio Lironi
Statua di D. Consalvo Oloa, Commendatore di Castiglia
La scena si finge in una locanda nelle vicinanze di Siviglia.

La musica del celebre sig. maestro Francesco Gardi.

MUTAZIONI DI SCENE

Atto primo

Galleria nella locanda, che serve d'ingresso a varie camere.
Recinto campestre destinato a' sepolcri de' Grandi, con varie urne e statue, in mezzo a cui è la gran statua equestre del Commendatore Oloa.
Camera.
Sala terrena con tavola apparecchiata.

Atto secondo

Galleria nella locanda.
Campagna.
Boschereccia.
Recinto campestre con urne e statue e cavallo senza la statua del Commendatore, che sta nel mezzo di una tavola apparecchiata di nero, con teste d'idre, serpenti, ec.

Le scene saranno tutte nuove d'invenzione
del sig. Lorenzo Sacchetti.

ATTO PRIMO

Scena prima

Galleria nella locanda, che serve d'ingresso a varie camere.

Tisbea, pescatrice, seduta da una parte; dall'altra Donn'Anna.
D. Giovanni, D. Masone e Zucasecca in piedi.

D. GIO: / D. MAS: / ZUC:	Si contorce la spagnuola, freme sola e nulla dice; la vezzosa pescatrice manifesta gran furor.
D. AN: / TIS:	Di soffrir tanti strapazzi sono stanca ed annoiata, per cagion di un'alma ingrata, d'un perverso mancator.
D. GIO:	Zuccasecca, Don Masone, fate voi da mediatori; lor donate questi fiori *(una rosa e un gelsomino)* e placatele così.
ZUC:	Proverò . . . (Che intrigo è questo!) *(prende il gelsomino)*
D. MAS:	Tenterò . . . (Vuol esser bella.) *(prende la rosa)*
D. GIO:	Tu per questa e tu per quella.
D. MAS: / ZUC:	L'ho capita, signor sì.
ZUC:	Alla vaga pescatrice *(a Tisbea)* offro un bianco gelsomino.
D. MAS:	A quel petto alabastrino *(a D. Anna)* destinato è questo fior.
TIS:	Dallo a un cane!
D. AN:	Non seccarmi!
TIS:	Non lo voglio.
D. AN:	Non l'accetto.
D. MAS: / ZUC:	Ci vuol altro che un fioretto per la rabbia di costor.
D. GIO:	Ma pregate un altro poco.
	Col pregar non si fa nulla.
D. MAS:	Nobilissima fanciulla,

ZUC: Leggiadrissima
lo volete sì o no?

D. AN:
TIS: L'insistenza poi m'offende.

D. MAS:
ZUC: Anzi effetto è di buon core.

D. AN:
TIS: Temerario ambasciatore,
uno schiaffo ti darò. *(dando uno schiaffo D. Anna a D. Masone e Tisbea a Zucasecca)*

D. MAS:
ZUC: Ti darò! . . . Se me lo dava,
gentilmente m'ammazzava.

D. GIO: Ma pregate un altro poco.

D. MAS:
ZUC: Basta, basta in verità.

D. GIO: Via, care, via, belle,
la pace sia fatta.

D. AN:
TIS: Così non si tratta,
bugiardo, infedel.

D. GIO: Ti volgi, mio bene. *(a D. Anna)*
Mi guarda, mia vita. *(a Tisbea)*

D. AN:
TIS: L'aspetto m'irrita
d'un mostro crudel.

A 5: Ah lo sdegno e la rabbia è sì forte,
che le/mi accende e lor/mi bolle nel core,
ch'ogni prego e protesta d'amore
più rabbios e/a e sdegnat e le/a mi fa.

D. GIO: Calmatevi una volta.
Se così seguitate, io non resisto.
Credetemi, mie belle,
dolcissime fanciulle,
che se meco più placide sarete,
il costante amor mio voi sole avrete. *(parte)*

D. AN: Iniquo! Ai tradimenti
egli unisce gli scherni.

Ma saprò vendicarmi. Andrò a Siviglia,
dirò com'egli il genitor m'uccise,
come con lui mi trasse
e come . . . Ma non posso
l'aspetto tollerar più di costei.
La rabbia mi divora.
Vanne, vil pescatrice, alla malora. *(parte)*

Scena ii

Tisbea, Zucasecca e D. Masone

D. MAS: Non partite, Donn'Anna,
fermatevi, sentite. Oh come è snella!
Non partì, no, precipitò la bella.

ZUC: Eh, lasciatela andar. Basta che voi,
carissima Tisbea,
più bella compagnia facciate a noi.

D. MAS: Dice ben Zuccasecca.
Allegra, allegra state.

ZUC: Allegra mia Tisbea . . . Ma sospirate?

TIS: In mezzo a tai strapazzi, e a tai martiri
come volete mai ch'io non sospiri?

Io sospiro l'onore perduto,
io sospiro la pace smarrita.
Il tranquillo tenor di mia vita,
giusti dei, come mai si cangiò?
Dove siete, ami, reti, capanne,
rive care del fiume natio?
Quanto sdegna l'afflitto cor mio
l'empia man che da voi mi staccò.

Scena iii

Zucasecca, Don Masone

ZUC: Udiste, Don Masone? Poverella!
Piange l'onor perduto.

D. MAS: Ella ha ragione.
Don Giovanni Tenorio,
nostro padrone, a dir la verità,
è un uom troppo goloso.
Vuol di niuna e di tutte esser lo sposo.

ZUC: Mi fa pietà Tisbea.

D. MAS: Mi fa pietà Donn'Anna.
Povera principessa!

ZUC: Povera pescatrice!

D. MAS: Andiamo, andiamo a consolarle.

ZUC: E come?

D. MAS: Con raccontar ad esse le istorielle
di tante e tante belle,
che senza gli sponsali,
senza i patti solenni e i testimoni,
hanno saputo far dei matrimoni.

ZUC: Eh, altro che istorielle.
Invitiamole, caro Don Masone,
con buona grazia a far anche con noi
cotesti matrimoni.
Io vado da Tisbea
per rallegrar il core
di quella poverina.
Forse il rimedio mio sarà migliore.

Un dì la mamma disse
ad una vecchia amica,
"Ah, tu che savia sei,
soccorri ai mali miei.
Il mio marito ingrato
ricusa starmi a lato
e mi fa sospirar."
L'amica a questi detti
rispose prestamente,
"Convien [con] altri oggetti
distrar un po' la mente."
Non so cos'abbia fatto;
so che la mamma a un tratto
cessò di spasimar. *(parte)*

D. MAS: Bravissimo, il mio caro Zuccasecca.
Io subito mi appiglio
al tuo savio consiglio.
Tu andasti da Tisbea.
Io vado da Donn'Anna. Ma pian piano.
Mi sovvengon due versi
d'un poeta romano:
"Non si ricorda del mio amor costei;
io mi ricordo di quel schiaffo ancora."
Ma da bravo, Masone,
coraggio, su, coraggio nonostante.
Poco importano i schiaffi a un vero amante.

Scena iv

Donna Isabella, Donna Betta e Comino

D. ISA: Deh, concedi, amor tiranno,
qualche pace a questo sen.
In me cessi il lungo affanno
o la vita cessi almen. *(languida si mette a sedere)*

D. BET: Dite, che cosa ha mai
questa vostra padrona?

COM: È stanca, anzi è ammalata,
anzi, a dirvela schietta, è innamorata.

D. BET: Avranno questi mali
il lor rimedio. Ma saper vorrei
e nome e grado e titoli e fortune
di questa forestiera,
per adempir con lei
tutti i dover di buona locandiera.

COM: È Isabella di Napoli, la figlia
di Artemidoro, duca di Campalto,
conte della Fossetta.
Son quattro anni e due mesi
che gira per l'Europa
in traccia dell'amante, che si chiama . . .

D. ISA: Olà, Comino, olà!

COM: Che cosa brama?
D. ISA: Converrà che a tacere alfin t'insegni.
Intanto voi, signora locandiera,
fate che la mia stanza a me si assegni.
D. BET: Subito, mia signora.
Entrate là. Pronta a servirvi io sono,
e se vi offesi mai, chiedo perdono. *(parte)*

Scena v
Don Giovanni, poi Donna Betta

D. GIO: Poffar il mondo! Io vidi
da lontano una donna
di leggiadra figura
entrar nella locanda.
Chi sarà mai? Deh, tu m'assisti, amore;
tu non hai nel tuo regno uomo migliore.
Tu sai che a prima vista
sempre le donne m'han colpito e sai
che tutte sul principio amo all'eccesso,
ma morirei se non cangiassi spesso.
Voglio saper chi sia.
Servitori, staffieri,
Don Mason, Zuccasecca, camerieri,
Betta, Betta, ove siete?
Presto, correte qua! Crepo di voglia
di rimirar in faccia
colei che sol di dietro
veduta per un poco
mi accese in mezzo al core un sì gran foco.
Olà, olà, olà!
D. BET: Cosa strillate?
Che diavolo avete?
Che premura, che fretta!
D. GIO: Volea vederti, la mia cara Betta.
D. BET: Eh, signor caro, se voi siete accorto,
io semplice non sono.
Vedova e locandiera, a fondo a fondo

anch'io conosco il mondo.
Forse, chi sa!, vedeste . . .
Ma ditemi alle corte:
quando volete farmi vostra sposa?

D. GIO: Quando meco sarete
più dolce, più discreta e men gelosa.

D. BET: Tutto per voi sarò.

D. GIO: Vengo alla prova. *(le prende la mano)*

D. BET: Oh Dio! Che mai volete?

D. GIO: Da quella forestiera
tosto m'introducete.

D. BET: Questo appunto da voi, questo attendeva.
Oh misera la donna che vi crede,
uomini senza onor e senza fede.

Quando sul labbro avete,
bugiardi, il dolce riso,
nel tristo cor chiudete
sensi di crudeltà.
"Cara, morir mi sento,"
sapete dir talora;
ma parla in quel momento
la vostra falsità. *(parte)*

Scena vi
D. Giovanni, poi Comino

D. GIO: Che collera, che stizza!
Ma placarla saprò. Basta un mio sguardo,
un sorriso, un momento . . .
Ma costui certamente è un servitore
di quella forestiera. Ora vogl'io
interrogarlo. Buon amico, addio.
(Comino risaluta piegando la testa)
Ma voi non rispondete? Addio, vi dico.
Che figura di stucco!
Dissimuliam. Mio dolce amico, dite,
che nome ha la padrona che servite?

Rispondete, vi prego.
Ma non vuoi favellar? Se taci ancora,
su quel deforme grugno
io t'impronto a momenti un forte pugno.

COM: Signor, calmatevi,
che muto io sono;
se non rispondovi,
chiedo perdono.
Ecco, osservatemi,
lingua non ho.
"Se alcun t'interroga, *(fra sè)*
tu non favella;"
così prescrissemi
Donna Isabella,
e fedelissimo
servirla io vuo'. *(parte correndo, e D. Giovanni lo raggiunge per i capelli)*

D. GIO: Tu non mi fuggirai.
COM: Deh, per pietà . . .
D. GIO: Tu sei
un gran birbo o un gran pazzo.
Voglio però di tanta impertinenza
punirti ad ogni modo.
Ma chi giugner vegg'io? *(lo lascia)*
COM: *(fra sè)* La mia padrona.
Salva, salva; s'io resto ancora qua,
o che parli o che taccia
ella o costui m'accoppa in verità. *(parte)*

Scena vii
Donna Isabella e D. Giovanni in disparte.

D. ISA: Meschina me! Quando sarò tranquilla?
Non so trovar riposo,
non so trovar oggetto
che possa consolar l'anima mia;

tutto, tutto mi fa malinconia.
Qui voglio passeggiar. Trovassi almeno
da divertirmi in questa galleria . . .
Che pittura gentil. *(osserva un quadro)*
D. GIO: Che donna bella.
(prima con disinvoltura, poi con sorpresa)
D. ISA: Ah, che vedo!
D. GIO: Ah, che miro!
D. ISA: È desso!
D. GIO: È dessa!
D. ISA: Don Giovanni, sei tu?
D. GIO: Sei tu, Isabella?
D. ISA: Barbaro, e tu potesti
tradirmi, abbandonarmi? O mio rossore!
Vanne, vanne, perverso,
torna lungi da me.
D. GIO: Placati, ascolta.
D. ISA: Non ti voglio sentir.
D. GIO: Almen, ti prego,
senti le mie ragion.
D. ISA: Che dir potrai?
D. GIO: Napoli abbandonai perchè vedea
d'essere là invidiato.
E poi . . . dirò . . . tu sai che un cavaliero
ora deve viaggiar. Questo costume,
che divien legge, anch'io volli seguire.
Ma ne' miei viaggi, o cara,
a te sempre rivolto ebbi il pensiero;
anzi tutta la Francia
girai di regno in regno
per ritornar a te, di te più degno.
D. ISA: Che graziosi pretesti!
Io so che da per tutto
in mezzo a mille donne ognor vivesti.
D. GIO: Conosci il genio mio.
(Giustificarsi e insieme
prevenirla convien.) Osservo il mondo,
amo la compagnia, le donne io stimo,

ma, credimi, a te sola
questo tenero cor sempre sen vola.

Passerello innamorato
scherza in mezzo all'erba verde
or con questa ed or con quella
vezzosetta passerella,
ma di volo mai non perde
la diletta che il piagò.
Io così di donne a lato
scherzo, rido e fingo amore,
fingo sdegni e gioie e pene;
ma tu sei sempre il mio bene,
e a te serba questo core
quella fede che giurò. *(parte)*

Scena viii

D. Masone, Zuccasecca, Donna Isabella; poi D. Giovanni

D. Isa: E credergli poss'io?
Ma perchè mi abbandona in questo istante?
D. Mas: Signore, ah, non partite.
Presto, presto, correte da Donn'Anna.
Zuc: Da Tisbea per pietà, padrone, andate.
D. Mas: Io la consiglio in vano . . .
Zuc: Consolarla io non posso . . .
D. Mas: Freme, sbuffa, delira . . .
Zuc: Piange, smania, sospira . . .
D. Mas: E dice che voi siete . . .
Zuc: E dice che per voi . . .
D. Gio: Sciocchi, tacete.
D. Isa: Anzi, tutto svelate,
chè saperlo vogl'io.
In quel momento, oh Dio,
che tu mi giuri amore,
in quel momento istesso
io ti scopro un iniquo, un traditore.
Che donne son costoro?

Che pretendon da te? Parla.

D. GIO: Con queste
io scherzo e mi diverto
e il passerello imito.
È vero, Zuccasecca?
È vero, Don Masone?

ZUC: È vero.

D. MAS: È vero.

D. ISA: Due birbi siete voi, tu un menzognero.

Non sai che cosa sia
l'amar un solo oggetto;
questo innocente affetto
tu non provasti ancor.
Deh, questa gioia, oh Dio,
tu prova almen per poco,
prova sì dolce foco,
prova sì caro amor.
Ma no, non è capace
quel tuo perverso cor. *(parte)*

D. GIO: Quanto mi spiace non aver trovata
una donna novella!
Questa, che un tempo amai,
ora non sembra agli occhi miei più bella.

D. MAS: Signor, ecco Donn'Anna.

ZUC: Ecco Tisbea.

D. GIO: Tosto partiam. Non voglio
più garrir con costoro.
Voi seguitemi. Andrò per la campagna
con voi di nuove femmine alla caccia.
Tu mio scudier sarai, tu capocaccia. *(parte)*

Scena ix

Donn'Anna, Tisbea; poi Donna Betta

TIS: E mi lascia così?

D. AN: Così mi fugge?

TIS: Barbaro.
D. AN: Iniquo.
TIS: Io tosto
da lui voglio partir.
D. AN: Sola a Siviglia
subito andar io voglio.
TIS: Servi della locanda!
D. AN: Donna Betta!
TIS: Non mi risponde alcun?
D. AN: Betta non viene?
TIS: Più non posso frenar gli sdegni miei.
D. AN: Io con le proprie man mi ammazzerei.
D. BET: Cos'è questo furor? Cosa volete?
TIS: Voglio andar via di qua.
D. AN: Partir io voglio.
D. BET: Che cosa è nata mai?
D. AN: E con chi parlo? Stupida voi siete?
Voglio andar a Siviglia.
D. BET: Chi vi trattiene? Andate ove volete.
D. AN: Ove volete? Intendo.
Troppo a voi piacerebbe
con Don Giovanni qui vedervi sola.
Ma non avrete voi questo diletto.
Voglio restar per far a voi dispetto.
TIS: Per questo appunto anch'io
più non voglio partir.
D. BET: Che gioco è questo?
Perchè dunque chiamarmi?
Queste, o signore mie,
a dir la verità, sono pazzie.
D. AN: E con tanta insolenza osa parlarmi
una vil locandiera?
Così manca al dover, manca al rispetto?
D. BET: Pazzie, pazzie, signora, io ve l'ho detto.
D. AN: L'amor di Don Giovanni,
femmina rea, ti rende troppo altera.
TIS: È ver, voi siete . . .
D. BET: Io sono Donna Betta,
la locandiera dalla lingua schietta. *(parte)*

TIS: Veramente è colei
con noi troppo arrogante.
D. AN: Con noi? Vorresti meco
metterti al paragon?
TIS: Vorreste voi
ora meco altercar?
D. AN: Quel che più volte
ti dissi, or ti ripeto. A te nemica
io per sempre sarò. Quando all'amore
di Don Giovanni tu rinunzierai,
tua protettrice e amica tua mi avrai.

Io, che sono principessa,
con un Grande unir mi voglio.
In me sento un giusto orgoglio,
che comanda a questo cor.
Tu rispetta l'amor mio,
tu non far quel che non lice;
siegui a far la pescatrice
e t'unisci a un pescator.
Bada agli atti, al portamento,
bada ai vezzi, bada a me.
Sai con grazia passeggiar,
presentarti innanzi a un re,
il ventaglio maneggiar?
Sai ballar il minuè,
alle carte sai giocar?
No, no, no, rispondi affè.
Tutto questo se non sai,
all'amore come fai
con un nobile signor?

TIS: O pescatrice o principessa, io voglio
Don Giovanni sposar. Intesi a dire
da un certo letterato
quando sposò la figlia d'un pastore:
"Ogni dissuguaglianza agguaglia amore." *(parte)*

Scena x

Recinto campestre destinato a' sepolcri de' Grandi, con varie urne e statue, in mezzo a cui è la gran statua equestre del Commendatore Oloa.

D. Giovanni, D. Masone, e Zuccasecca

D. MAS: Piano, deh, piano per pietà. Sapete
che a me da lungo tempo un certo imbroglio
non permette di far troppo cammino.
ZUC: Ma, signor, dove andiam?
D. GIO: Son disperato.
Il primo giorno è questo
che nella caccia mia restai deluso.
D. MAS: Qui non so cosa voglia.
ZUC: Io son confuso.
D. MAS: Signor, badate bene:
alle femmine andate a dar la caccia,
oppur venite qui di morti in traccia?
ZUC: Di morti? Ah, signor mio, torniamo indietro;
vi prego inginocchione. *(s'inginocchia)*
D. GIO: Sorgi, sorgi. Che temi? Io vedo adesso
che innoltrati ci siamo
nel luogo, poche miglia
discosto da Siviglia,
che ai sepolcri de' Grandi è destinato.
Ma qual novella statua io vedo eretta?
Don Mason, Zuccasecca,
riconoscete voi
quella fisonomia?
ZUC: Sì, signore. Somiglia a . . . a . . . a . . .
D. MAS: A Don Consalvo Oloa,
quondam Commendatore di Castiglia.
ZUC: Appunto, appunto a quello
che ammazzaste in duello.
Fuggiam, fuggiam di qua.
D. GIO: Che temi, sciocco?
È statua.
ZUC: Quando è statua, io nulla temo.
D. GIO: Leggi quell'iscrizione.

ZUC: Ch'io legga? Voi da ridere mi fate.
D. GIO: Come? Perchè?
ZUC: Perchè legger non so.
D. GIO: Dunque leggete voi.
D. MAS: Mi proverò.
"O tu che ucciso m'hai, morte t'aspetta.
Questa attendo dal ciel giusta vendetta."
D. GIO: Vendetta attendi? E quale?
Nè nume in ciel nè giudice nel mondo
punir mi può. T'uccisi
in singolar tenzon da cavaliero.
Dovevi esser più forte o men severo.

Discendi dal destriero
e la tua spada impugna;
il core in nuova pugna *(getta un guanto)*
la mia ti passerà.
D. MAS: / ZUC: Invita il cavaliero
la statua ad un duello,
e intanto il suo cervello
in aria se ne va.
D. GIO: Ma resta; io ti perdono,
chè cavalier son io.
D. MAS: / ZUC: Fa bene, signor mio,
se in collera non sta.
D. GIO: A cena lo invitate.
D. MAS. E ZUC: A cena?
D. GIO: Certamente.
D. MAS: / ZUC: Noi non faremo niente.
È pazzo in verità.
D. GIO: A cena lo invitate.
D. MAS: / ZUC: Proviam. Volete voi,
signor, cenar con noi?
Che dite? Sì o no? *(la statua piega la testa)*
Ahimè, ahimè, son morto!
D. GIO: Che confusion è questa?
D. MAS: Egli piegò la testa;

ZUC: l'invito egli accettò.
D. GIO: Io non vi credo nulla.
D. MAS:
ZUC: Voi dunque l'invitate.
D. GIO: Vili; se voi tremate,
l'invito io gli farò.
D. MAS:
ZUC: Egli piegò la testa;
l'invito egli accettò.
D. GIO: Meco a cenar t'invito;
Commendator, verrai?
Rispondimi.
STA: Verrò.
D. MAS:
ZUC: Qual suon! Qual voce mai
or mi spezzò l'udito!
Io resto, ohimè, stordito;
il core mi tremò.
D. GIO: Qual suon! Qual voce mai
or mi spezzò l'udito!
Non resto, no, avvilito;
nè il core mi tremò. *(partono)*

Scena xi
Camera nella locanda.

Donna Betta, poi Tisbea

D. BET: Vien notte, e Don Giovanni
ancora non si vede? Io temo assai
di qualche novità. Qui quattro donne
sospirano per lui.
Tutte volean partir, ma tutte alfine
non hanno avuto cor. Ma questa sera
veder decisa la mia sorte io voglio
e ad ogni modo uscir da questo imbroglio.
Tutto ho disposto per la cena. Intanto
vediamo cosa sia *(prende un libro)*
questo libro sì bello
ch'oggi mi regalò Don Pipistrello.

Delle rivoluzioni della danza,
opera filosofica divisa
in tre volumi. E tanto
si può scriver sul ballo?
Leggiamo qualche articolo: "Del modo
con cui gli antichi egiziani e i greci
ballavan la furlana e il minuè."
Tanta filosofia non fa per me. *(getta il libro)*

TIS: Don Giovanni dov'è? Deh, voi correte
a trattener Donn'Anna,
che si vuol ammazzar. È mia rivale,
e pur mi fa pietà.

D. BET: Io lascio che s'ammazzi in verità. *(parte)*

TIS: In mezzo alle sue furie
disse che questa sera
volea che Don Giovanni la sposasse.
Oh quanto a questo poi,
meglio sarebbe affè ch'ella crepasse. *(parte)*

Scena xii

Sala con tavola apparecchiata per la cena.

Donn'Anna, poi D. Masone

D. AN: Ho cangiato pensiero.
Più ammazzarmi non vuo'. L'ultima prova
facciasi questa sera.
S'egli a me non darà la man di sposo,
io gli darò il veleno e via ne andrò.
E così da eroina
me stessa e il genitor vendicherò.
Ma giunge Don Masone. Egli m'adora.
Si lusinghi perciò. Ne' casi miei
forse di lui bisogno aver potrei.
Mio caro Don Masone, io vi saluto.
Ma dov'è Don Giovanni?

D. MAS: Andò a invitar a cena
la nuova forestiera.

D. AN: Dissimuliam. Ma voi che fate, o caro?
D. MAS: A me voi dite caro?
D. AN: Anzi carissimo.
D. MAS: Mi volete voi ben?
D. AN: Bene, benissimo.
Ma dite, s'io lasciassi Don Giovanni,
meco verreste voi?
D. MAS: Che dite mai? Felice me!
D. AN: Ma poi
come vivere? Come
farci servir?
D. MAS: Io meco condurrei
il migliore de' servi, Zuccasecca.
D. AN: Sarebbe egli contento?
D. MAS: Lo vado a interrogar in sul momento.

Una turba d'amorini
mi circonda in questo istante.
Chi mi salta sulle piante,
chi nel sen, chi sui ginocchi,
chi sul naso, chi sugli occhi,
l'un di qua, l'altro di là.
"Don Masone, su, coraggio,"
sento dir quel briconcello.
Ma quest'altro, ch'è più saggio,
grida poi, "Pian pian, bel bello."
S'ode intanto da ogni banda
un bisbiglio, un mormorio;
chi la pappa mi domanda,
chi mi dice, "ahi nonno mio,"
e chi grida, "ahi mio papà."
O mani tenere
come giuncate!
E luci fulgide
che m'incantate!
Guancie di porpora
che innamorate!
Ma vado subito,
non v'alterate,

corro . . . precipito . . .
ritorno qua. *(parte)*

Scena xiii

Donn'Anna, poi Zuccasecca

D. AN: E l'uno e l'altro lusingar mi giova.
Non m'avvilisco io già. Posso a mia voglia
vestirmi e dispogliarmi
del matronal decoro.
Posso sedurre, posso far sovente
quello che al basso popolo non lice,
chè alla mia nobiltà nulla disdice.
Ma giunge Zuccasecca.
Si prevenga. Vedesti Don Masone?

ZUC: Signora no.

D. AN: Non lo incontrasti? In traccia
egli venne di te. Molta premura
ha di parlarti. Ma perchè ti stai
così tristo e confuso?

ZUC: Perchè Tisbea crudel . . .

D. AN: Cosa ti ha detto?

ZUC: Mi diede un altro schiaffo maledetto.

D. AN: Ma tu perchè piuttosto
non fai meco all'amor?

ZUC: Con voi? Davvero?

D. AN: E perchè no? Vorresti
tu lasciar Don Giovanni e venir meco?

ZUC: Volontieri, mia bella.
Andiamo, andiamo subito.

D. AN: E la cena?

ZUC: Quanto alla cena poi,
pria cenerò, poscia verrò con voi.

Scena xiv

D. Masone e detti.

D. MAS: Ecco qui Zuccasecca.
Sappi, amico . . .
D. AN: Di tutto egli è informato,
e con noi si unirà.
ZUC: Dunque volete
venir ancora voi?
D. MAS: Certamente. Che sciocco. E non son io . . .
D. AN: Sì, Don Mason, voi siete amico mio.
Io dunque in questo istante
dell'uno e l'altro la parola accetto.
Ma come di denari
voi state, Don Masone?
D. MAS: Assai pochetti.
D. AN: E tu, mio Zuccasecca?
ZUC: Io n'ho quanti un poeta da sonetti.
D. AN: Come dunque vivremo? Voi sapete
che tutta la mia roba fu distrutta.
D. MAS: Io penso . . . Non saprei . . .
ZUC: Zitto, zitto, ecco il modo.
D. MAS: È modo onesto?
ZUC: Onesto o non onesto, il modo è questo.
Facciamo gli assassini.
D. AN: Io non ricuso.
D. MAS: Far gli assassini? E voi? . . . Resto confuso.
D. AN: Ma tu sapresti assassinar? In petto
hai coraggio bastante?
ZUC: Io tutto il mondo assassinar saprei.
D. AN: Don Masone proviam, se in questo almeno
ha spirito costui.
D. MAS: Come volete.
D. AN: Adunque, cominciam. Quest'è la selva,
campo del tuo valore.
Noi siamo i passeggier, tu l'aggressore.

Siam perduti. Dove siamo?
D. MAS: Dove andiam? Che strada è questa?

[D. MAS:]	Oh che orribile foresta!
[D. AN:]	Che spavento! Che terror!
ZUC:	Alto là, non vi movete.
D. MAS:	Ah, son morto.
D. AN:	Son spedita.
ZUC:	I denari oppur la vita
	o per forza o per amor.
D. AN:	Che ridicolo assassino!
D. MAS:	Che figura da buffone!
ZUC:	Provi dunque Don Masone.
ZUC:	Vedi
D. AN:	un po' come si fa.
D. MAS:	Dite
	(D. Masone s'imposta)
D. AN:	Chi dirige, chi conduce
ZUC:	due meschini passeggieri?
D. MAS:	Qua le chiavi de' forzieri,
	o v'ammazzo in verità.
D. AN:	Oh che bestia! Oh che stivale!
ZUC:	La carrozza non abbiamo.
D. MAS:	Siete a piedi?
D. AN. E ZUC:	A piedi siamo.
D. MAS:	Che vi ho dunque da rubar?
A 3:	Via, lasciam ch'ella c' / lasciate ch'io v' insegni.
	Apprendiamo / Apprendete da lei / me sola.
D. AN:	Vi darò la vera scuola.
A 3:	State / Stiamo attenti ad imparar.
D. MAS:	Due birbanti pellegrini
ZUC:	chi consiglia in questo loco?
D. AN:	V'arrestate o faccio foco.
D. MAS. E ZUC:	Ahi, siam morti.
D. AN:	Fermi là.

Voi compagni all'erta state.
(fingendo di parlare ad altri assassini)

D. MAS. E ZUC: Per pietà, non ci spogliate.
D. AN: Via, spogliatevi, birbanti.
D. MAS: Zuccasecca,
ZUC: D. Masone, che si fa?
[A 2:] Per tal sorta d'assassini
niente posso, niente vaglio.
Prendi tutto il mio bagaglio,
volontieri io te lo do.
A 3: Per figura, per mestiere,
per robusto e franco core,
assassin di me / voi migliore
la natura non formò.

Scena XV
D. Giovanni, Donna Isabella e detti.

D. GIO: Deh, non serbarti, o bella, *(a D. Isabella)*
così superba e altera.
La faccia tua severa
malinconia mi fà.
D. ISA: Dopo sì lunghi stenti
per ritrovarti, ingrato,
di cento donne a lato
alfin ti trovo qua.
D. GIO: Con altre scherzo e rido;
con te dico davvero.
D. AN: Ah falso, ah menzognero.
D. GIO:
D. MAS: Ahimè, ahimè, ahimè!
ZUC:
D. ISA: Risponda alla signora.
D. AN: Non serve che risponda.
D. MAS: Eh via, non si confonda.

ZUC: Eh, si rivolga a me.
D. GIO: Voi siete il mio tesoro. *(a D. Isabella)*
D. MAS. E ZUC: Voi caposquadra siete. *(a D. Anna)*
D. AN: Lasciatemi, tacete.
D. ISA: Finite di scherzar.
D. GIO:
D. AN:
D. ISA: Io temo che una lite
qui s'abbia a rinovar.
D. MAS:
ZUC: Io temo questa sera
che s'abbia a digiunar.

Scena xvi

D. Betta, Tisbea e detti.

D. BET:
TIS: Vorrei saper da voi *(a D. Giovanni)*
deciso il mio destino.
D. GIO:
D. MAS:
ZUC: Il resto del carlino
ci viene a divertir.
D. AN: Rispondi, menzognero.
D. ISA: Rispondi, ingannatore.
D. GIO: Ma donne del mio core,
che cosa posso dir?
LE 4 DONNE: Vogliam saper di noi
chi deve esser tua sposa.
D. GIO:
D. MAS:
ZUC: È critica la cosa
che vogliono saper.
D. GIO: Risponderò.
LE 4 DONNE: Favella.
D. GIO: Risponderò.
LE 4 DONNE: Ma quando?
D. GIO: Di tempo un dì domando
a dirvi il mio parer.
D. AN:
D. ISA: Un giorno ancor s'aspetti.

D. BET:
TIS:] S'aspetti un giorno ancora.

D. GIO:
D. MAS:
ZUC:] [Domani alla malora
dovranno tutte andar.

D. GIO: Sedete, mie dilette,
sedetemi vicine.
(corrono tutte per aver il primo posto)

D. ISA: Adagio, signorine,
che qui non han da star . . .

A 7: Un altro imbroglio nasce;
si torna ad altercar.
(si sentono tre gagliardissimi colpi alla porta)

D. MAS:
ZUC:] [Come restano tutti sorpresi
alla scossa, al rumor, che si sente!
Io prevedo un funesto accidente;
quasi tutta la casa tremò.

D. GIO: Mie fanciulle, di che mai temete?
Zuccasecca, Masone, che fate?
Alla porta voi subito andate
a veder chi sì forte picchiò.
(Zuccasecca e D. Masone partono con lume in mano)

D. GIO. E 4 DONNE:
Ma quale strepito,
quai grida io sento! *(Zuccasecca e Don Masone tornano tremando)*
Che vedo mai?
Che mai sarà?

D. MAS:
ZUC:] [Oh mamma mia!
Oh quanto orrore!
L'ombra del morto
Commendatore
in sulla porta
ritta si sta.

D. GIO: L'ombra s'avanzi.
Nulla m'importa;
ad incontrarla
io volo già.

(D. Giovanni parte con spada e lume in mano, e D. Masone e Zuccasecca si nascondono sotto la tavola)

Scena xvii

Statua del Commendatore e detti.

D. GIO: Non temete, donne belle;
vien quest'ombra a far la pace.
Tu t'assidi, se ti piace, *(all'ombra)*
con le femmine e con me.

D. AN: Alla paterna
immagine
D. ISA: A sì lugubre
D. BET: sento un torrente gelido,
TIS: che tutto il core innondami.
Tremo da capo a piè.

D. AN: Ah, padre dilettissimo,
pietà di me, perdono.

STA: No, padre tuo non sono;
va', scostati da me. *(siede)*

D. GIO: Zuccasecca, Don Masone,
dove siete? Uscite, uscite.
Presto presto all'ombra dite
se si degna di mangiar.
(sporgono la testa, indi escono tremanti)

ZUC: Statua molto riverita . . .

D. MAS: Mio signor Commendatore . . .

D. GIO: Ma cos'è questo timore?

D. MAS. E ZUC: No, non posso, ohimè, parlar.

D. GIO: Fanciulle amabili,
voi lo invitate.

LE 4 DONNE: Non so resistere,
parlar non so.

D. GIO: Almen calmatevi,
ch'io parlerò.
Commendatore,
s'io sono degno
di tanto onore,

di pace in segno
mangia, ti prego.

STA: Mangiar non vuo'.

D. GIO: Adunque un brindisi
io ti farò.
(parla in orecchio a D. Masone e Zuccasecca, e tutti tre prendono un bicchiere)

LE 4 DONNE: Non so resistere,
parlar non so.

D. GIO: Un bell'evviva
facciam di cor.

D. GIO., D. MAS., ZUC: Donn'Anna viva.
Viva l'amor.
(la statua s'alza, e D. Masone e Zuccasecca cascano per paura)

STA: O Cavalier, m'ascolta.
Io venni a cenar teco.
T'invito a cenar meco.
Dimmi, verrai?

D. GIO: Verrò. *(la statua vola via)*

D. GIO: / D. MAS: / ZUC: Quale prodigio!
Quale spettacolo!
La bianca statua,
presta qual fulmine,
lungi volò.

TIS: Sono confusa . . .

D. ISA: Sono tradita . . .

D. BET: Sono agitata . . .

D. AN: Sono stordita . . .

LE 4 DONNE: Chi mi sostiene?
Mancando vo.

A 6: Dove son? Che vidi mai?
Trema il piè, palpita il core.
Circondat(a/o) dall'orrore,
vado errando qua e là.

D. GIO: Che si fa? Che vedo mai?
Loro in sen palpita il core.

Circondati dall'orrore,
vanno errando qua e là.

fine dell'atto primo

ATTO SECONDO

Scena prima
Galleria nella locanda.

Tisbea e D. Giovanni

TIS: Oh che cena! Oh che notte!
Tremo ancor di paura,
ancor avanti agli occhi
ho quella bianca orribile figura.
Questa sera per certo
più non mi coglie. Io voglio farmi sposa
e subito partir. Che rispondete?
D. GIO: Sì, partirò. Farò quel che volete.
TIS: Qui non soffro altri torti,
nè voglia ho di cenar con altri morti.

Deh, tornate, idolo mio,
a veder la mia capanna,
a pescare con la canna;
là vi voglio ammaestrar.
Là contenti insiem vivremo,
pescatrice e pescatore,
nè verranno il nostro amore
altri morti a disturbar. *(parte)*

Scena ii
D. Giovanni e Donna Betta

D. BET: Il tutto intesi. Un traditor voi siete;
io non vi credo più.

D. GIO: Deh, se mi amate,
questa collera vostra ora frenate.
D. BET: M'adiro appunto perchè v'amo.
D. GIO: Adunque
seguite il mio pensier. Della locanda
voi lasciate la cura
al più fedel de' vostri camerieri.
Preparate a un viaggio
quanto può bisognar. Noi questa notte
insieme partiremo, e queste donne
qui resteran deluse;
in segreto però fate ogni cosa.
D. BET: Ma partirò così senz'esser sposa?
D. GIO: Farem le nozze altrove, non temete.
Voi l'idol mio, la vita mia voi siete.
D. BET: Vo dunque l'occorrente
subito ad allestir. Oh quanto v'amo!
La prima volta è questa
che fortunata in vita mia mi chiamo.

Cara speranza,
non ingannarmi,
fa' che non m'agiti
nuovo dolor.
Lieta sembianza
pria di mostrarmi,
leggi in quell'anima,
leggi in quel cor.
Ah, non offendavi
il mio sospetto.
No, più non dubito
del vostro affetto.
Voi conservatemi
sì dolce amor. *(parte)*

D. GIO: Che sciocca locandiera! Tu ti credi
di conoscere il mondo, ma t'inganni.
Se dal cielo scendesse
Venere stessa, a lei

dar la mano di sposo io non vorrei.
Ma chi giunge? Isabella.
Questa è un'amica tenera e fedele,
ma troppo annoia con le sue querele.

Scena iii

D. Isabella, e D. Giovanni in disparte.

D. ISA: Miei pensieri, e che si fa?
Me meschina liberate
da sì indegna servitù.
Voi gridate libertà.
Voi severi vendicate
l'avvilita mia virtù.

Ma che vedo? Tu a gemere m'ascolti,
e ti nascondi, ingrato?
D. GIO: A gemere? A cantar io v'ascoltai;
cantate pur, cantate.
D. ISA: E mi deridi ancor?
D. GIO: Anzi, v'ammiro.
D. ISA: Io t'intendo, crudel. Vuoi che ti lasci
delle tue donne a lato.
Ti lascierò, ma pensa
che i primi giuramenti
ebbi io da te, che non a caso il cielo
ti manda un'ombra a molestar le cene . . .
D. GIO: Basta, deh, basta. Io tremo, io son commosso.
(con affettazione)
D. ISA: Io più soffrirti, traditor, non posso. *(parte)*

Scena iv

D. Giovanni, D. Mason, Zuccasecca

D. MAS: Signor, che risolvete?
ZUC: E chi sposate?
D. GIO: Nessuna. Udite: io voglio
questa sera partir, e voglio insieme

tutte lasciar queste importune donne.
Mi raccomando a voi. Secretamente
gli altri servi avvisate,
e dalla locandiera
riceverete i forzieri,
che preparati avrà.

ZUC: Dunque, volete
lasciar Donn'Anna?

D. GIO: Sì.

D. MAS: Donn'Anna ancora?

D. GIO: Sì, vuo' tutte mandar alla malora.

ZUC: Che gioia!

D. MAS: Che piacer!

D. GIO: Questi forzieri
fate portar nel campo
dov'è la statua eretta
del gran Commendator. Voglio con lui
cenar, poscia partire,
per ricercar novelle donne altrove.
Capiste?

D. MAS: Sì signor.

D. GIO: Dunque vi lascio. *(parte)*

ZUC: Andate pur, andate.
Zuccasecca è con voi, non dubitate.

Scena v

Don Masone, Zuccasecca

ZUC: Giacchè dunque il padron lascia D. Anna,
io penso di sposarla.
Vedeste, Don Mason, come disposta
era a venir con me? Che bella scuola
essa diede a noi due! Come valente
si dimostrò per assaltar la gente!

D. MAS: Che sciocco! Che buffon! Volea D. Anna
condurti seco, è vero,
ma per suo servitor, non per amante.

ZUC: Voi scherzate o impazzite in questo istante.

D. MAS: Nè scherzo nè impazzisco, anzi ti dico
ch'io sposarla dovea.

ZUC: Voi v'ingannate,
Don Masone mio caro. Ella volea
meco far all'amore,
e sposata io l'avrei con tutto il core.

D. MAS: Tu Donn'Anna?
ZUC: Sì, signore.
D. MAS: Maritiamo il bel narciso.
Oh che viso! Che figura!
ZUC: Voi, signore, a dirittura
non potete esser papà.
D. MAS: Vuo' aggiustarti come va.
Vieni qua.
ZUC: Venir non voglio.
D. MAS: Io non posso esser papà?
E perchè?
ZUC: Per un imbroglio.
D. MAS: Tu Donn'Anna?
ZUC: Sì signore.
D. MAS: No signore.
A 2: No, no, no.
Sì, sì, sì.
D. MAS: Se ti arrivo, se ti acchiappo . . .
ZUC: Non mi cogli, non c'incappo.
D. MAS: Assassino, malandrino,
s'hai coraggio, vieni qui.
ZUC: Canta, ch'io qual chitarrino
t'accompagno trinc trinc tri.
D. MAS: Furfantone, maledetto.
ZUC: Non strillare, Don Masone,
o l'imbroglio cascherà.

Scena vi
Donn'Anna e detti.

D. AN: Che strepitate qua?
D. MAS: Per voi, Donn'Anna,
qua si combatte, ed io
il punto sosterrò col sangue mio.
D. AN: Col sangue?
D. MAS: A dirittura.
ZUC: Ed io difenderò le mie ragioni
con le mani, coi piedi e coi polmoni.
D. AN: Ma di che mai si tratta?
D. MAS: Zuccasecca sostiene
che voi l'amate.
ZUC: E non è forse vero?
D. AN: Di Zuccasecca io non mi curo un zero.
D. MAS: Dall'allegrezza io sono
fuori di me.
ZUC: Che dite? Non m'amate?
Non diceste iersera? . . .
D. AN: Allor scherzai.
ZUC: Ah, questo, oh dei, non m'aspettava mai.
Vanne, barbara donna, in Barbaria.
Io t'odio e ti detesto.
Ti dirò poi qualche altro giorno il resto. *(parte)*

Scena vii
Donn'Anna, Don Masone

D. MAS: Che bestia! Egli volea
contrastarmi il possesso
del vostro cor.
D. AN: Egli è una bestia in vero,
ma voi, mio caro Don Masone . . .
D. MAS: Io v'amo,
e so che voi mi amate.
Sappiate in confidenza

che Don Giovanni parte questa sera,
e tutte vi abbandona.

D. AN: Come? Che dite? Io corro sul momento
a rinfacciargli un tanto tradimento.

D. MAS: No, per pietà, sentite.
Se mi amate davvero,
prudenza usar dovete. Egli m'ammazza,
se sa ch'abbia svelato a voi l'arcano.

D. AN: Dunque, che devo far?

D. MAS: Attenta state
quando partiam, e poi ci seguitate,
ma da lontano. Io vado a lento passo,
e potete raggiungerci. Con voi
m'unirò, prenderemo un'altra strada,
lascieremo il padrone,
e Donn'Anna starà con Don Masone.

D. AN: Freniamoci . . . Io farò quel che volete.

D. MAS: Bravissima, mia bella.
Sentite come il cor mi balza in petto;
io quasi casco qua dal gran diletto.

Vedeste un farfallone
girarsi intorno a un lume?
Scherza e dappresso vola
al foco che il consola;
ma poscia arde le piume,
e morto casca là.
Così fa questo core,
che vola intorno a voi.
A quelle due pupille
fa mille feste e mille;
ma non resiste poi,
e alfin mancando va.
Ah, se più tardo,
voi m'uccidete,
altrove il guardo
deh, rivolgete;
abbian quegli occhi
di me pietà. *(parte)*

Scena viii

Donn'Anna, poi D. Giovanni e Zuccasecca

D. AN: Oh tradimenti! Oh inganni!
Oh quanto stolta io fui
a credere a colui! Ma giunge ei stesso.
Voglio dissimular, voglio sentire
quel mancator di fè cosa sa dire.

D. GIO: *(in disparte a Zuccasecca, che entra coi facchini)*
Tu, Zuccasecca, va secretamente
con costoro a ricevere i forzieri,
e avvisa Don Masone.

ZUC: Il tutto intesi.
Lasciate fare a me. *(parte)*

D. GIO: Che fate, o cara?
Perchè così pensosa?
Vi spiace forse diventar mia sposa?

D. AN: Ahimè! Il dissimular quanto mi costa!

D. GIO: Che rispondete, o bella?

D. AN: Io sospiro i momenti
che possano aver fine i miei tormenti.

Sì, sarò la vostra sposa;
sì, voi siete la mia vita.
(Dall'ingrato io son tradita,
ma convien dissimular.)
Ma voi fisso mi guardate?
Voi restate pensieroso?
Io vi credo, caro sposo,
incapace d'ingannar.
Qual novo contento!
Qual gioia mi sento
destarsi nel core!
Che fede! Che amore!
Che tenero affetto!
No, sposo diletto,
non so dubitar.
Il mondo da voi
apprenda ad amar.

Scena ix
D. Giovanni, Zuccasecca

D. GIO: Che Donn'Anna sospetti
ch'io partir voglio? Que' confusi detti . . .
ZUC: Signor, ecco i forzier. Con Don Masone
io vi attendo di fuori. Donna Betta
ora mi disse che saper volea
a qual ora pensate di partire.
Crede che questa notte . . .
D. GIO: Basta, intendo.
Tu fa' quel che t'ho detto.
ZUC: Andiamo dunque, eroi compagni, andiamo.
(ai facchini coi forzieri, e partono)
D. GIO: Pian pian vi sieguo anch'io.
Anna, Tisbea, Betta, Isabella, addio. *(vuol partir)*

Scena x
D. Isabella, D. Giovanni

D. ISA: T'arresta. Dove vai?
D. GIO: (L'ultima volta
soffriam costei.)
D. ISA: Di', que' forzier son tuoi?
Pensi partir? Abbandonar mi vuoi?
D. GIO: Son que' forzieri d'un amico mio,
che parte per Siviglia.
Come volete mai ch'io v'abbandoni?
Troppo ingrato sarei. Voglio sposarvi
a dispetto di tutte. Andate, o cara,
e nella vostra stanza m'attendete.
D. ISA: Io non vi credo nulla.
D. GIO: A me credete.
Lo giuro a quel bel ciglio,
a quel labbro vermiglio, ai sommi dei,
al mio decoro, agli avi vostri e ai miei.

Giuro che sol Cupido
anima questo core;
giuro che senza amore
pace non so trovar.
Solo all'idea di perdere
quel ch'è d'amore il somite,
da cento furie indomite
mi sento trasportar. *(parte)*

D. ISA: Tu mi lusinghi invan. Voglio da lungi
seguir i passi tuoi.
Troppo tu mi giurasti, e troppo io lessi
i tradimenti tuoi sul volto espressi. *(parte)*

Scena xi

D. Anna, poi D. Betta e poi Tisbea

D. AN: Perfido Don Giovanni.
Barbaro! Traditor! Pur troppo è vero
quanto mi disse Don Mason. Tu parti.
Sono fuori di me, fremo di rabbia.
Ma non mi fuggirai;
raggiungerti saprò. *(parte)*

D. BET: Che vedo mai?
La nuova forestiera
e Donn'Anna van dietro a Don Giovanni?
Che mai sarà? Che queste
scoperto abbian l'arcano?
Ch'egli non torni indietro?
Si dovea questa notte . . . Ah, qual sospetto
m'assale in quest'istante!
Tu non ritorni più, tu m'hai tradita!
Teco tu porti, oh Dio,
il mio cor, la mia roba e l'onor mio.
Ma trema, anima vile,
trema di Donna Betta:
soccomberà, ma saprà far vendetta.

TIS: Cos'è? Cosa vuol dir questo scompiglio?

D. BET: Siam tradite, Tisbea.
Don Giovanni partì.
TIS: Che intendo? Oh Dio!
D. BET: Ma lo voglio seguir. *(parte)*
TIS: Lo sieguo anch'io. *(parte)*

Scena xii
Campagna.

D. Giovanni, D. Masone, Zuccasecca con altri servi e facchini che portano forzieri.

D. GIO: Via, camminate, via.
Mi sembrate pigrissime marmotte.
ZUC: Via, facchini agghiacciati, galoppate.
(urta i facchini e fa loro cadere i bauli)
D. MAS: Oh meschinelli!
D. GIO: Oh bestia! E che hai tu fatto?
ZUC: Soccorrerli io volea.
D. MAS: Che bel soccorso!
D. GIO: Presto i forzier riprendano sul dorso.
D. MAS: Adagio, poverini,
che con questa nebbiaccia maledetta
non potran camminar con tanta fretta.
(Venisse almen Donn'Anna!)
D. GIO: Quanto devo aspettar? Di', Zuccasecca.
Vuoi tu ch'io ti bastoni?
ZUC: Oh questa è buona.
Sempre con me l'avete, *(D. Masone ride)*
e quel vecchio stivale . . .
D. MAS: Che vorresti tu dir? Parla, animale.
ZUC: Questo rider in faccia a un galantuomo
è insolenza maiuscola.
D. MAS: Guardate
se tal faccia non chiama le sassate!
ZUC: Oh corpo di Pluton! Se qualche sasso
qui trovassi, vorrei farne una bella.
D. MAS: Che vorresti tu far?

ZUC: Romperti il capo.
D. MAS: Oh corpo di Proserpina! Son stanco . . .
D. GIO: Don Masone, finisce questa scena?
D. MAS: Ma colui mi cimenta; e non vedete? . . .
ZUC: No, signor, non è vero.
D. GIO: Orsù, tacete;
e ciascuno di voi meco cammini.
D. MAS: Vengo. (O sorte bisbetica e tiranna!)
ZUC: O tomo inaspettato! Ecco Donn'Anna.
D. GIO: Come? Donn'Anna è quella?
D. MAS: È dessa.
ZUC: E vien con lei Donna Isabella.

Scena xiii

Donn'Anna, Donna Isabella e detti.

D. ISA: Fermati, traditor.
D. AN: Fermati, iniquo.
D. ISA: Dove fuggir volevi?
D. AN: Dove ti nascondevi?
D. ISA: Parla.
D. AN: Favella.
D. ISA: Non tardar.
D. AN: Rispondi.
D. ISA: Ma ti veggo arrossir?
D. AN: Ma ti confondi?
ZUC: (Che bella scena seria!)
D. MAS: (Che caso da tragedia!)
D. GIO: (Che sorpresa fatal che m'imbarazza.)
D. ISA: Parla tu. *(a Don Masone)*
D. AN: Parla tu. *(a Zuccasecca)*
D. MAS:]
ZUC:] Che? Siete pazza?
D. GIO: Donne, sentite . . . (Ohimè, confuso io sono.)
D. ISA: Che dobbiamo sentir?
D. AN: Che saprai dirci?
D. GIO: Non so . . .
D. ISA: Crudel!

D. GIO: Dirò . . .
D. AN: Infedel!
D. GIO: Direi . . .
Oh avverso ciel!

D. MAS:, ZUC: Oh impertinenti dei!

D. MAS:, ZUC:
Son restato qual corno da caccia
fra le man d'un meschin principiante,
che mi suona col labbro tremante,
e, stuonando, mi tocca in befà.

D. AN:, D. ISA:
Son restata qual flauto traverso,
che ha di polve ogni buco turato;
mando il suono tant'aspro ed ingrato,
che ciascun da me lungi sen va.

D. GIO:
Ed io son qual viola d'amore,
col cantin[1] che ogni tanto si strappa;
la pazienza se or ora mi scappa,
fo crepar chi suonarmi non sa.

A 5:
corno
Senti, senti il mio flauto che suona.
la viola
Come stuona! Che diavolo fa?

D. AN: Son di pretesti stanca.
D. ISA: Ho tollerato assai.
D. AN: Parlami schietto omai.
D. ISA: Dimmi che intendi far.
D. MAS:, ZUC:
Che brutta sinfonia
si sente strepitar!
D. GIO: Risolvere conviene.
D. AN., D. ISA: Ebben, che mi destini?
D. GIO: Agli alberi, facchini,
venitele a legar.
(i facchini legano le donne agli alberi)
D. AN., D. ISA: Oh nero tradimento!
ZUC: Oh questa me la godo.
D. MAS: Pietà, signor . . .

---

1. The highest pitched string of the instrument.

D. GIO: Non t'odo.
D. MAS: Pietà . . .
D. GIO: Non mi seccar.

D. MAS:, D. AN:, D. ISA:
Ah, qual barbaro piacere!
Qual studiata tirannia!
Gli assassini per la via
son men sordi alla pietà!

D. GIO:, ZUC:
Oh che gusto! Oh che piacere!
Che bizzara fantasia!
Presto presto andiamo via,
non abbiam di lor pietà.

D. GIO: Don Mason, mi seguite. Io vel comando. *(parte)*
D. MAS: Poverelle! Io vi lascio con cordoglio. *(parte)*
ZUC: Un poco con costor rider io voglio.

Scena xiv
Zuccasecca, D. Anna, D. Isabella

D. AN: Deh, Zuccasecca mio!
D. ISA: Deh, caro amico!
D. AN: Pietà di me.
D. ISA: Tu questi lacci sciogli.
ZUC: S'anche crepaste, non m'importa un fico.
D. ISA: Ah! Non esser con me tanto crudele.
D. AN: Ah! Soccorri una donna che ti adora.
ZUC: Lasciate ch'io rifletta.
D. ISA: Che risolvi?
D. AN: Che fai?
ZUC: Rifletto ancora.
D. ISA: Compensarti io saprò.
D. AN: Sempre sarai
la mia vita, il mio bene, il mio diletto.
D. ISA:, D. AN: E non risolvi ancora?
ZUC: Ancor rifletto.
D. ISA: O servitor malvagio,
intieramente eguale al tuo padrone!

D. AN: O Zuccasecca ingrato!
Così lasci un'amante, una fanciulla?

ZUC: Ciancia pur, ciancia; io non ti credo nulla.

Misera spagnuoletta,
il tuo destin non sai.
Ah, non le dite mai
l'amante suo dov'è.
Come in un punto, oh Dio,
tutto cangiò d'aspetto!
Tu fosti il mio diletto;
mi rido ora di te.[2]
Guarda la lista
di tutte quelle
vaghe donzelle
ma troppo buone,
che il mio padrone
innamorò.
Tu come prima
sei nella cima;
a te vicina
quella meschina
si collocò.
Ora un balletto
a tuo dispetto,
donna stizzosa,
donna rabbiosa,
qui voglio far.
Guarda che salto
ardito ed alto;

2. The first two stanzas are a parody of Metastasio (*Demofoonte,* III.v).

Misero pargoletto
il tuo destin non sai.
Ah! non gli dite mai
qual era il genitor.
Come in un punto, oh Dio,
tutto cambiò d'aspetto!
Voi foste il mio diletto,
voi siete il mio terror.

guarda, spagnuola,
che capriola,
che bel scappar! *(parte)*

Scena xv

D. Anna, D. Isabella; poi Comino

D. Isa: Oh che affanno!
D. An: O che rabbia! Almen potessi
queste funi spezzar . . .
D. Isa: Giungesse almeno
alcun . . . Ma chi vegg'io?
Ah, ne soccorri tu, Comino mio.
Com: Che spettacolo è questo?
Chi fu colui che in così strano modo
v'ha qui legate?
D. Isa: Un empio.
D. An: Un assassino.
Com: Ecco sciolte voi siete. *(le scioglie)*
D. An: Dammi, dammi quel ferro,
(gli vuol togliere il ferro con cui le sciolse)
che immergere lo voglio
nel petto al traditor.
Com: Ah, no, fermate.
D. An: Cedi adunque quest'arma; io vo da forte
(gli toglie una pistola)
l'oltraggio a vendicar con la sua morte.
D. Isa: Corri, ah, corri, Comino, e la trattieni.
Il core in petto palpitarmi io sento.
Com: Coraggio, io la raggiungo in sul momento.

Scena xvi

Donna Isabella

Ch'ella uccida il mio ben! Gelo in pensarlo.
In che fieri momenti
abbandonata io sono!

Benchè un ingrato adori,
tutte le smanie più crudeli io sento,
nè ritrovo conforto al mio tormento.
Mio cor, sospiri? Ah, scordati d'un empio,
d'un mancator di fè. Ragion ti grida
che lasciarlo tu dei;
ma tu ragion non odi,
e l'alma resta intanto
dal duol oppressa, e mi abbandono al pianto.

  Dolce calma, afflitto core,
cerchi invano in tante pene.
Ah, se perdi il caro bene,
che sarà di te, mio cor?
  Non conosco più me stessa.
Son tradita e sono amante.
Dite voi, se in questo istante
fa pietade il mio dolor.
  Ferma il colpo, o donna ingrata;
da lei fuggi, o caro amante;
ah, no, torna al seno mio;
ah, no, vanne, torna, oh Dio!
Dite voi, se in questo istante
fa pietade il mio dolor. *(parte)*

Scena xvii
Boschereccia.

D. Giovanni, D. Masone, Zuccasecca

D. GIO: Si portino i forzieri nel recinto
dove sono quell'urne.

D. MAS: Quanto mi spiace aver così lasciate
quelle meschine agli alberi legate!

ZUC: Ma, signor, questa sera
dove cenar volete?

D. GIO: E nol tel dissi?

Tu meco cenerai
da Don Consalvo Oloa, Commendatore.

ZUC: Grazie, grazie a voi due di questo onore.
Intesi a dir che i morti
mangiano poco o niente, e voi sapete
che il vostro Zuccasecca e Don Masone
mangiano almen per ventisei persone.

D. GIO: Non temer, mangierai.

D. MAS: Ma chi giunge?

ZUC: Chi vedo?

D. GIO: E qual funesto
nuovo imbarazzo, Don Masone, è questo?

Scena xviii

D. Anna, Don Giovanni, Don Masone, Zuccasecca

D. AN: V'ho raggiunti, traditori.
Fermi là, non vi scuotete,
o quest'arma quanti siete *(una pistola)*
in un colpo ammazzerà.

D. GIO:, D. MAS:, ZUC: Quale sdegno, qual furore
vi trasporta in questo istante!
Ammazzare un fido amante
saria troppa crudeltà.

D. AN: Dal tuo labbro menzognero
più non soffro esser tradita.
Vuo' vederla qua finita,
vuo' la man di sposo qua.

D. MAS:, ZUC: Ecco qua; vincesti, ingrata. *(offrendo la mano a D. Anna)*

D. AN: Da voi, sciocchi, io non la voglio.

D. GIO: Io mi trovo in grande imbroglio.

D. MAS:, D. AN:, ZUC: Cosa vuole? Cosa fa?
Cosa pensa? Cosa fa?

D. GIO: Che decido? Che si fa?

D. GIO: Deh, mi concedi, o bella,

un sol momento almeno,
e poi contenti appieno
i tuoi desir farò.

D. AN: Ad un de' vezzi tuoi,
ad uno sguardo, a un detto,
io sento in mezzo al petto
che sdegno più non ho.

D. GIO: Mio ben, di me ti fida.

D. AN: Quest'alma in te riposa.

D. GIO: Quando sarai mia sposa,
felice allor sarò.

D. AN: Se mi farai tua sposa,
felice allor sarò.
Andiam, mia vita, andiamo.
Resister più non so. *(partono)*

Scena xix

D. Masone, Zuccasecca; poi Donna Betta e Tisbea

D. MAS: Sposo caro, avete visto?

ZUC: Sposo bello, avete inteso?

A 2: Al novizio ora sia reso
quell'onore che gli va.

D. MAS: Conduttori degli armenti . . .

ZUC: Zappatori di campagna . . .

A 2: . . . accorrete alla cuccagna,
chè costui le nozze fa.

[ZUC:] Fate quello che conviene.

D. MAS: Su, portate quel paniere . . .

ZUC: Su, recate quel bicchiere . . .

A 2: . . . con rispetto e civiltà.

[ZUC:] Ah, da ridere mi viene,
ah, ah, ah!

D. BET: / TIS: Che fai qua? Dimmi, o sei morto, *(ognuna con un pugnale)*
scelerato servitore
di padrone assai peggiore,
Don Giovanni dove andò?

D. MAS., ZUC: Qual sorpresa!
D. BET., TIS: Non rispondi?
D. MAS., ZUC: Io tremante tutto dico,
ma lontan stia quest'intrico, *(il pugnale)*
o dir nulla io non potrò.
D. BET., TIS: Parla.
D. MAS., ZUC: Parlo.
D. BET., TIS: Ho già risolto
d'ammazzarti, se m'inganni.
D. MAS: / ZUC: Mille grazie. Don Giovanni
per colà s'incamminò.
D. BET: / TIS: Se colui fuggemi,
tu trema, o perfido,
ch'io torno subito,
morto a distenderti
in mezzo qua.
D. MAS: / ZUC: Dunque ti supplico,
pietosa femmina,
qual capra subito,
se vuoi raggiungerlo,
corri per là.
D. BET., TIS: Se colui fuggemi, ec. *(partono)*

Scena xx

Donna Isabella, Don Masone e Zuccasecca

D. ISA: In che barbara maniera
mi trattò quel core ingrato!
Pur io tremo del suo stato,
e mi sento, oh Dio, mancar.
D. MAS: Zuccasecca,
ecco Isabella.
ZUC: Don Masone,
Come piange! Come geme!
Son commosso, andiamo insieme
l'infelice a consolar.
D. ISA: Sono in mezzo a traditori.

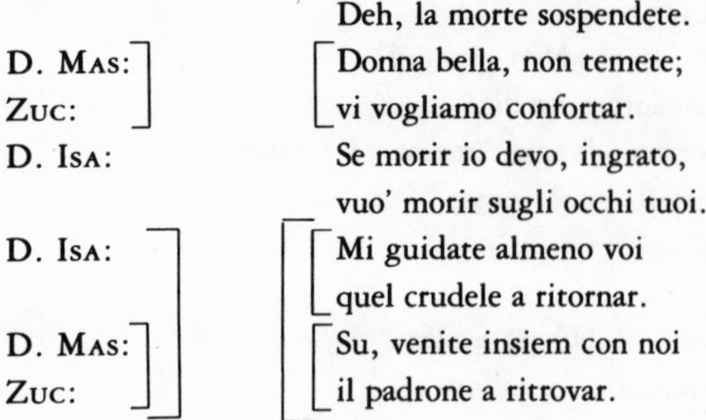

Deh, la morte sospendete.

D. MAS: / ZUC: Donna bella, non temete;
vi vogliamo confortar.

D. ISA: Se morir io devo, ingrato,
vuo' morir sugli occhi tuoi.

D. ISA: Mi guidate almeno voi
quel crudele a ritornar.

D. MAS: / ZUC: Su, venite insiem con noi
il padrone a ritrovar.

Scena ultima

Recinto campestre con urne e statue e cavallo senza la statua del Commendatore, che sta nel mezzo di una tavola apparecchiata di nero, con teste d'idre e serpenti, ec.

Statua, D. Giovanni, D. Anna, D. Betta, Tisbea; e poi Donna Isabella, D. Masone e Zuccasecca

D. AN: / D. BET: / TIS: Che vuol dir questo apparato?
Ahimè! Dove io m'innoltrai?

D. AN: Questo è il padre
che mirai,

D. BET: / TIS: Questa è l'ombra
quando meco a cena fu.

D. GIO: Non temete.

D. AN: / D. BET: / TIS: Io qui non resto.

D. GIO: Io qui adempio a un dovere.
Ma un illustre cavaliere
come a cena accogli tu?

D. MAS: / ZUC: / D. ISA: Deh, signore, consolate
questa donna meschinella,
o la povera Isabella
senza voi non vive più.

D. ISA: Ma che vedo?

D. MAS., ZUC: Dove sono?

D. AN: / D. BET: / TIS: Scelerato, cosa fai?

LE 4 DONNE: No, che in mezzo a tanti guai
io resister non potrò.

D. GIO: Forte in mezzo a tanti guai
io resister qui saprò.

STA: Dimmi tu, sei cavaliero?

D. GIO: Io lo son.

STA: Dammi la mano.

D. GIO: Atterrirmi pensi in vano.
Pronto a te la man io do. *(D. Giovanni dà la mano alla statua)*

D. GIO: Ahi, qual mano possente m'afferra!

STA: Qua deponi quel misero orgoglio,
qua ti penti.

D. GIO: Pentirmi non voglio.

STA: Dunque a Pluto sotterra ten va.

STA: Vedi
come da' cardini suoi

TUTTI GLI ALTRI: Ahimè,
smossa tutta traballa la terra!
Degli abissi l'orror si disserra,
tutto Averno vedere si fa.
(sparisce la statua, e sortono le furie)

A 7: Le fiamme a vortici
stridenti s'alzano.
Fischian dall'Erebo
i draghi orribili.
Le fiere Eumenidi
le faci scuotono.
Morte implacabile
sopra mi sta.
(si apre la terra, e D. Giovanni piomba all'inferno in mezzo alle furie)

fine del dramma

Il capriccio drammatico

Giovanni Valentini
Giovanni Bertati

1787

IL CAPRICCIO
DRAMMATICO

rappresentazione
per musica
di Giovanni Bertati
per la seconda opera
da rappresentarsi
nel Teatro Giustiniani
di S. Moisè
il carnovale dell'anno 1787

In Venezia
Appresso Antonio Casali

Con licenza de' superiori

ATTORI

Policastro, impresario
Il sig. Giovanni Morelli, virtuoso di S.A.R. l'Infante di Duca Parma, ec.
Guerina
La sig. Giulia Gasperini
Ninetta
La sig. Irene Tomeoni Duttilieu
(Guerina, Ninetta: prime buffe a vicenda)
Pasquino, primo mezzo carattere
Il sig. Paolo Mandini
Valerio
Il sig. Antonio Baglioni
Calandra
La sig. Elisabetta Marchesini
(Valerio, Calandra: altri attori dell'opera buffa)
Il suggeritore dell'opera
Il sig. Vincenzo Pavia

Il Cavalier Tempesta, protettore
Il sig. Antonio Marchesi

Un maestro di cembalo, che non parla.

La scena è in una città della Germania.
La musica è tutta nuova di vari signori maestri.
Il scenario è del sig. Gerolamo Mauro.
Il vestiario del sig. Carlo Grifolana.

ATTO PRIMO

Scena i
Camera di Policastro

Policastro, che passeggia malinconico; poi Ninetta, indi Calandra e Valerio

POL: Sia maledetto quando
il diavolo avversario
di fare l'impresario
mi venne un dì a tentar!
Il publico talora
si mostra indulgentissimo;
talor difficilissimo
è poi da contentar.
Ma adesso siamo in ballo
e qui convien ballar. *(in questo Ninetta)*
NIN: Riverisco l'impresario.
POL: A lei faccio anch'io un inchino.
NIN: E così di buon mattino
voi mi fate ricercar?
POL: Compatite questo incomodo. *(con ironia)*
NIN: Ma perchè sì di buon'ora?
POL: Ci verranno gli altri ancora
perchè a tutti ho da parlar. *(in questo Calandra e Valerio)*
CAL. E VAL: Siam qui pronti a veder, signor mio,
cosa sia questa gran novità.
POL: Novità certamente, dich'io,
che la testa girare mi fa.
NIN: Diventar voi mi fate curiosa.
CAL: Io patisco, se a dirlo tardate.
NIN: / CAL: / VAL: Dite, via, più aspettar non ci fate;
stiamo a udire che cosa sarà.
POL: Tanta voglia, che adesso mostrate,
appagata fra poco sarà.
GLI 3 SUD: Un orgasmo mi sento terribile,
che crescendo via più in sen mi va.
A 4: In me sento una pena indicibile,

che crescendo via più in sen mi va.

POL: Io volea veramente,
per dirvelo, aspettar che gli altri ancora
qua uniti si trovassero;
ma non importa già.
Vi spiegherò qual sia la novità.
NIN: Sentiamola, sentiamola.
POL: La novità, signori, è che qui vogliono
mutazion di spettacolo.
Parliamoci alla schietta. Io qui in Germania
men vado consumando
quello che in altri tempi ho guadagnato.
Voi non piacete, ed io son disperato.
NIN: Io non piaccio!
CAL: Io non piaccio!
POL: Piano, non vi scaldate.
Del merito voi tutti
io dico anzi che avete.
Colpa vostra non è se non piacete,
ma . . .
NIN: Che ma? Voi parlate in generale.
POL: Vi dirò . . .
CAL: Voi direte
delle insolenze. Non piacete? Oh capperi!
Io faccio la mia parte
quanto può farla ogn'altra;
e se tutti facessero
quello che faccio io, signor mio caro,
il teatro, il teatro, a parlar sodo,
se ne andrebbe per certo in miglior modo.

Ho cantato e ricantato
in Italia, Francia e Spagna,
in Olanda, in Allemagna,
e mi feci sempre onor.
A Milan per sopranome
mi dicevan la Canerina,
a Turin la Campanina,

a Francfort la Rondinella,
a Madrid la Farfarella,
non stupisca, mio signor.
    Basta dir che dei sonetti
a me fatti in più occasioni
mi fodrai tre mantiglioni,
due sottane, due corpetti,
e qualcun ne avanza ancor.[1] *(parte)*

Scena ii
Policastro, Ninetta e Valerio

POL: Ecco qua; mi ha lasciato
terminar il discorso!
NIN: Sentite, signor caro, io credo certo
d'esser compatita.
VAL: Io posso dire
che a battermi le mani
ho veduto dei nobili soggetti,
e a Legnago ed a Lugo ebbi i sonetti.
POL: Volete o non volete
lasciarmi terminare?
Che vi venga la rabbia!
NIN: Dite pure.
VAL: Io non parlo.
POL: Voi siete tutti bravi
dal primo fin'all'ultimo,
sono i drammi bellissimi,
la musica è eccellente.
Tutto è buono, ma infin non piace niente.
NIN: Dunque il mal vien dal publico.
POL: E che? Volete ch'io
col publico la prenda? Oh non son pazzo!
Bisogna rispettarlo,
e tutto s'ha da far per contentarlo.
VAL: Ma contentarlo come?

1. Occasional sonnets were often printed on silk.

POL: Col mutar lo spettacolo.
NIN: E cosa s'ha da far?
POL: In questa piazza
non hanno ancor veduta
quella commedia in musica
ridotta a un atto solo
che si fece in Provenza.
Voi tutti la sapete, ond'io vorrei
che fra noi qui, provandola alla presta,
questa sera in teatro
si recitasse poi.
NIN: Io . . . per me . . . fate voi.
VAL: Fate voi.
POL: Dunque, io vado
di sì fatto spettacolo novello
a fare che si esponga ora il cartello. *(per partire)*
NIN: Piano. Questa commedia è il *Don Giovanni?*
POL: Appunto. È *Il convitato*
di pietra.
NIN: Uhm! } *(stringendosi nelle spalle)*
VAL: Uhm! }
POL: Che?
NIN: Potrebbe darsi
che qui in Germania . . . Ma . . .
POL: Temete forse
del suo incontro?
NIN: Moltissimo.
L'azione è inverisimile, il libretto
è fuori delle regole,
la musica non so che cosa sia;
ed in fatti preveggio
che con questa si andrà di male in peggio.
POL: Ma credete voi forse
che si badi alle regole?
Si bada a quel che piace, e spesse volte
si fanno più denari
con delle strampalate

di quello che con cose
studiate, regolate e giudiziose.

VAL: Quel che dite sarà, ma il *Convitato,*
o signor impresario,
certo non si può far.

POL: Per qual ragione?

VAL: Perchè adesso ci manca
un buffo caricato. E qual ripiego
c'è a questo, signor mio?

POL: Da buffo caricato farò io.

NIN: Voi?

VAL: Voi?

POL: Io, io.

NIN: Ah, ah! *(ridendo forte)*

VAL: Ah, ah! *(ridendo forte)*

POL: Ridete?
Ridete, sì; ma poi
il buffo saprò far meglio di voi.
La parte la so a mente, e ci scometto
ch'io cavo più risate
di tutti quanti voi che recitate.
Quanto al cantar di musica,
m'ingegnerò ancor io. Non mi confondo.
Ed anzi, perchè debba
ciascun di voi restar qui stupefatto,
voglio cantarvi un'aria mia sul fatto.

In teatro siamo adesso,
pronta sta la compagnia,
suona già la sinfonia,
il sipario in alto va.
Di Bologna un duttoraz
or son'io, guardate qua.
"Cospetton! Cospettonaz!
An' se fà sta sort d'azion
al Dottor de Balanzon.
Oh che toch de mascalzon!
Sosterrò le me rason

con Marc Tulli Giceron,
con Pittagora e Platon."
Già va dentro il dottorazzo,
ecco in scena il Pantalon.
"Son qua, son qua, fia mia;
e cò te digo, fia,
el resto za se sa."
Il Pulcinella or viene
a fare le sue scene,
e alla napolitana
guardate come fa.
"Nè nè, què què, frabutta;
sta ccà Polecenella.
Te caccia la lenguella,
e dice fatte ccà."
Per far il buffo, or ditemi,
ho qualche abilità?
Or dunque, miei signori,
se manca un personaggio,
io mi darò il vantaggio
di farlo come va. *(parte)*

Scena iii
Ninetta e Valerio

NIN: Che ne dite, Valerio?
VAL: Voi che ne dite?
NIN: Io resto
quasi maravigliata.
VAL: Vedremo ancora questa.
Compiacerlo conviene
perch'è un buon galantuom. Ma qui in Germania
io non ci vengo più.
NIN: Oh, nemmen io.
In Italia, in Italia
dove in tutti i teatri
mi feci sempre onore;
e non solo i sonetti

in seta ebbi a Turino,
ch'ebbi i piccioni ancor col campanino.
Io specialmente poi
a tutti gl'impresari
feci coll'aria mia degli augellini
a cappellate sempre far zecchini.
Sentitela, sentitela,
e se non piace poi dove noi siamo,
o sordi o senza gusto io poi li chiamo.

Bel vedere in sul mattino
a spuntare i fior novelli,
bel sentire i dolci augelli
l'alba intorno a salutar!
Tra le fronde un uscignolo
là si sente a gorgheggiar,
di qua s'ode un cardellino,
un fanello, un calandrino,
e fra l'erbe ruggiadose
sta il ruscello a gorgogliar.
Tutte insieme queste cose
un'orchestra van formando,
che per l'aria risuonando
vi fa l'alma giubilar. *(parte)*

Scena iv
Valerio solo.

Dice bene. Le donne
su' teatri d'Italia
quando son belle, ancor che non sian buone,
trovano compassione.
Ma gli uomini poi,
che questo privilegio aver non sanno,
hanno solo del canchero;
e chi sa quante volte per disgrazia
è a me toccata ancor sì bella grazia.

Un mare è il teatro,
e sempre è in tempesta.
Ben spesso contrario
il vento si desta
allor che si crede
di averlo in favor.
D'entrar lieto in porto
non è alcun sicuro;
di qua se fa chiaro,
di là poi fa oscuro,
e sempre il pericolo
tremar vi fa il cor. *(parte)*

Scena v
Camera di Guerina.

Pasquino e Guerina

PAS: Dunque, avete risolto
di farmi disperar?
GUE: Farmi crepare
dunque è vostro pensiero?
PAS: Un amor come il mio . . .
GUE: Sì, un bell'amore!
Sempre rimproverarmi e farmi piangere
senza motivo!
PAS: Che? Senza motivo?
La sera nel teatro
chi vi parla all'orecchio,
chi vi baccia la mano
e chi d'occhio vi fa stando lontano.
Il giorno in casa poi chi va, chi viene;
e questa è cosa certa,
che a quanti san venir la porta è aperta.
GUE: E chi può dispensarsene?
PAS: Voi, se mi amaste.
GUE: Io v'amo,
ma se rendermi poi

incivile e ridicola cercate,
dico che siete voi che non mi amate.

PAS: Son di teatro, è vero,
ma faccio un giuramento
che a donne di teatro
non mi attacco mai più.

GUE: Giuro ancor'io,
e lo giuro per Bacco,
che a gente come voi più non m'attacco.

PAS: Dunque, è fatta?

GUE: Certissimo.
Siam d'accordo.

PAS: È finita.

GUE: Sì, è finita.

PAS: Addio. *(ciascuno per partire; poi si fermano*

GUE: Addio. *in qualche distanza e si voltano)*

PAS: Eh?

GUE: Che?

PAS: M'avete voi chiamato?

GUE: Io? Nemmen ho parlato.

PAS: Sentite. Già men vado,
ma vi dico sol questo:
soddisfatevi pure,
attaccatevi pur con chi volete,
sì, ma un altro Pasquin non troverete.
(per partire come sopra)

GUE: Ed un'altra Guerina
nemmen voi certamente.

PAS: Sentite, io già non dico . . . che . . . Ma basta,
giacchè abbiam da lasciarci,
così in collera almen non ci lasciamo.

GUE: Bene. Amici restiamo,
ma amorosi non più.

PAS: No, no; contenta
in tal modo sarete.

GUE: Io? Voi, che quello siete
che mi lascia.

PAS: Anzi, voi mi discacciate.

GUE: Voi siete un pazzo.

PAS: E voi dunque sognate.

A 2: Quando amor due cori accende
d'un affetto ch'è sincero,
così a un tratto non è vero
che si possa disamar.

GUE: È costante la mia face.
PAS: Il mio amor non è mendace.
A 2: Il lasciarvi, amato bene,
mi faria tra mille pene
questa vita terminar.

GUE: Io v'amo e lo vedete,
ma la vostra continua gelosia
mi è poi troppo molesta.

PAS: Ecco che viene il Cavalier Tempesta.
Protettor del teatro,
ridicolo, ignorante,
non viene che a seccarci ad ogni istante.

Scena vi

Il Cavalier Tempesta e detti.

C. TEM: Bella Guerina, addio. Schiavo, Pasquino.
GUE: Son serva al cavaliere.
PAS: A voi m'inchino.
C. TEM: Da seder presto presto,
ch'io voglio che parliamo
di questa novità che mi ha sorpreso.
GUE: Cos'è quel che di nuovo avete inteso?
C. TEM: Diggià il nuovo cartello
vidi alla piazza esposto. *Don Giovanni*
o sia Il convitato
di pietro.
GUE: No. *Di pietra*.
C. TEM: O pietro o pietra,
così dice il cartello.
Commedia d'un sol atto.
In musica. Ah ah! Come può essere

una commedia in musica? Le opere
in musica si fan; ma le commedie
si fanno sempre in prosa, ed io decido
che questa vostra sia
una bella e stupenda porcheria.

GUE: E il signor impresario,
senza prima passar meco parola,
vuol dar nuovo spettacolo?
Oh, ci sono io che qua ci mette ostacolo. *(si alza sdegnata)*

C. TEM: Voi avete ragione.

GUE: Egli avrà ben parlato
con l'altra prima donna,
e non parla con me! Se viene a dirmelo,
adesso gli rispondo
che non vo' recitar, cascasse il mondo.

C. TEM: Voi avete ragione.

PAS: Ed io non sono forse il primo uomo?
Lo sono, ed alla fin senza il mio assenso
non può far novità, per quel ch'io penso.

C. TEM: Voi avete ragione.

GUE: Pasquino, a cercar tosto
dell'impresario andate.
Dite a sua signoria che favorisca
di portarsi da me, che venga subito,
che non tardi, che preme.
Andate, e qua con lui tornate insieme.

PAS: Ma trovarlo . . . Chi sa . . . Forse egli stesso
se ne verrà fra poco.

GUE: Andate, io dico,
e fatelo venire.

PAS: E voi col cavaliere
sola restar volete?

GUE: Eterna seccatura,
caro Pasquin, voi siete.

PAS: Via, non andate in collera.

GUE: E chi può tollerarvi?

PAS: Via, che tutto farò per contentarvi.

Parto, Guerina mia,
ma quei begli occhi amati
vorrei veder placati
innanzi di partir.
Parto, ma ben saria
che il cavaliere anch'esso
coll'impresario istesso
venisse a conferir.
(Ah, che di gelosia
mi sento, oddio, morir!)
Non turbate quel viso adorato. *(a Guerina)*
Lei perdoni s'io sono incivile. *(al cavaliere)*
Voi sapete che ho il core piagato; *(a Guerina)*
mi dovete, mio ben, compatir. *(parte)*

Scena vii

Il Cavaliere e Guerina

C. TEM: È di voi innamorato, e fa il geloso
il mio caro Pasquino.
Che sciocco! Che buffon! Che babbuino!
Ritorniamo a sedere, e discorriamo
della commedia in musica.

GUE: E che volete voi di ciò discorrere,
se non ne avete idea?

C. TEM: Che spropositi dite!
Io non ne ho idea! Noi altri
ne sappiam d'ogni cosa
senz'averla studiata e senz'ancora
averla mai veduta. Sì, signora.

GUE: Ebbene. Discorretene
dunque con l'impresario,
ch'io non vo' sapere.

C. TEM: Via, via, non vi sdegnate,
cara la mia Guerina, e discorriamo,
che maledettamente, o bella, io v'amo.

GUE: Grazie alla sua bontà.

C. TEM: Mi disprezzate?

GUE: No, signore.
C. TEM: Mi amate?
GUE: No, signore.
C. TEM: Mi volete
nemico?
GUE: No, signore.
C. TEM: Mi volete, via, via, per protettore?
GUE: Protettore amo il publico.
Compatita esser bramo da ciascuno
e non già disgustar tutti per uno.
Ma adesso ci penso
questa mattina ancora. *(si alza)*
Non ho fatto esercizio. Mi permetta
ch'io me ne vada un poco alla spinetta.
C. TEM: Eh, restate un po' qua.
GUE: A a a a a a. *(modulando a piacere)*
C. TEM: V'è tempo di studiare.
GUE: A a a a a a.
C. TEM: Ma questa cosa
rassembrami impolita.
GUE: Se non v'aggrada, è per di là l'uscita,
A a a a a a.
C. TEM: Via, via, cara Guerina,
gorgheggiate anche in fin doman mattina.
Ma giacchè avete voglia di cantare,
almeno qualche arietta
fatemi un po' sentire.
GUE: Sì, signore, vi voglio in ciò servire.

La donna ch'è amante
si lagna, sospira,
languisce, delira,
lontan dal suo ben;
ma poi la speranza
in dolce sembianza
il cor dagli affanni
ristora nel sen. *(parte)*

Scena viii
Il Cavaliere solo.

Canta bene, fa bene,
ma se con me non vuol far all'amore,
io mi farò d'un'altra protettore.
E quando io proteggo,
sempre in teatro, sia buona o cattiva,
la mia protetta a trionfar arriva.

Delle virtuose io sono
il principal sostegno,
e quando ch'io m'impegno,
non v'è da dubitar.
Fo scrivere al poeta
il libro a modo mio;
la musica il maestro
la fa come vogl'io;
fo battere le mani
a chi mi piace e par.
Ma a quelle non protette
fischiate maledette;
sussurro quando cantano,
distraggo gli uditori,
e a forza di rumori
le faccio ancor stuonar. *(parte)*

Scena ix
Sala con porte praticabili in casa di Guerina.

Valerio dando di braccio a Calandra, indi Ninetta servita dal maestro di cembalo; poi il suggeritore con scartafaccio in mano.

VAL: Eccoci. Siamo i primi
alla prova venuti.
CAL: Di Guerina
chiuse ancor son le stanze.
Convien che la signora

se ne stia a letto ancora.
VAL: Picchiamo.
CAL: Oibò, oibò.
Già con lei volontieri io non ci sto.
NIN: Son serva a tutti due. Vuol l'impresario
che si provi alla presta,
ma gli altri non ci sono.
La signora Guerina
non si lascia veder; alfin de' fini
sono anch'io prima donna quanto lei,
e se mi degno io
di venir qui a provare in casa sua,
per creanza almen parmi
che dovrebbe venir ad incontrarmi.
VAL: Che sia fuori di casa?
CAL: Qui non si vede alcuno.
VAL: Si potrebbe picchiar.
NIN: No, no, aspettiamo
che vengano qui gli altri, anzi sediamo.
(siedono; in questo il suggeritore)
SUG: Umilissimo servo.
CAL: Addio.
VAL: Chi ricercate?
SUG: La casa è questa ove si fa la prova?
NIN: È questa.
SUG: E l-or sig-nori
s-ono li virtuosi?
VAL: Appunto.
Chi diavolo è costui?
SUG: L'in-vito, di-cano,
non è a quest'ora?
VAL: Ebben? Cosa volete?
SUG: Ho io oggi l'o-nore
d'essere, s-ignor m-io, s-uggeritore.
CAL: Voi il suggeritore? Saria bella!
NIN: Ma il solito non c'è?
SUG: C'è. È m-io fratello.
Ma egli è ancora u-bbriaco da ier sera;

ond'io, per-chè n'ho pratica,
s-on venuto in s-ua v-ece.

CAL: Staremo freschi.

VAL: E come
suggerir voi volete?

SUG: Non si d-ubiti,
padr-one riverito,
che ne' teatri anc-ora ho s-uggerito. *(si ritira ad una parte)*

Scena x

Policastro, Guerina, Pasquino e detti.

POL: Ma voi, signori miei,
come foste invitati,
se aveste favorito in casa mia,
esposto ora il cartello
senza vostra saputa non saria.

GUE: A un'ora così incomoda
si aveva da sortire?

PAS: Il mio bisogno io non potea dormire,
e tosto una raucedine
mi sarei acquistata.

GUE: E s'io mi fossi alzata
prima del consueto un'ora sola,
ora mi sentirei star mal di gola.

POL: Via, faceste benissimo
dunque a starvene a casa.
Ma lasciam di altercare,
e cominciam la prova.

GUE: Ma cosa pretendete
di far col *Don Giovanni*? A terra, a terra!

Scena xi

Il Cavaliere e detti.

C. TEM: E a terra dico anch'io.

POL: Ma perchè, signor mio?

C. Tem: Informato mi son, caro impresario.
Ce la volete dar per cosa nuova,
ed è vecchia all'opposto
più ancor dell'invenzion del menarrosto.
La fanno i commedianti
da due secoli in qua con del schiamazzo,
ma solamente per il popolazzo.

Pol: Signor sì, ve l'accordo.
Ma la nostra commedia,
ridotta com'ell'è fra la spagnuola
di Tirso de Molina,
tra quella di Molière
e quella delli nostri commedianti,
qualunque sia, non fu veduta avanti.

C. Tem: È poi d'un atto solo.

Pol: Per la musica basta.
Certo che ancora in questa
vi sono mille e mille inconvenienti,
ma gli animi gentili,
se qual cosa di buono
trovano nella musica,
nelle decorazioni e nei soggetti,
compatire sapran gli altri difetti.

Gue: Ma io per questa sera
di recitarla non mi trovo al caso.

Pol: Ed io son persuaso
che piena di clemenza *(con ironia)*
anzi favorirete. (Oh, che pazienza!)

Siete cara e siete bella,
siate ancora compiacente;
nè vogliamo alfin per niente
star qui insieme ad altercar.

Gue: Io per me fissato ho il chiodo . . .

Pas: Faccio anch'io quel che fa lei . . .

a 2: . . . e ragione aver mi par.

Nin: Serva sua, padroni miei.
Non si prova e si contrasta;
ho aspettato quanto basta,

e non voglio più aspettar.

POL: Aspettate.

C. TEM: Non andate.

CAL: Anch'io vado con Ninetta.

POL: Non abbiate tanta fretta,
ma vi prego a pazientar.

NIN: Prima donna sono anch'io,
e non fo la puntigliosa.
È lei pure una virtuosa, *(additando Calandra)*
nè s'ha ciò da tollerar.

VAL: Anch'io sono un virtuoso,
e non faccio il puntiglioso
quando s'ha da faticar.

PAS: Anche questa saria bella!
Cosa lei vorrebbe dir? *(a Valerio)*

GUE: Cosa c'entra questa e quella, *(a Policastro)*
se ho ragion io di garir?

GUE. E PAS: Che sen vadano anche subito,
se non vogliono sentir.
(uno dopo l'altro volendo andarsene, Policastro ed il cavaliere li trattengono e li riconducono al loro primo sito)

NIN: Ecco qua, s'io faccio presto.

POL: Via, non fate.

CAL: Io qua non resto.

C. TEM: No, restate.

VAL: Io me ne vo.

C. TEM. E POL: Via, che tutt'io aggiusterò.

GUE: Vado io, non dubitate.

POL: No, Guerina, qua restate.

PAS: Io vo certo.

C. TEM: Nemmen voi.

NIN., CAL., PAS., GUE. E VAL:
Queste scene a dirla poi
non si ponno sopportar.
(si dividono di qua e di là per andarsene; Policastro ed il cavaliere restano nel mezzo adirati)

POL: Ma se andar volete poi,
io vi mando a far squartar.

C. TEM: Ma se vogliono andar poi,

che si vadan far squartar.

POL: Presto, andate, galoppate,
ma il quartale non sperate
di poter da me tirar.
(ciascuno affettando dolcezza ritorna pian piano al proprio sito)

CAL: Io resto, non parto.

NIN: Io son compiacente.

VAL: Son io un agnellino.

PAS. E GUE: Son io certamente
la stessa bontà.

C. TEMP. E POL: Trovato ho/ha un rimedio
che buoni li fa.

GUE: Per farvi vedere (*a Policastro*)
ch'io son di buon core,
per voi, mio signore,
di tutto farò.

POL: Gentil, gentilissima
voi siete, lo so.

PAS: Ci manca un attore.

POL: Io faccio per quello.

GUE: Il suggeritore?

SUG: Signori, son qua.
Per-chè m-io fratello
sen sta incomodato,
per lui mi ha mandato.

POL. E C. TEMP: Per burla sarà. *(tutti siedono)*

SUG: La m-usica ancora
a in-tendere a-rrivo,
e intuono il motivo
con quel che ci va.

PAS., NIN., GUE., CAL., C. TEMP., VAL:
Evviva! Bravissimo!
Benissimo andrà!

POL: Facciamo la prova
con questo duetto,
(cava di saccoccia delle carte di musica)

ch'è quel di Giorgietto.
Voi già lo sapete. *(a Ninetta)*
Tenete, tenete. *(al maestro di cembalo)*
Mettetevi là. *(al suggeritore, situandolo dietro il maestro)*

LI 6 SUD.: Che abbiamo da ridere
m'immagino già.
(il suggeritore suggerisce; ma di quando in quando per il suo naturale difetto di lingua si ferma sopra alcune sillabe e le ripete più volte, interrompendo gli attori che cantano)

NIN: "Ser Giorgietto, vi ho da dire
che co . . . co . . . co . . . co . . ." Ma cosa? *(al suggeritore)*

SUG: "Che con me voi la sbagliate . . ."

NIN: Se così voi v'imbrogliate,
proseguire non si può.
Più spedito, e a capo io vo.
"Ser Giorgietto, v'ho da dire
che con me voi la sbagliate
e mi fate disgustar.

POL: Cara mia, non vo' soffrire
che a . . . a . . . a . . . a . . ." Ma avanti. *(al suggeritore)*

SUG: "Che altri amanti . . ."

NIN. E POL: Che si canti
con costui non si può dar.

PAS: Via, torniamo a incominciar.

POL: "Cara mia, non vo' soffrire
ch'altri amanti voi trattiate.
Spendo e solo voglio star.

NIN: Mi offendete.

POL: Parlo schietto.

NIN: Non avete per me affetto.
POL: Sta . . . sta . . . sta . . ." Ma quanti sta? *(al suggeritore)*

GLI ALTRI: Ah ah ah ah ah ah ah ah!
Così avanti non si va.

SUG: "Star con voi non vo' così."

POL: Ho capito, signor sì.
Papagallo mio carissimo,
voi potete andar benissimo
alle capre a suggerir.

SUG: Siete un co-

POL: Con quel che segue?

SUG: Un co-co-rto intenditore.

GLI ALTRI: È un co co il suggeritore,
che non sa ben proferir.

A 7: Se in teatro così noi facciamo,
—O che strepito! Oimè che fracasso!—
nè la tromba nè più il contrabasso
si potrebbono udire a suonar.
Sollevarsi ad un tratto veggiamo
tutto insieme il parterre e i palchetti;
"zitto là, zitto là," con fischietti
s'udirebbe qua e là replicar.

SUG: Co- co- co- co- co- co- con tai detti
mi vorrebbon così screditar.

fine dell'atto primo

Don Giovanni
o sia
Il convitato di pietra

Giuseppe Gazzaniga
Giovanni Bertati

1787

DON GIOVANNI
o sia
IL CONVITATO DI PIETRA

ATTORI

D. Giovanni
D. Anna, figlia del Comendatore d'Oliola
D. Elvira, sposa promessa di D. Giovanni
D. Ximena, dama di Villena
Il Comendatore, padre di D. Anna
Duca Ottavio, sposo promesso della medesima
Maturina, sposa promessa di Biagio
Pasquariello, servo confidente di D. Giovanni
Biagio, contadino, sposo di Maturina
Lanterna, altro servo di D. Giovanni
Servitori diversi che non parlano

La scena è in Villena nell'Aragona.

ATTO PRIMO

Scena i

Parte di giardino a cui corrisponde l'appartamento di D. Anna, con porta socchiusa.

Pasquariello involto nella sua cappa, che passeggia; indi D. Giovanni e D. Anna, che lo tiene afferrato per il mantello.

PAS: La gran bestia è il mio padrone!
Ma il grand'asino son'io,
che per troppa soggezione
non lo mando a far squartar.
Invaghito di Donn'Anna,
là di furto sì è introdotto;
ed io gramo, chiotto chiotto,
qui ad attenderlo ho da star.
Sento fame, sento noia . . .
Ma che venga alcun già parmi.
Che sia lui vo' lusingarmi,
ma non vogliomi fidar.
(si ritira da una parte; in questo D. Giovanni e D. Anna dalla porta che introduce nell'appartamento)

D. GIO: Invano mi chiedete
ch'io mi discopra a voi.

D. AN: Un traditor voi siete,
un uomo senza onor.

D. GIO: Se fosse il Duca Ottavio
nemmeno parlereste.

D. AN: Azioni disoneste
non fece il duca ancor.

D. GIO: Lasciatemi.

D. AN: Scopritevi.

D. GIO: Voi lo sperate in vano.

D. AN: Vi strapperò il mantello.

D. GIO: Vi stroppierò la mano.

D. AN: Aiuto! Son tradita!
Soccorso, genitor!

D. GIO: Acchetati, impazzita.

Non ho d'alcun timor.

PAS: Oimè! La bestia ardita
va ancora a far rumor.

(in questo il Comendatore; al comparir del medemo, D. Anna lascia D. Giovanni e si ritira)

Scena ii

Il Comendatore e D. Giovanni, che sfodra la spada; Pasquariello in disparte.

COM: Qual tradimento! Perfido! Indegno!
Sottrarti invano speri da me.

(alla prima parola del Comendatore, D. Giovanni con un colpo gli smorza il lume, ed all'oscuro si battono)

D. GIO: Vecchio, ritirati, ch'io non mi degno
del poco sangue che scorre in te.

PAS: (Ah, che ci siamo!)

COM: Non fuggirai.

D. GIO: Ch'io da vil fugga non pensar mai.

(sempre combattendo, D. Giovanni ferisce mortalmente il Comendatore)

COM: Un'alma nobile, no, in te non v'è.

PAS: (Per dove fuggasi non so più affè.)

COM: Ahi, che m'ha infissa mortal ferita!
Sento a mancarmi diggià la vita.
Sen fugge l'anima . . . Già vo a spirar . . .

(il Comendatore cade sopra un sasso)

D. GIO: Di mortal piaga ferito il credo;
che già traballa fra l'ombre io vedo;
solo singulti d'udir mi par.

PAS: Io tremo tutto. Son qua di gelo.
Ad arricciarsi mi sento il pelo.
Più non si sentono . . . nemmen fiatar.

D. GIO: Zh zh!

PAS: Eh?

D. GIO: Pasquariello!

PAS: Siete voi?

D. GIO: Sono io.

PAS: Vivo o morto?

D. GIO: Che bestia!
E non senti ch'io parlo?
PAS: E il vecchio? Se n'è ito?
D. GIO: È morto, o mortalmente io l'ho ferito.
PAS: Bravo! Due azioni eroiche:
Donn'Anna violentata
e al padre una stoccata.
D. GIO: Ehi, te l'ho detto ancora
che non vo' rimostranze.
Seguimi e taci. Andiamo.
PAS: Sì, signore.
(Simular mi convien perchè ho timore.)

Scena iii

Il Duca Ottavio e D. Anna preceduti da servi con torcie.

D. OTT: Ecco, col sangue istesso . . . Ah, che rimiro!
(tiene la spada in mano)
D. AN: Oimè, misera! Oimè, padre! Oddio, padre!
D. OTT: Signor! Ah! Dov'è l'empio
che vibrò il fatal colpo!
D. AN: Ah! Che di morte
il pallore sul viso ha già dipinto!
Il cor più non ha moto. Ah, il padre è estinto!
(cade fra le braccia del duca)
D. OTT: Servi, servi, togliete agli occhi suoi
così funesto oggetto. E se alcun segno
scopresi in lui di vita,
medica man tosto gli porga aita.
(due servi portano in casa il corpo del Comendatore)
D. AN: Duca, estinto è mio padre; e ignoro, o misera,
l'empio che lo ferì.
D. OTT: Ma in qual maniera
s'introdusse l'iniquo
ne' vostri appartamenti?
D. AN: A voi, Duca, stringendomi
la promessa di sposa, io me ne stava
ad aspettarvi nel mio appartamento

pel nostro concertato abboccamento.
La damigella uscita
era per pochi istanti, allor che tutto
nel suo mantello involto
uno ad entrar nella mia stanza io vedo,
che al primo tratto, o Duca, io voi lo credo.

D. OTT: Che ascolto mai! Seguite.

D. AN: A me s'accosta, e tacito
fra le sue braccia stringemi. Io arrossisco,
mi scuoto e dico: "Ah! Duca,
che osate voi? Che fate?"
Ma colui non desiste; anzi, mi chiama
suo ben, sua cara, e dicemi che m'ama.
Resto di gelo allora. Egli malnato
ne volea profittar; io mi difendo,
lo vo' scoprir, lo afferro; palpitante
chiamo la damigella.
Egli allor vuol fuggir; lo seguo, voglio
smascherar per lo meno il traditore
e chiamo in mio soccorso il genitore.
Al suo apparir io fuggo, e l'assassino,
per compir l'esecrando suo delitto,
misera, oddio!, lo stese al suol trafitto.

D. OTT: Ardo di sdegno e tutto d'ira avvampo
per sì enorme misfatto. Ignoto a lungo
non resterà l'iniquo. Il suo castigo
sarà eguale al delitto, e voi, Donn'Anna,
se un rio destino il genitor v'invola,
nell'amor d'uno sposo
il sollievo cercate.

D. AN: Di ciò, Duca, per or più non parlate.
Finchè il reo non si scopre e finchè il padre
vendicato non resta, in un ritiro
voglio passar i giorni;
nè alcun mai vi sarà che men distorni. *(parte colli servi)*

Scena iv
Il Duca solo.

D. Ott: Qual doppio eccesso è questo
di sventura per me! Tutto si faccia
per scoprir l'empio intanto e non si lasci
Donn'Anna senz'aita in questo stato.

Vicin sperai l'istante
d'entrar felice in porto,
ma appena il lido ho scorto,
che torno in alto mar.
Cede l'amore in lei
ai moti del dolore,
e il misero mio core
ritorna a palpitar. *(parte)*

Scena v
Campagna con case rustiche e nobile casino fuori delle mura di Villena.

D. Giovanni e Pasquariello

D. Gio: Posto che non mi parli
più del Comendatore o di Donn'Anna,
la libertà ti lascio
di potermi ora dir quello che vuoi.
Pas: Quand'è dunque così, veniamo a noi.
Sapete voi ch'io son scandelezzato
della vita che fate!
D. Gio: Come! Qual vita faccio?
Pas: Buona. Ma se non più con giuramenti,
con inganni, e con cabale
sedur quanto potete . . .
Cercando tutti i dì qualche conquista,
mi par che sia una vita al quanto trista.
E poi, qui discorrendola, il burlarsi
come voi d'ogni legge, o signor caro . . .
D. Gio: Basta, basta così, mastro somaro.

Sai tu perchè venuto
son fuori delle porte?

PAS: Per non andar a letto
e per farmi crepar dal patimento.

D. GIO: Come sei tu poltrone!
Tieni, tieni una doppia
per il sonno che perdi.

PAS: Questo po' di cordiale
mi corrobora al quanto. Ebben, sentiamo
perchè siete ora qui.

D. GIO: Perchè invaghito
son di Donna Ximena. Ella sen venne
ieri qui al suo casino
per poter meco aver qualche colloquio
con maggior libertà.

PAS: Prudentemente.

D. GIO: Ma vedi una signora
che smonta di carrozza.

PAS: Dunque, pria che qui giunga,
entriamo nel casino
per non esser veduti.

D. GIO: Oibò. Vogl'io
qui in disparte osservar anzi chi sia.
Vieni, e mettiamci qui fuor della via. *(si ritirano)*

Scena vi

D. Elvira con due servitori; D. Giovanni e Pasquariello in disparte, che poi si avanzano.

D. ELV: Povere femmine,
noi siam chiamate
cervelli istabili,
anime ingrate,
cori volubili
nel nostro amor.
Ma sono gli uomini
che fan gli amanti
di noi più deboli,

più assai incostanti;
anzi son perfidi,
son senza cor.
Siamo pur misere
se noi li amiamo,
se ci fidiamo
del loro ardor.

In questo borgo io penso
trattenermi piuttosto
ch'entrar nella città. Là in quell'albergo
prenderò alloggio intanto
che scopro gli andamenti
dello sposo infedele,
che dopo avermi la sua fè giurata,
mi lasciò il terzo giorno abbandonata.

D. Gio: Oh cielo! *(restando sorpreso nel riconoscere D. Elvira)*
D. Elv: Ah! Don Giovanni!
Pas: Oh! Veh!
D. Elv: Cotanto
vi sorprende il vedermi?
D. Gio: Io vi confesso *(affettando disinvoltura)*
che tutt'altro qui adesso
aspettava che voi.
D. Elv: Ed io tutt'altro
aspettava d'aver che un tradimento.
Fin a questo momento
non fu il mio che un sospetto,
ma la vostra sorpresa or qui ad un tratto
più non mi lascia dubitar del fatto.
D. Gio: Donna Elvira, scusatemi,
ma voi foste una pazza a far il viaggio
con un così magnifico equipaggio.
Pas: (A proposito.)
D. Elv: È questo
quel che mi rispondete? Anima ingrata!
Fate ch'io senta almen qual fu il motivo
che da Burgos partiste, abbandonandomi
tacito, a precipizio,

dopo la data fè di sposalizio.
D. GIO: Oh, quanto a questo poi, qui Pasquariello
vi dirà la ragione.
PAS: Io?
D. GIO: Sì, tu. Digliela,
digliela.
PAS: Ma . . .
D. GIO: Ti dico
che gliela dici. Ed io perdon vi chiedo,
se un premuroso affar, con mio tormento,
vuol ch'io debba lasciarvi in tal momento. *(entra nel casino)*

Scena vii
D. Elvira e Pasquariello

D. ELV: E mi lascia così? Parla tu, dimmi
la cagione qual fu del suo abbandono,
e pensa ben che disperata io sono.
PAS: Per me . . . Sentite . . . Vi dirò . . . Siccome . . .
D. ELV: Non confonderti.
PAS: Oibò, non v'è pericolo.
Siccome, io dico, che Alessandro il Grande . . .
D. ELV: E che c'entra Alessandro?
PAS: C'entra, e statevi cheta.
Siccome, io dico, che Alessandro il Grande
non era giammai sazio
di far nuove conquiste, il mio padrone,
se avesse ancora cento spose e cento,
sazio non ne saria, nè mai contento.
Egli è il Grande Alessandro delle femmine,
onde, per far le sue amorose imprese,
spesso spesso cangiar suol di paese.
D. ELV: Dunque ha dell'altre femmine!
PAS: Ih, ih! Se voi volete averle in vista,
ecco, signora mia, quest'è la lista.
(getta una lista di alcune braccia di carta)

Dell'Italia ed Alemagna
ve ne ho scritte cento e tante;
della Francia e della Spagna
ve ne sono non so quante
fra madame, cittadine,
artigiane, contadine,
cameriere, cuoche e guattere,
perchè basta che sian femmine
per doverle amoreggiar.
Vi dirò ch'è un uomo tale,
se attendesse alle promesse,
che il marito universale
un dì avrebbe a diventar.
Vi dirò che egli ama tutte,
che sian belle o che sian brutte;
delle vecchie solamente
non si sente ad infiammar.
Vi dirò . . .

D. ELV: Tu m'hai seccata.
PAS: Vi dirò . . .
D. ELV: Non più! Va' via.
PAS: Vi dirò che si potria
fin domani seguitar.
D. ELV: Il mio cor da gelosia
tutto sento a lacerar. *(Pasquariello parte)*

Scena viii
D. Elvira sola.

Infelice ch'io sono! E tanti torti
potrà soffrir quest'anima gelosa?
No. Il diritto di sposa
farò valer; e qual si sia rivale
che giungerò a scoprire
farò tremar, nè mi saprò avvilire. *(parte)*

Scena ix
D. Giovanni e D. Ximena, dal casino.

D. GIO: Più di ciò non si parli,
dolcezza del mio cor. Io, vostro sposo,
nuotando fra i contenti,
sarò il più fortunato fra i viventi.
D. XIM: Oh quanto sono dolci
queste vostre espressioni!
Ma quando seguiranno
i sponsali fra noi?
D. GIO: Quando! Vorrei che subito
qua ci fosse un notaro,
riguardo al genio mio; ma un certo affare
mi obbligherà con sommo mio martire
ancora qualche giorno a differire.
D. XIM: Ricordatevi bene
il vostro giuramento. Rammentate
ch'io son d'umor geloso,
che voi siete mio sposo,
e che non soffrirei
nemmen per civiltà che a un'altra donna
voi toccaste la man, nemmen col guanto.
D. GIO: Che dite mai! Mi vanto
d'esser io il più fedele, il più costante
uomo che vi sia al mondo.
Non temete, mio ben, che d'ora in poi
ogn'altra donna io fuggirò per voi.

Per voi nemmeno in faccia
io guardarò le belle;
se fossero ancor stelle,
io gli occhi abbasserò.
Voi sola, voi, mia cara,
porto scolpita in petto;
voi siete il solo oggetto
che amar da me si può.
Mio idolo, mio bene,
mia fiamma, mio tesoro,

per voi mi struggo e moro,
più pace al cor non ho.
(Pur questa nel catalogo
a scrivere men vo.) *(parte)*

Scena x
D. Ximena

Or che sicura io son della sua fede,
chi di me è più contenta?
Se amor per lui m'impiaga,
amor per lui mi sanarà la piaga. *(parte)*

Scena xi
Maturina, Biagio e villani che suonano le nacchere; indi Pasquariello

MAT: Bella cosa per una ragazza
è il sentirsi promessa in isposa,
ma più bella diventa la cosa
in quel giorno che sposa si fa.

TUTTI: Tarantàn, tarantàn, tarantà.
Su via, allegri, balliamo e saltiamo, *(ballano)*
che quel giorno ben presto verrà.

MAT: Bella cosa per una ragazza *(in questo Pasquariello in disparte)*
è l'aver un amante che adora,
ma più bella diventa in allora
che in marito a pigliarlo sen va.

TUTTI: Tarantai, tarantai, tarantà.
Su via, allegri, balliamo e saltiamo, *(ballano)*
che quel giorno ben presto verrà.
(Pasquariello si caccia anch'esso tra li villani, prende Maturina per la mano e balla)

PAS: Bella cosa, cospetto di Bacco,
è il trovar una femmina bella,
ma facendo la tantarantella
molto meglio la cosa sen va.

TUTTI: *(eccettutato Biagio, che mostra dispetto)*

Tarantàn, tarantai, tarantà.
Su via, allegri, balliamo e saltiamo,
che un piacere maggior non si dà.

BIA: Oh oh! Poffar Diana!
Tralasciate voi altri e andate in casa. *(li villani partono)*
E voi, cosa venite, o signor caro,
a meschiarvi con noi
ed a pigliar per man le nostre femmine?
PAS: Oh oh! Poffar Mercurio,
che ti faccia andar stroppio! E crederesti
ch'io fossi come te qualche facchino?
Son cavaliero e son . . . Don Giovannino.
MAT: È un gentiluomo, senti?
Dunque, lascialo fare.
BIA: Come lasciarlo fare! Io non intendo
che punto s'addomestichi
colle donne che sono a noi promesse,
nè che tarantellar voglia con esse.

Scena xii
D. Giovanni, Maturina, Biagio e Pasquariello

D. GIO: Cosa c'è? Cosa c'è?
PAS: (Cedo majoribus.)
BIA: Quest'altro cavaliero
vien con la nostra sposa
a far l'impertinente.
MAT: Eh, non c'è male, non c'è mal per niente.
D. GIO: Quel cavaliero là? Questo si prende
così per una orecchia . . .
PAS: Ahi, ahi! Che fate? *(Biagio ride forte)*
(Diavolo che sel porti!)
D. GIO: V'insegnerò, ser cavaliero selvatico,
a far l'impertinente
con le belle ragazze. *(Biagio seguita a ridere)*
PAS: Ma se . . .

D. GIO: Zitto. Le belle si accarezzano *(si accosta a Maturina; la piglia per la mano)*
gentilmente così. Quanto mai siete
vezzosa e graziosina!
Che delicata e morbida manina!

MAT: Ah, signor, voi burlate.

BIA: *(frapponendosi)* Eh! Dico io . . .

D. GIO: Che dici?

BIA: Dico, corpo di Bacco,
che voi fate di peggio.

MAT: Biagio, non riscaldarti.

BIA: Anzi, vo' riscaldarmi. Animo, parti.

D. GIO: Eh eh! *(allontanando Biagio con una spinta)*

BIA: Come! Cospetto! A me una spinta!

D. GIO: Va' via. *(gli dà uno schiaffo)*

BIA: Come! Uno schiaffo! *(Pasquariello ride forte)*

D. GIO: Va' via. *(gli dà un altro schiaffo; Pasquariello seguita a ridere forte)*

BIA: Come! Anche un altro!
E tu, trista, lo sopporti?
Niuno m'ha fatto mai simili torti! *(piangendo)*
Avete voi ragione
che adesso son poltrone,
ma mi vendicherò dell'insolenza.

D. GIO: Taci e va' via. *(minacciando di batterlo ancora; Biagio si salva dietro a Maturina)*

MAT: Va', Biagio, abbi pazienza.

BIA: A me schiaffi sul mio viso,
a me far un tal affronto!
Ma gli schiaffi non li conto
quanto conto, fraschettaccia,
che tu stai con quella faccia
a vedermi maltrattar.
Ma aspettate, ma lasciate *(a D. Giovanni)*
ch'io mi possa almen sfogar.
Da tua madre, da tua zia,
da tua nonna adesso io vado,
vo da tutto il parentado

la facenda a raccontar.
Maledetto sia quel ridere, *(osserva Pasquariello, che ride)*
che di più mi fa arrabbiar!
Sì, sì, vado, più non resto,
vado subito di trotto;
sento il sangue sopra e sotto
che si va a rimescolar. *(parte)*

Scena xiii
Maturina, D. Giovanni e Pasquariello

MAT: Con vostra permissione. *(per partire)*
D. GIO: Oibò. Restatevi,
anima mia.
MAT: A me?
D. GIO: Sì, a voi, mia cara.
MAT: Signore, io mi vergogno
a sentirmi parlar teneramente
quando un altro vi sia che tutto sente.
PAS: Poverina!
D. GIO: Ecco, subito . . . *(voltandosi a Pasquariello)*
PAS: Signore,
non state a incomodarvi
di dirmi niente affatto,
che capisco per aria e me la batto.
(Va', che stai fresca!) *(parte)*

Scena xiv
D. Giovanni e Maturina

D. GIO: Ehi, dico, *(dietro a Pasquariello)*
statene qui d'appresso.
In due soli restati eccoci adesso. *(la prende per la mano)*
MAT: Ma signor . . .
D. GIO: Oh, mia gioia!
E voi con quegli occhietti così belli,
con quel bocchin di rose,

questa sì cara mano
darete ad un villano?
No, mia dolcezza, no. Voi meritate
un assai miglior stato,
e di voi già mi sento innamorato.

MAT: Ah, signor! Mi dà gusto
quello che voi mi dite, ed io vorrei
che quello che mi dite fosse vero;
ma sempre mi fu detto
che voi altri signori
per lo più siete falsi e ingannatori.

D. GIO: Oh! Io non son di quelli. Il ciel men guardi!

MAT: Sentite, io sono, è vero,
povera paesana,
ma però non per questo avrei piacere
di lasciarmi ingannar; e poi il mio onore
più di tutto mi preme.

D. GIO: Ed io che avessi
un'anima sì trista
per ingannarvi, o cara? Oh, in questo poi
son troppo delicato.
Son di voi innamorato,
e posso ben giurarvi
che mio solo disegno è lo sposarvi.

MAT: Voi mel giurate?

D. GIO: Sì, ch'io ve lo giuro
per il cielo, o mio ben. E se volete
che ve lo giuri ancor per qual cos'altro,
ditelo voi.

MAT: No, no. Comincio a credere
a quel che voi mi dite,
e da questo momento
innamorata anch'io di voi mi sento.

Se pur degna voi mi fate
di goder d'un tanto onore,
sarò vostra, o mio signore,
e di core v'amerò.
Sento già che in riguardarvi

tutto il sangue in me si move.
Tal dolcezza in sen mi piove
che spiegarla, oddio, non so.
Caro, caro, che vel dico,
ma di core, ma di voglia!
Niun fia mai che mi distoglia
dal gran ben che vi vorrò.
(partono ed entrano in casa di Maturina)

Scena xv
Pasquariello, poi D. Ximena; indi D. Giovanni

PAS: Io penso ad ogni modo
che il lasciar questa bestia è necessario
a costo ancor di perdere il salario.
Sento a far un gran strepito
per il Comendator, che fu ammazzato,
e se il diavolo fa . . . Servo obbligato.

D. XIM: Pasquariello, mi ascolta,
e sincero mi parla. Anzi, ora vedi
come voglio impegnarti
a parlar schiettamente. *(gli dà alcune monete)*

PAS: Due doppie! E chi, cospetto,
non avrebbe con voi da parlar schietto?

D. XIM: Innamorata io son del tuo padrone.
Ei giurò di sposarmi,
ma di lui tante cose a dirmi io sento,
che da due ore in qua tutta pavento.

PAS: Per esempio, di lui vi avranno detto
ch'è un discolo, un briccone, un prepotente,
un cane . . . *(avvertendosi di D. Giovanni, che si avvanza)*
Oibò, non date retta a niente.
Il mio padrone è un vero galantuomo,
uno che ha tutti i numeri;
e se a me non credete . . . Eccolo appunto;
domandatelo a lui.

D. GIO: Costui che dice?

PAS: E che ho da dire? Io faccio
giustizia al vostro merito,
ma tante male lingue . . .

D. GIO: E che, mia cara?
Forse talun . . .

D. XIM: No, no, sposo adorato,
del vostro cor non ho mai dubitato.

Scena xvi

D. Elvira e detti.

D. ELV: Signor mio, una parola.

D. GIO: Oh! Donna Elvira . . .

D. ELV: Vi trovo, ingrato, alfin.

D. GIO: Zitto, tacete,
adorata mia sposa. È quella dama
una che m'importuna, e godo appunto
della vostra venuta.

D. XIM: Don Giovanni,
che avete voi con quella?

D. GIO: È una bisbetica,
che mi viene a seccar. Entrate in casa,
che son tosto da voi.

D. XIM: Vado per compiacervi, ma badate
ch'io vi starò a guardar dalla finestra. *(parte)*

PAS: (Vedo il turbine in aria, e piano piano
prudentissimamente mi allontano.) *(parte)*

Scena xvii

D. Elvira e D. Giovanni, poi Maturina

D. ELV: E credereste voi d'infinocchiarmi,
ingratissimo sposo?
No. Tremate di me . . .

D. GIO: No, che voi siete
in errore, mio ben. Statevi cheta,

che v'amo, che v'adoro, e che col rito
io domani sarò vostro marito.

MAT: Con vostra permissione.
E che parlate voi, signor, con quella
di essere marito?

D. GIO: Anima mia,
quella dama è una pazza,
e nella sua pazzia si raffigura
di essere mia sposa.

D. ELV: Favorite.
E quai segreti avete
con quella contadina?

D. GIO: Ah ah! Quella meschina
è una povera matta,
che si è cacciata in testa ch'io la sposi.

MAT: Ma vi prego . . .

D. GIO: È gelosa
sin ch'io parli con voi.

D. ELV: Eh, a me badate.

D. GIO: Se vi volete divertire un poco, *(a D. Elvira)*
con lei parlate. Io intanto pien d'affetto,
sposa, mio bene, a casa mia vi aspetto.
Se volete un po' ridere, *(a Maturina)*
parlatele di me. Addio, sposina,
i sponsali farem doman mattina. *(parte)*

Scena xviii
D. Elvira e Maturina

D. ELV: Per quanto ben ti guardo,
davver pietà mi fai;
ma forse guarirai
col farti salassar.

MAT: Proprio così va detta,
ma c'è una differenza,
ch'è pazza sua eccellenza
e stenterà a sanar.

D. ELV: Ah ah! Sì, sì, meschina.

MAT: Ah ah! No, no, carina.
A 2: Ah ah! Così per ridere
la voglio stuzzicar. *(apparte)*
D. ELV: Già Don Giovanni io mi figuro
che a te di sposo la man darà.
MAT: No. Don Giovanni già per sicuro
è sposo vostro, che ben si sa.
D. ELV: Qui non v'è dubbio.
MAT: Ah ah ah ah!
A 2: Ecco qua appunto, ragazza / signora mia,
dove consiste la tua / sua pazzia!
Tutto il tuo / suo male sta dentro là! *(additando la testa)*
MAT: (Che matta vana!)
D. ELV: (Che pazza ardita!)
A 2: [Voi vi potete / Ti puoi, figliuola,] leccar le dita,
ma un tal boccone per voi / te non fa.
D. ELV: Vanne via, va', pazzarella,
ch'ei non ama una sardella.
MAT: Via pur voi, correte in fretta,
ch'ei non ama una polpetta.
D. ELV: Temeraria.
MAT: Voi insolente.
D. ELV: Mi rispetta.
MAT: Non fo niente.
[MAT: Usi lei più civiltà.
D. ELV: Faccio or ora una viltà.]
A 2: Ma no, no, che alfin si tratta
d'altercar con una matta,

e mi fai tu / fate ben pietà.
(partono)

Scena xix
Luogo rimoto circondato di cipressi dove nel mezzo si erige una cupola sostenuta da colonne con urna sepolcrale sopra la quale statua equestre del Comendatore.

Il Duca Ottavio con carta in mano ed un incisore.

Questo mausoleo, che ancor vivente
l'eroe Comendatore
apprestare si fece,
un mese non è ancor ch'è terminato.
Ed oh, come ben presto
servì di tomba a lui che l'ha ordinato.
Su quella base intanto
a caratteri d'oro
sian queste note incise.
(dà carta allo scultore, che va a formare l'iscrizione)
Tremi pur chi l'uccise,
se avvien che l'empio mai
di qua passi e le scorga,
e apprenda almen che, se occultar si puote
alla giustizia umana,
non sfuggirà del ciel l'ira sovrana. *(parte)*

Scena xx
D. Giovanni e Pasquariello

PAS: Io non so, detto sia
con vostra permissione,
se dir me lo lasciate,
qual diavolo di uom, signor, voi siate.
D. GIO: E perchè?
PAS: Non parliamo

delle amorose imprese,
che già son bagatelle . . .

D. GIO: Oh, bagatelle
sicurissimamente. E che?

PAS: Parliamo . . .
Zitto . . . Aspettate . . . Piano . . . Non vi basta
(lo scultore, in questo frattempo avendo formata l'iscrizione, parte)
che l'abbiate ammazzato,
che vi viene anche voglia
di andar vedere la sua sepoltura?
Ma questo non è un far contro natura?

D. GIO: Che stolido! Che sciocco!
Che male c'è, se vengo
a veder per diporto
come sta ben di casa ora ch'è morto?
Ecco, ecco. *(additando il mausoleo)*

PAS: Oh, cospetto! Ora vedete
tanti ma tanti ricchi,
per viver nobilmente,
guardan per fino un soldo; e poi non guardano
di spendere a migliara li ducati
per star con nobiltà dopo crepati.

D. GIO: Bravo! Qui dici bene. Ma vediamo
quell'iscrizion maiuscola.
"Di colui che mi trasse a morte ria, *(legge)*
dal ciel qui aspetto la vendetta mia."
Oh vecchio stolto! E ancor di lui più stolto
quel che la fece incidere!
La vendetta dal ciel? Mi vien da ridere.

PAS: Ah, signor, che mai dite!
Osservate, osservate che la statua
par proprio che vi guardi
con due occhi di foco al naturale.

D. GIO: Ah, ah, ah! Che animale!
Va', va' a dire alla statua
che della sua minaccia io non m'offendo,
anzi rido. E perchè veda ch'io rido
di questo a bocca piena,
meco l'invita questa sera a cena.

PAS: Chi?
D. GIO: Il Comendatore.
PAS: Eh, via!
D. GIO: Invitalo, dico. Animo, presto!
PAS: Ora vedete che capriccio è questo.

Signor Comendatore . . .
(Io rido da una parte,
dall'altra ho poi timore,
e in dubbio me ne sto.)
D. GIO: E quanto ancora aspetti?
PAS: Adesso lo farò.
A cena questa sera
v'invita il mio padrone,
se avete permissione
di movervi di qui.
(la statua china la testa replicatamente)
Ahi, ahi, ahi, ahi!
D. GIO: Cos'hai?
PAS: La testa sua è movibile,
e fecemi così.
D. GIO: Va' via, che tu sei matto.
PAS: Così, così ha fatto.
D. GIO: No.
PAS: Sì.
D. GIO: No.
PAS: Sì.
D. GIO: No.
PAS: Sì.
A 2: Che ostinazion frenetica!
Che capo è mai quel lì!
D. GIO: Aspetta, o stolido, che per convincerti
io colla statua favellerò.
V'invito a cena, Comendatore;
se ci venite, mi fate onore.
Ci venirete?
LA STATUA: Ci venirò.
PAS: Ah, [ah,] mio signore, per carità,
andiamo subito lontan di qua.

Per me certissimo più non ci sto.
D. Gio: Un'illusione quest'è diggià.
Non posso crederla mai verità.
Di te il più stolido trovar non so. *(parte)*

Scena xxi
Camera di D. Giovanni.

Lanterna, che apparecchia la tavola; poi D. Elvira

Lan: È la gran vita quella di servire
a un padron come il mio! Qui non si trova
mai ora destinata
nè al dormir nè al mangiare.
E quello che fa lui bisogna fare.
Guai a chi fa al contrario!
Quello ch'è peggio, non vien mai il salario.
Qualche mancia così per estro pazzo,
ma assai più del denaro è lo strapazzo.
(si sente a battere)
Picchiano. E chi mai diavolo vuol essere?
Vediamo. *(va ad aprire e nel vedere D. Elvira resta sorpreso)*
Oh poffar Bacco!
Illustrissima! Voi?
D. Elv: La tua sorpresa
non è senza ragione.
Avverti ch'io qui sono il tuo padrone.
Lan: Non è ancora arrivato,
vel giuro in verità. Ma zitto, io credo
che giusto adesso arrivi. È lui sicuro,
ed in cucina io me ne vado tosto
perchè si apprionti subito l'arrosto. *(parte)*

Scena xxii

D. Giovanni e D. Elvira, Pasquariello in disparte.

D. GIO: Voi, Donna Elvira, qui! Brava! La vostra
è una sorpresa amena.
Meco così restar potrete a cena.
D. ELV: No, Don Giovanni. In me vedete adesso
un'altra Donna Elvira,
dalla prima diversa. Io già non vengo
nè più a rimproverarvi,
nè più a cercar da voi l'adempimento
del vostro giuramento;
ma l'interesse vostro, il vostro bene
solo mi guida a voi, che ho tanto amato,
e tutto obblio quel ch'è fra noi passato.
PAS: (Povera donna!)
D. GIO: Dite.
D. ELV: A me dei vostri
prevertiti costumi
tutto è noto il complesso; ah, che perfino
da ognun voi l'uccisore
siete creduto del Comendatore.
L'orror de' vostri falli
scosse il mio core, e del mio error, pentita,
in un ritiro io vo a passar la vita.
Ma un estremo dolore
nel mio ritiro ancora io sentirei,
se voi, che tanto amai,
diveniste assai presto
un esempio funesto
di quell'alta giustizia e di quell'ira
che sovra di sè ogn'empio al fin s'attira.
PAS: (Povera donna!)
D. GIO: Avanti.
D. ELV: Ah, in ricompensa
di tanto amor ch'ebbi per voi, non chiedo
che il vostro pentimento,
non per me, ma per voi. Sì, vi scongiuro
colle lagrime agli occhi,

per quell'amor che per me aveste un giorno,
per quel ch'è più capace
di toccare il cor vostro,
che, richiamando la virtù smarrita,
pensar vogliate ad emendar la vita.

PAS: (Povera donna!)

D. GIO: Proseguite.

D. ELV: Ho detto
quello ch'io dir voleva.

D. GIO: Ebben, fa tardi,
o cara Donna Elvira; e perciò anch'io
vi prego, vi scongiuro,
per quell'amor che per me aveste un giorno
e per quel che il cor vostro
più movere potria,
di alloggiar questa notte in casa mia.

D. ELV: No, Don Giovanni, no. La mia carrozza
mi attende. Io vado. E se voi stesso amate,
a voi soltanto, e non più a me, pensate.

Sposa più a voi non sono,
spento è già in me l'ardore,
placido sento il core,
l'alma tranquilla ho in me.
Ben v'amerò lontana,
se alla virtù tornate.
Io parto. Addio. Restate, *(a D. Giovanni, che con caricatura vorrebbe accompagnarla)*
fermo tenete il piè.
Ah, vedo che, misero,
di me vi ridete;
di tigre le viscere
già vedo che avete.
Ma forse che il fulmine
lontano non è. *(parte)*

Scena xxiii
D. Giovanni, Pasquariello e Lanterna

D. GIO: Lo sai tu, Pasquariello,
che la sua voce languida
e quegli occhi piangenti
m'aveano quasi quasi in sen svegliato
un resto ancora dell'estinto affetto?
PAS: Ma però tutto al vento è quel che ha detto.
(va a sedere alla tavola)
D. GIO: Presto presto, alla cena.
PAS: Sì, signor, sì, signore.
D. GIO: Per altro, Pasquariello,
pensar bisogna ad emendarsi.
PAS: Oh, questo
è quel che anch'io diceva.
D. GIO: In fede mia,
che bisogna pensarci. Altri trent'anni
di bella vita, e poi
sicuramente penseremo a noi.
(Lanterna porge le piattanze a Pasquariello, e questo le mette in tavola)
PAS: Tutto sta, signor mio,
che il conto non falliate.
D. GIO: Eh? Che vorresti dir?
PAS: Niente. Cenate.
(nel mettere un piatto sulla tavola si prende una polpetta e la mette in bocca)
D. GIO: Che cos'hai? Tu mi sembra
ch'abbi una guancia gonfia.
Da quando in qua? Cos'hai?
PAS: Niente, signore.
D. GIO: Ti è venuto un tumor? Lascia ch'io senta.
(si alza e gli tocca la guancia; prende il coltello; Pasquariello sputa la polpetta)
È un tumore sicuro,
e tagliarlo convien perch'è maturo.
Ah, briccone che sei!
PAS: In verità, signore,

ch'io soltanto volea sentir un poco
se troppo sal ci aveva posto il cuoco.

D. GIO: Bene, bene. Ora, via. Vedo, meschino,
che tu hai molta fame, e dopo cena
io bisogno ho di te. Siedi pertanto,
e meco mangia qui.

PAS: Dite davvero?

D. GIO: Siedi e mangia.

PAS: Ubbidisco al dolce impero. *(siede alla tavola)*
Ehi, Lanterna. Posata e tovagliolo.

LAN: (Gode il favor sovrano
solo costui perchè gli fa il mezzano.)

D. GIO: Olà! Finchè si mangia
voglio che il mio concerto di stromenti
sentir si faccia.

PAS: Bravo! Ottimamente!
Mangiaremo così più allegramente.
(segue concerto di stromenti; Don Giovanni e Pasquariello mangiano; Lanterna, a misura che Pasquariello gira la testa, subito gli cambia il piatto)

PAS: Ma potere del mondo!
Sei troppo attento per cambiar di tondo!
Guarda, Lanterna mio, che nel mostaccio
questo piatto tal quale or or ti caccio.

D. GIO: Da bere. *(viene servito)*

PAS: Animo, presto,
da bere ancora a me. *(un servitore gli presenta un bicchiere; Pasquariello vuol bere, e D. Giovanni lo trattiene)*

D. GIO: Fermati, piano.

PAS: Cosa c'è?

D. GIO: Pria di bere,
un brindisi hai da fare.

PAS: Ora vengo. Aspettate. L'ho trovato:
"Alla salute del mio signor nonno."

D. GIO: Oibò, oibò!

PAS: Ma, dunque,
a chi farlo conviene?

D. GIO: L'hai da far, l'hai da far . . . Sentimi bene.

Far devi un brindisi alla città
che noi viaggiando di qua e di là
abbiamo trovato ch'è la miglior,
dove le femmine, tutte graziose,
son le più belle, le più vezzose,
le più adorabili del sesso lor.

PAS: Questo vostr'estro non disapprovo.
Senza pensarci diggià la trovo,
e ci scommetto che già la so.
Quest'è in Italia.

D. GIO: Dici benissimo.

PAS: Questa è Venezia.

D. GIO: Bravo bravissimo!
Tu già l'hai detta.

PAS: Oh benedetta!

PAS: Io farò il brindisi come potrò.
D. GIO: Via, su, fa il brindisi, ch'io sentirò.
LAN: Io "viva" al brindisi risponderò.

PAS: Faccio un brindisi di gusto
a Venezia singolar.
Nei signori il cor d'Augusto
si va proprio a ritrovar.
V'è nell'ordine civile
quel che v'ha di più gentile,
e nel ceto anche inferiore
v'è il buon core e il buon trattar.
(suonano gli stromenti da fiato; Pasquariello vuol bere, e D. Giovanni lo trattiene)

D. GIO: Piano, piano.

PAS: Cos'è stato?

D. GIO: Tu ti scordi del bel sesso.
Pria di ber, anche allo stesso
devi il brindisi indrizzar.

PAS: Sì, signore. *(beve tutto il vino)*

D. GIO: Cosa fai?

PAS: Rifondete adesso il vino.
Mascolino e femminino
non vo' insieme mescolar.
(vien riempito di nuovo il bicchier di Pasquariello)

PAS: Alle donne veneziane
questo brindisi or presento,
che son piene di talento,
di bellezza e d'onestà.
Son tanto leggiadre
con quei zendaletti
che solo a guardarle
vi movon gli affetti.
Se poi le trattate,
il cor ci lasciate;
non han che dolcezza,
che grazia e bontà.
(suonano li strumenti; Pasquariello beve)
(in questo si sente a battere replicatamente alla porta)

LAN: Signor, signor, sentite.

D. GIO: A un'ora sì importuna
non ha creanza alcuna
chi a batter vien così.

LAN: Sentite nuovamente.

D. GIO: Va' a dire all'insolente
che adesso non ricevo,
che torni al nuovo dì. *(Lanterna parte, poi torna spaventato correndo e casca in terra)*

PAS: Ma se per accidente
mai fosse qualche bella?

D. GIO: / PAS: [Si cangieria favella,
e si faria star qui.]

LAN: Ahimè! Ahimè!

D. GIO: Cos'hai?

LAN: Ahimè!

PAS: Ma cosa è stato?

D. GIO: Costui è spiritato;
va' tu a veder cos'è.
(Pasquariello parte, poi subito ritorna spaventato ancor esso)
Via, parla, su, animale,
che cosa hai tu veduto? *(a Lanterna)*

PAS: Ahimè, ch'è qui quel tale . . .
Quel tale si è venuto . . .
Cioè, quello . . . Ahimè, che spasimo!

Oh poveretto me!
(D. Giovanni prende il lume e va per affacciarsi alla porta; in questo il Comendatore; Pasquariello si caccia sotto la tavola)

Scena xxiv
Il Comendatore e detti.

D. GIO: Siedi, Comendator. Mai fin ad ora
credere non potei che dal profondo
tornasser l'ombre ad apparir nel mondo.
Se creduto l'avessi,
troveresti altra cena.
Pure se di mangiar voglia ti senti,
mangia, che quel che c'è t'offro di core,
e teco mangierò senza timore.

COM: Di vil cibo non si pasce
chi lasciò l'umana spoglia.
A te guidami altra voglia,
ch'è diversa dal mangiar.
D. GIO: Pasquariello, dove sei?
Torna subito al tuo sito.
PAS: Non mi sento più appetito.
D. GIO: Vieni fuori, non tardar.
(Pasquariello esce e si mette in disparte)
PAS: Se la febre avessi indosso,
non potrei così tremar.
D. GIO: Tu non mangi, tu non bevi. *(al Comendatore)*
Cosa brami or qui da noi?
Canti e suoni, se tu vuoi,
io ti posso far servir.
COM: Fa' pur quello che ti aggrada.
D. GIO: Pasquariello, fatti avanti.
D. GIO: Che si suoni e che si canti
per poterlo divertir.
PAS: Tutti i muscoli ho tremanti,
non poss'io più bocca aprir.
COM: Basta così. M'ascolta.

Tu m'invitasti a cena;
ci venni senza pena.
Or io te inviterò;
verrai tu a cena meco?

PAS: Oibò, signor, non può.

D. GIO: Non ho timore in petto.
Sì, che il tuo invito accetto.
Verrò col servo.

PAS: Oibò!

COM: Dammi la man per pegno.

D. GIO: Eccola. Oimè, qual gelo!

COM: Pentiti; e temi il cielo,
che stanco è omai di te.

D. GIO: Lasciami, vecchio insano.

COM: Empio, ti scuoti in vano.
Pentiti, Don Giovanni.

D. GIO: Ahi, quai crudeli affanni!
Ma il cor non trema in me.

COM: Termina, o tristo, gli anni,
vedi il tuo fin qual'è.

PAS: Ah, di theriaca[1] i panni
m'empio di sotto affè.

(segue trasformazione della camera in infernale, restandovi solo le prime quinte dove Pasquariello spaventato si rifugia; D. Giovanni tra le furie)

Ahi, che orrore! Che spavento!
Ah, che barbaro tormento!
Che insoffribile martir!
Mostri orrendi, furie irate,
di straziarmi, deh, cessate!
Ah, non posso più soffrir.

(sparisce l'infernale e torna come prima la camera di D. Giovanni)

1. Theriac, a molasseslike medicinal substance.

Scena ultima

Lanterna, Maturina, D. Elvira, D. Ximena, Duca Ottavio, Pasquariello

MAT., D. OTT., D. ELV., D. XIM:
Qual strepito è questo che abbiamo sentito?
Lanterna che dice, che qui ci chiamò?

PAS: Oimè! Già son morto, già sono arrostito.
Un pelo, un capello in me più non ho.

LAN: Qui qui l'ho veduto ed io son fuggito.
Lui dicavi il resto, ch'io niente più so.

PAS: I diavoli, il foco, il Comendatore . . .
Sentite il fetore che indosso averò.

D. OTT: Che diavolo dici?

D. ELV: Tu fai confusione.

D. XIM: Dov'è Don Giovanni?

MAT: Dov'è il tuo padrone?

PAS: Signori, aspettate, ch'io tutto dirò.
Di lui pian pian vel dico,
non se ne parli più.
Coi brutti *barabai*
qui se n'è andato giù.
Ah, non avessi mai
veduto quel che fu!
E chi non crede al caso
a me che accosti il naso,
che dell'odor diabolico
io credo ancor d'aver.

GLI ALTRI: Misero! Resto estatic a/o,
ma è meglio di tacer.

TUTTI: Più non facciasi parola
del terribile successo,
ma pensiamo in vece adesso
di poterci rallegrar.
Che potressimo mai far?

DONNE: A a a, io vo' cantare.
Io vo' mettermi a saltar.

D. OTT: La chitarra io vo' suonare.

LAN: Io suonar vo' il contrabasso.
PAS: Ancor io per far del chiasso
il fagotto vo' suonar.
D. OTT: Tren, tren, trinchete trinchete tre.
LAN: Flon flon flon flon flon flon.
PAS: Pu pu pu pu pu pu pu.
TUTTI: Che bellissima pazzia!
Che stranissima armonia!
Così allegri si va a star.

fine

4

Don Juan in Music: Performance Data, 1669 to 1800

Herewith follows a list of performances with music of the Don Juan legend from the earliest, *L'empio punito,* in 1669 to 1800, an arbitrary cutoff date. Each entry includes, if available, a year of performance, a season or specific date, a title followed by an indication in parentheses of the genre, a city and theater of first performance, a composer and a librettist or choreographer. While I have tried to be as precise and as complete as possible, details are often sketchy or simply unavailable, nor are all sources totally reliable. Since I have not been able to verify every piece of information, I have given the source of each listing. Titles for the same work sometimes vary from source to source. I have not tried to make them uniform but have left them as reported. Genre specifications likewise depend, at times, on source indications and not on my own observation. Some listings include a comments section in which problems concerning the entry are discussed or additional information about it is furnished.

I have taken particular care to supply as much information as possible about Don Juan ballets—a program, a list of scene changes, a list of characters—since this sort of data is rare in and of itself and very hard to locate. I have not included performances of Mozart's *Don Giovanni* or any of its spin-offs, since such information is beyond the scope of the present study.

Sources have been identified only by the author's last name and a short title. Detailed information can be found in the Bibliography.

Items are listed in chronological order beginning with the year. Within each year, the most comprehensive date is always listed first; so "1792, Spring" precedes "1792, April." Entries with identical dates are then listed alphabetically by city.

I have drawn considerably from the thirty-six volumes of the *Indice de' spettacoli teatrali* and the *Indice de' teatrali spettacoli* published in Milan between 1764 and 1800. While items included in *Indice* entries seem to be generally reliable, it is evident that there were many errors of omission. The same cities are not listed every year in every volume; in some volumes, performance information for cities as important as Venice is lacking altogether; there is relatively little interest in what is happening outside Italy; some volumes list ballets, some do not. I do not pretend, therefore, that the present list is in any way exhaustive; further investigation would certainly turn up additional items. There must have been, for example, many more *foire* performances than those included here. Yet even if the present list is incomplete, it nonetheless indicates the great popularity of the legend during the latter decades of the eighteenth century.

Year: 1669 Date: 17 February; several additional performances
Title: *L'empio punito* (opera)
City: Rome Theater: Palazzo Colonna
Composer: Alessandro Melani
Librettist: Filippo Acciaiuoli, Giovanni Filippo Apolloni
Source: Macchia, *Vita avventure,* 81.
Comments: Parsons *(Mellen Opera Reference* 3:1180) is certainly in error listing the first performance as having taken place at the Teatro Cocomero, Florence, 1675.

Year: 1684
Title: *Le Festin de Pierre* (play with ballet)
City: Chambord, France
Text: Molière, Thomas Corneille
Music: ? Choreographer: Sieur de Lastre
Source: Singer, *Don Juan Theme,* 113; program in *Le Moliériste,* 11–16.
Comments: Performed by the Troupe Royale de Chambord. The entertainment is advertised as "le veritable et dernier festin de Pierre." The original program describes the action of the ballet as follows: "Premier intermede: Le Theatre represente une campagne & dans l'enfoncement une mer flottante avec des rochers sur le rivage, c'est sur cette mer que D. Jüan a fait naufrage, où plusieurs matelots qui l'ont sauvé se réjoüissent entr'eux de l'argent qu'ils en ont receu par une entrée de Ballet dont l'air & les pas conviennent merveilleusement au sujet. . . . Second intermede: Des débauchés amis de D. Jüan font connoître leur joye par une danse toute pleine de mouvemens conformes à leurs humeurs emportées. . . . Troisieme intermede: Quatre des Statües qui accompagnent le tombeau se détachent par des pas de desespoir & des figures pleines de leur douleur, expriment l'horreur de l'assassinat commis en la personne du Commandeur & semblent par leurs pas faire des voeux au Ciel pour la punition d'un tel assassin. . . . Quatrieme intermede: Des Païsans d'un hameau voisin font voir leur joye par

une danse fort agreable; cette entrée n'est pas une des moins belles et des moins divertissantes de ce grand spectacle. . . . Cinquieme et dernier intermede: Trois demons paroissent & témoignent par une entrée de Ballet de la plus grande force & du mouvement le plus vîte, la joye qu'ils ressentent d'avoir dans leur possession l'Athée, ce qui finit le divertissement."

Year: 1713 Date: 3 February
Title: *Le Festin de Pierre* (vaudeville musical)
City: Paris Theater: Foire Saint-Germaine
Music: Based on popular airs, arranger unknown Text: Le Tellier
Source: Lagrave, "Don Juan," 272; Spaziani, *Don Giovanni dagli scenari,* 73–95. Spaziani publishes three surviving manuscripts and discusses the difficult problem of performance dates.

Year: 1714
Title: *Le Festin de Pierre* (vaudeville musical)
City: Paris Theater: Foire Saint-Germaine
Music: Based on popular airs, arranger unknown Text: Le Tellier
Source: Spaziani, *Don Giovanni dagli scenari,* 73–95.
Comments: Also played at the Foire Saint-Laurant.

Year: 1720
Title: *Le Festin de Pierre* (vaudeville musical)
City: Paris Theater: Foire Saint-Germaine or Saint-Laurant
Music: Based on popular airs, arranger unknown Text: Le Tellier [?]
Source: Spaziani, *Don Giovanni dagli scenari,* 73–95.

Year: 1720 Date: September
Title: *Le Festin de Pierre* (opéra comique)
City: Paris Theater: Château de Bercy
Composer: ? Librettist: Le Tellier
Source: Brenner, *Bibliographical List of Plays,* #8475.

Year: 1721
Title: *Le Festin de Pierre* (vaudeville musical)
City: Paris Theater: Foire Saint-Germaine
Music: Based on popular airs, arranger unknown Text: Le Tellier [?]
Source: Spaziani, *Don Giovanni dagli scenari,* 73–95.

Year: 1734 Season: carnival
Title: *La pravità castigata* (opera)
City: Brno Theater: Teatro Novissimo della Taverna

Composer: Eustachio Bambini Librettist: ?

Source: Opera libretto, University Library, Brno

Comments: Sartori's recently issued *I libretti italiani* (4:457) lists a *Pravità castigata,* "rappresentazione morale per musica," given in Prague in 1730. No composer or librettist is identified. I was not able to obtain a copy of the text before publication.

Year: 1746 Date: 19 February

Title: *L'Athée foudroyé* (pantomime)

City: Paris Theater: Foire Saint-Germaine

Composer: ? Librettist: ?

Source: Brenner, *Bibliographical List of Plays,* #393.

Comments: I assume this is a Don Juan version only because of its title.

Year: 1746 Date: 19 September

Title: *Le Grand festin de Pierre ou L'athée foudroyé* (pantomime)

City: Paris Theater: Foire Saint-Laurant

Composer: ? Librettist: Le Tellier [?]

Director of Troupe: Jean Restier and Jean-François Colin

Source: Brenner, *Bibliographical List of Plays,* #1365; Singer, *Don Juan Theme,* 154.

Comments: According to Singer, this was a "pantomime, ballet, spectacle, with fireworks."

Year: 1750

Title: *La pravità castigata* (opera)

City: Strasbourg

Composer: Eustachio Bambini Librettist: ?

Source: Steiger, *Opernlexikon* 3:972; opera libretto, Reiss-Museum der Stadt Mannheim, Theatersammlung.

Comments: According to the libretto: "Da rappresentarsi in Argentina, nel nuovo theatro." Bambini was appointed Director of Italian Opera in Strasbourg in 1750. The cast of characters listed in the libretto indicates that the part of Rosalba was taken by Anna Tonelli. She was Bambini's wife. Unlike the 1734 version, the roles of Don Giovanni and Manfredi, king of Naples, are now sung by men; the role of Don Ottavio is taken by a woman.

Year: 1761 Date: 17 October

Title: *Don Juan ou Le festin de Pierre* (ballet)

City: Vienna Theater: Burgtheater

Composer: Gluck Choreographer: Angiolini

With: Regnard's *Le Joueur*

Year: 1761
Date: 18, 21, 22, 25 October; 3, 15, 16, 18, 24 November; 1 December
Title: *Don Juan ou Le festin de Pierre* (ballet)
City: Vienna Theater: Burgtheater
Composer: Gluck Choreographer: Angiolini
Source: Croll, "Glucks *Don Juan* Freigesprochen," 15.
Comments: Croll is the first to date the repeat performances in Vienna accurately. He indicates that none was at the Kärntnertor Theater as commonly believed and that the fire that destroyed that theater on 3 November 1761 was not due to the infernal flames of Gluck's ballet, as is always stated, but to those of a comedy with the same title by Gottfried Prehauser.

Year: After 1761
Title: *Don Juan ou Le festin de Pierre* (ballet)
City: Paris
Composer: Gluck Choreographer: ?
Source: Engländer, *Don Juan/Semiramis,* x.

Year: 1762 Date: 8 February
Title: *Don Juan ou Le festin de Pierre* (ballet)
City: Vienna Theater: Burgtheater
Composer: Gluck Choreographer: Angiolini
Source: Engländer, *Don Juan/Semiramis,* x.

Year: 1762 Date: 12 November
Title: *Don Juan ou Le festin de Pierre* (ballet)
City: Vienna Theater: Burgtheater
Composer: Gluck Choreographer: Angiolini
Source: Engländer, *Don Juan/Semiramis,* x.

Year: 1763–67
Title: *Don Juan* (ballet)
Composer: ? Choreographer: A. Sacco, after Angiolini
Source: *Enciclopedia dello spettacolo: Indice-repertorio,* 253.

Year: 1763 Date: 5, 7 April
Title: *Don Juan ou Le festin de Pierre* (ballet)
City: Vienna Theater: Burgtheater
Composer: Gluck Choreographer: Angiolini
Source: Engländer, *Don Juan/Semiramis,* x.

Year: 1763 Date: 4 October
Title: *Don Juan ou Le festin de Pierre* (ballet)
City: Vienna Theater: Schönbrunner Schloßtheater
Composer: Gluck Choreographer: Angiolini
With: Traetta's *Ifigenia in Tauride*
Source: Engländer, *Don Juan/Semiramis*, x.
Comments: Engländer's list includes a ballet performance with Traetta's opera in 1763. He then lists a second ballet performance specifically on 4 October 1763 but without mentioning an accompanying opera. The two ballet performances were really the same one. Traetta's opera was first presented on 4 October. Angiolini did the choreography for the opera as well.

Year: 1765
Title: *Don Juan oder das steinerne Gastmahl* (ballet)
City: Parma
Composer: Gluck Choreographer: ?
Source: Farinelli, *Don Giovanni*, 141.

Year: 1766 Season: carnival
Title: *Il convitato di pietra* (ballet)
City: Turin Theater: Teatro Regio
Composer: Giuseppe Antonio Le Messier, based on Gluck's score.
Choreographer: Vincenzo Galeotti, based on Angiolini's version. Galeotti studied with Angiolini.
With: Bertoni's *Tancredi*
Source: *Enciclopedia dello spettacolo*, s.v. "Galeotti"; opera libretto, Library of Congress
Comments: The opera libretto indicates that the ballet contained the following scenes: "Strada con case. Bosco. Sepolcri con statua equestre. Sala per il convito. Di nuovo sepolcri. Infernale."

Year: 1768
Title: *Maschinen-ballet Don Juan* (ballet)
City: Cologne
Composer: ? Director: Joseph Félix von Kurz
With: *Der Kavalier und die Dame, oder die zwei gleicher edlen Seelen*
Source: Gendarme de Bévotte, *La Légende de Don Juan*, 367. Singer's similar entry (*Don Juan Theme*, 42) does not include Kurz's name.

Year: from 1769
Title: *Don Juan oder der steinerne Gast* (ballet)
City: Vienna, Leipzig
Composer: Gluck [?]

Choreographer: Friedrich Ludwig Schröder with the Ackerman Troupe

Source: Haas, "Die Wiener Ballet," 32; Singer, *Don Juan Theme,* 164; Litzmann, "Don Juan als Ballet."

Comments: A repertory item. Litzmann's summary of a ballet program from Hanover, 26 April 1773, makes it clear that this ballet had little to do with Angiolini's version.

> Don Philippo kommt mit Musikanten, um seiner Geliebten Donna Anna eine Serenade zu bringen. Don Juan mit seinem Diener sieht ihn, ersticht ihn, nimmt seinen Mantel, giebt Befehl, den Leichnam fortzuschaffen und die Musikanten herbeizuführen. Don Juan in's Haus. Serenade. Beim Schluß derselben Lärm im Innern, Don Pedro, Anna's Vater erscheint, Don Juan mit dem Degen verfolgend. Don Juan ersticht ihn und flieht. Im zweiten Akt kommt Don Juan zu hochzeitfeiernden Bauern, verliebt sich in die Braut, entführt fie. Das Theater verwandelt sich: Don Pedro's Monument, Don Juan mit der entführten Braut von den Bauern verfolgt, das Mädchen sträubt sich, er ersticht sie und entfernt sich. Nach Abgang der Bauern tritt er wieder auf, "besieht das Monument, bittet die Statue zu Gaste: sie antwortet ihm unter einem Blitz mit Kopfnicken. Don Juan entfernt sich bestürzt, der Diener folgt ihm." Scenenverwandlung: Gaststube: Spanier tanzen, wollen sich zu Tische setzen. Don Juan mischt sich unter sie. Es klopft, die Statue erscheint, "alles läuft davon, nur Don Juan nöthiget ihn unerschrocken zu Tische." Die Statue bittet Don Juan bei dem Monument zu erscheinen und geht. Don Juan zwingt seinen Bedienten eine Laterne zu holen und ihn zu begleiten. Scenenverwandlung: Das Monument. "Die Statue steht neben dem Pferde." Flucht des Dieners. "Der Geist vermahnt Don Juan, von seinem ruchlosen Leben abzustehen, da dieser alle Warnungen verachtet, ergreift ihn der Geist bei der Hand und schleudert ihn von sich. In dem Augenblick verwandelt sich das Theater in den Schlund der Hölle, eine Schaar Furien peinigen den Don Juan und stürzen sich mit ihm in den Höllenschlund."

Year: 1769 Date: 12 January; 17 June

Title: *Don Giovanni Tenorio* (ballet)

City: Naples Theater: San Carlo

Composer: ? Choreographer: Onorato Viganò

Source: Roscioni, *Il Teatro di San Carlo,* 52, 54.

Year: 1770

Title: *Don Juan ou Le festin de Pierre* (ballet pantomime)

City: Cassel; Court of Landgrave Frederick II of Hesse-Cassel

Theater: Komödienhaus

Composer: various Choreographer: Etienne Lauchery

Source: Olivier, *Les Comédiens français,* 53, 99.

Comments: Cast of characters: Don Juan, Inès, Sganarelle, la statue du Commandeur, Dona Elvire, Don Silvestre, un paysan, Mathurin, Jacqueline.

Year: 1772 Date: June
Title: *Don Juan ou Le festin de Pierre* (ballet)
City: Vienna Theater: Schönbrunner Schloßtheater
Composer: Gluck Choreographer: Vincenzo Rossi
Source: Haas, "Der Wiener Bühnentanz," 85–86.
Comments: A four-scene version with expanded servant role. A handwritten manuscript in the Paris Conservatory, Ms. N. 20, may be a later version of this one by Rossi. It too is in four scenes with an expanded servant role. Unfortunately, no date has been established for it. The text, as published by Marks ("Reform of Subject and Style," 179–81), is as follows.

Programm du Ballet de Dom-juan, ou bien, du festin du pierre, pour l'intelligence de la musique, que le Sr. Gluck a faite à Vienne sur ce sujet. La scene represente une place publique de Madrid. On voit d'un coté la maison du Commandeur et de l'autre coté une promenade. Dom-juan avec son valet precedent une troupe de musiciens, que ce dernier place sous les fenetres de la niece du Commandeur. Les musiciens commencement leur serenade avec des guitares, sans autre instrument; la nièce du Commandeur paroit à la fenetre, et fait ouvrir la porte à Dom-juan, qui entre dans la maison du Commandeur tandis que la serenade se continue. Le Commandeur surprend Dom-juan avec sa niece, et veut le tuer. Celui-ci met l'épée à la main dans la maison du Commandeur pour défendre sa vie. On entend le cliqueti des épées dans la rue. La porte du Commandeur s'ouvre, les musiciens le voyent l'épée à la main à la poursuite de Dom-juan, se sauvent. Le combat entre le Commandeur et Dom-juan est continue dans la rue. Le Commandeur est blessé, et se retire du coté opposé à sa maison, en tombant à chaque pas, et s'apuyant sur son épée pour se relever. La scene change et represente une salle de la maison de Dom-juan, où l'on voit tous les aprêts d'une fête. Les amis de Dom-juan la célèbrent par leur danses tandisque l'on prépare le festin. Il y a un pas de deux entre Dom-juan et la nièce du Commandeur. Le valet de Dom-juan avertit que l'on est servi; comme on se met à table, on entend fraper fortement à la porte. Le valet de Dom-juan prend une bougie pour aller voir qui c'est; il est epouvanté en apercevant la statue du Commandeur qui s'avance gravement vers Dom-juan jusqu'auprès de la table. Les amis de Dom-juan, et la nièce du Commandeur ainsi que le valet de Dom-juan, épouvantées, prennant la fuite et laissent Dom-juan seul avec la statue. Il l'invite à se mettre à table et à manger. La statue s'assesit; comme elle voit Dom-juan pret à la servir, elle se leve et invite Dom-juan à venir souper avec elle dans le mausolée du Commandeur. Dom-juan promet de s'y rendre et reconduit la statue, qui s'en retourne. Pendant que Dom-juan l'accompagne, ses amis reviennent, et expriment par leur gestes la crainte, dont ils sont encore saisis. Dom-juan reparoit triomphant; à sa vue la terreur s'empare encore de tous ses amis, qui fuyent de nouveau et le laissent seul avec son valet, qu'il arrête comme il tâche de l'esquiver. Dom-juan, qui veut sortir pour se rendre dans le mausolée où il doit souper avec la statue, fait signe à son valet d'aller chercher son chapeau et son épée. Le valet les apporte. Dom-juan lui fait signe de le suivre au mausolée. Le valet refuse en alleguant sa peur. Dom-juan insiste, le valet souffre toutes sortes de violences sans ceder. Dom-juan prend le parti d'y aller seul. Le valet le laisse sortir, et par ses démonstrations envoye à tous les diables un maitre, qui veut le forçer à participer au danger, auquel il va s'exposer de son propre mouvement. La scene change et represente le mausolée du Commandeur. Dom-juan y arrive. A l'aspect de ce lieu, terrible par l'horreur du silence, qui y regne, Dom-juan chancelle sur le parti qu'il doit prendre; la peur paroit s'emparer de ses sens. La statue du Commandeur paroit; à sa vue, Dom-juan rapelle son courage, et la vanité le fait triompher de sa terreur. La statue du Commandeur, qui semble lire dans l'âme de Dom-juan qu'il n'agit que par les mouvemens d'une fausse et vaine gloire, lui montre le ciel, et le serrant tendrement entre ses bras, lui met à differentes reprises la main sur son coeur, qu'elle cherche à toucher par ses remonstrances. Dom-juan les meprise. La statue fait des nouveaux efforts pour soustraire Dom-juan à sa perte, que son obstination semble rendre inevitable. Tout cela est inutile, Dom-juan repond en haussant les epaules et regarde la statue d'un air moqueur. Elle lui fait entendre les gemissements des ames qui subissent la peine due à leur impieté. Dom-juan n'en est point touché, ni meme emu. Le Commandeur entre en fureur; il saisit Dom-juan par le bras, et frape violemment du pied, en lui montrant la terre prete à s'ouvrir pour l'engloutir dans l'abime qui va se creuser sous ses pieds jusqu'aux Enfers. Dom-juan est toujours le meme. Enfin la statue du Commandeur voyant la mesure de l'impieté de Dom-juan comblée, le livre à son mauvais destin en le prècipitant dans le gouffre qui s'entrouve sous ses pieds. La scene change et represente les Enfers, où l'on voit Dom-juan se debattre au milieu des demons qui dansent autour de lui la torche à la main, et qui le poursuivent sans cesse. Dom-juan paroit enfin ouvrir les yeux sur l'horreur de sa situation. Il est au desespoir d'avoir causé lui meme sa perte par son entetèment. Il cherche une issue pour s'echaper des Enfers; comme il croit en avoir trouvé une, il est arreté dans la fuite par une troupe de furies, qui lui barrent le chemin, et font siffler autour de lui les serpens dont elles ont la tête environnée, et qu'elles excitent avec leur flambeaux. Dom-juan ne se connoit plus, il donne toutes les marques du plus affreux desespoir, et dans l'exces de sa rage il regarde comme son unique ressource la fureur des demons, auxquels il se livre et s'abandonne de lui meme pour decider enfin son sort. Il est enchainé par les demons, et precipité par eux dans le plus profond des Enfers, d'où l'on voit de temps en temps sortir des tourbillons de la flamme qui le consume.

Year: 1772 Date: 28 December
Title: *Don Juan oder das klägliche Ende eines Verstockten Atheisten* (musical farce)
Composer: ? Librettist: Justinus Knecht
Source: Singer, *Don Juan Theme,* 109; Farinelli, *Don Giovanni,* 145.

Year: 1775 Date: October
Title: *Il convitato di pietra* (ballet)

City: Padua Theater: Teatro Nuovo
Composer: ? Choreographer: Giuseppe Forti
With: Gazzaniga's *L'isola di Alcina*
Source: Brunelli, *I teatri di Padova,* 175; *Indice,* 1775–76, 24.

Year: 1776 Season: carnival
Title: *Il convitato di pietra o sia Il dissoluto* (opera)
City: Prague Theater: Il Reggio Teatro di Praga
Composer: Vincenzo Righini Librettist: Nunziato Porta
Source: Opera libretto, Krimice, Czechoslovakia
Comments: *Indice,* 1775–76, 80, lists the title as *Il Don Giovanni.* See chap. 2, note 39, for a discussion of Porta's authorship of the libretto.

Year: 1777–78 Season: carnival
Title: *Il convitato di pietra* (ballet)
City: Florence Theater: Teatro della Pergola
Composer: ? Choreographer: Paolo Franchi
Source: Morini, *La R. Accademia,* 68.

Year: 1777
Title: *Don Juan* (ballet)
City: Munich
Composer: Gluck Choreographer: Crux
Source: Price, "Don Juan," 105.

Year: 1777
Title: *Il convitato di pietra o sia Il dissoluto / Das steinerne gastmahl oder Der ruchlose* (opera)
City: Prague Theater: Königliches Theater in der Kotzen
Composer: Vincenzo Righini Librettist: Nunziato Porta
Source: Opera libretto in Italian and German, Library of Congress; Sonneck, *Catalogue* 1:318, for theater.

Year: 1777 Season: carnival
Title: *Il convitato di pietra* (opera)
City: Venice Theater: Teatro Tron di San Cassiano
Composer: Giuseppe Calegari Librettist: ?
Source: Opera libretto, Library of Congress.

Year: 1777 Date: 21 August
Title: *Il convitato di pietra o sia Il dissoluto* (opera)
City: Vienna Theater: Kärntnertor Theater
Composer: Vincenzo Righini Librettist: Nunziato Porta

Source: Opera libretto, Library of Congress; Sonneck, *Catalogue* 1:318, for specific date and theater.

Year: 1778 Date: May through August
Title: *Don Juan, czyli bankiet Piotra* [*Don Juan or Peter's Banquet*] (ballet)
City: Warsaw
Composer: Hart Choreographer: Caselli
Source: Bernacki, *Teatr, dramat i muzyka* 2:326–27.
Comments: Also performed: 1779; 28 Jan., 22 Feb. 1781; 3 May 1789; 24 Jan., 9 March, 2 Sept., 27 Dec. 1790; 15 Feb. 1791; 15 May, 20 June, 15 Sept., 14 Nov. 1792; 11 Aug., 5 Oct., 19 Nov., 19 Dec. 1793.

Year: 1779–80
Title: *Don Juan oder der steinerne Gast* (ballet)
City: Salzburg
Composer: Gluck Choreographer: Peter Vogt with Johannes Böhm's theater company
Source: Bacher, "Ein Frankfurter Szenar," 574.

Year: 1780 Season: carnival
Title: *Il convitato di pietra* (ballet)
City: Como
Composer: ? Choreographer: Giuseppe Castagna
With: Paisiello's *La frascatana* and *L'innocente fortunata*
Source: *Indice, 1779–80*, 60.

Year: 1780 Season: carnival
Title: *Il convitato di pietra* (ballet)
City: Florence Theater: Teatro della Pergola
Composer: ? Choreographer: Domenico Rossi
With: *La Nitteti*, various composers
Source: *Indice, 1779–80*, 65–66; Sartori, *I libretti italiani* 4:239.

Year: 1780 Date: second half of year
Title: *Il Don Giovanni* (probably) (opera)
City: Warsaw Theater: Teatr Narodowy
Composer: Gioacchino Albertini (probably)
Librettist: Nunziato Porta (probably)
Source: Raszewski, "Rondo alla Polacca," 179.
Comments: See chap. 2, note 51, for additional information.

Year: 1780 Date: 4 November
Title: *Il convitato di pietra* (ballet)

City: Naples Theater: San Carlo
Composer: Gluck Choreographer: Domenico Rossi
Source: Roscioni, *Il Teatro di San Carlo,* 78; Engländer, *Don Juan/Semiramis,* x.
Comments: Engländer lists this performance as Gluck's *Don Juan.* He gives the year and city but no theater or choreographer. Roscioni gives a specific date, title, theater, and choreographer but lists no composer.

Year: 1781–90
Title: *Don Juan oder der steinerne Gast* (ballet)
City: Frankfurt and elsewhere in Germany
Composer: Gluck Choreographer: Peter Vogt with Johannes Böhm's theater company
Source: Bacher, "Ein Frankfurter Szenar," 570–74.
Comments: This five-act ballet is at once an expansion of Angiolini's version (and so acknowledged by Vogt) and a return to a more traditional and less original story line. The following synopsis is from a *scenario* published in Frankfurt and reprinted by Bacher (572–73).

> Kurzer Inhalt. Erster Aufzug. Gasse bey Nachtszeit. Don Juan bringt Amarillis, des Gouverneurs Tochter eine Nachtmusik, unter welcher er sich in ihr Haus schleicht. Pedrillo, sein Diener, schreibt diese Eroberung auf ein langes Verzeichnis, aus dem schon die übrigen von seinem Herrn verführten Mädchen stehen. Es wird Lärm und die Musik flieht. Don Pedro verfolgt den Schänder seiner Ehre mit bloßem Degen, empfängt aber von Don Juan einen tödlichen Stich, der ihm sein Leben raubt. Zweyter Aufzug. Großer Saal in einen Gasthause auf dem Lande. Eine Hochzeit von Schäfern hält ihren Einzug. Don Juan, der sich seines begangenen Mordes halber flüchten mußte, Kömmt in den nemlichen Gasthof. Er mischt sich unter die Tanzenden, entführt aber zuletzt die Braut, die die Brautleute, da sie es bemerken, von Pedrillo mit Gewalt zurückfordern, der sie ihnen auch auf eine lächerliche Art wieder zu schaffen verspricht. Dritter Aufzug. Garten mit der prächtigen Statue Don Pedros zu Pferde. Don Juan beredet die Braut ihn zu lieben. Sogleich erscheint Pedrillo und meldet den Lärm, der im Gasthofe sey. Die Braut entflieht, und Don Juan, der ihr nach will, erblickt die Statue. Er befiehlt Pedrillo sie zum Essen einzuladen, welches dieser nach vielen Drohnungen mit Furcht und Zittern verrichtet. Der Stein winkt ihm sein Ja zu, worüber er vor Schrecken außer sich davonläuft. Vierter Aufzug. Der obige Saal mit gedeckter Tafel. Eben will man sich zu Tische setzen, als drey starke Schläge gehört werden. Pedrillo, der sehen muß was es sey, stürzt zurück herein, und der Geist Don Pedros folgt ihm auf dem Fuße nach. Er vertreibt alle Gäste und ladet den frechen Don Juan in der Mitternachtsstunde auf den nächsten Gottesacker, wohin ihm dieser auch voll Ausgelassenheit zu folgen verspricht. Fünfter Aufzug. Ein Kirchhof. Don Juan erscheint, und erblickt den Geist, der ihn sanft zur Buße mahnt. Er hingegen spottet seiner so lange, bis sich die Bühne in die offene Hölle verwandelt. Don Pedro versinkt und Don Juan endet sein ruchloses Leben unter tausend feurigen Martern und der äußersten Verzweiflung.

Year: 1781
Title: *Don Juan* (ballet)
Composer: ? Choreographer: F. Rosetti [?]
Source: *Enciclopedia dello spettacolo: Indice-repertorio,* 253.

Year: 1781 Season: carnival
Title: *Il convitato di pietra* (ballet)
City: Naples Theater: San Carlo
Composer: ? Choreographer: Domenico Rossi
Source: *Indice, 1780–81,* 83.

Year: 1781 Date: July through September
Title: *Il convitato di pietra o sia Il dissoluto* (opera)
City: Esterháza
Composer: Vincenzo Righini Librettist: Nunziato Porta
Source: Opera libretto, Harvard University
Comments: This text from Esterháza is the only Don Juan libretto bearing Porta's name. The performance was prepared by Joseph Haydn, who introduced changes and additions. He added a chorus, probably not his own, to the opening scene of act one. Also in act one, for Elisa's "Se voi, mio caro," he substituted "Amor tristarello" by Luigi Bologna; in place of Donna Anna's "Tutte le furie unite" he put "Odio, furor, dispetto" by Niccolò Jommelli. Of his own he added a *scena* for Donn'Isabella in act two (the text can be found in chap. 3, Righini's *Convitato,* note 7), and in the same act he recomposed the music for scene ix (his scene x). The words of this scene were no longer in praise of the Prague nobility, but of Haydn's own local patron. Haydn's music has not survived. See Landon, *Haydn* 2:437–38, for additional details. Landon notes that five performances were given. It is sometimes implied that Haydn had earlier written another Don Juan opera. Haydn's draft catalog lists and links together three compositions that he called comedies: "*La Vedova, Il dottore, Il Scanarello.*" They were composed sometime in the early 1760s. It is extremely unlikely that *Il Scanarello* had anything to do with either the Don Juan legend or Molière's Sganarelle. The work seems to be part of several commedia dell'arte scenarios. It would also have been unheard of not to use the customary and proper Italian title of *Il convitato di pietra.* The music no longer exists. In 1763, Haydn composed a comedy entitled *La Marchesa Nespola.* It included two soprano arias for a character called Scanarello. Once again, from the title of the comedy and from the text of the two arias, it is evident that there is no connection with the legend. See Landon, *Haydn* 1:371–72, 434–36, 646.

Year: 1781 Date: 29 October
Title: *Don Juan* (ballet)
City: Copenhagen Theater: Kongelige Theater

Composer: Gluck and others   Choreographer: Vincenzo Galeotti
Source: Jersild, "Le ballet d'action italien," 80.

Year: 1782
Title: *Don Juan* (ballet)
City: Berlin
Composer: Gluck   Choreographer: Lanz
Source: *Enciclopedia dello spettacolo: Indice-repertorio,* 253; Price, "Don Juan," 105, for city and composer.

Year: 1782
Title: *Il convitato di pietra* (opera)
City: Eisenstadt, Austria
Composer: Vincenzo Righini   Librettist: Nunziato Porta
Source: Bartha and Somfai, *Haydn als Opernkapellmeister,* 98.

Year: 1782   Date: Easter through 1 November 1783
Title: *Il convitato di pietra* (opera)
City: Braunschweig
Composer: Vincenzo Righini   Librettist: Nunziato Porta
Source: Cramer, *Magazin der Musik* 1:373–74.

Year: 1782   Date: 10 May
Title: *Don Juan; or, The Libertine Destroy'd* (pantomime)
City: London   Theater: Drury Lane
Composer: "Chevalier Clough" [Gluck]
Director: Charles Antony Delpini and Alessandro Zuchelli
With: Congreve's *The Old Bachelor*
Source: *London Stage,* pt. 5, vol. 1.
Comments: Cast of characters: Don Juan, Don Henriques, Don Pedro, Governor, Covielo the clown, Leonora. Concludes with a dance of the furies. In two acts.

Year: 1783 or 1784
Title: *Il convitato di pietra o sia Il dissoluto* (opera)
City: Hanover
Composer: Vincenzo Righini   Librettist: Nunziato Porta
Source: Loewenberg, *Annals,* 358.

[Year: 1783
A "probable" performance in Parma of a *Convitato di pietra* mentioned by Engländer (*Don Juan/Semiramis,* x), based on Farinelli (*Don Giovanni,* 142), is evidently a confusion with

the Parma performance of 1784. No 1783 ballet is listed by Ferrari (*Spettacoli drammatico-musicali*), who does, however, list my 1784 entry.]

Year: 1783 Season: carnival
Title: *Il convitato di pietra* (ballet)
City: Milan Theater: La Scala
Composer: ? Choreographer: Domenico Rossi
With: Sarti's *Idalide.*
Source: Opera libretto, Carvalhães Collection, Accademia Santa Cecilia, Rome
Comments: The libretto indicates the following scene changes: "1. Strada con casa del Commendatore Loyoa. Notte. 2. Campagna. 3. Mausoleo con statua equestre del Commendatore. 4. Gran sala illuminata per il festino, e la cena di Don Giovanni Tenorio. 5. Padiglione lugubre. 6. Inferno."

Year: 1783 Season: carnival
Title: *Il convitato di pietra* (opera)
City: Naples Theater: Il Nuovo Teatro de' Fiorentini
Composer: Giacomo Tritto Librettist: Giambattista Lorenzi
With: Tritto's *Li due gemelli*
Source: Opera libretto, Fondazione Cini, Venice.

Year: 1783 Date: 23, 25 Feb.; 9, 19 March; 18 May; 16 Sept.; 18 Nov.
Title: *Don Juan, albo libertyn ukarany* (*Don Juan or The Libertine Punished*) (opera)
City: Warsaw Theater: Teatr Narodowy
Composer: Gioacchino Albertini
Librettist: Translated and adapted by Wojciech Bogusławski from an Italian libretto by Nunziato Porta
Source: Opera libretto, 1783, in *Teatr Polski;* Bernacki, *Teatr, dramat i muzyka* 2:227.

Year: 1783 Season: spring
Title: *Il convitato di pietra* (ballet)
City: Novara Theater: Nuovo Teatro di Novara
Composer: ? Choreographer: Domenico Rossi
With: Giordano's *L'epponnina*
Source: Sartori, *I libretti italiani* 3:35.

Year: 1783 Season: autumn
Title: *Il convitato di pietra* (ballet)
City: Cremona Theater: Nuovo Teatro della Società di Casalmaggiore
Composer: Gluck Choreographer: Domenico Rossi
With: Sarti's *Medonte*
Source: Sartori, *I libretti italiani* 4:120.

[Year: 1784
Title: *Il Don Giovanni* (opera)
City: Venice
Composer: Gioacchino Albertini Librettist: Nunziato Porta
Source: Schmidl, *Dizionario universale* 1:28.
Comments: This performance, mentioned only by Schmidl, is probably in error. It is not listed by Wiel (*I teatri musicali veneziani*), whose listings ought to be, by the very nature of his book, more precise than Schmidl's. No opera titles are listed for Venice in *Indice, 1783–84* or *1784–85*.]

Year: 1784 Season: carnival
Title: *Il convitato di pietra* (ballet)
City: Parma Theater: R. D. Teatro di Corte
Composer: ? Choreographer: Domenico Rossi
With: Romani's *Il vecchio geloso.*
Source: Opera libretto, Carvalhães Collection, Accademia Santa Cecilia, Rome
Comments: The libretto indicates the following scene changes: "Strada con palazzo del Commendatore. Campagna amena e deliziosa. Mausoleo col deposito del Commendatore. Camera magnifica per la cena di Don Giovanni. Camera a lutto. Infernale."

Year: 1784 Season: carnival
Title: *Il convitato* (ballet)
City: Pavia Theater: Teatro delli Quattro Signori Associati Cavalieri
Composer: Gluck Choreographer: Eusebio Luzzi
With: Calvi's *Ezio*
Source: Opera libretto, Library of Congress.

Year: 1784 Season: carnival
Title: *Il convitato di pietra* (ballet)
City: Rome Theater: Torre Argentina
Composer: Luigi Marescalchi Choreographer: Onorato Viganò
With: Gazzaniga's *Tullo Ostilio*
Source: Opera libretto, Library of Congress.
Comments: Viganò danced in the first performance of the Gluck-Angiolini version.

Year: 1784 Season: carnival
Title: *Don Giovanni o sia Il gran convitatto* [sic] *di pietra* (ballet)
City: Verona Theater: Accademia Filarmonica
Composer: ? Choreographer: Giuseppe Banti
With: Giordani's *Pizzarro nell'Indie*
Source: *Indice, 1783–84*, 106–7; Sartori, *I libretti italiani* 4:444–45.

Year: 1784 Season: autumn
Title: *Il convitato di pietra* (opera)
City: Palermo Theater: Santa Cecilia
Composer: Giacomo Tritto Librettist: Giambattista Lorenzi
With: Tritto's *Li due gemelli*
Source: Leone, *L'opera a Palermo,* 32–33; Sartori, *I libretti italiani* 2:432, for season.

Year: 1785
Title: *Don Juan ou Le festin de Pierre* (ballet)
City: Milan
Composer: Gluck Choreographer: ?
Source: Engländer, *Don Juan/Semiramis,* x.

Year: 1785
Title: *Il convitato di pietra* (opera)
City: Palermo
Composer: Giacomo Tritto Librettist: Giambattista Lorenzi
With: Tritto's *Li due gemelli*
Source: Kunze, *Don Giovanni vor Mozart,* 79. Not listed in Leone (*L'opera a Palermo*), who has an identical entry for 1784.

Year: 1785 Season: carnival
Title: *Il convitato di pietra* (ballet)
City: Florence Theater: Teatro della Pergola
Composer: ? Choreographer: Domenico Rossi
Source: Catalogue of the Carvalhães Collection, Accademia Santa Cecilia, Rome (libretto missing).

Year: 1785 Date: 12, 29 March; 5, 14, 28 April; 10 May
Title: *Il convitato di pietra* (ballet)
City: London Theater: King's Theater
Composer: Gluck Choreographer: Charles Lepicq
With: Anfossi's *Nitteti* and then various other operas
Source: *London Stage,* pt. 5, vol. 2.
Comments: Three other performances at the King's Theater in this same period bear different titles: 7 April—*Don Juan or the Libertine Destroyed;* 28 May, 9 June—*Don Juan.* I assume that these are also Lepicq's version.

Year: 1785 Season: spring
Title: *Il convitato di pietra* (ballet)
City: Lodi
Composer: ? Choreographer: Alessandro Guglielmi

With: Sarti's *Il Medonte re di Pirro*
Source: *Indice,* 1785–86, 74–75, which adds: "30 recite dal 3 aprile in avanti."

Year: 1785 Season: spring
Title: *Il convitato di pietra* (ballet)
City: Mestre
Composer: ? Choreographer: Giuseppe Scalesi
With: Paisiello's *Teodoro re di Corsica in Venezia*
Source: *Indice,* 1785–86, 83–84.

Year: 1785 Date: 15, 18, 29 April
Title: *Don Juan* (pantomime)
City: London Theater: Haymarket Theater
Composer: Gluck Director: Charles Antony Delpini
With: *The Deserter,* a ballet
Source: *London Stage,* pt. 5, vol. 2, which indicates that these performances are the same as the one on 10 May 1782.

Year: 1785 Season: summer
Title: *Il convitato di pietra* (ballet)
City: Treviso Theater: Teatro Delfino
Composer: ? Choreographer: "Li balli furono composti e diretti dal Sig. Giuseppe Scalesi."
With: Paisiello's *Teodoro re di Corsica in Venezia*
Source: *Indice,* 1785–86, 174–75.
Comments: An odd entry. Beneath the ballet's title is written: "Di Mr. Viganò."

Year: 1785 Season: summer
Title: *Il convitato di pietra* (ballet)
City: Udine
Composer: ? Choreographer: Giuseppe Scalesi
With: Paisiello's *Teodoro re di Corsica in Venezia*
Source: *Indice,* 1785–86, 181–82.

Year: 1786
Title: *Don Juan ou Le festin de Pierre* (ballet)
City: Munich
Composer: Gluck Choreographer: ?
Source: Engländer, *Don Juan/Semiramis,* x.

Year: 1786 Season: carnival
Title: *Il convitato di pietra* (ballet)

City: Carrara
Composer: ? Choreographer: Luigi Sereni
With: Anfossi's *La finta giardiniera*
Source: *Indice,* 1785–86, 25–26.

Year: 1787
Title: *Le Grand festin de Pierre ou L'athée foudroyé* (pantomime)
City: [Paris] Theater: Théâtre des Associés
Composer: ? Librettist: ?
Source: Brenner, *Bibliographical List of Plays,* #1367.

Year: 1787 Date: 5 February
Title: *Don Giovanni o sia Il convitato di pietra* (opera)
City: Venice Theater: Teatro Giustiniani di San Moisè
Composer: Giuseppe Gazzaniga Librettist: Giovanni Bertati
With: Valentini's *Il capriccio drammatico*
Source: Opera libretto, Library of Congress; Loewenberg, *Annals,* 441, for specific date.

Year: 1787 Date: 5 February
Title: *Il nuovo convitato di pietra* (opera)
City: Venice Theater: San Samuele
Composer: Francesco Gardi Librettist: Giuseppe Maria Foppa [?]
Source: Opera Libretto, Library of Congress; Loewenberg, *Annals,* 358, for specific date.
Comments: This libretto does not bear Foppa's name. See chap. 2, note 69, for a discussion of Foppa's authorship.

Year: 1787 Season: spring
Title: *Il convitato* (ballet)
City: Bologna Theater: Teatro Zagnoni
Composer: "Cristoforo Chluchè" [Gluck] Choreographer: Eusebio Luzzi
With: Anfossi's *Le gelosie fortunate*
Source: *Indice,* 1787–88, 15–16, which lists the title as *Il convitato di pietra;* Sartori, *I libretti italiani* 3:270. Also performed with Paisiello's *Il barbiere di Siviglia* (Sartori, *I libretti italiani* 2:397).

Year: 1787 Season: summer
Title: *Il convitato di pietra* (ballet)
City: Cento (Ferrara)
Composer: ? Choreographer: Gaetano Massini
With: Bianchi's *La villanella rapita*
Source: *Indice,* 1787–88, 32.

Year: 1787 Season: summer
Title: *Il convitato di pietra* (ballet)
City: Lugo (Ravenna)
Composer: ? Choreographer: Gaetano Massini
With: Bianchi's *La villanella rapita*
Source: *Indice, 1787–88*, 76–77.

Year: 1787 Date: July through April 1788
Title: *Don Juan; or, The Libertine Destroy'd* (pantomime)
City: London Theater: Royalty Theater
Composer: "The Songs, Duets and Choruses Mr. [William] Reeve. Music composed by Mr. Gluck." But according to Hopkinson (*Bibliography*, 72), none of the music is from Gluck's *Don Juan*.
Director: Charles Antony Delpini
Source: Program, Library of Congress, entitled *Don Juan; or, The Libertine Destroy'd: A Tragic Pantomimical Entertainment, in Two Acts;* Wotquenne (*Catalogue thématique*, 219) sets the first performance date at 12 August 1787.
Comments: The Royalty Theater, built and managed by John Palmer and opened on 20 June 1787, was not licensed to present plays. From 3 July 1787 and for about a year's time, it presented only songs, dances, vaudevilles, and musical pieces of all kinds. Palmer, who played the role of Don Juan, left the Royalty in April 1788 to return to Drury Lane. See *London Stage*, pt. 5, vol. 2, pp. 911–12. Therefore, this pantomime must have been performed between July 1787 and April 1788. Cast of characters: Don Juan, Commandant, Don Fernando, Scaramouch, Donna Anna, fisherwomen, furies. This list of characters is entirely different from the Delpini pantomimes of 1782 and 1785; the production is clearly a new staging of the legend. The story line bears almost no relationship to Shadwell's *The Libertine.*

Year: 1787 Season: autumn
Title: *Il convitato di pietra* (opera)
City: Rome Theater: Teatro Valle
Composer: Vincenzo Fabrizi Librettist: Giambattista Lorenzi
With: Fabrizi's *Il viaggiatore sfortunato*
Source: Kunze, *Don Giovanni vor Mozart*, 87; *Indice, 1787–88*, 157.

Year: 1787 Season: autumn
Title: *Il convitato di pietra ossia Il Don Giovanni* (opera)
City: Varese Theater: Regio Ducal Teatro di Varese
Composer: Giuseppe Gazzaniga Librettist: Giovanni Bertati
With: Valentini's *Il capriccio drammatico*
Source: Kunze, *Don Giovanni vor Mozart*, 129.

Year: 1787 Date: 29 October
Title: *Il dissoluto punito o sia Il D. Giovanni* (opera)
City: Prague Theater: National Theater
Composer: Wolfgang A. Mozart Librettist: Lorenzo Da Ponte
Comments: See Loewenberg, *Annals*, 448–57, for additional performances. *Indice, 1787–88*, 147, lists the title as *Il dissoluto corretto.*

Year: 1788
Title: *Il convitato di pietra* (opera)
City: Fano
Composer: Vincenzo Fabrizi Librettist: Giambattista Lorenzi
Source: Loewenberg, *Annals*, 358.
Comments: Perhaps this performance is really the one listed in *Indice, 1788–89*, 64, for carnival, 1789.

Year: 1788 Season: carnival
Title: *Il dissoluto* (ballet)
City: Livorno Theater: Teatro degli Armeni
Composer: ? Choreographer: Antonio Berti
With: Cimarosa's *Le trame deluse*
Source: *Indice, 1787–88*, 70–71.
Comments: I assume this is a Don Juan ballet only because of its title.

Year: 1788 Season: carnival
Title: *Il convitato di pietra* (ballet)
City: Vicenza Theater: Teatro Nuovo
Composer: ? Choreographer: Giuseppe Cappelletti
With: Alessandri's *I fratelli Pappamosca*
Source: *Indice, 1787–88*, 199.

Year: 1788 Season: spring
Title: *Il convitato di pietra* (opera)
City: Bergamo
Composer: Giuseppe Gazzaniga Librettist: Giovanni Bertati
With: *Il capriccio drammatico*, various
Source: *Indice, 1788–89*, 17.

Year: 1788 Season: spring
Title: *Don Giovanni o sia Il convitato di pietra* (opera)
City: Bologna Theater: Teatro Marsigli Rossi
Composer: Giuseppe Gazzaniga Librettist: Giovanni Bertati

With: Valentini's *Il capriccio drammatico*
Source: Kunze, *Don Giovanni vor Mozart,* 130.

Year: 1788 Season: spring
Title: *Il convitato di pietra ossia Il Don Giovanni* (opera)
City: Cittadella (Bergamo) Theater: Teatro di Cittadella
Composer: Giuseppe Gazzaniga Librettist: Giovanni Bertati
With: Valentini's *Il capriccio drammatico*
Source: Kunze, *Don Giovanni vor Mozart,* 130.

Year: 1788 Season: spring
Title: *Il Don Giovanni* (opera)
City: Civitavecchia Theater: Teatro Minozzi
Composer: Vincenzo Fabrizi Librettist: Giambattista Lorenzi
Source: *Indice, 1788–89*, 44.

Year: 1788 Season: spring
Title: *Il convitato di pietra* (ballet)
City: Milan Theater: La Scala
Composer: ? Choreographer: Luigi Dupen
With: Fabrizi's *Chi la fa l'aspetta*
Source: Opera libretto, Library of Congress.
Comments: The libretto lists the following scene changes: "1. Strada. 2. Villaggio. 3. Sotterranea. 4. Sala. 5. Camera a lutto. 6. Infernale."

Year: 1788 Season: summer
Title: *Il convitato di pietra* (opera)
City: Cremona Theater: Teatro della Nobile Società
Composer: Giuseppe Gazzaniga Librettist: Giovanni Bertati
With: Valentini's *L'impresario in rovina*
Source: *Indice, 1788–89*, 54.

Year: 1788 Season: summer
Title: *Il dissoluto* (ballet)
City: Sinigaglia Theater: Teatro degl'Illustrissimi Signori Condomini
Composer: ? Choreographer: Antonio Berti
With: Paisiello's *Il barbiere di Siviglia*
Source: *Indice, 1788–89*, 202; Sartori, *I libretti italiani* 1:398.

Year: 1788 Season: summer
Title: *D. Giovanni o sia Il convitato di pietra* (opera)
City: Treviso Theater: Nobilissimo Teatro Dolfin di Treviso

Composer: Giuseppe Gazzaniga Librettist: Giovanni Bertati
With: Valentini's *Il capriccio drammatico*
Source: Sartori, *I libretti italiani* 2:68.

Year: 1788 Season: summer
Title: *Il convitato di pietra* (opera)
City: Udine Theater: Nobile Teatro di Udine
Composer: Giuseppe Gazzaniga Librettist: Giovanni Bertati
With: *Il capriccio drammatico,* various
Source: *Indice, 1788–89,* 214, for title; Sartori, *I libretti italiani* 2:68.
Comments: The title of the second act, the Don Juan act, is not mentioned in the libretto itself.

Year: 1788 Season: autumn
Title: *Il convitato di pietra* (opera)
City: Albano Theater: Nuovo Teatro della Villeggiatura
Composer: various Librettist: ?
With: Bernardini's *Le quattro stagioni*
Source: *Indice, 1788–89,* 5.

Year: 1788 Season: autumn
Title: *Il convitato di pietra ossia Il Don Giovanni* (opera)
City: Cremona Theater: Teatro della Società di Casalmaggiore
Composer: Giuseppe Gazzaniga Librettist: Giovanni Bertati
With: Valentini's *Il capriccio drammatico*
Source: Kunze, *Don Giovanni vor Mozart,* 131.

Year: 1788 Season: autumn
Title: *D. Giovanni o sia Il convitato di pietra* (opera)
City: Padua Theater: Nobile Teatro Obizzi
Composer: Giuseppe Gazzaniga Librettist: Giovanni Bertati
With: Valentini's *Il capriccio drammatico*
Source: Kunze, *Don Giovanni vor Mozart,* 131.

Year: 1788 Season: autumn
Title: *Il convitato di pietra* (opera)
City: Rome Theater: Teatro Valle
Composer: various Librettist: ?
With: Masi's *Lo sposalizio per puntiglio*
Source: *Indice, 1788–89,* 185.

Year: 1789
Title: *Il convitato di pietra* (opera)
City: Milan
Composer: Vincenzo Fabrizi Librettist: Giambattista Lorenzi
With: Cimarosa's *L'impresario in angustie*
Source: Kunze, *Don Giovanni vor Mozart,* 87.

Year: 1789
Title: *Don Juan, albo libertyn ukarany* (opera)
City: Warsaw Theater: Teatr Narodowy
Composer: Gioacchino Albertini
Librettist: Nunziato Porta/Wojciech Bogusławski
Source: Bernacki, *Teatr, dramat i muzyka* 2:227.

Year: 1789 Season: carnival
Title: *Don Giovanni o sia Il convitato di pietra* (opera)
City: Corfù Theater: Teatro di San Giacomo
Composer: Giuseppe Gazzaniga Librettist: Giovanni Bertati
With: Valentini's *Il capriccio drammatico*
Source: Kunze, *Don Giovanni vor Mozart,* 132; Sartori, *I libretti italiani* 2:68.

Year: 1789 Season: carnival
Title: *Il convitato di pietra* (opera)
City: Fano
Composer: Vincenzo Fabrizi Librettist: Giambattista Lorenzi
With: Cimarosa's *L'impresario in angustie*
Source: *Indice, 1788–89*, 64.

Year: 1789 Season: carnival
Title: *Il convitato di pietra* (opera)
City: Ferrara Theater: Nobil Teatro Scroffa
Composer: Giuseppe Gazzaniga Librettist: Giovanni Bertati
With: Cimarosa's *L'impresario in angustie*
Source: Sartori, *I libretti italiani* 3:419.
Comments: Several modern commentators state that Gazzaniga wrote an *Impresario in angustie,* and they cite this performance in Ferrara in 1789: *L'enciclopedia dello spettacolo, Die Musik in Geschichte und Gegenwart, New Grove Dictionary,* and Steiger, *Opernlexikon,* who lists the title under Gazzaniga but calls it a *pasticcio.* The libretto clearly states that the music for *L'impresario* is by Cimarosa.

Year: 1789 Season: carnival
Title: *Don Giovanni Tenorio* (opera)

City: Florence Theater: Regio Teatro degli Intrepidi detto della Palla a Corda
Composer: Vincenzo Fabrizi Librettist: Giambattista Lorenzi
Source: *Indice, 1788–89*, 76.

Year: 1789 Season: carnival
Title: *Il Don Giovanni* (opera)
City: Livorno Theater: Teatro degli Armeni
Composer: Vincenzo Fabrizi Librettist: Giambattista Lorenzi
With: Cimarosa's *L'impresario in angustie*
Source: Sartori, *I libretti italiani* 3:419.

Year: 1789 Season: carnival
Title: *Il convitato di pietra* (opera)
City: Modena Theater: Teatro Rangone
Composer: Giuseppe Gazzaniga Librettist: Giovanni Bertati
Source: *Indice, 1788–89*, 121.

Year: 1789 Season: carnival
Title: *Il convitato di pietra* (opera)
City: Mortara (Pavia)
Composer: various Librettist: ?
With: *Il capriccio drammatico,* various
Source: *Indice, 1788–89*, 127–28.

Year: 1789 Season: carnival
Title: *D. Giovanni Tenorio o sia Il convitato di pietra* (opera)
City: Reggio Emilia Theater: Teatro dell'Illustrissimo Pubblico
Composer: Giuseppe Gazzaniga Librettist: Giovanni Bertati
Source: Kunze, *Don Giovanni vor Mozart,* 132.

Year: 1789 Season: carnival
Title: *Il convitato di pietra* (opera)
City: Siena Theater: Nobilissima Accademia degli Intronati
Composer: Vincenzo Fabrizi Librettist: Giambattista Lorenzi
With: Bernardini's *Gli amanti confusi*
Source: *Indice, 1788–89*, 199.

Year: 1789 Season: spring
Title: *Il convitato di pietra ossia Don Giovanni* (opera)
City: Forlì Theater: Pubblico Teatro
Composer: Giuseppe Gazzaniga Librettist: Giovanni Bertati

With: Valentini's *Il capriccio drammatico*
Source: Kunze, *Don Giovanni vor Mozart,* 131.

Year: 1789 Season: spring
Title: *Il convitato di pietra* (opera)
City: Rovereto
Composer: various Librettist: ?
Source: *Indice,* 1789–90, 197.

Year: 1789 Season: spring
Title: *Don Giovanni o sia Il convitato di pietra* (opera)
City: Trento Theater: Teatro di Trento
Composer: Giuseppe Gazzaniga Librettist: Giovanni Bertati
With: Valentini's *Il capriccio drammatico*
Source: Sartori, *I libretti italiani* 2:68.

Year: 1789 Date: 22, 28 May; 1, 6, 15, 18 June; 16 Sept.; 2 Nov.
Title: *Don Juan; or, The Libertine Destroyed* (pantomime)
City: London Theater: Covent Garden
Composer: Gluck, William Reeve Director: Charles Antony Delpini
With: Burgoyne's *The Heiress* and then various other titles
Source: *London Stage,* pt. 5, vol. 2.
Comments: Cast of characters for 22 May: Don Juan, Commandant, Don Fernando, Don Alonzo, Don Carlos, Pedrillo, fisherman, alguaziles, sailor, landlord, waiter, Scaramouch, Spanish lady, attendants, fisherwomen, Donna Anna. Delpini was not a part of the 22 May performance. Starting with 28 May, he took part in performances advertised as "Delpini's Grand, Tragic, Comic, Pantomimical Entertainment in 2 acts." From 28 May, the cast of characters was as follows: Don Juan, Don Pedro, Commandant, Spanish Grandees, Scaramouch, Donna Anna. On 11 November at the White Horse Inn, Parsons Green, Fulham, one scene was played as part of a "pantomimical interlude" (*London Stage,* pt. 5, vol. 2, p. 1205).

Year: 1789 Season: summer
Title: *Il convitato di pietra* (ballet)
City: Vercelli Theater: Teatro di Vercelli
Composer: ? Choreographer: Domenico Ballon
With: Cotti's *Il manescalco*
Source: *Indice,* 1789–90, 246; Sartori, *I libretti italiani* 4:60.

Year: 1789 Season: autumn
Title: *Il convitato* (opera)
City: Bagnacavallo (Ravenna)

Composer: Giuseppe Gazzaniga Librettist: Giovanni Bertati
With: Cimarosa's *L'impresario in angustie*
Source: *Indice,* 1789–90, 8.

Year: 1789 Season: autumn
Title: *Il convitato di pietra* (opera)
City: Bolzano
Composer: various Librettist: ?
Source: *Indice,* 1789–90, 24.

Year: 1789 Season: autumn
Title: *Il convitato di pietra* (opera)
City: Fiume
Composer: Giuseppe Gazzaniga Librettist: Giovanni Bertati
With: *L'impresario in rovina,* attributed to Gazzaniga
Source: *Indice,* 1789–90, 69.

Year: 1789 Season: autumn
Title: *D. Giovanni ossia Il convitato di pietra* (opera)
City: Milan Theater: Teatro alla Scala
Composer: Giuseppe Gazzaniga Librettist: Giovanni Bertati
With: Cimarosa's *L'impresario in angustie*
Source: Kunze, *Don Giovanni vor Mozart,* 132.

Year: 1789 Season: autumn
Title: *Il convitato* (opera)
City: Racunigi
Composer: various Librettist: ?
Source: *Indice,* 1789–90, 182.

Year: 1789 Season: autumn
Title: *Il convitato* (opera)
City: Rivarolo (Torino)
Composer: various Librettist: ?
Source: *Indice,* 1789–90, 190.

Year: 1789 Season: autumn
Title: *Il Don Giovanni* (opera)
City: Rome Theater: Teatro Valle
Composer: various Librettist: ?
With: Guglielmi's *Il medico burlato*
Source: *Indice,* 1789–90, 194.

Year: 1789 Season: autumn
Title: *Il convitato di pietra* (opera)
City: Turin Theater: Teatro Carignano
Composer: Giuseppe Gazzaniga Librettist: Giovanni Bertati
With: Cimarosa's *L'impresario in angustie*
Source: Kunze, *Don Giovanni vor Mozart*, 131; *Indice, 1789–90*, 220, for season.

Year: 1790–1800
Title: *Don Juan Tenorio ó por otro nombre El combidado de piedra* (ballet)
City: Madrid Theater: Coliseo de los Caños del Peral
Composer: ? Choreographer: Domingo Rossi
Source: Mitjana, *Discantes y Contrapuntos*, 60.

Year: 1790
Title: *Il convitato di pietra* (opera)
City: Naples
Composer: Vincenzo Fabrizi Librettist: Giambattista Lorenzi
With: Da Capua's *L'ultima che si perde è la speranza*
Source: Kunze, *Don Giovanni vor Mozart*, 87.

Year: 1790 Season: carnival
Title: *Don Giovanni Tenorio o sia Il convitato di pietra* (opera)
City: Faenza Theater: Nuovo Pubblico Teatro
Composer: Giuseppe Gazzaniga Librettist: Giovanni Bertati
With: Cimarosa's *L'impresario in angustie*
Source: Sartori, *I libretti italiani* 3:420.

Year: 1790 Season: carnival
Title: *Il convitato di pietra* (opera)
City: Forlì Theater: Pubblico Nuovo Teatro
Composer: Giuseppe Gazzaniga Librettist: Giovanni Bertati
With: Valentini's *L'impresario in rovina*
Source: *Indice, 1789–90*, 72.

Year: 1790 Season: carnival
Title: *Il convitato di pietra* (opera)
City: Imola
Composer: Giuseppe Gazzaniga Librettist: Giovanni Bertati
With: Anfossi's *La maga Circe*
Source: *Indice, 1789–90*, 81.

Year: 1790 Season: carnival
Title: *Il convitato di pietra* (opera)
City: Macerata
Composer: attributed to Paisiello and Cimarosa Librettist: ?
Source: *Indice,* 1789–90, 99.

Year: 1790 Season: carnival
Title: *Il convitato* (opera)
City: Pinarolo (Pavia)
Composer: various Librettist: ?
Source: *Indice,* 1789–90, 176.

Year: 1790 Season: carnival
Title: *Il convitato di pietra* (opera)
City: Rieti
Composer: ? Librettist: ?
Source: *Indice,* 1789–90, 187.

Year: 1790 Season: spring
Title: *Il D. Giovanni o sia Il convitato di pietra* (opera)
City: Pisa Theater: Teatro di Pisa dei Nobili Signori Fratelli Prini
Composer: Giuseppe Gazzaniga
Librettist: Giambattista Lorenzi/Giovanni Bertati
Source: Kunze, *Don Giovanni vor Mozart,* 133.
Comments: Kunze states that the libretto is Lorenzi's but with several large scenes inserted from Bertati's.

Year: 1790 Season: spring
Title: *Il D. Giovanni ossia Il convitato di pietra* (opera)
City: Verona Theater: Teatro Filarmonico
Composer: Giuseppe Gazzaniga Librettist: Giovanni Bertati
With: Cimarosa's *L'impresario in angustie*
Source: *Indice,* 1790–91, 244; Sartori, *I libretti italiani* 3:420–21.

Year: 1790 Date: 23 May
Title: *Don Juan, albo libertyn ukarany* (opera)
City: Warsaw Theater: Teatr Narodowy
Composer: Gioacchino Albertini
Librettist: Nunziato Porta/Wojciech Bogusławski
Source: Bernacki, *Teatr, dramat i muzyka* 2:227, 1:331, where it is indicated that the third act was revised for this performance.

Year: 1790 Season: summer
Title: *Don Giovanni Tenorio o sia Il convitato di pietra* (opera)
City: Lucca Theater: Pubblico Teatro di Lucca
Composer: Giuseppe Gazzaniga Librettist: Giovanni Bertati
With: Cimarosa's *L'impresario in angustie*
Source: Kunze, *Don Giovanni vor Mozart,* 134.

Year: 1790 Date: 8 July
Title: *Il convitato di pietra* (opera)
City: Barcelona
Composer: Vincenzo Fabrizi Librettist: Giambattista Lorenzi
Source: Loewenberg, *Annals,* 358.

Year: 1790 Date: October
Title: *Il D. Giovanni o sia Il convitato di pietra* (opera)
City: Perugia Theater: Teatro Civico del Verzaro
Composer: Vincenzo Fabrizi Librettist: Giambattista Lorenzi
With: Cimarosa's *L'impresario in angustie*
Source: Kunze, *Don Giovanni vor Mozart,* 133.
Comments: Kunze notes that some Gazzaniga numbers were added.

Year: 1790 Date: 26 Oct.; 1, 6, 9, 26 Nov.; 1, 23 Dec.
Year: 1791 Date: 12, 18 Feb.; 5, 12, 19 March; 16, 27 April
Title: *Don Juan; or, The Libertine Destroyed* (pantomime)
City: London Theater: Drury Lane
Composer: ? Choreographer: ?
With: Cobb's *The Haunted Tower* and then various other titles
Source: *London Stage,* pt. 5, vol. 2.
Comments: Characters: Don Antonio, Don Ferdinand, Don Juan, Don Guzman, Carlos, Perez, Pedrillo, Lopez, Gomez, Vasquez, host, Masaniello, Scaramouch, alguaziles, boatswain, sailors, Donna Anna, Isabella, Inis, Katharina, Viletta. "A revived Grand Pantomimical Ballet. To conclude with a superb Prospect of the Infernal Regions . . . and a Rain of Fire." Charles Delpini is not listed as having participated in this production.

Year: 1791–92
Title: *Il convitato di pietra* (opera)
City: Capua
Composer: ? Librettist: ?
With: *I due gemelli,* no composer listed
Source: *Indice,* 1791–92, 32.

Year: 1791
Title: *Il convitato di pietra* (opera)
City: Naples Theater: Il Teatro Nuovo sopra Toledo
Composer: Giacomo Tritto Librettist: Giambattista Lorenzi
With: Cimarosa's *L'impresario in angustie*
Source: Kunze, *Don Giovanni vor Mozart,* 79.
Comments: According to Kunze, this production was not entirely the same as the original.

Year: 1791 Season: carnival
Title: *Il convitato di pietra* (opera)
City: Ancona Theater: Nobile Teatro della Fenice
Composer: various Librettist: ?
With: Cimarosa's *L'impresario in angustie*
Source: *Indice, 1790–91*, 261.

Year: 1791 Season: carnival
Title: *Don Giovanni Tenorio ossia Il convitato di pietra* (opera)
City: Bologna Theater: Teatro Zagnoni
Composer: Vincenzo Fabrizi Librettist: Giambattista Lorenzi
Source: Opera libretto, Library of Congress.
Comments: The libretto indicates no composer; a perusal of it makes clear that the text is Lorenzi's. Sonneck (*Catalogue* 1:396) and Kunze (*Don Giovanni vor Mozart,* 87) indicate that the music is by Fabrizi. *Indice 1790–91*, 23, states that the opera at the Zagnoni was Gardi's *Il nuovo convitato di pietra;* Loewenberg (*Annals,* 358) mentions a performance of Gardi's opera in Bologna in 1791, as does Schmidl (*Dizionario universale* 1:597), who places it, however, at the Teatro Formagliari.

Year: 1791 Season: carnival
Title: *Il convitato di pietra* (opera)
City: Brescia Theater: Teatro della Illustriss. Accademia degli Erranti di Brescia
Composer: Giuseppe Gazzaniga Librettist: Giovanni Bertati
Source: Sartori, *I libretti italiani* 2:223.

Year: 1791 Season: carnival
Title: *Il convitato di pietra,* "intermezzo giocoso" (opera)
City: Florence Theater: Teatro di Borgo Ognissanti
Composer: Giuseppe Gazzaniga Librettist: Giovanni Bertati
Source: *Indice, 1790–91*, 63.

Year: 1791 Season: carnival
Title: *Il convitato di pietra* (opera)

City: Pergola Theater: Teatro della Luna
Composer: Giuseppe Gazzaniga Librettist: Giovanni Bertati
With: Anfossi's *La maga Circe*
Source: Sartori, *I libretti italiani* 2:223–24.

Year: 1791 Date: February
Title: *Il convitato di pietra* (ballet)
City: Padua Theater: Teatro Nuovo
Composer: ? Choreographer: ?
With: Cimarosa's *Giannina e Bernardone*
Source: Brunelli, *I teatri di Padova*, 279–80.

Year: 1791 Season: summer
Title: *Il convitato di pietra* (opera)
City: Milan [?] Theater: Teatro privato de' Due Muri
Composer: Francesco Gardi Librettist: Giuseppe Maria Foppa [?]
Source: Kunze, *Don Giovanni vor Mozart*, 84.
Comments: Amateur performance based on *Il nuovo convitato di pietra*.

Year: 1791 Season: autumn
Title: *Il convitato di pietra* (opera)
City: Crema Theater: Teatro di Crema
Composer: Giuseppe Gazzaniga Librettist: Giovanni Bertati
Source: Kunze, *Don Giovanni vor Mozart*, 134.
Comments: The opera was divided into two acts with two large ballets between them.

Year: 1791 Date: 5, 9, 25 Nov.; 2, 20, 27 Dec.
Title: *Don Juan: or, The Libertine Destroyed* (pantomime)
City: London Theater: Drury Lane at King's
Composer: ? Choreographer: ?
With: Burgoyne's *The Heiress* and then various other titles
Source: *London Stage*, pt. 5, vol. 2.
Comments: The cast of characters is essentially the same as for performances in 1790 at Drury Lane.

Year: 1792, 1794
Title: *Don Juan* (pantomime ballet)
City: Philadelphia Theater: Southwark Theater
Composer: Gluck, William Reeve Performers: The Old American Company
Source: Sonneck, *Early Opera*, 112. Sonneck indicates that this was the Delpini version of 1787.

Year: 1792 Season: carnival
Title: *Don Giovanni Tenorio ossia Il convitato di pietra* (ballet)
City: Ancona Theater: Teatro della Fenice
Composer: ? Choreographer: Eusebio Luzzi
Source: *Indice,* 1791–92, 6–7.

Year: 1792 Season: carnival
Title: *Il Don Giovanni ossia Il convitato di pietra* (opera)
City: Lisbon Theater: Teatro della Rua dos Condes
Composer: Giuseppe Gazzaniga Librettist: Giovanni Bertati
Source: Kunze, *Don Giovanni vor Mozart,* 135.

Year: 1792 Season: carnival
Title: *Don Giovanni Tenorio ossia Il convitato di pietra* (opera)
City: Reggio Theater: Teatro dell'Illustrissimo Pubblico
Composer: Giuseppe Gazzaniga Librettist: Giovanni Bertati
With: Valentini's *Il capriccio drammatico*
Source: Sartori, *I libretti italiani* 2:68–69.

Year: 1792 Season: carnival
Title: *Don Giovanni* (opera)
City: Rome Theater: Teatro Capranica
Composer: ? Librettist: ?
With: *La serva padrona,* no composer listed
Source: *Indice,* 1791–92, 154.

Year: 1792 Season: carnival
Title: *Il convitato di pietra* (opera)
City: Venice Theater: San Cassiano
Composer: Vincenzo Fabrizi Librettist: Giambattista Lorenzi
With: Da Capua's *L'ultima che si perde è la speranza*
Source: Opera libretto, Library of Congress.
Comments: The libretto reads: "La musica è di varj celebri Maestri." Kunze (*Don Giovanni vor Mozart,* 87) lists this version by Fabrizi.

Year: 1792 Season: carnival
Title: *Il convitato di pietra,* "intermezzo" (opera)
City: Volterra
Composer: ? Librettist: ?
Source: *Indice,* 1791–92, 191.

Year: 1792 Date: spring through carnival 1793
Title: *Il convitato di pietra* (opera)
City: Palermo Theater: Real Teatro detto da Santa Cecilia
Composer: Giacomo Tritto Librettist: Giambattista Lorenzi
With: Guglielmi's *La sposa contrastata*
Source: *Indice,* 1792–93, 136. These performances are not listed in Leone, *L'opera a Palermo.*

Year: 1792 Season: spring
Title: *Il Don Giovanni* (opera)
City: Florence Theater: Teatro della Pergola
Composer: ? Librettist: ?
With: Cimarosa's *L'impresario in angustie*
Source: *Indice,* 1792–93, 54.
Comments: The *Indice* entry reads as follows: " . . . tre Drammi Giocosi in musica intitolati / LA CIFRA / Musica del Sig. Maestro Salieri / IL MATRIMONIO PER INDUSTRIA / ossia IL SERVO ASTUTO / Musica del Sig. Maestro Rutini / IL DON GIOVANNI, / E L'IMPRESARIO IN ANGUSTIE." Neither composer nor librettist is mentioned for the last item, and no text of the performance exists. It is useful to speculate on whose Don Juan version it might have been, since this *Il Don Giovanni* has at times been thought to represent the first appearance in Italy of Mozart's own. It should be noted, first of all, that the opera must have been in one act only since it was performed in conjunction with another well-known one-act opera, *L'impresario in angustie.* Morini (*La R. Accademia,* 84) states that the *Don Giovanni* in question was Albertini's, but this hardly seems possible even though the title is the same. Albertini's was a full-length, three-act work. The Tritto-Lorenzi one-act version was twice linked, as is the opera here, with Cimarosa's *L'impresario in angustie,* but this version is not likely to be theirs since theirs was never called *Il Don Giovanni* but always *Il convitato di pietra.* In addition, Tritto's opera had a relatively limited diffusion. This version, then, is either the one by Gazzaniga and Bertati or the one by Fabrizi and Lorenzi, both of which were extremely popular in this period. Petrobelli ("*Don Giovanni* in Italia," 30) identifies the first Italian performance of Mozart's opera as having taken place in Rome at the Teatro Valle in the spring of 1811.

Year: 1792 Season: spring
Title: *D. Giovanni o sia Il convitato di pietra* (opera)
City: Genoa Theater: Teatro da Sant'Agostino
Composer: Giuseppe Gazzaniga Librettist: Giovanni Bertati
With: Anfossi's *La maga Circe*
Source: Kunze, *Don Giovanni vor Mozart,* 135.
Comments: Included some of the Fabrizi and Lorenzi version.

Year: 1792 Season: spring
Title: *Il convitato di pietra* (opera)
City: Gubbio Theater: Il Teatro della Fama
Composer: Giuseppe Gazzaniga Librettist: Giovanni Bertati
Source: *Indice,* 1792–93, 71.

Year: 1792 Season: spring
Title: *Il convitato di pietra* (opera)
City: Legnago
Composer: Giuseppe Gazzaniga Librettist: Giovanni Bertati
Source: *Indice,* 1792–93, 75.

Year: 1792 Season: spring
Title: *Il convitato di pietra* (opera)
City: Mantua Theater: Regio Ducal Teatro Vecchio
Composer: Giuseppe Gazzaniga Librettist: Giovanni Bertati
With: Cimarosa's *L'impresario in angustie*
Source: *Indice,* 1792–93, 94.

Year: 1792 Season: summer
Title: *Il convitato di pietra* (opera)
City: Aquila
Composer: ? Librettist: ?
Source: *Indice,* 1792–93, 9.

Year: 1792 Season: summer
Title: *Il Don Giovanni* (opera)
City: Pistoia Theater: Nobil Teatro degli Accademici Risvegliati
Composer: Giuseppe Gazzaniga Librettist: Giovanni Bertati
With: Cimarosa's *L'impresario in angustie*
Source: *Indice,* 1792–93, 150.

Year: 1792 Season: autumn
Title: *Il D. Giovanni Tenorio o sia Il convitato di pietra* (opera)
City: Lucca Theater: Pubblico Teatro di Lucca
Composer: Vincenzo Fabrizi Librettist: Giambattista Lorenzi
Source: Opera libretto, Accademia Santa Cecilia, Rome
Comments: Kunze (*Don Giovanni vor Mozart,* 136) notes that much music by Gazzaniga was integrated into this representation.

Year: 1792 Season: autumn
Title: *Il convitato di pietra* (ballet)

City: Turin Theater: Teatro Carignano
Composer: ? Choreographer: Antonio Berti
With: Paisiello's *Nina o sia La pazza per amore*
Source: Sartori, *I libretti italiani* 4:227.

Year: 1792 Date: 24 September
Title: [*Il convitato di pietra o Le Festin de Pierre*] (opera)
City: Paris Theater: Théâtre Feydeau
Composer: Giuseppe Gazzaniga Librettist: Giovanni Bertati
Source: Kunze, *Don Giovanni vor Mozart,* 134.
Comments: Kunze indicates that the performance was directed by Luigi Cherubini and included several pieces from Mozart's *Don Giovanni. Indice, 1791–92,* 134, clearly identifies the opera as Gazzaniga's *Il convitato di pietra* but furnishes very imprecise dates: "in tutto l'anno 1791 e carnevale 1792."

Year: 1793–97, 1799, 1800
Title: *Don Juan* (pantomime ballet)
City: New York Theater: John Street Theater, Park Theater
Composer: ? Performers: The Old American Company
Source: Sonneck, *Early Opera,* 90, table B.

Year: 1793
Title: *Il convitato di pietra* (opera)
City: Florence
Composer: Vincenzo Fabrizi Librettist: Giambattista Lorenzi
With: Da Capua's *L'ultima che si perde è la speranza*
Source: Kunze, *Don Giovanni vor Mozart,* 87.

Year: 1793 Season: carnival
Title: *Il convitato di pietra* (opera)
City: Anghiari (Arezzo) Theater: Teatro della Nobile Famiglia Corsi
Composer: Giuseppe Gazzaniga Librettist: Giovanni Bertati
Source: *Indice, 1792–93,* 8.

Year: 1793 Season: carnival
Title: *Il convitato di pietra* (opera)
City: Capodistria
Composer: Giuseppe Gazzaniga Librettist: Giovanni Bertati
Source: *Indice, 1792–93,* 32.

Year: 1793 Season: carnival
Title: *Il convitato di pietra* (opera)

City: Chioggia
Composer: Giuseppe Gazzaniga Librettist: Giovanni Bertati
With: Gazzaniga's *La modista raggiratrice*
Source: *Indice,* 1792–93, 38.

Year: 1793 Season: carnival
Title: *Il convitato di pietra* (opera)
City: Montepulciano Theater: Teatro dell'Accademia degli Intrigati
Composer: Giuseppe Gazzaniga Librettist: Giovanni Bertati
With: Cimarosa's *L'impresario in angustie*
Source: *Indice,* 1792–93, 117–18.

Year: 1793 Season: carnival
Title: *Don Giovanni Tenorio* (opera)
City: Mortara (Pavia) Theater: Teatro Scaramaglia
Composer: ? Librettist: ?
Source: *Indice,* 1792–93, 120.

Year: 1793 Season: carnival
Title: *Il convitato di pietra* (opera)
City: Naples Theater: Il Teatro di Capua
Composer: Giacomo Tritto Librettist: Giambattista Lorenzi
With: Cimarosa's *L'impresario in angustie*
Source: Opera libretto, Library of Congress.
Comments: Kunze (*Don Giovanni vor Mozart,* 79) indicates that the score for this performance underwent modifications.

Year: 1793 Season: carnival
Title: *Il Don Giovanni* (opera)
City: Novi (Alessandria)
Composer: ? Librettist: ?
With: *L'impresario in angustie,* no composer listed
Source: *Indice,* 1792–93, 128.

Year: 1793 Season: carnival
Title: *D. Giovanni ossia Il convitato di pietra* (opera)
City: Pavia Theater: Nuovo Teatro dei Quattro Signori Associati
Composer: Giuseppe Gazzaniga Librettist: Giovanni Bertati
With: Valentini's *L'impresario in rovina*
Source: Kunze, *Don Giovanni vor Mozart,* 136.
Comments: Between the two operas, a ballet entitled *Amor protettore di D. Gio. Tenorio anche dopo la morte* was performed.

Year: 1793 Season: spring
Title: *Il convitato di pietra* (opera)
City: Como
Composer: Giuseppe Gazzaniga Librettist: Giovanni Bertati
With: *L'impresario in rovina,* no composer given
Source: *Indice,* 1793–94, 34.

Year: 1793 Season: spring
Title: *Il convitato di pietra* (opera)
City: Mont'Alcino (Siena) Theater: Teatro degli Accademici degli Astrusi
Composer: Giuseppe Gazzaniga Librettist: Giovanni Bertati
With: Cimarosa's *L'impresario in angustie*
Source: *Indice,* 1793–94, 103.

Year: 1793 Season: summer
Title: *Il convitato di pietra* (opera)
City: Monza
Composer: ? Librettist: ?
With: *L'impresario in rovina,* no composer listed
Source: *Indice,* 1793–94, 105.
Comments: According to Kunze (*Don Giovanni vor Mozart,* 137), this version is by Gazzaniga.

Year: 1793 Date: July–August
Title: *Il convitato di pietra ossia Il Don Giovanni* (opera)
City: Lodi
Composer: Giuseppe Gazzaniga Librettist: Giovanni Bertati
With: *L'impresario in rovina,* no composer given
Source: *Indice,* 1793–94, 71–72.

Year: 1793 Date: 21 July; 16 October
Title: *Don Juan, albo libertyn ukarany* (opera)
City: Warsaw Theater: Teatr Narodowy
Composer: Gioacchino Albertini
Librettist: Nunziato Porta/Wojciech Bogusławski
Source: Bernacki, *Teatr, dramat i muzyka* 2:227.

Year: 1793 Season: autumn
Title: *Don Giovanni Tenorio ossia Il convitato di pietra* (opera)
City: Alessandria
Composer: ? Librettist: ?
Source: *Indice,* 1793–94, 2.

Comments: According to Kunze (*Don Giovanni vor Mozart,* 137), this version is by Gazzaniga.

Year: 1793 Season: autumn
Title: *Il convitato di pietra* (opera)
City: Codogno (Milan)
Composer: ? Librettist: ?
Source: *Indice,* 1793–94, 31.
Comments: According to Kunze (*Don Giovanni vor Mozart,* 137), this version is by Gazzaniga.

Year: 1793 Season: autumn
Title: *Il convitato di pietra* (opera)
City: Colle (Siena) Theater: Nobile Teatro dell'Accademia
Composer: Giuseppe Gazzaniga Librettist: Giovanni Bertati
Source: *Indice,* 1793–94, 32–33.

Year: 1793 Season: autumn
Title: *Il convitato di pietra* (ballet)
City: Varese
Composer: ? Choreographer: Eusebio Luzzi
With: Rutini's *Il matrimonio per industria*
Source: Opera libretto, Library of Congress.

Year: 1794
Title: *Don Juan* (ballet pantomime)
City: Charleston, South Carolina Theater: Charleston Theater
Composer: ? Choreographer: ?
Source: Sonneck, *Early Opera,* 124, table I.

Year: 1794 Season: carnival
Title: *Don Giovanni Tenorio* (ballet)
City: Alessandria
Composer: ? Choreographer: Eusebio Luzzi
With: *La Nina pazza per amore,* no composer listed
Source: *Indice,* 1793–94, 4.

Year: 1794 Season: carnival
Title: *Il Don Giovanni* (opera)
City: Arezzo
Composer: Giuseppe Gazzaniga Librettist: Giovanni Bertati

With: Cimarosa's *L'impresario in angustie*
Source: *Indice,* 1793–94, 7.

Year: 1794 Season: carnival
Title: *Il convitato di pietra* (opera)
City: Colle (Siena) Theater: Nobile Teatro dell'Accademia
Composer: Giuseppe Gazzaniga Librettist: Giovanni Bertati
With: Cimarosa's *L'impresario in angustie*
Source: *Indice,* 1793–94, 32–33.

Year: 1794 Season: carnival
Title: *Il convitato* (opera)
City: Viadana (Mantua)
Composer: Giuseppe Gazzaniga Librettist: Giovanni Bertati
With: Cimarosa's *L'impresario in angustie*
Source: *Indice,* 1793–94, 178–79.

Year: 1794 Date: 1, 8 March
Title: *Il Don Giovanni* (opera)
City: London Theater: King's Theater, Haymarket
Composer: Gazzaniga, Sarti, Federici, Guglielmi, Mozart
Librettist: Giovanni Bertati and Lorenzo Da Ponte
With: *Il capriccio drammatico*
Source: Kunze, *Don Giovanni vor Mozart,* 137; *London Stage,* pt. 5, vol. 3, pp. 1622–24.
Comments: The cast of characters listed in *London Stage* makes it clear that *Il capriccio drammatico* was actually Cimarosa's *L'impresario in angustie.* Kunze (137) quotes from the libretto: "*Il Don Giovanni,* a tragi-comic Opera in one act. The Music by Messrs. Gazzaniga, Sarti, Federici, and Guglielmi. The words are new, by L. da Ponte, poet of this theatre, except those that are not marked with inverted commas." The only music by Mozart was Leporello's catalog song. It was sung by Pasquariello.

Year: 1794 Season: spring
Title: *Don Giovanni Tenorio ossia Il convitato di pietra* (opera)
City: Lubiana Theater: Nobile Teatro Cesareo
Composer: Vincenzo Fabrizi Librettist: Giambattista Lorenzi
Source: Manferrari, *Dizionario universale* 1:363.

Year: 1794 Season: summer through autumn
Title: *Il convitato di pietra* (opera)
City: Fiume
Composer: Vincenzo Fabrizi Librettist: Giambattista Lorenzi

With: Cimarosa's *L'impresario in angustie*
Source: *Indice*, 1794–95, 39.

Year: 1794 Season: summer
Title: *Il Don Giovanni* (opera)
City: Trieste Theater: Teatro San Pietro
Composer: Giuseppe Gazzaniga Librettist: Giovanni Bertati
Source: Kunze, *Don Giovanni vor Mozart*, 137; *Indice*, 1794–95, 124, for year and season.

Year: 1795
Title: *Il convitato di pietra* (opera)
City: Catania
Composer: Giacomo Tritto Librettist: Giambattista Lorenzi
With: Tritto's *Li due gemelli*
Source: Kunze, *Don Giovanni vor Mozart*, 79.

Year: 1795 Season: carnival
Title: *Il convitato di pietra* (opera)
City: Corfù Theater: Nobile Teatro di San Giacomo
Composer: Francesco Gardi Librettist: Giuseppe Maria Foppa [?]
Source: Manferrari, *Dizionario universale* 2:25—Manferrari attributes the text to Bertati; *Indice*, 1794–95, 22.

Year: 1795 Season: carnival
Title: *Il convitato di pietra* (ballet)
City: Padua Theater: Teatro degli Obizzi
Composer: ? Choreographer: ?
Source: Brunelli, *I teatri di Padova*, 318.

Year: 1795 Season: carnival
Title: *Il convitato di pietra* (opera)
City: Rovigo Theater: Teatro Roncale
Composer: Giuseppe Gazzaniga Librettist: Giovanni Bertati
With: Cimarosa's *L'impresario in angustie*
Source: *Indice*, 1794–95, 110.

Year: 1795 Season: Lent
Title: *Il convitato di pietra* (ballet)
City: Milan Theater: La Scala
Composer: ? Choreographer: Nicola Ferlotti
With: Paisiello's *La frascatana;* Cimarosa's *Giannina e Bernardone*
Source: *Indice*, 1795–96, 79.

Year: 1795 Season: spring
Title: *Il convitato di pietra* (opera)
City: Viadana (Mantua) Theater: Teatro della Nobile Società
Composer: Giuseppe Gazzaniga Librettist: Giovanni Bertati
With: *Il capriccio drammatico,* various
Source: *Indice,* 1795–96, 155.

Year: 1795 Season: summer
Title: *Il D. Giovanni Tenorio o sia Il convitato di pietra* (opera)
City: Barga Theater: Nobil Teatro dell'Illustrissima Accademia de' Differenti
Composer: Vincenzo Fabrizi Librettist: Giambattista Lorenzi
Source: Kunze, *Don Giovanni vor Mozart,* 138.
Comments: Kunze notes that many numbers by Gazzaniga were added.

Year: 1795 Season: summer
Title: *Il convitato di pietra* (opera)
City: Modigliana (Forlì)
Composer: Giuseppe Gazzaniga Librettist: Giovanni Bertati
With: Cimarosa's *L'impresario in angustie*
Source: *Indice,* 1795–96, 91.

Year: 1795 Date: autumn through carnival 1796
Title: *Il convitato di pietra* (opera)
City: Venice Theater: San Samuele
Composer: Vincenzo Fabrizi Librettist: Giambattista Lorenzi
Source: *Indice,* 1795–96, 150.

Year: 1795 Season: autumn
Title: *Il convitato di pietra* (opera)
City: Fusignano
Composer: Giuseppe Gazzaniga Librettist: Giovanni Bertati
With: Cimarosa's *L'impresario in angustie*
Source: *Indice,* 1795–96, 48–49.

Year: 1795 Season: autumn
Title: *Il Don Giovanni,* "Ballo primo Eroico Pantomimo" (ballet)
City: Livorno Theater: Regio Teatro degli Accademici Avvalorati
Composer: ? Choreographer: Carlo Augusto Favier
With: Cimarosa's *Penelope*
Source: *Indice,* 1795–96, 59.

Year: 1795 Date: 7 December
Title: *Don Juan; or, The Libertine Destroyed* (pantomime ballet)
City: Boston Theater: Federal Street Theater
Composer: ? Choreographer: ?
Source: Singer, *Don Juan Theme,* 38; Sonneck, *Early Opera,* 144, table D, for date and theater.
Comments: Probably the Gluck, Reeve, and Delpini version. Gendarme de Bévotte (*La Légende de Don Juan,* 353) indicates that Joseph Grimaldi, Byron's friend, played the part of Scaramouche. Singer indicates that the work was advertised as "a grand pantomimical ballad, in two parts."

Year: 1796 Date: 2 January
Title: *Don Juan* (ballet)
City: Vienna Theater: Freihaus
Composer: Gluck Choreographer: Cecchi
Source: Engländer, *Don Juan/Semiramis,* x; Prod'homme, *Gluck,* 405.
Comments: Prod'homme notes that the ballet was given by Schikaneder's company.

Year: 1796 Season: carnival
Title: *Il D. Giovanni o sia Convitato di pietra* (opera)
City: Foligno Theater: Teatro dell'Aquila
Composer: Vincenzo Fabrizi Librettist: Giambattista Lorenzi
With: Guglielmi's *Il poeta di Villa*
Source: Kunze, *Don Giovanni vor Mozart,* 87–88; Sartori, *I libretti italiani* 2:391.
Comments: Kunze notes that this version included many additions from Gazzaniga.

Year: 1796 Season: summer
Title: *Il convitato di pietra* (opera)
City: Milan Theater: Teatro Canobbiana
Composer: Francesco Gardi Librettist: Giuseppe Maria Foppa [?]
Source: Manferrari, *Dizionario universale* 2:25—Manferrari attributes the text to Bertati; *Indice,* 1796–97, 58.

Year: 1796 Date: 7 June
Title: *Don Juan; or, The Libertine Destroyed* (pantomime)
City: London Theater: Drury Lane
Composer: ? Choreographer: ?
With: Coleman's *The Mountaineers*
Source: *London Stage,* pt. 5, vol. 3.
Comments: Cast of characters: Don Antonio, Don Ferdinand, Don Juan, Scaramouch, boatswain, Donna Anna, Isabella, Inis, Katharina, Viletta.

Year: 1796 Date: 20 July
Title: *Don Juan* (pantomime)
City: Norfolk, Virginia Theater: New Theater
Composer: ? Choreographer: ?
Source: Sonneck, *Early Opera,* 190.

Year: 1796 Season: autumn
Title: *Il Don Giovanni* (opera)
City: Foiano
Composer: Vincenzo Fabrizi Librettist: Giambattista Lorenzi
Source: *Indice,* 1796–97, 55.

Year: 1796 Season: autumn
Title: *Il convitato di pietra* (opera)
City: Lisbon Theater: San Carlo
Composer: Vincenzo Fabrizi Librettist: Giambattista Lorenzi
With: Cimarosa's *La finta ammalata*
Source: Kunze, *Don Giovanni vor Mozart,* 87; Catalogue, Carvalhães Collection, 88, Accademia Santa Cecilia, Rome, for season and theater.

Year: 1796 Date: 12 November
Title: [*Don Giovanni ossia Il convitato di pietra*] (opera)
City: Madrid Theater: Teatro los Caños del Peral
Composer: ? Librettist: ?
Comments: According to Kunze (*Don Giovanni vor Mozart,* 138), following Manferrari (*Dizionario universale* 2:42), this version is by Bertati and Gazzaniga. However, Loewenberg (*Annals,* 441) states that "according to the libretto" this is the Lorenzi and Fabrizi version. See also Loewenberg, *Annals,* 358.

Year: 1797–99
Title: *Don Juan* (pantomime ballet)
City: Charleston, South Carolina Theater: City Theater
Composer: ? Choreographer: ?
Source: Sonneck, *Early Opera,* 180, table J.

Year: 1797–98
Title: *Il Don Giovanni* (opera)
City: Porto (Portugal)
Composer: ? Librettist: ?
With: *L'impresario in angustie,* no composer listed
Source: *Indice,* 1797–98, 103–4.

Year: 1797 Season: carnival
Title: *Don Giovanni* (opera)
City: Urbino Theater: Nuovo Teatro dell'Accademia
Composer: Vincenzo Fabrizi Librettist: Giambattista Lorenzi
Source: *Indice,* 1796–97, 110.

Year: 1797 Season: spring
Title: *Il Don Giovanni* (opera)
City: Bastia
Composer: various Librettist: ?
With: *Il principe spazzacamino,* various
Source: *Indice,* 1797–98, 5.

Year: 1797 Season: ascension
Title: *Il convitato di pietra* (ballet)
City: Venice Theater: San Benedetto
Composer: Luigi Marescalchi Choreographer: Onorato Viganò
With: Portogallo's *Il ritorno di Serse*
Source: Opera libretto, Carvalhães Collection, Accademia Santa Cecilia, Rome.

Year: 1797 Date: 19 May
Title: *Don Juan; or, The Libertine Destroyed* (pantomime)
City: London Theater: Drury Lane
Composer: ? Choreographer: ?
With: Cowley's *The Belle's Stratagem*
Source: *London Stage,* pt. 5, vol. 3.
Comments: Same as 1796, Drury Lane.

Year: 1797 Date: 22 May; 27 Sept.
Title: *Don Juan* (ballet pantomime)
City: Boston Theater: Haymarket Theater
Composer: ? Choreographer: ?
Source: Sonneck, *Early Opera,* 148, table E.

Year: 1797 Date: 30 September
Title: *Don Juan* (pantomime)
City: Fredricksburg, Virginia Theater: New Theater
Composer: ? Choreographer: ?
Source: Sonneck, *Early Opera,* 189; Sonneck quotes: "The fireworks by Mr. T. West."

Year: 1798 through carnival 1799
Title: *Il convitato di pietra* (ballet)

City: Granata Theater: Reale Teatro
Composer: ? Choreographer: Leopoldo Banchelli
Source: *Indice,* 1798–99, 53.

Year: 1798 through carnival 1799
Title: *D. Giovanni Tenorio* (ballet)
City: Porto (Portugal) Theater: Real Teatro di San Giovanni della Battaglia
Composer: ? Choreographer: Luigi Chiaveri
Source: *Indice,* 1798–99, 115–17.

Year: 1798 Season: spring
Title: *Il Don Giovanni* (opera)
City: Bastia
Composer: various Librettist: ?
With: *Il principe spazzacamino,* various
Source: *Indice,* 1798–99, 10.

Year: 1798 Date: 11 May; 13 June
Title: *Don Juan; or, The Libertine Destroyed* (pantomime)
City: London Theater: Drury Lane
Composer: ? Choreographer: ?
With: Murphy's *Know Your Own Mind*
Source: *London Stage,* pt. 5, vol. 3.
Comments: Same as 1796, Drury Lane.

Year: 1798 Season: summer
Title: *Il Don Giovanni* (opera)
City: Pescia (Pistoia) Theater: Regio Teatro degli Accademici
Composer: Vincenzo Fabrizi Librettist: Giambattista Lorenzi
Source: *Indice,* 1798–99, 109.

Year: 1798 Season: autumn
Title: *Il Don Giovanni* (opera)
City: Alba
Composer: ? Librettist: ?
Source: *Indice,* 1798–99, 1.

Year: 1798 Season: autumn
Title: *Il Don Giovanni* (opera)
City: Colle (Siena)
Composer: Vincenzo Fabrizi Librettist: Giambattista Lorenzi
Source: *Indice,* 1798–99, 29.

Year: 1799 Season: summer
Title: *Il Don Giovanni* (opera)
City: Bologna Theater: Marsigli Rossi
Composer: ? Librettist: ?
Source: *Indice, 1799–1800*, 84.

Year: 1800 Season: carnival
Title: *Don Giovanni Tenorio* (opera)
City: Cesena Theater: Teatro Accademico
Composer: ? Librettist: ?
Source: *Indice, 1799–1800*, 34.

Year: 1800 Date: 2 June
Title: *Don Juan; or, The Libertine Destroyed* (pantomime)
City: London Theater: Covent Garden
Composer: Gluck, William Reeve Director: Charles Antony Delpini
With: Macnally's *Fashionable Levities*
Source: *London Stage*, pt. 5, vol. 3.
Comments: Characters: Don Juan, Governor, Don Fernando, fisherman, Spanish gents., alguazile, waiters, musicians, sailors, Scaramouch, Donna Anna, fishermen's wives.

Bibliography

Abert, Hermann. *Mozart's "Don Giovanni."* Trans. Peter Gellhorn. London: Eulenburg Books, 1976.

Ademollo, Alessandro. *I teatri di Roma nel secolo decimosettimo.* 1888. Reprint. Bologna: Forni, 1969.

Aitkin, George Atherton. "Shadwell, Thomas." In *The Dictionary of National Biography* 17:1278–81. Oxford: Oxford University Press, 1960.

Alberti, Luciano. "Note per la riproposta di una sintomatica opera buffa: *Il convitato di pietra* di Gazzaniga." *Chigiana* 29–30, nos. 9–10 (1975): 185–187.

Alborg, Juan Luis. *Historia de la literatura española.* Vol. 3. Madrid: Gredos, 1972.

Allacci, Lione. *Drammaturgia di Lione Allacci accresciuta fino all'anno MDCCLV.* 1755. Reprint. Turin: Bottega d'Erasmo, 1966.

Anderson, Emily, trans. and ed. *The Letters of Mozart and his Family.* 3d ed. New York: Norton, 1985.

Angelini, Franca. "Le raccolte di scenari e il mito di Don Giovanni." In *Il teatro barocco,* 254–59. Bari: Laterza, 1979.

Angiolini, Gasparo. *Dissertation sur les ballets pantomimes des anciens, pour servir de programme au ballet pantomime tragique de Semiramis.* Introduction by Walter Toscanini. 1765. Reprint. N.p.: Dalle Nogare e Armetti, 1956.

———. *Lettere di Gasparo Angiolini a Monsieur Noverre sopra i Balli Pantomimi.* Milan: Bianchi, 1773.

Austen, John. *The Story of Don Juan: A Study of the Legend and of the Hero.* London: Secker, 1939.

Bacher, Otto. "Ein Frankfurter Szenar zu Glucks Don Juan." *Zeitschrift für Musikwissenschaft* 7, nos. 9–10 (June/July 1925): 570–74.

———. *Die Geschichte der Frankfurter Oper im 18. Jahrhundert.* Frankfurt: n.p., 1926.

Balmas, Enea. *Il mito di Don Giovanni nel seicento francese.* Vol. 1, *Testi;* vol. 2, *Nascita ed evoluzione del mito, dagli scenari a Rosimond.* Milan: Cisalpino-Goliardica, 1977–78.

Baquero, Arcadio. *Don Juan y su evolución dramática.* 2 vols. Madrid: Editora nacional, 1966.

Barlow, Joseph W. "Zorrilla's Indebtedness to Zamora." *Romanic Review* 17 (1926): 303–18.

Bartha, Dénes, and László Somfai. *Haydn als Opernkapellmeister.* Mainz: Schott, 1960.

Bernacki, Ludwik. *Teatr, dramat i muzyka za Stanisława Augusta.* 2 vols. Lvov: Wydawnictwo zakładu narodowego imienia ossolińskich, 1925.

Berrio, Antonio García. "El Primer *Convidado de Piedra* no Español." *Revista de Filología Española* 50 (1967): 25–56.

Bibliographie des Musikschrifttums. 19 vols. Mainz: Schott, 1960–78.

Biographisch-Bibliographisches Quellen-Lexikon. Ed. Robert Eitner. 11 vols. Graz: Verlagsanstalt, 1959–60.

Bjurström, Per. *Feast and Theater in Queen Christina's Rome.* Stockholm: Bengtsons, 1966.

Borgman, A. S. *Thomas Shadwell: His Life and Comedies.* New York: New York University Press, 1928.

Brenner, Clarence D. *A Bibliographical List of Plays in the French Language 1700–1789.* 1947. Reprint. New York: AMS, 1979.

———. *The Théâtre Italien: Its Repertory, 1716–1793.* Berkeley: University of California Press, 1961.

Brunelli, Bruno. *I teatri di Padova dalle origini alla fine del secolo xix.* Padua: Draghi, 1921.

Cailhava de l'Estandoux. *De L'Art de la comédie, Nouvelle édition.* 1786. Reprint in 2 vols. Geneva: Slatkine, 1970.

Canning, Hugh. "Vadstena: A Castrato *Giovanni.*" *Opera* 37, no. 11 (November 1986): 1255–56.

Casanova, Giacomo. *History of My Life.* Trans. Willard R. Trask. 12 vols. New York: Harcourt Brace Jovanovich, 1966–71.

Caselli, Aldo. *Catalogo delle opere liriche pubblicate in Italia.* Florence: Olschki, 1969.

Chrysander, Friedrich. "Die Oper Don Giovanni von Gazzaniga und von Mozart." *Vierteljahrsschrift für Musikwissenschaft* 4 (1888): 352–435.

Chujoy, Anatole, and P. W. Manchester. *The Dance Encyclopedia.* New York: Simon and Schuster, 1967.

Chybiński, A. *Słownik muzyków dawnej Polski.* Kraków: Polskie wydawnictwo muzyczne, 1948–49.

Cooper, Martin. *Gluck.* 1935. Reprint. N.p.: Scholarly Press, 1978.

Corneille, Thomas. *Théâtre de Pierre et de Thomas Corneille.* Vol. 2. Paris: Didot, 1852.

Cramer, C. F. *Magazin der Musik* 1 (1783): 373–74.

Crinò, Anna Maria. "Documenti inediti sulla vita e l'opera di Jacopo e di Giacinto Andrea Cicognini." *Studi secenteschi* 2 (1961): 255–86.

Croce, Benedetto. "Intorno a Giacinto Andrea Cicognini e al *Convitato di pietra.*" In *Aneddoti di varia letteratura* 2:116–33. 2d ed. Bari: Laterza, 1953.

———. *I teatri di Napoli.* Bari: Laterza, 1916.

Croll, Gerhard. "Glucks *Don Juan* Freigesprochen." *Österreichische Musik Zeitschrift* 31, no. 1 (1976): 12–15.

Da Ponte, Lorenzo. *An Extract from the Life of Lorenzo Da Ponte.* New York: Grey, 1819.

———. *Memorie e altri scritti.* Ed. Cesare Pagnini. Milan: Longanesi, 1971.

———. *Tre libretti per Mozart.* Ed. Paolo Lecaldano. Milan: Rizzoli, 1956.

De la Fage, Adrien. "Notices sur Jacques Tritto." In *Miscellanées musicales,* 169–85. 1844. Reprint. Bologna: Forni, 1969.

Della Corte, Andrea. *L'opera comica italiana nel '700.* Bari: Laterza, 1923.

de Napoli, Giuseppe. *La triade melodrammatica altamurana: Giacomo Tritto, Vincenzo Lavigna, Saverio Mercadante.* Milan: n.p., 1931.

Dent, Edward J. *Mozart's Operas.* 2d ed. Oxford: Oxford University Press, 1973.

de Rinaldis, Aldo. *Lettere inedite di Salvator Rosa a G. B. Ricciardi.* Rome: Palombi, 1939.

Desboulmiers, Jean-Auguste Julien. *Histoire anecdotique et raisonnée du Théâtre Italien.* 1769. Reprint in 2 vols. Geneva: Slatkine, 1968.

Deutsch, Otto Erich. *Mozart: A Documentary Biography.* Stanford: Stanford University Press, 1965.

Dieckmann, Friedrich. "Erdbeben auf dem Hoftheater: Don Juan bei Gluck und Angiolini." *Musik und Gesellschaft* 37 (November 1987): 579–86.

Disher, M. Willson. *Clowns and Pantomimes.* 1925. Reprint. New York: Blom, 1968.

Dizionario biografico degli italiani. Rome: Treccani, 1960–.

Dizionario enciclopedico della letteratura italiana. Bari: Laterza, 1966–70.

Dizionario enciclopedico universale della musica e dei musicisti: Le biografie. Ed. Alberto Basso. 8 vols. Turin: UTET, 1985.

Dokoupil, Vladislav, and Vladimír Telec. *Hudební staré tisky ve fondech universitní knihovny v brně.* Brno: Universitní knihovna, 1975.

Edwards, Gwynne, ed. *The Trickster of Seville and the Stone Guest.* By Tirso de Molina. Warminster: Aris and Phillips, 1986.

Einstein, Alfred. *Gluck.* Trans. Eric Blom. Rev. ed. 1964. Reprint. New York: McGraw-Hill, 1972.

Enciclopedia della musica. Ed. Claudio Sartori. 4 vols. Milan: Ricordi, 1963–64.

Enciclopedia dello spettacolo. 9 vols. Rome: Le Maschere, 1954–62.

Enciclopedia dello spettacolo: Indice-repertorio. Rome: Unione editoriale, 1968.

The Encyclopedia of Dance and Ballet. Ed. Mary Clarke and David Vaughan. London: Pitman, 1977.

E[ngel], C[arl]. "Views and Reviews." *Musical Quarterly* 29, no. 4 (October 1943): 521–30.

Engländer, Richard, ed. *Don Juan/Semiramis, Ballets Pantomimes von Gasparo Angiolini.* Ser. 2, vol. 1 of *Sämtliche Werke* by Christoph Willibald Gluck. Kassel: Bärenreiter, 1966.

Farinelli, Arturo. *Don Giovanni.* 1896. Reprint. Milan: Bocca, 1946.

Fellmann, Hans Georg. "Die Böhmsche Theatertruppe und ihre Zeit, ein Beitrag zur deutschen Theatergeschichte des 18. Jahrhunderts." *Theater geschichtliche Forschungen* 38 (1928): 68–86.

Ferrari, Paolo-Emilio. *Spettacoli drammatico-musicali e coreografici in Parma, dall'anno 1628 all'anno 1883*. 1884. Reprint. Bologna: Forni, 1969.

Fétis, F. J. *Biographie universelle des musiciens*. 12th ed. Paris: Didot, 1866.

Fierz, Gerold. "Ein schwedischer Musiksommer: Melanis *L'empio punito (Don Juan 1669)* in Vadstena." *Opernwelt* 27, no. 10 (1986): 34–36.

Fitzlyon, April. *The Libertine Librettist: A Biography of Mozart's Librettist Lorenzo da Ponte*. London: Calder, 1955.

Foppa, Giuseppe Maria. *Appendice alle memorie storiche della vita di Giuseppe M.a Foppa viniziano scritta da lui medesimo*. Venice: n.p., 1842.

———. *Memorie storiche della vita di Giuseppe M.a Foppa viniziano scritte da lui medesimo*. Venice: Molinari, 1840.

Forti-Lewis, Angelica. "Il mito di Don Giovanni?" *Critica letteraria* 16, no. 3 (1988): 583–90.

———. "Parole o musica? Don Giovanni 'illuminato' da Goldoni e Mozart." *Italian Quarterly* 30, no. 117 (Summer 1989): 31–41.

Fournel, Victor. *Théâtre du Marais*. Vol. 3 of *Les Contemporains de Molière*. Paris: Firmin-Didot, 1875.

Fuà, Franco. *Don Giovanni attraverso le letterature spagnuola e italiana*. Turin: Lattes, [n.d.]

———. *L'opera di Filippo Acciajoli*. Fossombrone: Ceppetelli, 1921.

Fucilla, Joseph G. "*El Convidado de Piedra* in Naples in 1625." *Bulletin of the Comediantes* 10, no. 1 (Spring 1958): 5–6.

Galle, Leon. *Wojciech Bogusławski*. Warsaw: Areta, 1925.

Garbelotto, Antonio. "Piccola enciclopedia musicale padovana." *Padova e la sua provincia* 17 (October 1971): 20–25.

Gazzaniga, Giuseppe. *Don Giovanni o sia Il Convitato di Pietra*. Ed. Stefan Kunze. Kassel: Bärenreiter, 1974.

Geiringer, Karl. "From Guglielmi to Haydn: The Transformation of an Opera." In *Report of the Eleventh Congress of the International Musicological Society Copenhagen 1972*, 391–95. Copenhagen: Hansen, 1974.

Gendarme De Bévotte, Georges. *Le Festin de Pierre avant Molière*. Paris: Cornély, 1907.

———. *La Légende de Don Juan, son évolution dans la littérature des origines au romantisme*. 1906. Reprint. Geneva: Slatkine, 1970.

Gertsman, Lois. "Musical Character Depiction in Gluck's *Don Juan*." *Dance Chronicle* 1, no. 1 (1977): 8–21.

Gianturco, Carolyn. "Evidence for a Late Roman School of Opera." *Music and Letters* 56, no. 1 (January 1975): 4–17.

Glendinning, Nigel. *A Literary History of Spain: The Eighteenth Century*. London: Benn, 1972.

Goldin, Daniela. "Mozart, Da Ponte e il linguaggio dell'opera buffa." In *Venezia e il melodramma nel settecento*, 213–77. Florence: Olschki, 1981.

Goldoni, Carlo. *Don Giovanni Tenorio o sia Il dissoluto.* 2d ed. Vol. 9 of *Tutte le opere di Carlo Goldoni,* ed. Giuseppe Ortolani. Milan: Mondadori, 1960.

———. *Epistolario.* 2d ed. Vol. 14 of *Tutte le opere di Carlo Goldoni,* ed. Giuseppe Ortolani. Milan: Mondadori, 1969.

———. *Mémoires, Prefazioni di Carlo Goldoni ai diciassette tomi delle commedie edite a Venezia da G. B. Pasquali.* 5th ed. Vol. 1 of *Tutte le opere di Carlo Goldoni,* ed. Giuseppe Ortolani. Milan: Mondadori, 1973.

Gran Enciclopedia Rialp. Madrid: Ediciones Rialp, 1971–76.

Great Soviet Encyclopedia. 3d ed. New York: Macmillan, 1973.

Haas, Robert. *Gluck und Durazzo im Burgtheater.* Vienna: Peters, 1925.

———. "Die Wiener Ballet-Pantomime im 18. Jahrhundert und Glucks Don Juan." In *Studien zur Musikwissenschaft,* 6–36. Beihefte der Denkmäler der Tonkunst Österreich, vol. 10. Vienna: Zehntes Heft Universal-Edition, 1923.

———. "Der Wiener Bühnentanz von 1740 bis 1767." In *Jahrbuch der Musikbibliothek Peters für 1937,* 77–93. 1937. Reprint. Vaduz: Kraus, 1965.

———. *Die Wiener Oper.* Vienna, Budapest: n.p., 1926.

———, ed. *Don Juan, Pantomimisches Ballett.* Vol. 2 of *Werke* by Christoph Willibald Gluck. 1923. Reprint. Graz: Akademische Druck- und Verlagsanstalt, 1960.

Harich, János. "Das Repertoire des Opernkapellmeisters Joseph Haydn in Eszterháza (1780–1790)." *Haydn Yearbook* 1 (1962): 9–110.

Heartz, Daniel. "From Garrick to Gluck: The Reform of Theatre and Opera in the Mid-Eighteenth Century." *Proceedings of the Royal Musical Association* 94 (1968): 111–27.

———. "Goldoni, Don Giovanni and the dramma giocoso." *Musical Times* 120 (December 1979): 993–98.

Hoboken, Anthony van. *J. Haydn: Thematisch-bibliographisches Werkverzeichnis.* Vol. 2. Mainz: Schott, 1971.

Hodges, Sheila. *Lorenzo Da Ponte: The Life and Times of Mozart's Librettist.* New York: Universe Books, 1985.

Hopkinson, Cecil. *A Bibliography of the Printed Works of C. W. von Gluck 1714–1787.* 2d ed. New York: Broude Brothers, 1967.

Indice de' spettacoli teatrali. 22 vols. Milan: 1764–86.

Indice de' teatrali spettacoli. 14 vols. Milan: 1787–1800.

Jersild, J. "Le ballet d'action italien du XVIIIe siècle au Danemark." *Acta musicologica* 14 (1942): 74–94.

John, Nicholas, ed. *Don Giovanni* by Wolfang Amadeus Mozart. Opera Guide 18. London: Calder, 1983.

Kelly, Michael. *Reminiscences.* Ed. Roger Fiske. London: Oxford University Press, 1975.

Kirstein, Lincoln. *Dance: A Short History of Classical Theatrical Dancing.* 1935. Reprint. New York: Dance Horizons, 1969.

———. *Movement and Metaphor: Four Centuries of Ballet.* New York: Praeger, 1970.

Koegler, Horst. *The Concise Oxford Dictionary of Ballet.* London: Oxford University Press, 1977.

Kuhn, Rose Marie. "De la comédie à la morale: Le Don Juan français du dix-septième siècle et sa transformation dans le théâtre néerlandais." *Papers on French Seventeenth Century Literature* 13 (1986): 104–32.

Kunze, Stefan. *Don Giovanni vor Mozart.* Munich: Wilhelm Fink, 1972.

———. "Elementi veneziani nella librettistica di Lorenzo Da Ponte." In *Venezia e il melodramma nel settecento,* 279–92. Florence: Olschki, 1981.

———. "Su alcune farse di Giuseppe Foppa musicate da Francesco Gardi." In *I vicini di Mozart,* vol. 2, 479–88. Florence: Olschki, 1989.

L., P. H. Review of *Don Giovanni o sia Il Convitato di Pietra* by Giuseppe Gazzaniga, ed. Stefan Kunze. *Musical Quarterly* 62, no. 1 (January 1976): 125–34.

Lagrave, Henri. "Don Juan au siècle des lumières." In *Approches des lumières: Mélanges offerts a Jean Fabre,* 257–76. Paris: Klincksieck, 1974.

Landon, H. C. Robbins. *Haydn: Chronicle and Works.* 5 vols. Bloomington: Indiana University Press, 1976–80.

Lanfranchi, Ariella. "La librettistica italiana del Settecento." In *Storia dell'opera,* vol. 3, pt. 2: 47–141. Turin: UTET, 1977.

Lazzaro-Weis, Carol. "Parody and Farce in the Don Juan Myth in the Eighteenth Century." *Eighteenth-Century Life* 8, no. 3 (May 1983): 35–48.

Lea, Kathleen M. *Italian Popular Comedy: A Study in the Commedia dell'Arte.* 2 vols. Oxford: Clarendon Press, 1934.

Leone, Guido. *L'opera a Palermo dal 1653 al 1987.* 2 vols. Palermo: Publisicula Editrice, 1988.

Leydi, Roberto, and Renata M. Leydi. *Marionette e burattini.* Milan: Collana del "Gallo Grande," 1958.

Litzmann, Berthold. "Don Juan als Ballet," *National-Zeitung, Sonntags-Beilage,* 23 October 1887.

Loewenberg, Alfred. *Annals of Opera 1597–1940.* 3d ed. Totowa, N.J.: Rowman and Littlefield, 1978.

The London Stage 1660–1800. 11 vols. Carbondale, Ill.: Southern Illinois University Press, 1960–68.

Lynham, Deryck. *The Chevalier Noverre: Father of Modern Ballet.* London: Sylvan Press, 1950.

Macchia, Giovanni. *Tra Don Giovanni e Don Rodrigo.* Milan: Adelphi, 1989.

———. *Vita avventure e morte di Don Giovanni.* Bari: Laterza, 1966.

Mandel, Oscar, ed. *The Theatre of Don Juan: A Collection of Plays and Views, 1630–1963.* Lincoln: University of Nebraska Press, 1963.

Manferrari, Umberto. *Dizionario universale delle opere melodrammatiche.* 3 vols. Florence: Sansoni, 1954.

Marks, Paul F. "The Reform of Subject and Style in Ballet-Pantomime at Vienna between

1740–1767." In *Woman in the 18th Century and Other Essays,* ed. Paul Fritz and Richard Morton, 141–85. Toronto: Hakkert, 1976.

Maynard, Olga. "Don Juan and his Artistic Metamorphosis." *Dance Magazine* 51 (January 1977): 52–66.

Mendel, Herman. *Musikalisches Conversations—Lexikon.* Leipzig: List und Francke, 1870.

Mila, Massimo. *Lettura del Don Giovanni di Mozart.* Turin: Einaudi, 1988.

Miller, Jonathan, ed. *Don Giovanni: Myths of Seduction and Betrayal.* New York: Schocken Books, 1990.

Mitjana, Rafael. *Discantes y Contrapuntos.* Valencia: F. Sempere, [1905].

Molière. *Don Giovanni ovvero Il convitato di pietra.* Ed. and trans. Luigi Lunari. Milan: Rizzoli, 1980.

———. *Oeuvres complètes.* Ed. Georges Couton. Vol. 2. Mayenne: Gallimard, 1971.

———. *Oeuvres complètes.* Ed. Robert Jouanny. Vol. 1. Paris: Garnier, 1962.

———. *Oeuvres de Molière.* Ed. Eugène Despois and Paul Mesnard. Nouvelle édition. Vol. 5. Paris: Hachette, 1880.

Le Molièriste, revue mensuelle. Paris: Librairie Tresse, April 1886.

Molmenti, P. *Carteggi casanoviani: Lettere di Giacomo Casanova e di altri a lui.* Naples: Sandron, 1916.

Monaco, Vanda. *Giambattista Lorenzi e la commedia per musica.* Naples: Berisio, 1968.

Morini, Ugo. *La R. Accademia degli Immobili ed il suo Teatro La Pergola.* Pisa: Simoncini, 1926.

Mozart, W. A. *Briefe und Aufzeichnungen.* Ed. Wilhelm A. Bauer and Otto Erich Deutsch. 6 vols. Kassel: Bärenreiter, 1962–71.

Murata, Margaret. "Il carnevale a Roma sotto Clemente IX Rospigliosi." *Rivista italiana di musicologia* 12, no. 1 (1977): 83–99.

Die Musik in Geschichte und Gegenwart. Ed. Friedrich Blume. 17 vols. Kassel: Bärenreiter, 1949–86.

Musikalisches Conversations-Lexikon. Ed. Hermann Mendel. 11 vols. Leipzig: List und Francke, n.d.

The New Grove Dictionary of Music and Musicians. Ed. Stanley Sadie. 20 vols. London: Macmillan, 1980.

Nicole, Allardyce. *Masks, Mimes and Miracles.* New York: Cooper Square, 1963.

Olivier, Jean-Jacques. *Les Comédiens français dans les cours d'Allemagne au XVIIIe siècle.* Vol. 4. 1905. Reprint. Geneva: Slatkine, 1971.

Oreglia, Giacomo. *The Commedia dell'Arte.* New York: Hill and Wang, 1964.

Ortolani, Giuseppe. "Nota storica." In *Opere complete di Carlo Goldoni edite dal Municipio di Venezia* 23:353–60. Venice: Zanetti, 1926.

Osthoff, Wolfgang. "Gli endecasillabi villotistici in *Don Giovanni* e *Nozze di Figaro.*" In *Venezia e il melodramma nel settecento,* 293–311. Florence: Olschki, 1981.

Pandolfi, Vito. *La Commedia dell'Arte: Storia e testi.* 6 vols. Florence: Sansoni, 1957–61.

Parfaict, François, and Claude Parfaict. *Histoire de l'ancien théâtre italien, depuis son origine en France, jusqu'à sa suppression en l'année 1697*. 1767. Reprint. New York: AMS, 1978.

Parsons, Charles H. *The Mellen Opera Reference Index*. 12 vols. Lewiston, N.Y.: Edwin Mellen, 1986–.

Pestelli, Giorgio. *The Age of Mozart and Beethoven*. Cambridge: Cambridge University Press, 1984.

Petrobelli, Pierluigi. "*Don Giovanni* in Italia." In *Colloquium "Mozart und Italien."* Analecta Musicologica 18:30–51. Cologne: A. Volk, 1978.

Pietrucci, Napoleone. *Biografia degli artisti padovani*. 1858. Reprint. Bologna: Forni, 1970.

Pirrotta, Nino. *Don Giovanni in musica*. Venice: Marsilio, 1991.

Pizzari, Serafino. *Le mythe de Don Juan et la comédie de Molière*. Paris: Nizet, 1986.

Price, Curtis A. *Henry Purcell and the London Stage*. Cambridge: Cambridge University Press, 1984.

Price, Elizabeth. "Don Juan: A Chronicle of His Literary Adventures in Germanic Territory." Ph.D. diss., Washington University, 1974.

Prod'homme, Jacques Gabriel. *Gluck*. 1948. Reprint. New York: AMS, 1978.

Prosnak, Jan. *Kultura muzyczna Warszawy XVIII wieku*. Kraków: Polskie Wydawnictwo Muzyczne, 1955.

Raszewski, Zbigniew. "Rondo alla Polacca: Operowa działalność Wojciecha Bogusławskiego w Latach 1779–83." *Pamiętnik literacki* 61, no. 2 (1970): 177–91.

Reiss, Józef. *Podręczna Encyklopedia Muzyki*. Kraków: Wiedza, 1949.

Riemann Musik Lexikon. Ed. Hugo Riemann. 5 vols. Mainz: Schott, 1959–75.

Rivara, Annie. "Don Juan et la mort ou la difficulté d'être libertin (Dorimon, Villiers, Molière, Th. Corneille, Rosimond et les *Don Juan* de la Foire)." In *Etudes et Recherches sur le XVIIIe siècle*, 1–55. Aix-en-Provence: Université de Provence, 1980.

Rolandi, Ulderico. *Il librettista del "Matrimonio segreto" Giovanni Bertati*. Tricase: Raeli, 1926.

Roscioni, Carlo Marinelli, ed. *Il Teatro di San Carlo, la cronologia 1737–1987*. Naples: Guida, 1987.

Rousset, Jean. "Don Juan dans l'opéra avant Mozart." In *L'Opéra au XVIIIe siècle*, 97–109. Aix-en-Provence: Université de Provence, 1982.

———. *Le Mythe de Don Juan*. Paris: Colin, 1978.

Rushton, Julian. *W. A. Mozart "Don Giovanni."* Cambridge Opera Handbooks. Cambridge: Cambridge University Press, 1981.

Russell, Charles C. "The First Don Giovanni Opera: *La pravità castigata* by Eustachio Bambini." In *Mozart-Jahrbuch 1980–83*, 385–92. Kassel: Bärenreiter, 1983.

———. "The Libertine Reformed: *Don Juan* by Gluck and Angiolini." *Music and Letters* 65, no. 1 (January 1984): 17–27.

Sadie, Stanley. "Some Operas of 1787." *Musical Times* 122 (July 1981): 474–77.

Sáenz-Alonso, Mercedes. *Don Juan y el donjuanismo*. Madrid: Guadarrama, 1969.

Saint-Foix, Georges de. *W. A. Mozart, sa vie musicale e son oeuvre.* 2d ed. 5 vols. Belgium: Desclée, de Brouwer, 1946.

Salvioli, G. "Il primo *Convitato di pietra* e il vero autore del libretto *Il flauto magico.*" *Gazzetta musicale di Milano* 42 (1887): 379–80.

Salvioli, Giovanni, and Carlo Salvioli. *Bibliografia universale del teatro drammatico italiano.* Venice: n.p., 1903.

Sartori, Claudio. *I libretti italiani a stampa dalle origini al 1800.* Vols. 1–4. (A–Q). Milan: Bertola e Locatelli, 1990.

Schaffer, Aaron. "Thomas Corneille's Re-working of Molière's *Don Juan.*" *Modern Philology* 19 (1921): 163–75.

Schatz, Albert. "Giovanni Bertati." *Vierteljahrsschrift für Musikwissenschaft* 5 (1889): 231–71.

Scherillo, Michele. *L'opera buffa napoletana durante il settecento.* 2d ed. Naples: Sandron, 1914.

Schilling, Gustav. *Encyclopädie der gesammten musikalischen Wissenschaften.* Stuttgart: Röhler, 1840.

Schmidl, Carlo. *Dizionario universale dei musicisti.* 2 vols. Milan: Sonzogno, 1929.

Scott, Virginia. *The Commedia dell'Arte in Paris 1644–1697.* Charlottesville: University Press of Virginia, 1990.

Sehnal, Jiří. "Počátky opery na moravě." In *O divadle na moravě,* 55–77. Acta universitatis palackianae olomucensis. Facultas philosophica. Supplementum 21. Prague: Státní pedagogické nakladatelství, 1974.

Shadwell, Thomas. *The Complete Works of Thomas Shadwell.* Ed. Montague Summers. Vol. 3. London: Fortune Press, 1927.

Singer, Armand E. "Don Juan in America." *Kentucky Foreign Language Quarterly* 7 (1960): 226–32.

———. *The Don Juan Theme, Versions and Criticism: A Bibliography.* Morgantown: West Virginia University, 1965.

———. "Second Supplement to *The Don Juan Theme.*" *West Virginia University Bulletin: Philological Papers,* ser. 70, 17, no. 12-7 (June 1970): 102–70.

———. "Extra Pages to be Inserted in West Virginia Philological Papers Volume 17 (1970)." *West Virginia University Bulletin,* ser. 71, no. 8-7 (February 1971).

———. "Third Supplement to *The Don Juan Theme.*" *West Virginia University Bulletin: Philological Papers,* ser. 74, 20, no. 3-3 (September 1973): 66–106.

———. "Fourth Supplement to *The Don Juan Theme.*" *West Virginia University Bulletin: Philological Papers,* ser. 76, 22, no. 6-4 (December 1975): 70–140.

———. "Fifth Supplement to *The Don Juan Theme.*" *West Virginia University Bulletin: Philological Papers,* ser. 81, 26, no. 1-2 (July 1980): 1–112.

———. "The Present State of Studies on the Don Juan Theme." In *Tirso's "Don Juan": The Metamorphosis of a Theme,* ed. Joseph M. Sola-Solé and George E. Gingras, 1–31. Washington, D.C.: Catholic University of America Press, 1988.

Sloman, Albert E. "The Two Versions of *El burlador de Sevilla*." *Bulletin of Hispanic Studies* 42, no. 1 (January 1965): 18–33.

Smeed, J. W. *Don Juan: Variations on a Theme*. London: Routledge, 1990.

Smith, William C. *The Italian Opera and Contemporary Ballet in London 1789–1820*. London: Society for Theater Research, 1955.

Smith, Winifred. *Italian Actors of the Renaissance*. 1930. Reprint. New York: Blom, 1968.

Sonneck, Oscar G. *Catalogue of Opera Librettos Printed before 1800*. 2 vols. Washington, D.C.: U.S. Government Printing Office, 1914.

———. *Early Opera in America*. 1915. Reprint. New York: Blom, 1963.

Sowinski, Albert. *Les musiciens polonais et slaves*. Paris: Le Clere, 1857.

Spada, Stefania. *Domenico Biancolelli ou l'art d'improviser*. Naples: Institut Universitaire Oriental, 1969.

Spaziani, Marcello. "Un capitolo della storia di Don Giovanni: Molière parodiato da Biancolelli?" In *Mélange à la mémoire de Franco Simone* 2:279–94. Geneva: Slatkine, 1981.

———. *Don Giovanni dagli scenari dell'arte alla "foire."* Rome: Edizione di storia e letteratura, 1978.

———. "Don Juan à la foire." In *L'opéra au XVIIIe siècle,* ed. André Bourde, 111–35. Aix-en-Provence: Université de Provence, 1982.

Steele, Eugene. *Carlo Goldoni: Life, Work and Times*. Ravenna: Longo, [1982].

Steiger, Franz. *Opernlexikon*. 11 vols. Tutzing: Schneider, 1975–83.

Steptoe, Andrew. *The Mozart–Da Ponte Operas*. Oxford: Clarendon Press, 1988.

Storia della letteratura italiana. Ed. Emilio Cecchi and Natalino Sapegno. 9 vols. Milan: Garzanti, 1965–69.

Storia dell'opera. Ed. Alberto Basso. 3 vols. Turin: UTET, 1977.

Surian, Elvidio. Review of *Don Juan/Semiramis, Ballets Pantomimes von Gasparo Angiolini* by Christoph Willibald Gluck, ed. Richard Engländer. *Nuova rivista musicale italiana* 11, no. 3 (1977): 506–8.

Teatr Polski czyli zbior komedyi drammy tragedyi. Vol. 53. Warsaw: P. Dufour, 1794.

Tirso de Molina. *Obras dramáticas completas*. Ed. Blanca de Los Ríos. 2 vols. Madrid: Aguilar, 1962.

Toldo, Pietro. "Nella baracca dei burattini." *Giornale storico della letteratura italiana* 51 (1908): 1–93.

Tonelli, Franco. "Molière's *Don Juan* and the Space of the Commedia dell'Arte." *Theatre Journal* 37, no. 4 (December 1985): 440–64.

Tozzi, Lorenzo. "Attorno a *Don Juan* (1761)." *Chigiana* 29–30, nos. 9–10 (1975): 549–64.

———. *Il balletto pantomimo del settecento: Gaspare Angiolini*. L'Aquila: Japadre, 1972.

Trifilo, S. Samuel. "Influencias calderonianas en el drama de Zamora y De Cañizares." *Hispanofila* 11 (1961): 39–46.

Turchi, Guido. "*Don Giovanni* di Gazzaniga-Bertati." *Chigiana* 29–30, nos. 9–10 (1975): 189–95.

Verti, Robert. "The *Indice de' teatrali spettacoli,* Milan, Venice, Rome 1764–1823." *Periodica musica* 3 (Spring 1985): 1–7.

Wade, Gerald E., and Robert J. Mayberry. "*Tan Largo Me Lo Fiáis* and *El Burlador De Sevilla Y El Convidado De Piedra.*" *Bulletin of the Comediantes* 14, no. 1 (Spring 1962): 1–16.

Weaver, Robert Lamar. "Florentine Comic Operas of the Seventeenth Century." Ph.D. diss., University of North Carolina, 1958.

———. "*Il Girello,* a 17th-Century Burlesque Opera." *Quadrivium* 12, no. 2 (1971): 141–63.

———. "Materiali per le biografie dei Melani." *Rivista italiana di musicologia* 12, no. 2 (1977): 252–95.

Weilen, U. Von. Review of *Johann Joseph Félix von Kurz, genannt Bernardon* by F. Raab. *Euphorion* 6 (1899): 350–61.

Weinstein, Leo. *The Metamorphoses of Don Juan.* 1959. Reprint. New York: AMS, 1967.

Weinstock, Herbert. *Rossini: A Biography.* New York: Knopf, 1968.

Widmann, Wilhelm. "Don Juans Bühnenwallen." *Der Merker* 7, no. 4 (15 February 1916): 121–31.

Wiel, Taddeo. *Catalogo delle opere in musica rappresentate nel secolo xviii in Venezia.* 2 vols. Venice: 1892.

———. *I teatri musicali veneziani del '700.* Venice: Visentini, 1897.

Wilson, G. B. L. *A Dictionary of Ballet.* 3d ed. New York: Theater Arts Books, 1974.

Wilson, Margaret. *Tirso de Molina.* Boston: Twayne, 1977.

Wotquenne, Alfred. *Catalogue thématique des oeuvres de Chr. W. v. Gluck.* 1904. Reprint. Wiesbaden: Breitkopf und Härtel, 1967.

Zimmerman, Franklin B. *Henry Purcell 1659–1695: An Analytical Catalogue of His Music.* London: Macmillan, 1963.

Index

Index excludes performance data.

Acciaiuoli, Filippo, 56, 58
Agnelli, Pietro, 52n
Albertini, Gioacchino, 96–101, 104, 131, 277–88
Alceste (Calzabigi, Gluck), 75
Alessandri, Felice, 115
Alfieri, Vittorio, 108
Allacci, Lione, 12n
Americana in Olanda, L' (Porta, Anfossi), 88n
Andreini, Giambattista, 11–13
Anfossi, Pasquale, 89n, 115
Angiolini, Gasparo, 75–86, 104, 122
Apolloni, Giovanni Filippo, 56, 58
Arbore di Diana, L' (Da Ponte, Martín y Soler), 122
Ariosto, Lodovico, 217n
Armida abbandonata (Bambini), 67n
Armida abbandonata (Foppa, Bertoni), 109
Artaserse (Bambini), 67n
Artemisia (Calegari), 93n
Ateista fulminato, L' (*scenario,* Rome), 15, 31, 60n
"Autore a chi legge, L'" (Goldoni), 44n, 45n
Aveugle clairvoyant, L', 113
Badini, Carlo Francesco, 89n, 117–18
Baglione, Antonio, 113n
Ballet versions of the Don Juan legend, 75–86
Balmas, Enea, 19n, 23n, 29n, 30n, 32
Bambini, Eustachio, 67, 68, 73–74, 79, 131, 133–81
Bambini, Laura, 68
Baquero, Arcadio, 37, 59
Barone di Trocchia, Il (Cerlone, Gazzaniga), 112
Bartha, Dénes, 89n
Bassaglia, Giammaria, 52
Béjart, Armande, 29–30
Bellini, Vincenzo, 102
Berrio, Antonio García, 12n
Bertati, Giovanni, 31, 48n, 83, 84, 104n, 108, 112–13, 114–18, 120, 121–26, 131, 132, 381–405, 407–43
Bertoni, Ferdinando, 109
Bianchi, Franceso, 116n
Biancolelli, Domenico, 16–18, 53, 70
Biblioteca Nazionale (Florence), 12
Bocchini, Bartolomeo, 11
Bogusławski, Wojciech, 97–98, 100–101
Böhm, Johannes, 83
Bologna, Luigi, 88, 89n

Bologna, Matilde, 89
Brenner, Clarence, 53n
Burbero di buon core, Il (Da Ponte, Martín y Soler), 113
Burlador de Sevilla y Convidado de piedra, El (Tirso de Molina), 1–6, 7, 8, 11, 20, 35, 36, 37, 42, 69
Bustelli, Giuseppe, 86, 88

Cacciatrice brillante, La (Albertini), 96
Cailhava de l'Estandoux, 49–50, 53
Caldara, Antonio, 295n
Calderón de la Barca, 42, 44
Calegari, Giuseppe, 71, 93–95, 104, 105, 108, 131, 227–75
Calipso abbandonato (Porta, Bologna), 89n
Calzabigi, Ranieri, 75
Capriccio drammatico, Il (Bertati, Valentini, Gazzaniga), 112–13, 114–15, 118n, 119–21, 131, 132, 381–405
Capriccio drammatico, Il (London, 1794), 118n
Cardini, Rosa, 68
Casa Goldoni, 7, 52n, 115n
Casanova, Giacomo, 2–3, 76, 117
Casoni, Giovanni, 114n
Casti, Giambattista, 115–16, 118
Cavalli, Francesco, 6
Cencetti, Gio. Batta, 97
Cerlone, Francesco, 52, 112
Cesti, Antonio, 6, 56
Chigi, Cardinal Flavio, 56, 57
Christina of Sweden, Queen, 56, 57, 60
Cicognini, Giacinto Andrea, 6–11, 12, 12n, 13, 14, 20, 21, 25, 27, 36, 41, 44, 51, 52, 53, 60, 69, 70, 83, 91, 95, 120
Cicognini, Jacopo, 6–7
Cimarosa, Domenico, 101, 103, 113, 115
Circe ed Ulisse (Albertini), 96
Clarissa Harlowe (Richardson), 50
Clemente IX, Pope, 55, 56
Colloredo, Archbishop Hieronymus, 87
Colonna, Caterina, 57
Comica del cielo, La (Rospigliosi), 55
Commedia dell'arte versions of the Don Juan legend, 11, 13–18, 19, 44, 50, 51, 52, 53, 60, 66, 69, 70, 83, 90, 95, 122
Conservatorio Luigi Cherubini (Florence), 97, 131
Contrattempi, I (Porta, Sarti), 89n
Convitato di pietra, Il: with Domenico Locatelli, 16; with Tiberio Fiorilli, 11n
Convitato di pietra, Il (Andreini), 11–13
Convitato di pietra, Il (Biancolelli), 17–18, 70
Convitato di pietra, Il (Calegari), 93, 94–95, 108, 131, 227–75
Convitato di pietra, Il (Cicognini), 6–11, 44, 52, 60n, 69, 91, 95
Convitato di pietra, Il (Giliberto), 13
Convitato di pietra, Il (Lepicq, Gluck), 53–54
Convitato di pietra, Il (Lorenzi, Fabrizi), 93, 107–8
Convitato di pietra, Il (Lorenzi, Tritto), 101–2, 104–7, 131, 132, 289–326
Convitato di pietra, Il (Perrucci), 36, 70
Convitato di pietra, Il (*scenario,* Naples), 14–15, 60n, 70
Convitato di pietra, Il (*scenario,* Rome), 13–15, 60n
Convitato di pietra, opera reggia et esemplare, Il (Cicognini), 52n
Convitato di pietra o sia Il dissoluto, Il (Porta, Righini), 84, 86, 88–93, 98–101, 131, 183–226, 225–72
Córdova y Maldonado, Alonso de, 36–38, 41, 42, 43
Corneille, Pierre, 23, 29
Corneille, Thomas, 29–30, 44, 53, 82
Cosa rara, Una (Da Ponte, Martín y Soler), 90
Costanza in amore vince l'inganno, La (Caldara), 295n
Couton, Georges, 27, 29n
Crinò, Anna Maria, 6n
Crispin rival de son maître (Lesage), 52
Croce, Benedetto, 6n, 11n

Dante, 127
Da Ponte, Lorenzo, 6, 7, 8, 10n, 14, 17, 18, 20, 21–22, 25, 29, 32, 33, 34–35, 38, 40–41, 47–48, 49, 51, 52, 54, 57n, 65–66, 67, 68, 69, 71–74, 75, 83, 84–85, 86, 87–88, 89–90, 91, 92, 93, 94, 96, 103–4, 105, 107, 109, 112, 113–14, 115–18, 120, 121–27
De' Filistri da Caramondani, Antonio, 88
De la Rose, Claude. *See* Rosimond
De L'Art de la comédie (Cailhava de l'Estandoux), 49–50, 50n, 53
De los Rios, Blanca, 2n
Delpini, Charles Antony, 53–54
Demofoonte (Metastasio), 378n
Départ d'Enée ou Didon abandonnée (Metastasio, Angiolini), 76
Desboulmiers, Jean-Auguste Julien, 53
Descamps, Claude. *See* Villiers
Dissertation sur les ballets pantomimes des anciens, pour servir de programme au ballet pantomime tragique de Semiramis (Angiolini), 77n
Dissoluto punito o sia Il D. Giovanni, Il (Da Ponte, Mozart). *See Don Giovanni* (Da Ponte, Mozart)
Dokoupil, Vladislav, 67n
Dominique. *See* Biancolelli, Domenico
Dom Juan, oder Der steinerne Gast (Marinelli), 51
Dom Juan ou Le festin de Pierre (Molière), 17, 18, 26–30, 60n, 82
Don Giovanni (Da Ponte, Mozart), 7, 18, 20, 25, 28, 29, 32, 33, 34–35, 38, 40–41, 47–48, 51–52, 54, 65, 71–74, 78, 84–85, 90, 92, 94–95, 97, 104, 106, 107, 113n, 118, 119n, 122–27
Don Giovanni (puppet *scenario*), 51
Don Giovanni, Il (Albertini), 96–101, 131, 277–88
Don Giovanni il disoluto, ovvero Il castigo impensato, con Famiola disgraziato in amore (puppet *scenario*), 51
Don Giovanni o sia Il convitato di pietra (Bertati, Gazzaniga), 31, 48n, 84, 112, 113, 114, 115n, 116, 118, 119n, 121–26, 131, 132, 407–43
Don Giovanni Tenorio o sia Il dissoluto (Goldoni), 43–48, 98
Don Juan (Angiolini, Gluck), 75–86, 104
Don Juan, albo ukarany libertyn (Albertini), 96–98, 100–101
Don Juan legend, 2–3, 11, 18, 20, 31, 49–50, 52–53, 55, 75, 121
Don Juan; or, The Libertine Destroy'd (Delpini, Gluck), 53–54
Don Juan Tenorio (Zorrilla), 37, 42
Dori, La (Apolloni, Cesti), 56
Dorimond, 18–22, 23, 24, 25, 26, 27, 30, 31, 32, 33, 40, 42, 46, 58
Drammaturgia (Allacci), 12n
Drouin, Nicolas. *See* Dorimond
Dryden, John, 33
Due gemelli, Li (Tritto), 102
Durazzo, Count Giacomo, 75

Edwards, Gwynne, 2n
Empio punito, L' (Acciaiuoli, Apolloni, Melani), 55–66, 86
Enea nel Lazio (Gardi), 108
Engländer, Richard, 77n
Extract from the Life of Lorenzo Da Ponte, An (Da Ponte), 116n, 118n

Fabrizi, Vincenzo, 97n, 107–8
Farinelli, Giuseppe, 110
Federici, Vincenzo, 118, 119n
Festin de Pierre, Le: popularity, 115–16; at the Théâtre Italien, 53; title, 15
Festin de Pierre, Le (Corneille), 29–30
Festin de Pierre, Le (Le Tellier), 39–41
Festin de Pierre ou Le fils criminel, Le (Dorimond), 18–22
Festin de Pierre ou Le fils criminel, Le (Villiers), 19, 23–26
Filosofo punito, Il (Da Ponte, Righini), 87
Finta giardiniera, La (Mozart), 83
Finto cieco, Il (Da Ponte, Gazzaniga), 113–14
Fiorilli, Tiberio, 11n, 16n
Fogliazzi, Teresa, 76

foire versions of the Don Juan legend, 38–41, 53, 75
Foppa, Giuseppe Maria, 26, 31, 108, 109–12, 114, 121, 131, 327–79
Fournel, Victor, 30n
Fracastoro, Girolamo, 217n
Fra i due litiganti il terzo gode (Lorenzi, Sarti), 104

Galeotti, Vincenzo, 83
Galuppi, Baldassare, 115
Gardi, Francesco, 31, 108–11, 131, 327–79
Gazzaniga, Giuseppe, 31, 52n, 54, 71, 97n, 108, 112–14, 115, 118, 119n, 120, 121, 131, 407–43
Geiringer, Karl, 89n
Gendarme de Bévotte, Georges, 6n, 23n, 36, 36n, 44, 53n
Giasone (Cavalli), 6
Giliberto, Onofrio, 13, 23, 44, 60
Giornale delle due Sicilie, 101
Girello, Il (Acciaiuoli, Melani), 56
Giulietta e Romeo (Foppa, Zingarelli), 110
Gluck, Christoph Willibald, 53–54, 75, 76, 78, 79, 86, 104
Goldoni, Carlo, 13, 40, 43–48, 49, 52, 70, 90–91, 98, 99
Gran convitato di pietra ad uso d'almanacco, Il (Cicognini), 52n
Guardassoni, Domenico, 116
Gueullette, Thomas-Simon, 17
Guglielmi, Pietro, 88, 88n, 89n, 101, 103, 118

Hauptactionen versions of the Don Juan legend, 50–51
Haydn, Joseph, 88, 89, 199n, 213n
Hilverding, Franz, 76
Histoire anecdotique et raisonnée du Théâtre Italien (Desboulmiers), 53
Histoire de l'ancien théâtre italien (Parfaict), 16, 16n
History of My Life (Casanova), 3n
Hodges, Sheila, 119n

Idolo cinese, L' (Lorenzi, Paisiello), 103
Impresario in angustie, L' (Cimarosa), 113
Incontro inaspettato, L' (Porta, Righini), 89, 89n
Indice de' teatrali spettacoli, 90n, 96n, 113n, 115n
Inganno felice, L' (Foppa, Rossini), 110
Isola disabitata, L' (Metastasio, Calegari), 93n
Italiano a Parigi, L' (Bertati, Alessandri), 115

Jommelli, Nicolò, 88, 101
Joseph II, Emperor, 86
Joueur, Le (Regnard), 78, 81
Journal littéraire de Varsovie, 96

Kelly, Michael, 87
Kunze, Stefan, 109n, 110n, 132

Laclos, Choderlos de, 50
Landon, H. C. Robbins, 89n
Lanfranchi, Ariella, 103
Lepicq, Charles, 53–54
Lesage, Alain-René, 52
Le Tellier, 39–41, 120
Lettere di Gasparo Angiolini a Monsieur Noverre sopra i Balli Pantomimi (Angiolini), 78n
Leydi, Roberto and Renata, 51–52
Liaisons dangereuses, Les (Laclos), 50
Libby, Dennis, 101–2
Libertine, The (Shadwell), 15, 33–35, 53, 75
Locatelli, Domenico, 16, 18, 23
Longhi, Gioseffo, 52
Lorenzi, Giambattista, 83, 93, 101, 102–8, 120, 121, 131, 132, 289–326
Loret, 16n, 26n
Lynham, Deryck, 119n

Macchia, Giovanni, 6n, 17n, 58n
Mandel, Oscar, 27–28, 49
Marescalchi, Luigi, 78
Marinelli, Karl, 51
Marks, Paul F., 75n

Martín y Soler, Vicente, 113, 122
Matrimonio segreto, Il (Bertati, Cimarosa), 115–16, 118
Mattei, S., 93n
Mayr, Simone, 110
Melani, Alessandro, 56
Melani, Jacopo, 56
Mémoires (Goldoni), 43n, 44n
Memorie (Da Ponte), 88n, 89n, 90n, 113n, 114n, 115n, 116n, 117n, 118, 118n, 122
Memorie storiche della vita di Giuseppe M.a Foppa viniziano scritte da lui medesimo (Foppa), 109n, 110n
Mercadante, Saverio, 102
Mesmer, 87
Metastasio, Pietro, 75, 76, 93n, 111, 116, 214n, 372n
Mingotti, Angelo and Pietro, 66, 68, 79
Molière, 6, 15, 17, 18, 19, 25, 26–30, 31, 32, 33, 42, 44, 50, 58, 60n, 82, 104n, 120, 122
Monaco, Vanda, 103n, 105n, 131, 132
Morini, Ugo, 97n
Morning Chronicle, The (London), 119n
Morte di Dimone, La (Bertati, Tozzi), 114
Mozart, Leopold, 87n
Mozart, Wolfgang Amadeus, 6, 10, 14, 18, 20, 28, 34–35, 38, 40, 51, 54, 66, 68, 71, 72, 75, 78, 79, 83, 86, 87, 88, 90, 97, 98, 104, 107, 108, 113, 115, 116, 116n, 118, 119n, 120, 121, 122, 127

Napoli-Signorelli, Pietro, 102
Natal d'Apollo, Il (Mattei, Calegari), 93n
Nina o sia La pazza per amore (Da Ponte, Weigl), 103
Nina o sia La pazza per amore (Lorenzi, Paisiello), 103
No hay deuda que no se pague y Convidado de piedra (Zamora), 42–43
Nouveau festin de Pierre ou L'athée foudroyé (Rosimond), 19, 30–33
Noverre, Jean Georges, 119n
Novità, La (Bertati, Alessandri), 115
Nozze di Figaro, Le (Da Ponte, Mozart), 87, 104, 114
Nuovo convitato di pietra, Il (Cerlone), 52
Nuovo convitato di pietra, Il (Foppa, Gardi), 26, 31, 108, 109, 110–12, 131, 327–79

Operatic versions of the Don Juan legend. *See* individual titles
Opere teatrali (Lorenzi), 105n
Oracle, The (London), 119n
Orfeo ed Euridice (Calzabigi, Gluck), 75, 76
Orlando furioso (Ariosto), 217n
Orlando paladino (Porta, Guglielmi), 88, 88n, 89, 89n
Orlando paladino (Porta, Haydn), 89
Orontea (Cesti), 6

Paer, Ferdinando, 110
Paisiello, Giovanni, 101, 103, 115
Pantomime versions of the Don Juan legend, 53–54, 111
Parfaict, François and Claude, 16, 16n
Pariati, Pietro, 93
Paride ed Elena (Calzabigi, Gluck), 75
Parini, Giuseppe, 76
Partenope (Bambini), 67n
Passanti, Antonio, 14
Pavesi, Stefano, 110
Pazzie de' savi overo Il Lambertaccio, Le (Bocchini), 11
Pazzie di Orlando (Badini, Guglielmi), 89n
Pepoli, Alessandro, 108–9
Pergolesi, Giovanni, 67
Perrucci, Andrea, 35–36, 44, 52, 70
Pestelli, Giorgio, 66
Piccinni, Nicola, 103, 104, 112
Poniatowski, King Stanislaw August, 96
Poniatowski, Prince Stanislaw, 96
Porpora, Nicola, 112
Porta, Nunziato, 88–93, 94, 98–101, 105, 112, 115, 116, 120, 131, 183–226, 280n, 285n
Portogallo, Marco, 110
Pravità castigata, La (Bambini), 66–74, 79, 86, 131, 133–81

Prefazioni di Carlo Goldoni ai diciassette tomi delle commedie edite a Venezia da G. B. Pasquali (Goldoni), 44n
Prendarca, Enrico. *See* Perrucci, Andrea
Price, Curtis, 35
Price, Elizabeth, 50–51
"Programm du Ballet de Dom-juan, ou bien, du festin du Pierre" (Angiolini, Gluck), 85
Puppet versions of the Don Juan legend, 51–52
Purcell, Henry, 35, 75

Quaglio, Giovanni Maria, 78
Querelle des bouffons, 67

Radziwill, Prince Karol, 96
Raszewski, Zbigniew, 97n
Reeve, William, 54
Regnard, Jean François, 78
Ricco di un giorno, Il (Da Ponte, Righini), 89, 118
Richardson, Samuel, 50
Righini, Vincenzo, 71, 84, 86–89, 98–100, 104, 105, 118, 120, 131, 183–226
Robinet, 16n
Rolandi, Ulderico, 114
Rosa, Salvator, 57–58
Rosimond, 19, 30–33
Rospigliosi, Cardinal, 57, 60
Rospigliosi, Giulio. *See* Clemente IX
Rossi, Domenico, 83, 84
Rossi, Vincenzo, 85
Rossini, Gioacchino, 110
Russell, Charles C., 77n

Sacchini, Antonio, 112
Salieri, Antonio, 103, 115, 122
Sarti, Giuseppe, 89n, 104, 118
Savio, Francesco, 13
Scala di seta, La (Foppa, Rossini), 110
Schmidl, Carlo, 88n, 97n, 102
Schröder, Friedrich Ludwig, 84
Scipione africano (Albertini), 96
Scott, Virginia, 16n
Scuffiara, La (Lorenzi, Tritto), 103
Sereni, Sereno, 52
Serva onorata, La (Lorenzi, Piccinni), 104
Serva padrona, La (Pergolesi), 67
Shadwell, Thomas, 6, 15, 31, 32, 33–35, 38, 53, 75, 85, 120
Shakespeare, William, 110, 127
Sigismondo (Foppa, Rossini), 110
Signor Bruschino, Il (Foppa, Rossini), 110
Smith, William C., 119n
Socrate immaginario, Il (Lorenzi, Paisiello), 103
Somfai, László, 89n
Sorpresa amorosa, La (Righini), 87
Spaziani, Marcello, 13n, 17, 17n, 39, 53n
Spontini, Gaspare, 102
"Suite du festin de Pierre, La" (Biancolelli), 17n
Syphilis sive Moribus Gallicus (Fracastoro), 217n

Tancredi (Pepoli, Gardi), 108
¿Tan largo me lo fiáis? (Tirso de Molina), 1–2
Tarare (Da Ponte, Salieri), 122
Taylor, William, 118, 119n
Teatr Polski czyli zbior komedyi drammy tragedyi, 100n
Téllez, Gabriel. *See* Tirso de Molina
Times, The (London), 119n
Tirso de Molina, 1–6, 7, 8, 9, 11, 14, 20, 35, 36, 37, 42, 44, 46, 58, 60, 66, 69, 122
Tozzi, Antonio, 114
Tre gobbi rivali, I (Fabrizi), 107
Tritto, Giacomo, 52n, 71, 93, 101–2, 103, 107–8, 120, 131, 289–326
Turner, William, 35

University of Brno Library, 67

Valenti. *See* Valentini
Valentini, Giovanni, 113, 131, 381–405
Venganza en el sepulcro, La (Córdova y Maldonado), 36–38
Vergine vestale, La (Albertini), 96

Viganò, Onorato, 78
Villanella rapita, La (Bertati, Bianchi), 116n
Villiers, 19, 23–26, 27, 30, 31, 32, 33, 40, 42, 46, 120
Virginia (Albertini), 96, 96n
Vogt, Peter, 83, 84

Wade, Gerald E., 2
Weigl, Joseph, 103
Weinstock, Herbert, 110n
Wilson, Margaret, 2n

Zamora, Antonio de, 41–43, 49, 50
Zeno, Apostolo, 93
Zenobia in Palmira, La (Metastasio, Calegari), 93n
Zingarelli, Nicola, 110, 115
Zinzendorf, Count Karl, 78, 81–82, 85
Zorrilla, José, 37, 42